THE
DEATH
OF
WHITE
SOCIOLOGY
ESSAYS ON RACE AND CULTURE

THE
DEATH
OF
WHITE
SOCIOLOGY
ESSAYS ON RACE AND CULTURE

EDITED BY JOYCE A. LADNER

WITH AN
AFTERWORD BY BECKY THOMPSON

BLACK CLASSIC PRESS
BALTIMORE

First Published 1973
Published by Black Classic Press 1998
Introduction copyright 1998 by Joyce A. Ladner
Afterword copyright 1998 by Becky Thompson
All Rights Reserved
Library of Congress Card Catalog Number 97-73660
ISBN 1-57478-007-7

Cover design by Laurie Williams/A Street Called Straight

Founded in 1978, Black Classic Press specializes in bringing to light obscure and
significant works by and about people of African descent. If our books are not in
available in your area, ask your local bookseller to order them. Our current list of
titles can be obtained by writing:

Black Classic Press
c/o List
P.O. Box 13414
Baltimore, MD 21203

Visit our website at www.blackclassic.com

A Young Press With Some Very Old Ideas

Charles V. Hamilton for "Black Social Scientists: Some Contributions and Problems" from the *Amsterdam News*, September 18, 1971.

Black Law Journal, Volume No. 1, Summer 1971, for "Public Research and Racism: The Case of Racist Researchers" by Richard F. America.

Outerbridge and Dienstfrey, publishers, for "White Norms for Black Deviation" by Albert Murray from *The Omni-Americans: New Perspectives on Black Experience and Black Culture.*

Doubleday & Co., Inc., for an excerpt from *Tomorrow's Tomorrow: The Black Woman* by Joyce A. Ladner. Copyright © 1971, Doubleday & Co.

Black Scholar for "The Challenge of a Black Scholar" by Nathan Hare, December 1969; "The Ideology of Black Social Science" by Gerald Mc-Worter, December 1969; "The Sociology of Black Nationalism" by James Turner, December 1969; "Guidelines for Black Sociologists" by Joseph White, March 1970; "Assessing Race Relations Research" by Charles Saunders, March 1970.

INTRODUCTION

to the Black Classic Press edition
By Dr. Joyce A. Ladner

When *The Death of White Sociology* was first published in 1973, it created considerable discussion and debate. The provocative title alone caused numerous scholars and students alike to read many of the essays. I must admit, however, that the title was not my creation. When a friend of mine, who was an editor at a major publishing company, asked me what title I intended to give the anthology, I told him it would be called *An Introduction to a Black Perspective in Sociology*. He was not impressed. "Why don't you give it an exciting and stimulating title?" he asked. "Your book should be called *The Death of White Sociology*." I was so intrigued by his suggestion that I decided to use the title even though I knew that the book's contents did not signal the end to mainstream (White) sociology as we knew it. Rather, the book was my attempt to publish a volume that would capture some of the debate and protest over the ways that traditional sociology (and some of the other social sciences) has stigmatized African Americans.

This book was published during the Civil Rights and Black Power eras. The structured inequality in race and class was the target of mass protests by activists and government officials who sought to rid U.S. society of its legalized discriminatory practices. The changes in the wider society had a profound impact on college campuses. Black students protested against a multitude of issues: for example, they claimed that there were too few minority professors and that the views of the professors who taught them did not reflect their cultural experiences. Historically, Black intellectuals were confined to Black institutions for the most part. Only a relatively small number found employment outside the Black colleges in the South and the border states.

The outcomes of the protests against these inequalities changed academic institutions profoundly. Many colleges and universities recruited minority faculty to run newly established Black studies programs as a response to student demands. Major universities began to hire Black scholars in significant numbers. The increased racial and ethnic diversity of majority higher educational institutions has provided a more expansive set of roles for African American professors. Black protests also gave rise to protests by women who demanded women's studies programs for basically the same reasons that Black students had demanded the establishment of Black studies programs. Feminists made the same clarion for more women to be hired as a way of rectifying the absence of the experiences of women in mainstream scholarship. Gay students demanded their rights within the halls of academia. Radical sociologists also challenged their colleagues to confront their social class biases by including Marxist analyses in their scholarship. Thus, the book reflects the mood of an era when protest against all types of inequalities regularly occurred.

African American professors now teach in majority institutions across the nation. As time passed, the number of Black faculty increased, and they penetrated the major disciplines in the social sciences, humanities, engineering, and science. The Black studies programs, in many cases, became departments, giving rise to the institutionalization of curricula leading to undergraduate and graduate degrees. What started as a protest against the exclusion of African Americans in majority institutions has, a generation later, resulted in respected degree-granting departments. Many campuses have gone a step further by making efforts to include the experiences of Blacks across the curriculum. The cross-fertilization of scholarship, that is, the influence of African American culture and scholarship, has had an important impact on most of the disciplines and on the institutions as a whole. There are also more Black students on White campuses than ever. Another important outcome is that women, Hispanics and other minorities, gays and lesbians, the elderly, and the developmentally challenged forced society to view and respond to their needs as well.

Despite the enormous gains, however, numerous problems continue to exist. Many Black students still complain about feeling marginal on the campuses of majority institutions. The concept of institutional racism that was used widely in the sixties and seventies has been supplanted among today's students and faculty by the concept of cultural insensitivity. It has been, indeed, disappointing to learn that less change had occurred than expected. After the anthology had been out of print for roughly two decades, this generation of students and some professors are dealing with issues that are not dissimilar to those of my generation. Therefore, the content of the book remains virtually unchanged, except for the inclusion of a paper written by Becky Thompson, a sociologist whose assessment of the impact of this work serves as an appropriate afterword.

The essays in the anthology provoked healthy debates over a range of issues: Does Black sociology exist? If so, what are its theoretical assumptions, and what is the range of subject matter it covers? Is it proper to attempt to develop a course of study based so heavily on the *rejection* rather than the *affirmation* of traditional sociology and the social sciences? Others asked why it was necessary to build a discipline that was limited to examining the singular experiences of African Americans, especially when Blacks were attempting to integrate into the mainstream of society. Graduate students, in particular, identified with the anthology. Douglas Davidson's essay, "The Furious Passage of the Black Graduate Student," resonated not only with students across racial lines, but with female students also. Indeed, Davidson captured many of their own experiences and emotional reactions to the difficult challenges they faced in graduate school. In many cases, Black students and women students were dealing with the fallout from being the first generation to enter graduate school in large numbers, partly as a result of the implementation of affirmative action programs. Therefore, *The Death of White Sociology* provided them with an alternative way of examining the race, class, and to a lesser extent, gender issues that they were experiencing on professional and personal levels.

Some of the authors in the anthology attacked the sacred cows in their fields of study. An issue that was hotly debated was whether the scholar could be value-free. Should the author's subjectivity be condoned? Or does it interfere with the scientific process in which the researcher's individual bias is controlled? Kenneth Clark's essay on the unavoidable role of subjectivity in his classic work on life in Harlem, titled "Dark Ghetto," provided fuel for the fire, in a manner of speaking. Clark wrote eloquently about how his experiences as a lifetime resident of Harlem shaped his views. He also noted that his prior experiences enhanced his scholarship rather than serving as an obstacle. I addressed the same issue in an excerpt from *Tomorrow's Tomorrow: The Black Woman*. This was one of the toughest challenges I faced personally, and one in which I arrived at the same conclusion as Clark.

What the proper role of the Black intellectual should be is a topic that generated considerable discussion and debate. E. Franklin Frazier, who was the first of two Blacks to be elected president of the American Sociological Association (William Julius Wilson was the other), challenged African Americans to consider their intellectual and social responsibilities for other Blacks. Thus, the idea that scholarship should be used to promote the common good was addressed by several authors. Historian Lerone Bennett and political scientist Ron Walters also analyzed the racial bias that individuals bring to their scholarship, both wittingly and unwittingly.

The concept of *double consciousness* that W. E. B. DuBois introduced in his classic work, *The Souls of Black Folk* (1903), is also a theme in the anthology. DuBois stated that Blacks are socialized to have two warring, irreconcilable identities—American and Negro. And he explored the constant pressures to adapt to both cultures. Some of the scholars in this anthology echo this theme as they grapple with their proper roles and responsibilities and the duality of being a product of both the minority and mainstream intellectual communities. The idea of double consciousness is still relevant, and this is somewhat troubling because the optimism that fueled the debates on race, class, and gender in the seventies has been replaced with a degree of pessimism. Racial progress has been slower than we had all anticipated. A large Black underclass exists today—one that is more entrenched than might be expected. There have been so many attacks on affirmative action that we have forgotten that White women have realized greater gains than have Blacks. Unfortunately, the stigma of race is still a very powerful symbol that tends, perhaps more than any other concept, to separate rather than to unite disparate groups in this society.

Many individuals who read this work will seek answers to the resolution of the problems and issues described. There are no "magical" solutions or "quick fixes." To paraphrase Frantz Fanon, the Martinican psychiatrist, each generation must define its mission —fulfill or betray it. It is my hope that the next generation of students and scholars who read these essays will be able to do so as they contemplate the issues of their times and work toward solutions that are appropriate.

Acknowledgments

I owe much gratitude to Robert Staples for his critical comments and suggestions; to Anne Freedgood for her editorial suggestions; and to Wilma Perry for her invaluable technical aid as my research assistant.

I want to express special thanks to all of the contributors to this volume, without whose cooperation the book would not have been possible.

I am also indebted to my colleagues at Howard University for the assistance they provided. G. Franklin Edwards always found the time to clarify my questions concerning the work of E. Franklin Frazier, with whom he spent many years at Howard, as well as that of other pioneering Black sociologists.

Ralph Gomes and Johnny Daniel served as patient listeners and provocative critics.

Andrew Billingsley deserves special thanks for his unselfish attention to this and all the projects I have undertaken. He has provided eager interest in the ideas combined with technical assistance in executing them.

I wish also to thank a special friend, who would perhaps prefer to go unnamed, for suggesting the title to this anthology.

Finally, I owe much gratitude to Walter Carrington, who often disagrees with some of my ideas, but always provides me with support and encouragement because that is the way he is.

To Lerone Bennett and Horace Mann Bond and
Fannie Lou Hamer and Margaret Walker Alexander
and Black students everywhere.

It is necessary for us to develop a new frame of reference which transcends the limits of white concepts. It is necessary for us to develop and maintain a total intellectual offensive against the false universality of white concepts, whether they are expressed by William Styron or Daniel Patrick Moynihan. By and large, reality has been conceptualized in terms of the narrow point of view of the small minority of white men who live in Europe and North America. We must abandon the partial frame of reference of our oppressors and create new concepts which will release our reality, which is also the reality of the overwhelming majority of men and women on this globe. We must say to the white world that there are things in the world that are not dreamt of in your history and your sociology and your philosophy.
—Lerone Bennett, *The Challenge of Blackness*

Contents

Introduction

Why a book on "Black sociology"? Is there such a discipline? Many readers, indeed, will argue that sociology, like physics, is without color and can validly apply the same methodology and theoretical framework, regardless of the ethnic, racial and other backgrounds of the group under investigation.

But sociology, like history, economics and psychology, exists in a domain where color, ethnicity and social class are of primary importance. And, as long as this holds true, it is impossible for sociology to claim that it maintains value neutrality in its approach.

The purpose of this anthology is to present a set of statements that attempt to define the emerging field of Black sociology and to establish basic premises, guidelines, concerns and priorities which can be useful to those who have an interest in understanding and applying these to their study and work.

Black sociology is an emerging field of study. It evolved for two reasons: (1) as a reaction to, and revolt against, the biases of "mainstream" bourgeois, liberal sociology; and (2) as a positive step toward setting forth basic definitions, concepts, and theory-building that utilize the experiences and histories of Afro-Americans.

Because Black sociology is an outgrowth of, and reaction to, mainstream sociology, it is impossible to divorce the two. Mainstream or "white" sociology has, in the main, upheld the status quo and seldom advocated the kinds of progressive changes that would insure that Blacks no longer experience the subjugated status in American society to which they have been subjected. One of the prevailing premises in mainstream sociology has been that Blacks are a minority group which would, in time, become part of the "melting pot" in much the same manner that European ethnic groups have done. There has been an almost total negation of the different historical conditions that differentiate Blacks from European minorities. The salient factor that Africans came to America *involuntarily*, that they were enslaved and subsequently granted second-class citizenship, which, for the most part, still exists, means that they cannot be analyzed in the same way as Europeans who *voluntarily* came to the United States seeking better lives. The further fact that the later European immigrants had the same skin color as the early American colonists and came from roughly similar cultures enhanced their assimilation.

Another crucial distinction to be made is that Africans who came to the United States in chains have always lived in segregated surroundings, among themselves, and have therefore created a strong culture that exists, to varying degrees, outside or on the fringes of the mainstream.[1]

---

[1] For a fuller discussion of Black culture, refer to Charles Keil, *Urban Blues* (Chicago: University of Chicago Press, 1966), pp. 191-92; Robert Blauner, "Negro Culture: Myth or Reality," *Black Experience: The Transformation of Activism* (*Trans-action* publication, New Brunswick, 1970); Melville Herskovits, *The Myth of the Negro Past* (Boston: Beacon Press, 1958); Joyce A. Ladner, *Tomorrow's Tomorrow: The Black Woman* (New York: Doubleday and Company, 1971), pp. 32-39 and 270-73.

Traditional sociological analyses have failed to explore the unique experiences and culture of Blacks when they were the subject of investigation, and have excluded Blacks from the general framework of American sociology. The refusal to address Black culture and experience has caused the distortion that we see today in sociological literature. Historically, sociologists have portrayed Blacks as disorganized, pathological, and an aberrant group. The myths of "cultural deprivation," "innate inferiority," "social disadvantagement," and "tangle of pathology" characterize the writings of many sociologists up to the present time.

The stigmatizing labels have perpetuated the white majority's treatment of Afro-Americans as inferior. For example, the so-called "matriarchal" family structure, with its "culturally deprived" members, has been the target of many social intervention strategies whose designs strongly reflect these biases and are not wholly relevant to the recognition and fulfillment of the family's needs and desires.

There are many historical antecedents for these conceptual and methodological inaccuracies. Too many white social scientists have accepted the premise that the historical, political and social conditions to which Blacks were subjected would forever prevent them from conforming to the ambiguous model of the "ideal" American. This inherent bias, which can be observed in all the social sciences, was particularly evident in the early writings of some of American sociology's founding fathers. For example, in 1924, Robert E. Park and Ernest Burgess, two of the influential urban sociologists from the famed "Chicago School," wrote in their book *Introduction to the Science of Sociology:*

The temperament of the Negro as I conceive of it consists in a few elementary but distinctive characteristics, determined by physical organizations and transmitted biologically. These characteristics manifest themselves in a genial, sunny, and social disposition, in an interest in and attachment to external, physical things rather than to subjective states and objects of introspection, in a disposition for expression rather than enterprise and action.[2]

It is interesting to note that Park and Burgess still maintain highly respectable positions in the history of American sociology, despite their theory of genetic determinism in Blacks.

Edward B. Reuter, another American sociologist, held a similar view. In 1927 he wrote:

[The Negroes] were without ancestral pride or family tradition. They had no distinctive language or religion. These, like their folkways and moral customs, were but recently acquired from the whites and furnished no nucleus for a racial unity. The group was without even a tradition of historic unity or of racial achievement. There were no historic names, no great achievements, no body of literature, no artistic productions. The whole record of the race was one of servile or barbarian status apparently without a point about which a sentimental complex could be formed.[3]

One could argue that the doctrines of racial inferiority which these men sought to document scientifically have been disposed of. Yet a search of the recent literature reveals strongly prejudiced positions, albeit not nearly so harsh as those expressed in the 1920's.

Notable among contemporary sociologists who espouse the view that Blacks lack some of the necessary "stuff" for acceptance into America's mainstream are those who maintain that Blacks have no cultural heritage. They argue that Blacks must continue to fight for equality and seek to *assimilate* into the mainstream. They do not advocate "cul-

---

[2] Robert E. Park and Ernest Burgess, *Introduction to the Science of Sociology* (Chicago: University of Chicago Press, 1924), pp. 138-9.
[3] Edward B. Reuter, *The American Race Problem* (New York: Thomas Y. Crowell, 1970), p. 365. (Originally published in 1927.)

tural pluralism," or the affirmation and appreciation of *Black* culture. In *Beyond the Melting Pot,* Daniel P. Moynihan and Nathan Glazer state the modern-day version of the 1920's view. Originally published in 1963, the book makes the provocative statement that

. . . It is not possible for Negroes to view themselves as other ethnic groups viewed themselves because—and this is the key to much in the Negro world—the Negro is only an American, and nothing else. *He has no values and culture to guard and protect.*" (Italics added)[4]

Although the authors go on to say that the problems of the Negro are everyone's, because the Negro is a product of this society, they still *negate* the African past and deny Blacks everything except what they can garner from American whites.

Blacks have always been measured against an alien set of norms. As a result they have been considered to be a deviation from the ambiguous white middle-class model, which itself has not always been clearly defined. This inability or refusal to deal with Blacks as a part and parcel of the varying historical and cultural contributions to the American scene has, perhaps, been the reason sociology has excluded the Black perspective from its widely accepted mainstream theories.

Mainstream sociology, in this regard, reflects the ideology of the larger society, which has always excluded Black lifestyles, values, behavior, attitudes, and so forth from the body of data that is used to define, describe, conceptualize and theorize about the structure and functions of American society. Sociology has in a similar manner excluded the totality of Black existence from its major theories, except insofar as it has *deviated* from the so-called norms.

[4] Nathan Glazer and Daniel P. Moynihan, *Beyond the Melting Pot* (Cambridge, Mass.: MIT Press, 1965), p. 53.

The emergence of Black sociology comes at a time when Blacks in sociology and other disciplines, including social work, psychology, history, political science and economics, have found it necessary either to organize "caucuses" within the established associations of the disciplines or to organize "separate" all-Black organizations such as the National Association of Black Social Workers and the Association of Black Psychologists.

Black sociologists organized the "Caucus of Black Sociologists" in 1968 and elected to remain *within* the American Sociological Association instead of establishing an all-Black organization outside of it. This disenchantment with the way social and behavioral science disciplines related to Blacks (or did not relate to them) was influenced by the advent of the civil rights movement in the sixties, when questions were raised about hiring practices, full participation in the affairs of the associations of the various disciplines, and the concern that Black scholars who had produced important sociological works be granted long-overdue recognition.

Another influence on the dissent among Black scholars was the thrust toward "Black awareness." As the civil rights movement progressed, many Blacks began demanding the recognition and revitalization of Black values and culture. They argued that the civil rights movement must ultimately address itself to the area of Black culture and seek to affirm and preserve its existence. Hence, many Blacks, who were eventually labeled "cultural nationalists," emerged on the national scene to advocate that stronger cultural links be established with African countries. They also organized programs to revitalize African cultural traditions within the United States. Many Afro-Americans, especially the young, embraced this new thrust and today continue to portray some of its symbols in their personal appearance and programs. Indeed, the thrust gave rise to strong "Black nationalism" ideologies, which have become systematized into viable policies and programs. Black sociologists were influenced personally and intellectually by the Black culture and "awareness" thrust, and some of them sought to understand and interpret this phenomenon as *sociologists*.

A final factor which gave impetus to the development of Black sociology was the Black student movement's demand for Black Studies programs. The late 1960's saw the disruption of numerous Black and white college campuses where students demanded more relevant programs of study, including Black-oriented curricula, Black faculty and the abolition of unnecessary requirements. One of their strong demands was for more pragmatic, community-oriented programs which would remove them from the "ivory towers" of the university and place them in the poor, oppressed Black urban communities where they could apply some of the sociology they learned in the classroom. In sum, they demanded that the content of the Black experience become a vital part of the sociology, history, political science and economics they were studying.

They raised the questions: Why should we study classical sociological theory and be taught nothing about the history of Black sociological thought, including the works of W. E. B. DuBois, Charles S. Johnson, E. Franklin Frazier, Oliver C. Cox and others? Why should we be taught courses on deviance, social disorganization and social problems which take as given that Blacks should be defined as the perpetrators and creators of social pathology and not as its victims? Why a course on the family which, when studying the Black family, views the female head of the household as a "matriarch," and the male head as a shadow in the background?

The demands, of course, were endless because they covered practically every area of specialization in sociology and the other social sciences.

Black students also took up a defense of Black communities, which had been targets of considerable sociological research. They joined residents in complaining that research had rarely helped to solve the communities' problems and had, more often than not, merely distorted the nature of those problems. They charged that many of the intervention strategies that were derived from research findings had acted to exacerbate the problems, not to solve them. All too often the "white perspective," which has assumed that the Black community is *the* center of social pathology, has been the *modus operandi,* and social researchers have produced data consistent with this perspective.

These influences have led a growing number of sociologists to question the efficacy of the discipline. Is sociology serving the purposes for which it is intended? Is its analysis of the social phenomena that are affecting Blacks *relevant?* Can mainstream sociology continue to take the position that its role is simply to observe, classify and analyze these phenomena instead of engaging in the active promotion of social change? Certain white sociologists have challenged these traditional roles by establishing the Union of Radical Sociologists.[5] A growing number of Black sociologists have also taken great issue with the traditional roles, structure and content of the discipline.

Black sociologists and others who wish to utilize the "Black perspective" have many tasks ahead of them. Fortunately, many of the issues, concerns and challenges have arisen out of the broader context of those articulated by Black communities. Sociologists, as the theorists and forerunners of social change, can no longer ignore the goals the masses have espoused. Black sociologists must act as advocates of the demands the masses are making for freedom, justice and the right to determine their destinies.

Black sociologists must also become more concerned with intergroup relations in the Third World, especially Africa.

[5] For a discussion of the Union of Radical Sociologists position, refer to *Radical Sociology,* J. David Colfax and Jack L. Roach, eds., (New York: Basic Books, 1971).

America's race problem stretches beyond her borders to Southeast Asia and Latin America. As members of an oppressed minority, Black sociologists can play an important role in analyzing these problems and promoting solutions for them.

Black sociologists must develop new techniques and perspectives, as those which are no longer functional are discarded. One of the dominant themes the authors in this anthology address is that there must be a conciliation between culture (theory) and politics (practice), or, as Nathan Hare has described it, the "uniting of the Black academy and the street."[6] Hence, Black sociology must become more political than mainstream sociology has been. Black sociology must also develop theories which assume the basic posture of eliminating racism and systematic class oppression from the society. The myth of "value-free" sociology becomes relevant to the Black sociologist, because he must become "pro-value," by promoting the interests of the Black masses in his research, writings and teachings.

The Death of White Sociology is an early statement on the development of Black sociology. It seeks to examine some of the historical forces which have acted upon Black sociologists, and to explicate some of the issues which are central to this new discipline.

Part I is devoted to "The Socialization of Black Sociologists." The works of major Black sociologists, from the turn of the century to around 1950, and the sociopolitical climate in which they operated are examined. E. Franklin Frazier, Nathan Hare and Douglas Davidson, representing three generations of Black sociologists, discuss some of the dilemmas which they faced.

Part II is a discussion of "The Sociological Victimization of Black Americans." This section addresses itself to some

---

[6] Nathan Hare, "A Torch to Burn Down a Decadent World," *The Black Scholar*, Vol. 2, No. 1 (September 1970), pp. 2–5.

of the philosophical premises upon which American sociology was founded, and the systematic way it has oppressed Blacks. The greatest critics of mainstream sociology have been literary men, not sociologists. Two Black writers, Ralph Ellison and Albert Murray, provide provocative critiques. Two sociologists, Rhett Jones and Sidney Willhelm, discuss other dimensions of this victimization.

Part III examines some of the basic tenets of Black sociological theory. The authors of these chapters discuss nationalism, radicalism, the development of a Black social science, the relationship of ideology to Black social science, and sociology as a science of liberation. Traditional sociological analyses are seriously questioned for their relevance to Blacks, and alternative modes of analysis are proposed.

Part IV is devoted to a short discussion of "Black Psychology." The two authors, Joseph White and William E. Cross, Jr., set forth the premise that psychology must become a field of study which is devoted to Black liberation.

Part V, "Toward a Black Perspective in Social Research," discusses some of the fallacies embodied in mainstream methodological techniques that have been utilized with Black subjects. More important, however, most of the authors propose *concrete* methodological alternatives for those social scientists who intend to conduct research among Blacks. The topics examined include nation-building, decolonization, the utilization of quantitative methods in Black communities, formal organizational research and problems involved in the study of "deviant" communities.

In Part VI, two authors (including the anthologist) describe the *subjective* states involved in conducting research. Kenneth Clark provides a moving description of his personal feelings and reactions to his study of Harlem, *Dark Ghetto.* Clark and I take the position that it is not necessary for the scholar to remain detached from that which he studies.

In "Institutional Racism," Part VII, two authors examine racism in social research, in individual case studies. Andrew

Billingsley provides a penetrating analysis of the way in which Black families have been discriminated against, through distortion and omission, in mainstream literature. Richard F. America takes corporate research organizations to task for their discriminatory policies and practices toward Blacks. He uses as his model one of the nation's largest public-oriented research organizations.

The concluding section is a brief summary of new directions and priorities for Black social scientists.

JOYCE A. LADNER

CONTRIBUTORS

ABD-L HAKIMU IBN ALKALIMAT (GERALD MCWORTER) teaches sociology at The University of Akron.

RICHARD F. AMERICA is an adjunct professor of business at Georgetown University.

ANDREW BILLINGSLEY is a Fulbright Fellow at the University of Ghana, and author of *Climbing Jacob's Ladder: The Enduring Legacy of Black American Families.*

ROBERT BLAUNER is a Professor Emeritus in the Department of Sociology at the University of California at Berkeley. He is author of the classic, *Racial Oppression in America.*

JOHN H. BRACEY, JR., is a professor at the University of Massachusetts.

KENNETH B. CLARK is Professor Emeritus of psychology at City College, New York. He has published numerous books, including the widely acclaimed *Dark Ghetto.* He is past president of the American Psychological Association.

WILLIAM E. CROSS, JR., is a professor in the Department of Student Development and Pupil Personnel Services in the School of Education at the University of Massachusetts, Amherst.

DOUGLAS V. DAVIDSON is a professor at Eastern Michigan University.

RALPH ELLISON was author of the classic novel *Invisible Man* and *Shadow and Act,* a collection of essays. He was Albert Schweitzer Professor in the Humanities at New York University at the time of his death.

DENNIS FORSYTHE is the author of numerous articles in journals including *Presence Africaine* and *The Black Scholar.* He is currently practicing law in Jamaica.

E. FRANKLIN FRAZIER was a member of the sociology department at Howard University from 1934 until his death in 1962, serving as chairman for most of this period. He was president of the American Sociological Association in 1948—the first Black to be elected to that position. Frazier wrote the classic works, *The Negro Family in the United States* and *Black Bourgeoisie.*

CHARLES HAMILTON is professor of political science at Columbia University. He is coauthor, with Stokely Carmichael, of *Black Power: The Politics of Liberation, The Black Preacher in America,*

Professor in the Humanities at New York University at the time of his death.

DENNIS FORSYTHE is the author of numerous articles in journals including *Presence Africaine* and *The Black Scholar*. He is currently practicing law in Jamaica.

E. FRANKLIN FRAZIER was a member of the sociology department at Howard University from 1934 until his death in 1962, serving as chairman for most of this period. He was president of the American Sociological Association in 1948—the first Black to be elected to that position. Frazier wrote the classic works, *The Negro Family in the United States* and *Black Bourgeoisie*.

CHARLES HAMILTON is professor of political science at Columbia University. He is coauthor, with Stokely Carmichael, of *Black Power: The Politics of Liberation, The Black Preacher in America,* and *Adam Clayton Powell, Jr.: The Political Biography of an American Dilemma*.

NATHAN HARE, sociologist and psychotherapist, was the founding publisher of *The Black Scholar*, a journal of Black studies. He is author of *The Black Anglo-Saxons* and *The Miseducation of the Black Child*.

*JERRY HARRIS is assistant to the dean and instructor in the department of community development at Livingstone College, Rutgers University. He has taught a course in quantitative methods in urban and community analysis.

RHETT JONES is professor of history at Brown University.

*WILLIAM D. McCULLOUGH, now retired, was associate professor in the department of community development at Livingstone College, Rutgers University.

AUGUST MEIER is Professor Emeritus at Kent State University.

ALBERT MURRAY is well-known for his essays on the South and is author of *The Omni-Americans* and *South to a Very Old Land Place.*

ELLIOTT RUDWICK, now deceased, was a professor of history and sociology at Kent State University.

*CHARLES SAUNDERS lives in Hamilton, Ontario, and works as a research assistant in the psychiatry department at McMaster University.

ETHEL SAWYER is associate dean at Forest Park Community College in St. Louis. She was a graduate student in sociology at Washington University, St. Louis.

JOSEPH SCOTT is professor of Afro-American studies at the University of Washington in Seattle. He has also taught at the University of Notre Dame and the University of Ibadan, Nigeria.

WALTER STAFFORD is associate professor in the School of Public Management at New York University. Trained in sociology and urban planning, he has published articles in *The Journal of the American Institute of Planners* and *Social Policy.* His most recent monograph is *Black Civil Society in New York.*

ROBERT STAPLES is Professor Emeritus of sociology at the University of California, San Francisco. He is author of *Black Families at the Crossroads: Challenges and Prospects* and editor of *The Black Family: Essays and Studies.*

JAMES TURNER is on the faculty in the African–Africana studies department at Cornell University. He is a past chairman of the African Heritage Studies Association and has published in *The Black Scholar* and numerous other journals.

RONALD WALTERS is a professor in the Department of African American Studies at the University of Maryland at College Park. He is author of *Pan Africanism in the African Diaspora.*

DAVID WELLMAN is a professor of sociology at the University of Oregon. He is author of *Portraits of White Racism.*

***SIDNEY WILLHELM** is author of *Who Needs the Negro?* He is associate professor at the State University of New York at Buffalo.

*At the time of the original publication in 1973

PART I

The Socialization of Black Sociologists

John Bracey, August Meier and
Elliott Rudwick

The Black Sociologists:
The First Half Century

The first Black sociologist was W. E. B. DuBois, who was also an historian and social protest leader. In 1899 he published the classic work *The Philadelphia Negro*, the first study of Blacks in the urban community. Indeed, DuBois conceived of the field of sociology, which he called the "science of society," before the discipline was officially established in the United States.

In the succeeding years DuBois was joined by other Black sociologists who made important contributions to the study of Blacks, despite the racist climate of the time. The following essay analyzes the social and academic backgrounds of these pioneers, the influences upon them, and their achievements.

The half century from the appearance of W. E. B. DuBois's *The Philadelphia Negro* in 1899 to the publication of St. Clair Drake and Horace Cayton's *Black Metropolis* in 1945 can appropriately be described as the golden age in the sociology of blacks in America. It included the pioneering work of W. E. B. Du Bois; the contributions of George Edmund Haynes, Bertram W. Doyle, Ira De A. Reid, Oliver Cromwell Cox and Allison Davis; and the classic volumes by Charles S. Johnson, E. Franklin Frazier, St. Clair Drake, and Horace Cayton. . . . From the work of these

3

scholars came four sociological classics—Du Bois's *The Phil-adelphia Negro*, Johnson's *The Negro in Chicago*, Frazier's *The Negro Family in the United States*, and, most highly re-garded of all, Drake and Cayton's *Black Metropolis*. . . .

The sociological study of black America was born in a climate of extreme racism—both in popular thought and among intellectuals and social scientists. As the nineteenth century drew to a close the Negro's position in American society was deteriorating steadily. Disfranchisement, lynch-ings, Jim Crow laws, farm tenancy, and peonage were the black man's lot in the South. Throughout the country, labor unions excluded him from the skilled trades. After 1900, race riots became commonplace in both North and South. It was the most oppressive era in the history of black Ameri-cans since the Civil War; historian Rayford Logan has ap-propriately called it "The Nadir." The movement for Oriental exclusion and the overseas imperialism against col-ored peoples in the Caribbean and the Pacific only rein-forced this general racism of the period. Southern propa-gandists held that not only were blacks an innately inferior, immoral, and criminal race, but that in fact freedom caused a reversion to barbarism; many of them justified lynching on the basis of the black man's allegedly increasing tendency toward rape and believed that colonization of American blacks in Africa or the Caribbean was the only alternative to violent extermination. In the North weighty scholarly opin-ion in the biological sciences supported Southern racist doc-trines, and eminent historians and political scientists reinter-preted Reconstruction and the triumph of white supremacy in a manner favorable to the white South. Almost alone among prominent social scientists, the anthropologist Franz Boas maintained that innate racial differences were inconse-quential.

With the exception of W. I. Thomas, sociological theory prevalent before World War I stressed the biological su-periority of the white race and the "primitiveness" of the "inferior" Negro's "racial temperament," which predisposed him toward "shiftlessness and sensuality," rendering him basically unassimilable. Thus, for example, articles in the *American Journal of Sociology* not only justified white supremacy doctrines but presented them as necessary fortifications for the preservation of racial purity. As E. Franklin Frazier has described the situation, the "general point of view" of the first sociologists who directed their attention to the black man was that "the Negro was an inferior race because of either biological or social heredity or both; that the Negro because of his physical characteristics could not be assimilated; and that physical amalgamation was bad and therefore undesirable. These conclusions were generally supported by the marshalling of a vast amount of statistical data on the pathological aspects of Negro life." In short, as Frazier said, "The sociological theories which were implicit in the writings on the Negro problem were merely rationalizations of the existing racial situation."[1]

The early sociological study of race relations and the black community was part of a broader sociological concern with social problems and their amelioration. At the turn of the century the discipline of sociology was just emerging as an academic specialty out of a more generalized field of "social science" that included political economy, government, the study of social problems, and even history. The first formal department of sociology was organized in 1892 at the University of Chicago; the American Sociological Society was not founded until 1905 when sociologists separated from the American Economic Association. Thus in the 1890s sociology, economics, the study of social problems, and the field of social ethics were closely intertwined, and often not sharply distinguished. Impressed by the ability

1 E. Franklin Frazier, "Race Contacts and the Social Structure," *American Sociological Review*, XIV (February 1949), p. 2; Frazier, "Sociological Theory and Race Relations," *American Sociological Review*, XII (June 1947), p. 268.

of the physical scientists to understand and manipulate man's environment for man's benefit, most of the early sociologists exhibited a strong interest in using their knowledge to uplift the lot of man by solving society's social problems. This interest was reformist rather than radical and was closely related to the developing field of social work.

W. E. B. DuBois,[2] best known as the leading propagandist of the black protest during the first third of the twentieth century, was also the first black sociologist. Educated at Fisk, the University of Berlin, and Harvard—where he received a Ph.D. in history in 1895—DuBois was exposed to the best in social science training offered at the time, and, like his contemporaries, clearly combined the scientific and melioristic in his own work. As he later recalled:

I determined to put science into sociology through a study of the condition and problems of my own group. I was going to study the facts, any and all facts, concerning the American Negro and his plight, and by measurement and comparison and research, work up to any valid generalization which I could.[3]

DuBois's opportunity came in 1896 when municipal reformers in the Philadelphia settlement house movement decided that a painstaking statistical study of Philadelphia's blacks could serve as a guideline to improve their social conditions. For fifteen months DuBois was a participant observer in a slum where one-fifth of the city's Negroes lived. Using a lengthy questionnaire, he personally interviewed hundreds of people and compiled voluminous data on such matters as family structure, income, occupations, and prop-

[2] For more detailed treatment of DuBois as sociologist, see Elliott Rudwick, "Note on a Forgotten Black Sociologist: W. E. B. DuBois and the Sociological Profession," *The American Sociologist*, IV (November 1969), pp. 303–306.

[3] W. E. B. DuBois, *Dusk of Dawn* (New York, 1940), p. 51.

erty holdings. The results added up to a vivid portrait of unemployment, poverty, and family breakdown. In *The Philadelphia Negro*, DuBois criticized whites for offering "platitudes" and "sermons" rather than providing jobs without discrimination or giving extensive financial assistance. More important, he believed that whites must recognize Negro business and professional men as race leaders and grant them the status and power to solve the race's problems. Such a black "aristocracy" would administer social services like day nurseries and sewing schools; develop building and loan associations, newspapers, labor unions, and industrial enterprises; and would thus be in a position to uplift the masses by working to eliminate pauperism and crime within the race. Here DuBois the social scientist became DuBois the social reformer recommending solutions to the race problem. In short, foreshadowing his famous theory of leadership by the "Talented Tenth" of the race, DuBois preached a philosophy of Negro self-help and solidarity, a program of racial self-elevation under the leadership of an educated black elite.

DuBois conceived of *The Philadelphia Negro* as the start of a large research program. Speaking before the American Academy of Political and Social Science in the fall of 1897 he declared that "the first effective step toward the solving of the Negro question will be the endowment of a Negro college which . . . [will be] a centre of sociological research, in close connection and cooperation with Harvard, Columbia, Johns Hopkins, and the University of Pennsylvania."[4] White sociologists did not respond to this appeal; as E. Franklin Frazier remarked years later, "It appears that there was a feeling, perhaps unconscious and therefore all the more significant, that since the Negro occupied a low

---

[4] W. E. B. DuBois, "The Study of the Negro Problems," *Annals of the American Academy of Political and Social Science*, XI (January 1898), p. 22.

status and did not play an important role in American
society, studies of the Negro were of less significance from
the standpoint of social science."[5] Nevertheless, DuBois,
who had accepted a post at Atlanta University, embarked
alone upon an ambitious plan to investigate the life of the
black community. Considering that the University was a
struggling and impoverished institution, it is a tribute to
DuBois's determination as both a social scientist and a social
reformer that between 1897 and 1914 he actually supervised
the preparation of sixteen Atlanta University sociological
monographs on topics ranging from the black family
through the Negro church and Negro education to black
economic and business development.

Obliged to use only unpaid investigators on a part-time
basis, it is not surprising that DuBois's monographs were of
uneven quality. They are notably lacking in sociological
theorizing. Yet they represent a serious effort to introduce
systematic induction into the field of race relations, when
other sociologists were merely speculating about the Negro.
The publications also carried the recommendations of an
annual conference that brought educated blacks, and a
sprinkling of sympathetic whites, to the campus for a discussion of the topic researched that year and its relevance
to the future uplift of the race. Like *The Philadelphia
Negro*, both the research and the annual conference resolutions dwelt upon the value of racial solidarity and self-help
in advancing the black man's status in America.

Despite the seriousness of DuBois's commitment to sociology, he was, in the main, overlooked by the profession.
The *American Journal of Sociology*, founded at the University of Chicago in 1895, devoted many pages to social
welfare problems. But it clearly considered DuBois's work
of minor importance. It ignored the monumental piece of
research, *The Philadelphia Negro*, and during the sixteen

---

[5] E. Franklin Frazier, "Race Contacts and the Social Structure," p. 3.

years DuBois was associated with the Atlanta publications, only two were reviewed in the *Journal.* On the other hand, the editors did publish glowing reviews of some frankly racist books, as well as articles with an avowedly Southern white view on slavery and race relations. Thus, ironically, DuBois, who by training and research orientation toward both empiricism and reform, was part of the mainstream of American sociology as the discipline was emerging at the turn of the century, found himself relegated to the periphery of the profession. Except for reasons of racism it is difficult to account for his thus being shunted aside. Disillusioned, DuBois turned from calm scholarship to overt protest and propaganda; in 1910 he left Atlanta University to take a full-time post as director of research for the NAACP and editor of its principal organ, *The Crisis.*

Thus it is not surprising that DuBois's plea that the American Sociological Society and other learned organizations "put themselves on record as favoring a most thorough and unbiased scientific study of the race problem in America"[6] went unheeded. Nonetheless, a few careful studies, along the lines pioneered by DuBois in his research on Philadelphia blacks, were made of the Negro communities in New York and Boston. These studies—by Mary White Ovington (*Half a Man: The Status of the Negro in New York,* 1911), George Edmund Haynes (*The Negro at Work in New York City: A Study in Economic Progress,* 1912), and John Daniels (*In Freedom's Birthplace: A Study of the Boston Negroes,* 1914)—were made by individuals directly involved in attempts to deal with the problems of Northern urban blacks. Of the three, one—Haynes—was a Negro. The first black man to earn a Ph.D. in sociology (he received his degree in 1912), he was educated at Columbia University. He became the first professor of sociology at

---

[6] W. E. B. DuBois, untitled remarks at "Symposium on Race Friction," *American Journal of Sociology,* XIII (May 1908), p. 836.

Fisk University and at the same time held a post with the National Urban League, thus combining, as did Ovington and Daniels, careful research and social work. In addition to studying the economic life of blacks in New York, Haynes conducted early studies of black migration to the Northern cities prior to and during the First World War. In his career, the applied aspects of his interests soon overshadowed the scholarly. By the 1920s he had joined the staff of the Federal Council of Churches; he spent most of his career as a race relations expert for that organization. . . .

Like Haynes, Ira De Augustine Reid (who also earned his Ph.D. at Columbia University, and who served as vice president of the American Sociological Society and president of the Eastern Sociological Society) conducted a considerable amount of survey research on the condition of blacks in various parts of the country. From 1924 to 1934 he worked for the National Urban League. During this period he published *Negro Membership in American Labor Unions* (1930). His major works are *The Negro Immigrant* (1939), a study of West Indian migrants to New York; *In a Minor Key: Negro Youth in Story and Fact* (1940); and *Sharecroppers All* (1941), written in collaboration with the noted Southern white authority on farm tenancy, Arthur Raper.

DuBois's plea for an objective study of American blacks and American race relations became the hallmark of the next stage in the history of the sociology of the black community—the monographs emanating from the famous Chicago school of American sociology. From the end of World War I until the middle 1930s, under the leadership of Robert E. Park and others, the University of Chicago's department of sociology dominated the field. One of Park's major interests was in race relations, and it was the University of Chicago that produced those five distinguished students of American blacks—Charles S. Johnson, E. Franklin Frazier, Bertram W. Doyle, St. Clair Drake, and Horace

Cayton. All of these men, except Drake, were students of Park's.

Park, after a decade in journalism, had pursued graduate training and taken his Ph.D. at Heidelberg in 1904. Soon afterwards he became secretary of the Congo Reform Association, which publicized and campaigned against the atrocities which the Belgians committed against blacks in the Congo. Meanwhile he came to know Booker T. Washington, principal of Tuskegee Institute in Alabama. At Washington's invitation, Park made his headquarters at Tuskegee, spending several years investigating the race problem in the South. In 1914, at the age of fifty, Park joined Albion Small and W. I. Thomas in the Department of Sociology at the University of Chicago. As a leading figure in the most influential sociology department in the nation, Park enjoyed an unusual opportunity to advance the sociological study of the black man in America. While sociologists like E. A. Ross of the University of Wisconsin were still upholding Anglo-Saxon purity and inveighing against blacks or Orientals, Park demanded that sociology cast off bias and emotional agitation and study race relations in varied societal contexts. In his cultivation of a spirit of objective inquiry, Park addressed not only the extreme racists but also students who were strong fighters for the black man's rights. To the latter group, Park reiterated his conviction that scientific knowledge could help to solve race problems, but that only detachment in research would produce scientific knowledge. Under his influence students attempted to analyze with as much objectivity as possible various forms of race prejudice, discrimination, and even interracial violence.

Given the rampant racism of the period and the prejudiced attitudes of most American social scientists, Park's advocacy of detached scientific studies was very attractive to men like Johnson and Frazier. Probably no other person could have facilitated the transition of mainstream sociology's stance from racism to an attempt at objectivity in racial studies as easily as Robert E. Park. It should be made clear that he was no militant in the cause of racial equality. Indeed, as sociologist Ralph Turner points out, "For all of his concern with race relations, it is striking that the achievement of social and economic equality never emerges as a dominant goal in Park's thought."[7] This moderation, combined with Park's eminence in the field of sociology, served to legitimize the serious and scientific study of race relations among professional sociologists.

On the other hand, it should be pointed out that there was a practical and mildly reformist element in Park, who served as the first president of the Chicago Urban League. His research orientation included a strong interest in social problems. Much of the work of the Chicago school was directed toward studying the subject of urban social disorganization and urban pathology; and Park himself saw detached sociological knowledge as essential for the decisions of policy makers. According to Ernest W. Burgess, one of his colleagues at the University of Chicago, Park was drawn to the field of race relations precisely because he wanted "more than anything else to come to grips with a significant [practical] problem."[8]

If Park's emphasis upon urban studies and social problems is reflected in the work of his students who made race the focus of their interests, so also are his conceptual and methodological views. Park placed American race relations in a world-wide framework; he held that black-white relations in the United States, far from being a unique phenomenon, followed a sequential pattern that occurred whenever different races came into contact. In his methodol-

[7] Ralph H. Turner, ed., *Robert E. Park on Social Control and Collective Behavior* (Chicago, 1967), p. xvii.

[8] Ernest W. Burgess, "Social Planning and Race Relations," in Jitsuichi Masuoka and Preston Valien, eds., *Race Relations, Problems and Theory: Essays in Honor of Robert E. Park* (Chapel Hill, 1961), p. 15.

ogy he stressed the anthropological techniques of participant observation and studying the total life of a community; he emphasized also the importance of understanding the relevant historical background of social institutions. He advocated the use of the case study approach of investigation, and was critical of quantified techniques. He believed it was the duty of the sociologist to ascertain the "natural history" of a phenomenon—to abstract from unique events the generalized patterns that characterized such things as the development of social institutions, the course of revolutions, or patterns in race relations. Specific conceptualizations of Park's in the area of race that influenced the work of his students included the notions of racial conflict, competition, and accommodation. Park maintained that when large populations of diverse races came into contact, conflict and competition invariably resulted. Stabilization occurred when one race became dominant and the other accommodated to an inferior position. As part of the mechanism of accommodation there developed an "etiquette of race relations" which maintained "social distance" between the races, enabling them to coexist, although not on an egalitarian level. While competition and conflict produced prejudice and accommodation in the short run, the process of assimilation would inevitably occur. Park, studying the racial situation of his own time in the United States, dealt chiefly with the mechanisms of competition and accommodation, and never tried to explain how assimilation would ultimately be achieved.

The two leading black sociologists trained by Park were Charles S. Johnson (1893–1956) and E. Franklin Frazier (1894–1962). Johnson, the son of a Baptist minister in Bristol, Virginia, received his A.B. degree in 1916 from Virginia Union University, at the time a leading liberal arts institution for Negro youth, and took an undergraduate degree at the University of Chicago a year later. He worked closely with Park for about four years (1917–1921). The

1919 race riot in Chicago led to the creation of the Chicago
Commission on Race Relations, to which Johnson was appointed Associate Director. Under his supervision, the
Commission published in 1922 the classic, *The Negro in
Chicago: A Study of Race Relations and a Race Riot.* From
1923 to 1929 he was editor of *Opportunity* magazine and
research director for the National Urban League; for two
decades, 1928 to 1948, he was chairman of the Department
of Social Sciences at Fisk University, and most of his major
sociological works date from this period. In 1947, he was
elected president of Fisk University. Frazier, the son of a
Baltimore bank messenger, attended Howard University on
a scholarship. Receiving his A.B. in 1916, he taught at secondary schools for three years; took an A.M. at Clark University in Massachusetts in 1920; and in the fall of 1922
went to Atlanta as instructor in sociology at Morehouse
College and director of the Atlanta University School of
Social Work. From 1927 to 1929 he pursued advanced work
at the University of Chicago, receiving the Ph.D. in 1931
with his *The Negro Family in Chicago* (published 1932).
From 1929 to 1934 he worked under Charles S. Johnson at
Fisk University, and then returned to Howard University
to head the Department of Sociology until 1959. Frazier
remained in the department as a professor until his death
in 1962.

Though the work of each man was quite distinctive,
both owed much to Robert E. Park. Frazier's books on the
black family (*The Negro Family in Chicago,* 1932, *The
Free Negro Family,* 1932; and *The Negro Family in the
United States,* 1939) and on *Race and Culture Contacts in
the Modern World* (1957), and all of Johnson's most important books (*The Negro in Chicago,* 1922; *Shadow of the
Plantation,* 1934; *Growing up in the Black Belt,* 1941; and
Patterns of Negro Segregation, 1943) were written in the
spirit of scientific detachment urged by Park. Both Frazier
and Johnson continued, in the tradition pioneered by

DuBois, to make essentially nonstatistical empirical studies; however, in contrast to DuBois's works, the normative elements—the specific recommendations for social change—are virtually absent. Johnson's work, *The Negro in Chicago*, though dealing with a highly emotional subject, appeared to contemporaries to demonstrate that race relations could be studied objectively and scientifically, so dispassionate was its tone. The low-keyed quality of Johnson's writing is so remarkable that, as one friend wrote, "All through his studies he has kept his own detachment. . . . This 'scientific objectivity' surprises people. His colored friends scold him for being a calm student rather than a rabid reformer. White people get mad at his presumption in understanding them and their customs better than they do themselves." . . .

Yet, like DuBois, both Johnson and Frazier thought of their scholarship as a means for advancing the race; like Park, they had an abiding concern with social problems; and like DuBois and Park, both thought of their scholarship as providing the basis for social action. And despite their unemotional tone, the first books of both Johnson and Frazier were informed by a deep concern for the problems of racial discrimination which they described. Johnson became profoundly interested in social problems when in college; to learn more about these problems he turned to social work in Richmond and then to graduate study at the University of Chicago. Frazier developed an ambition to study sociology because it appealed to him as the social science which best analyzed social problems and most nearly provided an explanation of race and class conflicts.

Subsequently, Frazier served for several years as director of the Atlanta University School of Social Work prior to pursuing his Ph.D. at the University of Chicago; in later years he continued on occasion to engage in applied research—most notably when he served as survey director for the Mayor's Committee on Harlem after the Harlem race riot of 1935, and as Chief of the Division of Applied Social

Sciences of UNESCO (1951–1953). Johnson was even more involved in applied sociology. His longtime friend, Edwin R. Embree, has written of Johnson's University of Chicago period: "Before the end of his first year in Chicago he had started the research department of the new Urban League, created a fresh pattern in social study by an analysis of the Negro group in Milwaukee, and, under a Carnegie grant, launched a survey of the huge shifts in Negro population throughout the country."[9] Throughout his academic career, he performed important services to the United States government, including his report on Negro housing, which was prepared in connection with President Hoover's Conference on Home Building and Home Ownership and, most important, his 1937 report for President Roosevelt's Committee on Farm Tenancy. One of the finest examples of Johnson's concern for critical social problems is the slim volume he coauthored with Edwin Embree and Will Alexander, *The Collapse of Cotton Tenancy*.

Although Johnson later branched out to investigate the rural South—a field in which Park had an interest of long standing—the early work of both Johnson and Frazier reflected Park's predominant concern with the urban setting. From Park both men undoubtedly received their attachment to the use of the case study. Both men made important community studies—Johnson's *The Negro in Chicago, Shadow of the Plantation*, and *Growing Up in the Black Belt*; and Frazier's *Negro Family in Chicago* and *Negro Youth at the Crossways*. In these books, Johnson and Frazier clearly showed the influence of the anthropological approach and the use of individual life histories as well as other kinds of personal documents advocated by Park and W. I. Thomas. Both Johnson and Frazier displayed an awareness of the relevance of history to an understanding

[9] Edwin R. Embree, *Thirteen Against the Odds* (New York, 1944), p. 55.

of present-day race relations. Johnson evidenced this awareness most clearly in *The Negro in American Civilization* and *Shadow of the Plantation;* Frazier demonstrated it even more markedly in *The Negro Family in the United States, The Negro in the United States,* and *Black Bourgeoisie.*

Frazier probably displayed a greater tendency to use specific aspects of Park's theory than Johnson. His *Race and Culture Contacts in the Modern World* was an effort to do something Park had not himself done—test his model of a natural history of racial contacts by analysis of racial relationships throughout the modern world. His classic work *The Negro Family* is, as Burgess pointed out in his preface to the book, a specific application of the natural history of the family. G. Franklin Edwards, Frazier's longtime colleague at Howard University, observes that

the book analyzes the impact first of slavery and then of emancipation and urbanization upon the Negro family. These experiences produced in the Negro family variations from the dominant American family pattern—to wit, a more important role for the female; attachment of great significance to variations in skin color; and a higher incidence of illegitimacy, of common law relationships, and of other forms of family disorganization.[10]

By explaining these phenomena in sociological terms, it offered an important corrective to contemporary explanations which accounted for deviations from white middle-class norms in terms of alleged racial characteristics.

Johnson's last major work, *Patterns of Negro Segregation,* also owed much to Park's concepts. Park had stressed segregation as part of the accommodative nature of the patterns of race adjustment which were dominant in his era; and Johnson's analysis applied Park's concepts of social

---

[10] G. Franklin Edwards, "E. Franklin Frazier," *International Encyclopedia of the Social Sciences* (New York, 1968), V, p. 553.

distance and the etiquette of race relations—key aspects of the mechanism of accommodation which segregation represented. Park's ideas on racial etiquette had also been developed—and at greater length—in a book by Bertram Doyle, *The Etiquette of Race Relations in the South.* . . . Like Johnson and Frazier, Doyle, who received his Ph.D. at the University of Chicago, was not only a student of Park, but also taught at Fisk University. Subsequently he left the academic world to become a bishop in the Colored Methodist Episcopal Church.

In *Patterns of Negro Segregation,* as in other books, Johnson, like Frazier, clearly went beyond Park, and sought to show the impact of sociological forces upon the personality development of blacks. In *Shadow of the Plantation* and *Growing Up in the Black Belt,* he related the cultural influences of the plantation and the effects of racial status upon the personality of rural sharecroppers; in *Patterns of Negro Segregation,* he attempted to analyze the varying behavioral responses of different social classes in the black community to the system of racial separation and discrimination.

Both Frazier and Johnson went beyond Park most clearly in their interest in the black community's class structure and its impact on behavior and personality. Although social stratification was a relatively minor theme in Johnson's work, it had a major place in Frazier's writings. Frazier's long interest in Marxism, stemming from his student days at Howard University, when he was a member of the Intercollegiate Socialist Society, undoubtedly helped stimulate his abiding and critical interest in the class structure of the black community. His earliest analyses of the subject were written during the 1920s—his essay "Durham: Capital of the Black Middle Class," in Alain Locke's *The New Negro* (1925), and his "La Bourgeoisie Noire" (1929). His research on the subject culminated in his famous book *Black Bourgeoisie* (1957). He attacked the black middle and upper class for exploiting the black masses and hating the latter's way of life, for seeking to imitate white middle-class culture, and for covering up their inferiority complexes by an exaggerated emphasis upon their status and conspicuous consumption. The book contained many penetrating observations and suggestive hypotheses, but the basic thrust was impressionistic and polemical rather than scholarly. . . .

Although both Frazier and Johnson admired and owed much to Park, each developed in his own way and made his own particular contribution. They were, in fact, markedly different men. As a scholar, Johnson was preeminently the fact finder, the describer. In his spirit of extreme detachment, in his gradualist solutions to racial problems, he was closer to Park than was Frazier. Frazier, on the other hand, was the more theoretical; he was also the more boldly critical—not only of the foibles of the black bourgeoisie, but of white racism as well. Thus in "The Pathology of Race Prejudice," an article published in 1925, he referred to the projective mechanisms operative in white women who accused black men of attempted rape; the resulting furor among Atlanta whites forced his precipitate departure from the city and the loss of his job there.

Frazier's and Johnson's work was received with respect and often acclaim by the sociological profession. Johnson served as a president of the Southern Sociological Society, Frazier of the Eastern Sociological Society; Johnson rose to the position of vice president of the American Sociological Society, and in 1948 Frazier became president of that organization. Park's professional stature was undoubtedly a factor in projecting these two men, with their solid record of accomplishment, into the hierarchy of the profession; but the recognition they received was also due in part to the changing racial attitudes of American social scientists. Among sociologists the transition was epitomized by the work of Howard W. Odum, who in 1910 had written a doctoral dissertation at Columbia University, "Social and

Mental Traits of the Negro," that cloaked with scientific respectability the doctrine of inherent black inferiority; by the 1930s Odum had become both the leading Southern sociologist and a champion of racial equality. The work of both Johnson and Frazier had contributed to these changes in the attitudes of sociologists; Johnson in particular, through personal persuasion, was helpful in bringing his colleagues in the profession around to a more enlightened point of view. Both men (as well as Reid, Drake and Allison Davis) were on the staff that Gunnar Myrdal enlisted to help him in his research for the *American Dilemma* at the end of the 1930s; the publication of this opus in 1944, symbolizing the hegemony of the racial egalitarian point of view among sociologists of race relations, in a sense marks the end of an era.

. . . St. Clair Drake and Horace Cayton, while products of the University of Chicago, were not in the Park tradition. Drake, in particular, was most directly influenced by W. Lloyd Warner, the anthropologist whose strong interest was social stratification. In addition to *Black Metropolis*, Warner stimulated other major studies, including *Deep South*[11] by Allison Davis, the black social scientist, and two white scholars, Mary and Burleigh Gardner. *Deep South*, a detailed study of race, class, and community in Natchez, Mississippi, preceded *Black Metropolis* by several years; though focusing on the Negro community rather than the entire town, the Drake and Cayton study was a complementary investigation of a larger Northern metropolis, Chicago.

Black Metropolis exemplifies the Warner school's emphasis upon social stratification. Drake and Cayton, like Davis and the Gardners, adapted Warner's conceptualization of the white American class structure, modifying it

[11] St. Clair Drake's contribution, both in the field work and in the preparation of the manuscript, was incalculable. See the Foreword of *Deep South* (Chicago, 1941), pp. vii–viii.

to account for the differences in occupational distribution and wealth, and the divergent criteria of social stratification, in the white and black communities. Beyond this, *Black Metropolis* (like *Deep South*) is within the tradition of the holistic case studies of the black community, based upon participant observation, going back to DuBois's *The Philadelphia Negro*. In fact it marks the culmination of this approach to the sociological study of American blacks.

Both Drake and Cayton had spent many years in the black community of Chicago. Cayton, grandson of Hiram R. Revels, one of the two black Reconstruction senators of Mississippi, had originally come to Chicago from his home in Seattle, where he had been trained at the University of Washington. Drake had studied at Hampton Institute in Virginia, where he first became acquainted with Professor Allison Davis. While studying at the University of Chicago, both Drake and Cayton became involved in a WPA research project investigating the general social conditions surrounding the problem of juvenile delinquency in Chicago's black belt. This research expanded in scope and out of it ultimately came *Black Metropolis*.

As a result of their long years of residence and research in the community, they were able to use the technique of participant observation quite effortlessly. The result was an unequalled masterpiece, written with verve and profound understanding, describing and analyzing the historical evolution of the Chicago black community, the discrimination which Negro citizens faced, and the ways in which they coped with it, family life, job exclusion, ghetto housing, politics, class structure, and protest movements. All are analyzed with extraordinary insight.

Although Drake and Cayton did not say so, like their predecessors they were writing in the spirit of using scientific study that would lead to knowledge and understanding of the black community and race relations, and hopefully would form the basis for reform and advancement of the black man's status in the United States. All of the authors whose work is discussed here made it clear in their writings that blacks were human beings oppressed by a racist white society, though their tone ranged from the outright (though muted) criticism of DuBois's *The Philadelphia Negro* through the detached descriptions of Charles S. Johnson and the analytical theorizing of Frazier to the slightly ironic spirit of *Black Metropolis*.

Their writing clearly showed the social pathology arising from white oppression and discrimination—the poverty, the family problems, and the psychological fantasies of the black bourgeoisie. At the same time, these authors also described the richness and diversity of black life and the inventiveness which Negroes displayed in creating institutions and life-styles that enabled them to cope and survive in a racist society. Finally, all of the writers hoped that their published works, by reaching an influential white audience, would promote social change.

Douglas Davidson

The Furious Passage
of the Black Graduate Student

What kind of graduate training or socialization do Black students majoring in sociology receive? What are their reactions to mainstream American sociology? Why do many of them consider this training not to be "relevant" to their future pursuits? Indeed, what is it about this training that makes some of them "furious"?

Douglas Davidson, a young Black sociologist who left the University of California at Berkeley in 1971, describes some of the theoretical and practical concerns he had with the course of study he engaged in at one of the nation's most prestigious graduate sociology departments.

The University of California at Berkeley has made a concerted effort to recruit both graduate and undergraduate minority students since the academic years 1966–67. This paper conveys some of the reactions of Black graduate students after their entrance into the University; it evolved from the experiences, conversations and observations of the writer during his first two years as a graduate student in the Sociology Department.

23

Most of the Black graduates at Berkeley have come in the last two years. American racism and internal colonialism have already become *personally* visible, relevant, and infuriating in their undergraduate student lives and in the classroom itself at white college campuses. By the time they come to graduate schools most are already angry and the graduate experience serves in turn only to exacerbate this feeling. Naturally, both silent and violent confrontations with racism and colonial practices intensify their anger. But even the usual pressures of graduate school, because they come from the white world, have a special impact upon these Black graduates. Although racism and colonialism are two different realms of operation, they clearly do go hand in hand.

Racism is the personal, individual expression of prejudice, while colonialism, whether overt or covert, external or internal, is the social and cultural expression of racism. It is the institutionalization of racism which not only seduces the individual into at least minimal racist predispositions, but also acts as watchdog and relentless enforcer, much as a doomsday machine of white supremacy. The colonial model has gained widespread acceptance as a useful analogy since the appearance of the writings of Fanon, Carmichael and Hamilton, Blauner, Memmi, and others. In essence, the analogy argues that while the form is different, *the process of subjugation and domination is virtually the same for the classical colonialism of Western Europe and the internal treatment of nonwhites in the United States.*

One implication of this model of internal colonialism is that any white who acts in the role of colonizer is made by that role even more racist; the attitude of racism and the enforcement of racist policies are mutually reinforcing. Another implication is that racism is a slippery concept, hard to pin down, and thus a white can quite easily delude himself into believing he is free of it.

Covert colonialism (that is, internal colonialism or institutionalized racism) in the United States operates as a disorganizing agent in the life ways of all its minority peoples. But because this "melting pot" society is so rampantly color-conscious, the disorganizing effect is forced to occur most fully not among the Poles, Irish or Italians, but among the *colored* minority peoples. Precisely because of its psychological existence, the color line similarly serves as a filter which *transforms* virtually all of the common exploitative aspects of graduate school so that the resulting influence on the Black graduate student—already more oppressed than his white counterpart—becomes a difference in kind, not merely in degree. While the objective situation might be the same for both, the subjective state is actually quite different for Black and white students. Therefore, while most of what is discussed below occurs to white as well as to Black, we will be concerned primarily with the Black experience in graduate school and only occasionally with white graduate students.

Four conditions characterize the process of colonization:[1] (1) the colonized subjects did not enter the social system voluntarily but were forced or had it imposed upon them; (2) the subjects' indigenous culture is transformed or destroyed; (3) they are managed and controlled by persons outside their own ethnic status; and (4) racism prevails, i.e., a group seen as different or inferior in terms of alleged biological traits is exploited, controlled, and oppressed socially and psychologically by a subordinate group—a group which also defines itself as superior. One further indication of the not-too-subtle differences between Black and white graduate students should be noted. The faculty is a superordinate group which may or may not see itself as superior and which, acting more or less as a homogeneous mass, may or may not take advantage of its power to oppress *all* gradu-

---

[1] Robert Blauner, "Internal Colonialism and Ghetto Revolt," *Social Problems,* 16 (Spring 1969), pp. 393–408, esp. p. 398.

ate students. Only in this bare sense of the term can the student experiences of the white graduate begin to resemble the colonial elite's exploitation of the Black. These conditions give rise to racism and probable racism, and the colonial model is powerful and instructive in understanding their institutionalization.

Virtually every type of encounter, at any level, is unique to the Black graduate because of the simple fact that he is Black in white America—with its legacy of racism and its institutions of enforcement. But traditional, patterned responses of whites to Blacks as well as structured institutions in the formal sense also serve the usually insidious and never harmless subcultural propensity for racism. To the complacent white observer, many of the situations examined here might seem common to all graduate students and not in any way unique or especially oppressive to Blacks. But the following, to repeat, is a discussion of how Black graduate students respond to these situations.

Since they belong to the colonial elite by virtue of their academic position, Black graduate students do not experience the direct, blatant racist practices that their people experience back in such home communities as Georgia, Florida, Mississippi, Alabama, Texas, Pennsylvania, Massachusetts, and California—to mention only eight. Within the confines of the "hallowed" walls of the university, the Black graduate seldom encounters the overt racism that his people experience on the outside and seldom experiences the white policeman's billy club, his bullet, or his indiscriminate arrests which are so characteristic back home. He seldom experiences the fear evoked by cross-burnings and threats of beating, bombings, and killings; he hardly ever has to cope with unbridled hatred or be afraid for himself because of it. Thus, on the surface it would seem that the Black graduate should feel safe, secure, and content within the ivory tower —and some do: they develop a boundless love for the institution and never leave it. They can neither understand nor accept the "petty" reactions of what already is or will soon become the vast majority of Black graduates at Berkeley and other leading universities. But most of them take little interest in the University community, do not wish to be bothered by more than minimal contact with white professors and students, and want to get their degrees as quickly as possible. What are the reasons for these feelings and behavior? We shall now try to answer this question.

Most Black graduate students are aware of the relationship between racism and the conditions prevailing in their own communities. Although they enter the institutions of higher learning already very sensitized to racism, they are told to believe that no racism is found in those alleged bastions of liberalism known as colleges and universities. Yet they do find that there is racism, rampant racism, which is not at all mitigated by virtue of being covert rather than overt. That it is rampant and subtle makes it all the more insidious to the Black student. Carmichael and Hamilton note that covert racism is less identifiable in terms of specific individuals committing specific acts, but that it is no less destructive of human life:

[Covert racism] originates in the operation of established and respected forces in the society, and this receives far less public condemnation than [overt racist acts]. [Covert] or institutionalized racism relies on the active and pervasive operation of anti-black attitudes and practices. A sense of superior group position prevails; whites are "better" than blacks; therefore, blacks should be subordinate to whites. This is a racist attitude and it permeates the society, on the individual and the institutional level, covertly and overtly.[2]

---

[2] Charles Hamilton and Stokely Carmichael, *Black Power* (New York: Vintage Books, 1967), pp. 4–5. For other treatments of colonialism, see Frantz Fanon, *A Dying Colonialism* (New York: Grove Press, Evergreen Books, 1967) and *Black Skin, White Masks* (New York: Grove Press, Evergreen Books, 1967); and Albert Memmi, *The Colonizer and the Colonized* (Boston: Beacon Press, 1967) and *Dominated Man* (Boston: Beacon Press, 1969).

Just as internal colonialism is more covert than overt, so too is racism in everyday life. The difficulty of "proving" that an individual is racist reflects the insidious nature of "civility" and "tact" in the American way. It is his awareness of and sensitivity to the operation of covert, institutionalized racism that accounts for the "furious passage" of the Black student through graduate school.

For the purposes of this paper, the term "furious" refers to only two subjective states: (1) extreme anger, and (2) extreme inner turmoil generated by one's search for selfhood in a confusing, complex situation at a confusing and complex time in history. One can be especially furious in a confused and complex university in an overgrown town in a red-neck Disneyland. Although these social-psychological states are conceptually distinct, they often overlap in the everyday life of the student: one may become angry, for example, because he finds himself in a complex and confusing situation. This distinction should be noted despite their frequent joint occurrence in the situations discussed below.

Institutionalized Racism in its "Liberal" Academic Setting

Black graduate students become extremely angry when they see the relatively small number of Black undergraduates in predominantly white schools, and even angrier when they learn the pitifully small number of other Black graduate students (1,000[*], 5.5%; 369[**], 3.7%, respectively, at Berkeley, 1969–1970). They are angry because they know

---

[*] A. Billingsley, D. Davidson, and T. Loya, "Third World Studies at Berkeley," *California Monthly*, 80:4, p. 12 (June–July, 1970); California Alumni Association, University of California, Berkeley.

[**] Graduate Minority Office, University of California, Berkeley, 1970.

that this state of affairs is the result of institutionalized racism—colonialism, past and present; and that these few Blacks represent a fundamental contradiction—one of several which characterize Black existence in this country. The contradiction arises from the fact that the white colonizer has told generations of Black people to clean up, take a bath, study hard, correct their faulty grammar, and "we'll let you in"—into the educational institutions in particular and the society in general. Instead, he has lived up to his usual hypocrisies, and we have the proof right before our eyes: the small number of Black students in the white universities. We know that the immediate reasons we are so few in numbers are the various "smoke screens" set up by the colonizer to prevent us from ever entering *his* institutions in large, significant numbers in the first place. The "smoke screens" are *his* IQ tests, his College Boards, his Graduate Record Exams. They are smoke screens because they are culturally biased and thereby do not indicate what most prospective Black students can actually do in a class or with the subject matter. These devices were constructed on *white* populations, and they continue to be designed and "refined" by *white* academic experts. A white middle-class student is more easily able to pass through such smoke screens than is the case for Black and other Third World peoples. These examinations systematically fail to take into consideration the profound differences in subculture and subsociety; i.e., language, environment, values, and attitudes. The colonizer thereby insidiously *imposes* his standards upon Blacks and thereby denies them any real access to white institutions. (One might ask how the ethnocentric impact differs between Blacks in particular and the working-class white in general. Although one might argue that these factors equally oppress both groups, in the same mechanical fashion, there are at least two general types of differences which must be considered: (1) working-class whites forced into the "lesser" universities and colleges generally get a better education than the Blacks who are forced into one of "their" (Black) schools; and (2) working-class whites are socially, subculturally, and psychologically much closer to the "desired" middle-class norms than are the Blacks, and find the smoke-screen tests far less biased against themselves than the Blacks.

Attempts have been made to correct these "oversights," often with spectacular rises in Black enrollment at the undergraduate level (approximately $95 = 0.57\%$ to about $900 = 5.0\%$ at Berkeley from Fall, 1965, to Spring, 1969). At the graduate level the change has been less spectacular (about 30 students $= 0.3\%$ to about $369 = 1.97\%$ at Berkeley during the same period).* Of course, it is not easy to find qualified (in the sense of "white-like") Black college graduates (not to imply that many white graduate departments are looking for them). This problem is explained when we find that most of today's Black Ph.D.'s got their undergraduate training at *Black* colleges[3] which, in turn, were set up for the special needs of the white community (e.g., to help white missionaries live up to Christ's teachings; to develop a British system colonial elite for indirect rule; and to respond to the spirit, if not the letter, of the laws passed after the Civil War). We now begin to see the effects of past racism and their contribution to the fury of today's Black graduate student. But present racism deserves an even greater share of the credit for this fury.

Vice President Spiro Agnew denounced the University of Michigan's decision to achieve Black parity in a few years as a concession to radicals. Finding what he wanted in Dr. Arthur Jensen's notorious paper on racial differences, President Richard Nixon began policy changes; the mood

---

* These estimates come from the Admissions Office and the Educational Opportunity Program, University of California, Berkeley, 1970.

[3] Ford Foundation, Office of Special Projects, *A Survey of Black American Doctorates* (New York: Ford Foundation Office of Reports, 1970), cited in *Trans-Action*, 7:7 (May, 1970), p. 4.

of which[4] helped Governor Ronald Reagan to cancel all Educational Opportunity Program funds which were providing financial assistance to Black and other Third World students. Of all the public colleges and universities in California, it appears at this writing that only one campus, Berkeley, has the *possibility* of *eventually* having a Department of Ethnic Studies housed in a College of Ethnic Studies (at the present time there is only a "Division of Black Studies," among others, in a *Department* of Ethnic Studies). These are just three indications that a new form of control is only beginning to develop now that Blacks have begun to enter some white universities in relatively large numbers and make their presence felt and their opinions known.

Black graduate students become even angrier once they discover that the colonizer's intellectuals have run a tricky "game" on them, a "mash." The colonizer, through his smoke screens and propaganda, had convinced most of us that we would have extreme difficulty making it through *his* advanced degree program. When we begin to take *his* courses, the reality belies the myth; "higher education" becomes virtually nonsense. We lose our fear and become angry because we know that other Black students—high school friends of ours—could do this man's work easily, if only his system had allowed them to get a "good" B.A., if one at all. Because of the man's "mash" and smoke screens, otherwise "qualified" Black students never get into the *man's* graduate school. This is unfortunate and enraging, not because the man's education is so relevant, but rather because many Blacks *think* that it is and feel inferior because they don't have it. Thus, the educational institution at both the graduate and undergraduate levels is nothing but another colonial tool to perpetuate the colonizer's sense of

---

[4] See John Neary, "A Scientist's Variations on a Disturbing Racial Theme," *Life*, 68:22 (June 12, 1970), esp. p. 58D.

superiority and to induce a feeling of inferiority in the colonized subjects.

Brief consideration should be given here to the University as an institution in "interaction" with the Black and other Third World communities. In Berkeley, the University hires 1,641 Third World people in "staff" (as in "faculty, administrators, and staff") positions. The total staff is 5,261.[5] Apart from hiring, the University does little for the surrounding Third World communities other than create a housing shortage and force rents upward to a near-Manhattan level. It is already generally known that the universities do not practice as they preach and are actually often the most reprehensible of businessmen in their investments and in the wages they pay workers on the properties they own. In the highly politicized context of the student community at Berkeley, these corporate racist acts also feed the fires of fury.

Some Concrete Forms of Racism at the Departmental Level of the "Liberal" University

The Black graduate student usually reaches his most intense anger at the departmental level because it is here that he is most intimately exposed to the workings of institutional racism in the university in particular and by extension, white institutions in general. He is in a position here to observe and be a part of the academic white's specializations in and variations on exploitation, cultural imposition and "co-optation" (the latter is for Blacks really an enticement to coerced assimilation). He experiences and witnesses the academic colonialism applied to both Black students and the Black

[5] University of California (Berkeley) Personnel Office, special computer run, January 5, 1970.

community; he is especially aware of such colonialism being applied to the Black community if he is in one of the social sciences.

As Black graduate students we often observe and participate in academic exploitation; we learn that self-awareness is necessary for our own survival. We observe established academia using Black graduate students to go into Black communities to gather data for research. Most of us have participated in this type of exploitation and continued in it until we caught ourselves or had it mentioned to us. We did it under the illusion that we could somehow make a contribution to the needs of our people. We felt that if the all-powerful political colonizers would read and understand the academic colonizer's research report, it would result in some meaningful and necessary services being rendered to our communities. This was an illusion for several reasons. To begin with, the academic colonizer never really expected his research to have this type of impact. In almost every case, his primary concern was to test his particular theoretical model which, if supported, would help to enhance his professional status and yield substantial financial rewards; if all else failed, at least he might not "perish." Secondly, most of the political colonizers do not read his research report unless it presents data which they have reason to believe reinforce their racist beliefs, attitudes, and practices. This reinforcement often occurs either intentionally or unintentionally. For example, social scientists continue to write many volumes discussing the "social pathology" of the Black community. Many of these liberal academic colonizers have felt that they were making a contribution to the Black community by informing white America of the plight of Black people. These white liberal colonizers' "do-gooder" volumes have the actual effect of reinforcing the negative beliefs, attitudes, and practices held by the dominant racist white society; Republican Washington, D.C., was so eager for Banfield's *The Unheavenly City* that galleys of it were passed around as soon as they were available.[6] Banfield, renewing his membership in Glazer's and Moynihan's Cambridge Crowd, argues that it is the Black's fault that he has bad jobs (if any), poor educational attainment, and so on. If the Black man would but rid himself of his damnable culture, his troubles would be over.

Take one "objective" and sincere sociological piece; strain it through a government full of white politicians and policy-makers—Republicans at that; and you have an updated theory of the inherent inferiority of Black people. Black pride salvaged the civil rights movement but now Blacks must once again become ashamed of their subsociety and subculture; how else can they be kept in tow? Dialectically, the pendulum returns.

Again, in 1951, Kardiner and Ovesey published *The Mark of Oppression*, a work small in sample, sparse in cautions, and mammoth in its conclusions; after a few fleeting disclaimers, Kardiner launches into an impressive construction of the dynamics of the pathological "basic personality" of Blacks based on a sample of 25 psychiatric patients. This monograph serves as a negative example because there can be little doubt what the decision would have been if, three years later, Kardiner had testified instead of Kenneth Clark in *Brown v. Board of Education* before the Supreme Court: it would have been "demonstrated" that Blacks' educational difficulties were a result of their own psyche, rather than the result of insidious racist social-psychological dynamics. While it is apparent that it is not only the arrogant and unreasonably ethnocentric materials that are read, it is at the same time all too obvious that the "wait-just-a-minute-men" have been aided by "scholarly" works. (While the one-sidedness of both "good" and "bad" sociology sometimes derives from a lazy disregard for evidence rather than malicious racist intent, such laziness still plays into the hands

---

[6] *Newsweek*, 75:12 (March 23, 1970), p. 56.

of the racists eager to establish their claims about Black inferiority. Again, the subtlety of American racism is remarkable and should never be underestimated.)

Books such as Banfield's and Kardiner's have given racists the evidence necessary for the maintenance of their feeling of superiority in the midst of changing racial contexts. "Objective" tests of "innocent" theories enable flaming racists to continue in their myopic perceptions of Black people; the colonizers, active and passive, sighted and blind, can thereby preserve their racist beliefs with neither guilt nor doubt, nor awareness, because research "proves" that Blacks are indeed a dirty, inferior, and pathological people not merely unwilling (lazy), but apparently incapable of pulling themselves together.*

These studies also have the effect of producing a number of paternalistic white liberal colonizers who feel guilty about the conditions of Black people. They understand that the pathological conditions in the Black community arise from their own racism as well as their neighbors' and ancestors' racism; they all too readily and unwittingly adopt a condescending attitude toward Blacks, and try to convince us that they understand our problems and they want to help us. But these liberal paternalistic colonizers actually hold the *same attitude* toward the Black community as do their overtly racist counterparts, for they too perceive the Black community as a pathological cancer in America. They see nothing of value in the Black community. Regardless of their seemingly liberal intentions, *they in effect see nothing of value in Blackness.* They even recommend that Blacks should renounce their culture and become as white as pos-

---

* Even if Blacks do better work in sociology, whites would still more than likely hold to their notions, but they would always be off-balance. White sociologists are hardly willing to defer to Black ones, although this would be a most interesting situation to observe. Blacks might then have real sway over decisions affecting them. The tenuousness of this possibility only reinforces the sense of hopelessness among Black students.

sible in order to be eligible for admission into the "great American mainstream." The few possible exceptions, if more than merely possible, would only prove the rule; but they often show predictable and pessimistically expected racist assumptions, proving themselves equally unacceptable to Black students.

It is such awareness of and sensitivity to racism that increasingly angers Black graduate students in the social sciences, for they are no longer on the integration "trip"; they have been forced to realize that they and their people are expected to join gladly in American society not as advertised but as it is—perverted, decadent, and racist.

The myth of the great society is annihilated in the citadel of reason. The strength and depth of racism is seen in all its glory, not only in the way it distorts good intentions, but also in its consistent appearance in the point of view of studies of Blacks, and subsequent coloring (no pun intended) of conclusions. Racism is sooner or later seen as an integral part of white American culture, an arbiter of the actions and thoughts of all its people, whether they be aware of its existence or not. Beginning with relatively obvious racists acts, most Black students, graduate as well as undergraduate, become acutely capable of seeing racism in these infinitely more subtle and invidiously concealed realms of operation.*

The student also experiences, or at least witnesses, the subtle two-way dynamics between racism and exploitation. One brother in sociology told an interesting tale:

I had been in [the teacher's] class all quarter and at various times I'd mentioned thoughts that came to my mind. He

---

* The author had intended a few examples of unintentional racism but soon realized that it would be little better than useless to argue to a largely white audience that seemingly innocuous things that they do and say are racist. It is not our task to attempt to prove your racism to you. Our task is to sense that racism and thereby continue to survive.

had paused and listened each time, or I thought he was listening, but as soon as I finished he went on with what he had intended to say. I started to feel like I existed in another dimension or something. But one day I mentioned in class my ideas about [a particular subject], you know, the thing I was telling you about, and he sat up like his chair was wired. It was weird. He began questioning me extensively, and asked me to talk more about it with him some day soon. Two weeks later I was supposed to have also gone to talk with him about my paper and I realized I just didn't want to go. That's when I remembered his unusual interest. I didn't trust something about him, something connected with that thing in class. A few days after that I was talking with [a fellow Black sociology grad student] and he told me that [the professor] is doing some work on [that subject], trying to get a grant or something. I guess he realized I didn't appreciate his one-sided interest in me because he didn't bother me about talking with him any more; and that was cool with me. I'm glad he didn't; he just saved himself the trouble of bringing it up 'cause I wasn't gonna go.

The student's idea included some observations and opinions of Black society. In the remainder of the school year he discovered that similar experiences had been witnessed or experienced by every one of the other Black students he knew in sociology and other fields. Eventually, then, the Black graduate student learns that the white man will treat him as a nigger until he wants something from him, at which point he will still be a nigger. The form of interaction is then altered, but the racist assumptions remain the same. From such discoveries it is but a short step to recognize that the professor might readily use their term papers as sources of data to be included in his own "policy research" and ivory tower publications about Black people.

Many may hear of one or two clear-cut cases of this kind. A kind of non-paranoid paranoia becomes at times evident; non-paranoid because it is based in reality; but "paranoid" nonetheless, because it is excessive and sometimes demoralizing—a student might have trouble getting himself even to write the paper because of the fear that it will be later used for purposes of "intelligence" or "surveillance" aimed at Black people.

In this direct academic exploitation the Black graduate student receives none of the credit for his contribution. In the previous forms, in which he acts as a subsidiary exploiter, a go-between for the head researcher, he does receive some monetary rewards and occasionally, if he has been a "good boy" and has done a very good job, his name will be mentioned in a footnote or in the acknowledgements section of the colonizer's book.

In both forms of academic exploitation, the experiences of *all* graduate students have a high degree of similarity. Indeed, the experiences of Black and white alike are extremely galling. But in the white case, there is not so large a reservoir of already intense anger to be added to.* The levels of

---

* Jerry Rubin recently said that if young whites are not prepared to kill their parents, they are not really interested in revolution. His statement points up a critical point: any conflict between a white student and professor is all in the (racial) family. With nonwhites, it can never be in the "family," for they are perceived and treated as inferiors, an immature people who are first "boys" and "girls," then "aunts" and "uncles" in their lifetimes. Again, the reality of color and colonialism transforms both the objective and subjective reality of Black (and other Third World) graduates so that the "same" dynamics yield different results.

If you accept a man's assumptions you cannot win an argument from him. The white grad student, no matter what his former social class, has "bought" the "game" that was "run" on him. At Berkeley, many have obviously awakened to the assumptions they had implicitly accepted and are now struggling to free themselves. But from our point of view (the perspective of Simmel's outsider and Park and Stonequist's marginal man), they have a very long way to go.

These opinions are reinforced by the racism evident in the responses of many of these radicals to Blacks. They make the same type of blunders of stereotyping and racial imagery that their older brothers and sisters made in the "color-blind" liberalism of the 1950's in interacting with our older brothers and sisters during their stay in ivory white towers. (*Plus ça change. . . .*) The only difference is that today's

reality must be recognized: faculty members may fully intend to share ideas with the student and may be quite perplexed at his apparent lack of intellectual interest. The white student may feel hurt, angered, betrayed, or exploited. The Black student may feel all of these, plus additional anger, a too-ready cynicism, and further assurances of the nature of the white man.

Black graduate students at Berkeley and at other predominantly white institutions could probably add a few other examples of academic exploitation, but we will now turn to the colonial process of cultural imposition and indicate how it works in the colonizer's graduate schools.

Cultural imposition refers to the academic colonizer's practice of applying his traditional "universalistic" standards to the Black graduate student. They are particularly resented for a number of reasons. Because they are white-originated standards, they are seen as (a) an implied devaluation of Black values, (b) threats to Black individual identity, and (c) ruthless and dogmatic application of standards which are oppressive because they imply that Blacks are possibly "subhuman." These standards continue to be used to demonstrate that Blacks are "not ready," or that they are "pathological." From the time he submits his application for graduate admission to the time he acquires the advanced degree, he is subjected to the imposition of these standards; he is aware of the fact that only by demonstrating the ability to meet the standards of established white academia can he get inside the "sacred" walls. Once in the department, the Black graduate must demonstrate to the academic colonizer that he can do the prescribed work.

---

blunders are made at a different, probably better, plane of sociopolitical awareness. Like our older brothers and sisters, most of us pretend not to notice; but, unlike most of them, we do not continue to interact with white students once they have put their foot in their mouth.

The "Unattainable Standards of Scholarship" in Graduate School: A Case Study in the Smoke Screens and Shams of White Liberal Ideology

The Black graduate student (like his white counterpart) is usually ridden with anxiety because he was told or led to believe that graduate school is exceedingly difficult. His undergraduate professors have convinced him that the quality of work expected of him at the graduate level in an institution such as the University of California at Berkeley is extremely high. They tell the prospective graduate student how difficult it was for them to make it through their own Ph.D programs.* They seem to be saying to the prospective Black graduate student that it will be virtually impossible for *him* to make it in graduate school if the undergraduate professor—(and here is where Black and white part ways) who is obviously *much* more "intelligent" than the Black student—had a difficult time getting through. (Significantly, most of Berkeley's Black social science graduate students came not from Black colleges but from predominantly white ones, themselves crucibles of Black anger in ways quite similar to the graduate experience.) In addition, the prospective Black graduate is also often aware of the fact that the academic colonizer has supposedly lowered his standards to allow him to enter the department. He is therefore not only initially "uptight" and concerned about whether or not he is really graduate material, but also likely to feel inherently inferior all over again—a particularly infuriating irritation.

If the Black graduate gets an "A" or an "A—" average, he

* An alternative perspective would characterize the faculty as a status group attempting to protect its privileges from all comers, Black and white alike. They have, of course, been much more successful in defending against Blacks.

has incontrovertible proof that the inferiority "game" is exactly that: a racist colonial tool to subjugate Blacks. From another point of view, one hears more and more these days that white professors use a double standard of grading, a lower one for Blacks (so that a Black "A" is equivalent to, say, a white "B"). If these rumors are true, there are quite a few Black graduates at Berkeley alone who are ready and willing to be told, once again, that they are inferior. Such news would enliven graduate school and make it quite hilarious and entertaining; the laugh would do us good. More seriously, if these rumors are true, then white professors, wittingly or unwittingly, are serving the ends of the next dialectical* racist move: to once again attack the self-concept of the individual Black who has "gotten too big for his britches," and to destroy the burgeoning self-confidence and pride of Blacks as a people (heads, I lose; tails, you lose— but nobody wins). In either case the reality of colonialism is inescapable.

The cumulative effect of these experiences is that the Black graduate student gains insights into how cleverly the colonizer manipulates the colonized and convinces them of their inferiority. Once inside the institution he comes to know that graduate school is not "impossible," and comes to feel that his white counterparts are by and large merely "average" in intelligence; he discovers that there are only few white geniuses, contrary to the myth that has been mashed on him. (There is perhaps a more interesting point to be made here. The possibility that some professors may well be unwittingly participating in the racist dynamics of American society, as well as the certainty that social scientists have unwittingly done so, help point out the sub-cortical [routinized, non-conscious learning] entrenchment of racism, and the infra-cultural entrenchment of an internal,

---

* For a discussion of the dialectical nature of colonizer-colonized relationships, see "The Return of the Pendulum," Chapter 13 in Albert Memmi's *Dominated Man* (Boston: Beacon Press, 1969).

colonial-like system: their machinations are operative even in conditions believed to be free of the blight. This is no mean point, but it cannot be dealt with adequately in the present context. It should, however, be kept in mind; for example, the continuing racial blunders of white students, even after a decade of social and racial turmoil, is probably largely accounted for by the insidiousness of the colonial-racist mechanism. Or, again, the "background" level of anger and rage in Black students may be largely attributed to their sensitivity to this "background noise" of racism.)

The practice of cultural imposition leads Black graduate students to see how totally their careers are determined by white academic standards and to develop a sense of abject powerlessness in the department which allegedly is trying to help them advance as young professionals. The colonizer's standards determine the quality and acceptability of his work; they determine when he is "ready" to be evaluated for his M.A., when he is prepared for his Ph.D. orals, and whether his topic for a dissertation is even worthwhile. At every level, the colonizer's standards are used to determine whether he will continue, drop out or be forced out. Although these standards and procedural rules are also applied to whites, they have for the Black student the force of assimilating agents which must be accepted or he dies as a student. For Blacks these standards are bleaching or whitening agents which are perceived as virtually antithetical to one's self and one's experience. There is again here a subtle shift of forces which acts merely on the principles of the white graduate student but which attempts to descend to the very roots of Black identity and utterly remake it. Both the blindness and the insensitivity to the existence of alternative constructions of American life are typical of academic tradition; if a group of scholars in 1937 agreed that "this is so," then in no other light is "this" likely to be visible. But the Black student knows that it is also a devaluation of the Black world-view.

It is *de rigueur* in graduate school to attack the classical giants in the field but it sometimes happens that the Black student's academic work comes into conflict with the colonizer's standards. For example, the colonizing professor will give him an "A" if a paper uses traditional white colonizer theory in dealing with a problem in the Black community. That is, if the student uses the traditional white social scientist's approaches in studying the Black community without questioning their validity or legitimacy, he as often as not will receive good grades and be perceived as quite "bright" by the professor. But if he wants to question severely or even throw out an accepted sociologism, he must take great care to control his zeal lest he be seen as a Black militant or even a Black racist! He must, as it turns out, know the professor very well indeed if he is to survive *and* be intellectually honest in his graduate work. One well-known aspect of graduate school is sizing up the professor, but this is just another ridiculous aspect of mastering rigorous scholarly standards! Until he learns his professor's idiosyncrasies, the Black graduate who questions the validity of these approaches and goes on to demonstrate that they are brazen and racist is liable to receive great praise or severe condemnation—a bit extreme at both ends. Such is the volatility of racism in the United States.

There is a case in which a Black graduate student in Sociology wrote a paper which challenged the white sociologist's contention that there are large class cleavages in the Black community. The brother argued that there were large income differences, but in a racist society, the subjugated, oppressed group are treated the same, regardless of income. Thus, a Black millionaire is still a "nigger" and there are many places he cannot go and social events he cannot attend because he is a "nigger." The brother went on to argue that if there are class cleavages in the Black community, they were *imposed* from the outside, often by white sociologists. Those Blacks who accepted this "mash" are, according to the brother, living in a fantasy world created by white colonizers who benefit from creating cleavages in the Black community. The brother did not ask the white academic colonizer professor to argue with his theoretical approach, but to evaluate his logic in establishing a creative alternative perspective. The white academic colonizer told him that he had potential and that one day he *might be* a great *sociologist*, but a number of remarks and allusions in his paper bordered on *idiocy!!* The brother might someday be a great sociologist but his paper was somewhat idiotic; that doesn't speak very well for sociology. Furthermore, he merely asked for an evaluation of the *logic* used to create an alternative approach; the professor apparently could not consider a Black man's logic but chose rather to see only the "child-like simplicities" in the paper.

Incidents such as the one just described make it crystal clear to the Black graduate student that he is indeed powerless. To the extent that he plays the role of a colonized graduate student, he has no control over his destiny in the colonizer's institution of higher learning; his people lose him as a member of and contributor to the community. This serves the colonizer's purpose of destroying Black self-determination. Consequently, the Black graduate student experiences a very deep sense of demoralization and powerlessness, a painful sort of "double powerlessness." This kind of incident may make him vulnerable to the academic colonizer's schemes of co-optation.

Co-optation of the Black Graduate Student by the White Academic Colonizer

Co-optation refers to the process by which a dominant or powerful group nonviolently brings within its fold and, hence, control, an entire minority group, or individual members of that group which has challenged or may seriously challenge the power, myths, or *raison d'être* of the dominant group. The problem of co-optation is inherent in graduate school and as such is a problem each group, Black and white, men and women, must face from its own perspective. A distinction should be made here: in the contemporary context of Black-white relations, *it is whites who are co-opted.* Nonwhites are *assimilated*—taken into the white body through the educational-economic mouth and expelled as useless excrement after digestion and assimilation of all economic nutrients. In the case of *colonized* minorities, co-optation, while still at bottom the same process, becomes the "friendly persuasion" to accept forced assimilation; allegiances, subculture, and identity are sought out. The individual is in effect invited to sell his soul to the white "devil." The white belongs to the white American subsociety; he can never really be enticed completely out of his self because a substantial part of his cultural heritage created that world of co-optation. Black subsociety is quite obviously also a part of American society, but whether Blacks "belong" to the dominant subsociety is a moot question; they surely do not "belong" to it enough to reduce substantially the effect of the color filter on the co-optative processes in graduate school and elsewhere.

In the past it was fairly easy for the colonial-racist mechanisms, driven by ethnocentrism, easily to co-opt most of the Blacks who entered white universities. Since there were only a few Black students on a few white campuses, the ethic of color-blindness prevailed; they found themselves isolated from other Blacks and thus from the Black community. These Black intellectuals were engulfed in a sea of whiteness and some of them ultimately came to identify with the colonizer, believing that the elite white colleges and universities, far from being racist, were the realization of the melting pot ideal. While some went on to the point of today denying that they are in any way "Black," as compared with "Negro," others responded to the pressures by joining the American individualism bandwagon, or later, the liberal white entourage. Almost all of them believed that the only reason Blacks weren't in these schools in greater numbers was because they could not meet the standards; they simply didn't have enough self-pride and rugged individualism. Other Blacks knew that the fault could not possibly be blamed on Blacks alone; not all of them were ignorant. These more "sophisticated" Blacks believed instead that Blacks were "culturally deprived" or "culturally disadvantaged." This seemed to be a perfect answer, for neither the institutions nor individual Blacks were at fault; the absence of Blacks in white schools was just an unfortunate historical accident. (In *The Crisis of the Negro Intellectual*, Harold Cruse, in spite of the axe he has to grind, documents these trends to an extent that cannot be discussed here.)

Another distinction must be made here. Although all who "rise to the top" are colonial elite, not all colonial elite serve the interests of maintenance of the colonized *status quo*. The ideals and ethics of this *status quo* did prove to be true and legitimate, ironically enough, for many Black students—yet the acceptance of such ideals and ethics was at the expense of other Blacks, if not also of the individuals themselves: viz., the effective removal of Black people as a primary concern in their lives. Regardless of the specific forms that friendly conversion may take, this effect remains the lowest common denominator of nonwhite assimilation.

The process of forced assimilation still operates today, albeit less extensively, and it has taken on a new form. Blacks have been attacking these institutions as being racist. Many schools have at least tacitly agreed and are responding by stepping up recruitment of relatively large numbers of Blacks. Once he is on campus, the Black student continues to call the colonizer a racist, all the while receiving substantial financial aid and facing the full weight of cultural imposition, to which he must submit to some degree. This has the effect of making the Black graduate student very anxious: he wants to attack the colonizer verbally, but he also wants to acquire the degree. How can he resolve this dilemma? He notes that the professor to some extent wants him to act militant and radical, especially in public and *outside* the classroom. Once in the classroom, however, he must, and some do, become a quiet, concerned, nervous, and therefore traditional student. Gradually he begins to identify with the traditional success goals of the colonial academic institution. These actually become highly desirable to him, only to raise still higher his level of anxiety. He gradually becomes less and less militant in his attacks on the "man" in class. He still raps the militant rhetoric to his fellow Black students; he still attacks white graduate and undergraduate students. But he cultivates the friendship of his professors. The only time he disagrees with his liberal professors is during political discussions. He becomes a militant radical "house nigger." He portrays a militant revolutionary public front and a nervous and anxious student front. He is certain that both of these fronts are necessary to reach his ultimate goal—the cherished degree. Fortunately, these types of ambivalent brothers and sisters constitute a small minority of the Black graduate student population at Berkeley. The majority are struggling to retain and develop their Black perspective in an anti-Black environment.

Other new forms and mechanisms of forced assimilation add to the hostility of the environment as they become recognized by Blacks. For example, (1) Black Studies is tremendously over-controlled by the Administration; (2) both Third World demands *and* desires go virtually unheeded, no matter how well argued; and (3) there are constant assertions that hewing to tradition is apolitical, nonracial, and noncolonial. Some students quickly lose interest in participating in classes; they tire of having to spoon-feed the exigencies of their own and their people's experience so that the white liberal students and professors may understand.

For most Black graduate students, the inner turmoil is

virtually constant. It is exacerbated by the colonial and racist atmosphere, and given added force by the nearly universal discontent with the entire process of acquiring advanced degrees in this period of the Black liberation struggle. Like many other graduate students, we are never sure whether we should be in school or in the community contributing whatever we have to the struggle of our people. Our ambivalence is bound to exceed that of the whites because we generally dislike the school and all that goes with it much more than they do. Furthermore, our mobility produces not only personal tensions but also a dissonance-like tension growing out of the contradictions of our personal mobility as over against the relative immobility of Blacks as a group. We must be incessantly on guard against elitist attitudes and arrogance (all the while being to some degree self-aggrandizing in our mobility), and acutely aware that we are, by our "success," contributing to the self-doubt and sense of hopelessness of some of our brothers and sisters back home.

The nature of graduate training in predominantly white institutions intensifies the turmoil for those of us who view the educational system as little more than just another colonial tool to maintain the *status quo;* we find it difficult to continue in a "business as usual" manner. Those of us who have become interested in implementing Black Studies find we are studying and learning theories, methods, and techniques of teaching which we regard as obsolete or non-functional for Black students. The feedback we receive from our Black community about our graduate careers leads us to feel that we are acquiring an education which may very well be inadequate for the needs of Black people and which we may have to negate, or purge from our minds. This education is not meeting and will not meet the needs of the mass of Black people. Consequently, we feel that Black students must begin to develop alternative approaches in order to meet these needs. This task is difficult, if not impossible, within the context of the prevailing academic requirements; we do not have the time to explore our individual concerns because we are confined to meeting a long list of requirements for our advanced degrees. In sociology, specific course requirements occupy two full years with absolutely no leeway to venture into experimental, creative endeavors; one must be first of all certified before he can offer whatever he has. Indeed, the whole, newly streamlined procedure is so structured as to chain one to the Department for at least the first three years, doing book work rather than actual field work. There is no provision for or any apparent value placed on giving students the opportunity to learn sociology by doing. It seems to be much more important in the eyes of white professors and administrators that Black students be indoctrinated by the sociological catechism for three years rather than that they be allowed also to go out and develop their own ideas.

Yet we feel that it is necessary for us to attain these degrees. If we do not, we can never expect our people to grant any degree of legitimacy to our experimental alternatives; they respect and are willing to grant legitimacy to those of us who have demonstrated the ability to acquire these degrees in the colonizer's institutions. We are beset by an ambivalence and turmoil that has no apparent resolution whether we stay or go.

To further compound this already anxiety-producing situation, the Black graduate finds himself responding to those segments of the Black community who say that education is irrelevant; that we should be in the streets organizing our people "for the revolution." The student knows that the "people" respect education. The "people" have struggled all their lives to make it possible for him to attend these institutions. Thus, the "people" feel that a graduate student has *arrived*; he's made it. Yet the Black graduate knows this belief is another part of the colonizer's mash which the people have accepted. The man has convinced

them that education is "the answer." But an educated nigger
is still a nigger; in this sense, those in the Black community
who charge that education is irrelevant are to some extent
correct.

The Role of the Black Student in the
Struggle for Black Liberation

Again, how does one resolve this general state of inner turmoil? The answer is that one never does. The Black graduate student comes to realize that there are a number of alternatives open to him. (1) Obviously, he can drop out of
school, or (2) he can become co-opted and say that he is not
concerned with his people, that he is really only concerned
with becoming a scholar or, simply, individually successful.
If he chooses the first option, he will find it difficult to live
with himself. We must accept the fact that to an extent we
have accepted the colonizer's mash about our inferiority. If
we cannot convince ourselves, the colonizer, and, most im-
portantly, our people that we can properly jump through
the hoops for these degrees, we will never be happy with
ourselves. For many of us our goal is to develop a Black
nation, in one sense or another. To do this we will need people with certain skills and abilities; therefore we should
strive to acquire them, even though it be supreme drudgery
and supremely infuriating. To acquire these skills, we must
struggle to make Black Studies relevant to the Black community. If we are to construct viable alternatives to meet
the needs of our people, to repeat, we must first have their
respect. To drop out or allow ourselves to be ingested may
very well have the effect of making us irrelevant to the
needs of our people.

The other alternatives that the Black graduate student has
are: (3) to continue to work for the degrees and resolve to
work for change afterward, or (4) continue to work for

the degrees, and simultaneously work for change in his department, the university, and whatever other special interests he may have, homework or not. In order to function within either of these last two alternatives, especially the latter (which is more an ideal than a real possibility), the student must be adept at playing "games"; he has to have the ability to convince the academic colonizer that he is a serious student, properly concerned with intellectual problems both classical and contemporary, and in fact do well as a student, all the while feeling that the whole process is an obsolete ritual.

None of these alternatives are likely to resolve the dilemmas and contradictions involved in being a Black graduate student at a white school. However, they may reduce somewhat the intensity of the anger and turmoil so that one is able to attain some semblance of functioning well. As Blacks we must realize and remember that we were born into struggle and chaos and that we have no reason whatsoever to believe that the status of graduate student should be free of these hallmarks. We must have the strength, courage and insight utilized by our forefathers in their struggles for survival in an even more hostile environment. We must at once possess the strength to struggle and the vision of a new world in which Black people can grow and develop to the peak of their abilities. This can occur only through our commitment to develop our own Black institutions and hopefully, ultimately, the Black nation.

UMOJA!*

* Unity

E. Franklin Frazier

The Failure of
the Negro Intellectual

E. Franklin Frazier is the most outstanding Black sociologist America has produced, rivaled only by W. E. B. DuBois. Frazier achieved great fame in his discipline and served a term as the president of the American Sociological Association. As a product of the "Chicago School of Sociology" from which he received his Ph.D., he was influenced by Robert Park, Ernest Burgess, William F. Ogburn, Ellsworth Faris, George H. Mead, Louis Wirth and Herbert Blumer.

Frazier was greatly concerned with the problems and failures of Black intellectuals. Although in the following essay, written in 1962, he does not speak directly to the failure of Black sociologists, one can infer the implications of his writing for this group as well.

During the past forty years the relations of Negroes to American society have undergone fundamental changes. The tempo of these changes has been accelerated during the past two decades. The changes in the relationships of Negroes to American society have been the result of changes in the economic and social organization of American life which have in turn had their repercussions upon the Negro community and its institutions.

As a result of the changes in the character of the Negro community all the platitudes and clichés about Negroes and race relations have lost their meaning and relevance. The changes in the Negro community and American society have reached a stage where we are beginning to see in rather clear outlines the real problem of Negroes in American society.

There can be no question at the present time that the Negro must be integrated into the American community. But the integration of the Negro into the economic and social organization of American life is only an initial stage in the solution of some of the problems of the Negro.

There still remains the problem of the assimilation of the Negro, which is a more important and more fundamental problem. It is with this second problem that I am primarily concerned. But in order to clarify the issue it will be necessary to make clear the distinction between integration and assimilation. . . .

It is relevant at this point to say something concerning integration and the Negro community. . . . In the generally accepted meaning of the term, integration involves the acceptance of Negroes as individuals into the economic and social organization of American life. This would imply the gradual dissolution of the Negro community, that is, the decline and eventual disappearance of the associations, institutions and other forms of associated life in what constitutes the Negro community.

We do not expect anything approaching this to occur in our lifetime. Moreover, any discerning person will be aware of the fact that certain aspects of the organized aspects of Negro community life will be affected sooner and more fundamentally than other aspects.

For example, Negroes have always been forced to depend upon the economic institutions in the American community for employment and a living. Despite the vain hopes that Negroes have had concerning Negro business as a means to economic salvation and independence, the integration of Negroes into the industry and as white collar workers into the manufacturing and commercial institutions of the country has increased the economic welfare of Negroes and provided them with more business experience than all the so-called Negro business enterprise in the country.

On the other hand, there are certain cultural institutions such as the church and the fraternal organizations that will not dissolve or disappear. However, it has already appeared that in those sections of the country where newspapers carry news about Negroes as normal human beings and Negro reporters are employed, the circulation of Negro newspapers is declining.

I mention these facts concerning the Negro community because it is necessary to emphasize the fact that integration involves more than individuals, but the organized life of the Negro community vis-à-vis the organized white community. . . .

How does integration differ from assimilation? Assimilation involves, of course, integration for it is difficult to see how any people or group can become assimilated without being integrated into the economic and social organization of a country.

But assimilation involves integration into the most intimate phases of the organized social life of a country. As a consequence, assimilation leads to complete identification with the people and culture of the community in which the social heritages of different people become merged or fused.

In 1908, Charles Francis Adams stated in a lecture in Richmond that the theory of the complete assimilation and absorption of all peoples because of the absence of fundamental racial differences had broken down in the case of the Negro.

The Negro, according to Adams, could only be partially assimilated or, in our language, integrated but not assimilated. When he spoke of absorption he was evidently referring to amalgamation.

In recent years there has been much talk about the integration of the Negro but hardly any attention has been given to his assimilation. There have been some wild guesses about the amalgamation or absorption of the Negro and his disappearance in 300 to 500 years. It is to the question of the assimilation of the Negro that I want to devote the remainder of this talk.

It may seem strange if I tell you that the question of integration and assimilation of the American Negro has not been considered or raised by American Negroes but by African intellectuals. Only recently at a luncheon in Washington an African intellectual spoke on the subject and afterwards asked me to write an article on the subject. But the contrast between the attitude and orientation of American Negro intellectuals and African intellectuals was revealed most sharply at the congresses of Negro writers held in Paris in 1956 and in Rome in 1959.

At these congresses the African, and I might add the West Indian intellectuals, were deeply concerned with the question of human culture and personality and the impact of Western civilization on the traditional culture of Negro peoples. It was to be expected that African intellectuals would be concerned with such questions.

But the amazing thing was that American Negro intellectuals who were imbued with an integrationist point of view were not only unconcerned with this question but seemingly were unconscious of the implications of the important question of the relation of culture and personality and human destiny.

I insist that these are the fundamental questions with which all thinkers should be concerned and that it is unfortunate that Americans have not concerned themselves with these questions. The lack of interest in this important question or lack of understanding of it is responsible for much of the confusion in regard to integration which is changing the entire relationship of the Negro to American society.

As far as I have been able to discover, what Negro intellectuals have had to say concerning integration has been concerned with the superficial aspects of the increasing participation of Negroes in the economic and social and political organization of American society.

Practically no attention has been directed to the rather obvious fact that integration involves the interaction of the organized social life of the Negro community with the wider American community.

Moreover, there has been an implied or unconscious assimilationist philosophy, holding that Negroes should enter the mainstream of American life as rapidly as possible leaving behind their social heritage and becoming invisible as soon as possible. This has been due, I think, to the emergence of a sizeable new middle class whose social background and interests have determined the entire intellectual orientation of educated Negroes.

In my *Black Bourgeoisie* I have considered this phenomenon and it is unnecessary to go into the question here. There are certain phases of this phenomenon which are relevant to this discussion.

The first aspect is that the new Negro middle class is the stratum of the Negro population that is becoming integrated most rapidly because of its education and its ability to maintain certain standards of living. In its hope to achieve acceptance in American life, it would slough off everything that is reminiscent of its Negro origin and its Negro folk background.

At the same time integration is resulting in inner conflicts and frustrations because Negroes are still outsiders in American life. Despite integration, the middle class, in escaping from its sheltered and privileged position in the Negro community, has become more exposed to the contempt and discriminations of the white world. Thus, the new Negro middle class is confronted with the problems of assimilation and their intellectuals have not provided them with an understanding of the problems.

This lack of understanding on the part of the so-called intellectual fringe of the new middle class is due partly to the general anti-intellectualism of this class and partly to the desire to achieve acceptance in American life by conformity to the ideals, values, and patterns of behavior of white Americans.

This is no speculation on my part. Every study that has been made reveals that they think very much the same as white Americans, even concerning Negroes.

Moreover, so-called Negro intellectuals continue to repeat such nonsense as "No race has made as much progress as the American Negro in the same period and that his remarkable progress has been due to oppression."

Yet, anyone knows that after 250 years American Negro intellectuals cannot measure up to African intellectuals.

It was the white scholar, Buell Gallagher, in his book, *Color and Conscience*, who showed clearly that Negroes in every part of the world where they enjoyed freedom had achieved more intellectually and artistically than the American Negro. All of this drive towards conformity to dominant beliefs and values is implicit or unconscious striving of the middle class to become assimilated.

The great difference between the orientation of the African intellectual and the American Negro intellectual is striking when one considers their starting point in their analysis of the position of the people for whom they are supposed to provide intellectual leadership.

All African intellectuals begin with the fact of the colonial experience of the African. They possess a profound understanding of the colonial experience and its obvious effects upon not only their traditional social organization, but of the less obvious and more profound effects upon the culture and the African personality.

The American Negro intellectual goes his merry way discussing such matters as the superficial aspects of the material standard of living among Negroes and the extent to which they enjoy civil rights. He never begins with the fundamental fact of what slavery has done to the Negro or the group which is called Negroes in the United States.

Yet it is as necessary for the American Negro intellectual to deal with these questions as it is for the African intellectual to begin with the colonial experience.

The American Negro intellectual is even more remiss in his grasp of the condition and fate of American Negroes. He has steadily refused to recognize what has been called the "mark of oppression." It was the work of two white scholars that first called attention to this fundamental aspect of the personality of the American Negro. Moreover, it was the work of another white scholar, Stanley M. Elkins, in his recent book on *Slavery*, who has shown the psychic trauma that Negroes suffered when they were enslaved, the pulverization of their social life through the destruction of their clan organization, and annihilation of their personality through the destruction of their cultural heritage.

Sometimes I think that the failure of the American Negro intellectual to grasp the nature and the significance of these experiences is due to the fact that he continues to be an unconscious victim of these experiences. After an African intellectual met a group of Negro intellectuals, he told me that they were really men who were asleep.

All of this only tends to underline the fact that educated Negroes or Negro intellectuals have failed to achieve any intellectual freedom. In fact, with the few exceptions of literary men, it appears that the Negro intellectual is unconscious of the extent to which his thinking is restricted to sterile repetition of the safe and conventional ideas current in American society.

This is attributable in part, of course, to the conditions under which an educated and intellectual class emerged in the American society. This class emerged as the result of white American philanthropy. Although the situation has changed and the Negro intellectuals are supported through other means, they are still largely dependent upon the white community. There is no basis of economic support for them within the Negro community. And where there is economic support within the Negro community it demands conformity to conservative and conventional ideas.

Witness, for example, the vote of the National Medical Association in New York City against placing medical care for the aged under social security. The action of this group might be attributable partly to ignorance and what they conceived to be their economic interests; nevertheless, it was done under the domination of the American Medical Association which ignored the whining complaints of Negro doctors against racial discrimination.

I could cite other examples which more clearly represent the absence of intellectual freedom in regard to national and international issues. Most Negro intellectuals simply repeat the propaganda which is put out by people who have large economic and political interests to protect.

Of course, Negro intellectuals are in a different position from the standpoint of employment. If they show any independence in their thinking they may be hounded by the F.B.I. and find it difficult to make a living. At the present time many of them find themselves in the humiliating position of running around the world telling Africans and others how well-off Negroes are in the United States and how well they are treated.

One is reminded of the words of Langston Hughes in *Ask Your Mama*, where he says that the African visitor finds that in the American social supermarket blacks for sale range from intellectuals to entertainers. Thus, it appears that the price of the slow integration which the Negroes are experiencing must be bought at the price of abject conformity in thinking.

One of the most important results of the lack of freedom

on the part of Negro intellectuals has been their failure to produce men of high intellectual stature who are respected by the world at large.

We have no philosophers or thinkers who command the respect of the intellectual community at large. I am not talking about the few teachers of philosophy who have read Hegel or Kant or James and memorized their thoughts. I am talking about men who have reflected upon the fundamental problems which have always concerned philosophers such as the nature of human knowledge and the meaning or lack of meaning of human existence.

We have no philosophers who have dealt with these and other problems from the standpoint of the Negro's unique experience in this world. I am not talking about the puerile opportunistic rationalizations of the Negro's effort to survive in a hostile world. The philosophy implicit in the Negro's folklore is infinitely superior to the opportunistic philosophy of Negro intellectuals who want to save their jobs and enjoy material comforts.

The philosophy implicit in the folklore of the Negro folk is infinitely superior in wisdom and intellectual candor to the empty repetition of platitudes concerning brotherly love and human dignity of Negro intellectuals who are tyrants within the Negro world and never had a thought in their lives.

This brings me to say something of what Negro intellectuals or scholars have failed to accomplish as the intellectual leaders of Negroes.

They have failed to study the problems of Negro life in America in a manner which would place the fate of the Negro in the broad framework of man's experience in this world. They have engaged in petty defenses of the Negro's social failures. But more often they have been so imbued with the prospect of integration and eventual assimilation that they have thought that they could prove themselves true Americans by not studying the Negro.

Since integration has become the official policy of the

country they have shunned more than ever the study of the Negro. They have remained intellectually sterile while propounding such meaningless questions as: Should Negro scholars study the Negro? Should Negro painters paint Negro subjects? Should Negro writers and playwrights write Negro novels and plays about Negroes?

This is indicative of the confusion among Negro intellectuals. But more important still, it has meant that Negro intellectuals have cut themselves off from a vastly rich source of human experience to which they had access.

It is scarcely believable that the only significant studies of Negroes in politics have been the work of white scholars. I have already mentioned other fields of interest in which scholars have made significant contributions. Of course, some of this failure has been the result of ignorant administration of Negro schools which have refused the intelligent proposals of Negro scholars.

Let us take the case of James B. Conant's book, *Slums and Suburbs*, which deals with the tragic position of Negroes in America. As long as 25 years ago I pointed out that urbanization had changed the entire relationship of Negroes to American society and that comprehensive and fundamental research should be done on Negroes in cities. But those Negroes who have controlled the destiny of Negro intellectuals ignored this and even today no Negro college or university is concerned with this fundamental problem.

Conant's book, which reveals the poverty, ignorance and social disorganization of Negroes, emphasizes a phase of the integration and assimilation of Negroes to which I have only vaguely referred. It deserves special attention in what I am undertaking to discuss.

Not only has Conant devoted attention to the position of Negroes in slums, but I have noted that Harry S. Ashmore has published a book dealing with this problem and the frustrations of the Negro middle class.

The significance of the large proportion of unemployed,

impoverished and socially and personally disorganized Negroes in cities for our discussion cannot be overemphasized. It shows clearly that whereas a relatively large middle class is emerging in our cities, at the same time a large degraded proletariat is also appearing.

It reveals the wide economic and social cleavage which is becoming more manifest between the middle class and the masses of Negroes.

These Negroes have little education, practically no skills, and what is more, they have never known a normal family life. Because of their lack of socialization, they can hardly take advantage of the educational institutions, they are unprepared for employment in an industrial society, and they are unfit for normal social life.

Conant is afraid that they will become susceptible to Communist propaganda, but he does not know Negroes. If they were to become Communist their lives would be organized about objectives and goals which would have some stabilizing influence.

But most of these Negroes will become the victims of liquor, dope, and disease and they will engage in all forms of crime and anti-social behavior. Those who seek an escape from their frustration and bewilderment will not join communist movements; they will join all types of religious sects and cults, some of which will have nationalistic or racial aims.

In fact, the growth of the Black Muslim movement represents disillusionment on the part of Negroes concerning integration and a repudiation of the belief in assimilation which is so dear to the middle classes.

Recently we have been hearing about the revolt against the leaders of the Negro. The most significant symptom of this revolt has been the revolt of Negro youth against the old respectable and conventional leadership which acted as mediators between the Negro community and the white community.

The most dramatic aspect of the revolt has been the "sit-in" movements which are a direct attack upon segregation. The aim is integration and ultimately assimilation, if I gauge correctly the aims of the leaders. This seems to emphasize the failure of Negro intellectuals. They can only see assimilation beyond integration. But there are problems of American life that Negroes will have to meet in becoming integrated and assimilated and they concern the economic and social organization of American life.

I pointed out at the beginning that whatever change had occurred in the status of Negroes was due to changes in the economic and social organization of American life. American Negro intellectuals seem to be unconscious of this fact and seemingly believe that integration and ultimate assimilation will solve the problems of the Negro.

It is very important for our discussion on integration and assimilation that the leaders of the non-violence technique have gone to India for philosophical and ideological justification of their revolt against segregation and discrimination in American society.

That the technique should be non-violent is natural since Negroes, who are outnumbered by whites and threatened by the armed might of whites, could not resort to violence or revolutionary tactics.

I do not think that it represents any moral superiority on their part. Moreover, I do not think that Gandhism is really applicable to the Negro's situation in the United States.

Nevertheless, I recognize that it achieves a certain moral respectability because of its religious basis. This is especially important where Negroes confront the guilt-ridden respectable white middle classes. In analyzing the movement and in seeking its religious and moral inspiration, we should recognize that it has its roots in the religious experiences and culture of the Negro folk.

The leaders may speak in philosophical and ideological terms that are drawn from an alien culture but the dynamics of the movement are to be found in the religious experiences of the Negroes. When Negroes are forced to face hostile white mobs, they do not sing Indian hymns, they sing Negro Spirituals and the hymns of their fathers which embodied the faith of their fathers in a hostile world.

That the Negro leaders should turn to an alien culture for the philosophical and ideological justification of their revolt shows the extent to which Negro intellectuals are alienated from the masses. It is also an indication of the failure of the intellectual leaders to perform their role in relation to the Negro. They have failed to dig down into the experience of the Negro and provide the soul of a people.

With exceptions, and I will name Langston Hughes as a conspicuous example, they have tried to escape from the Negro heritage. It was their duty to put this heritage in history books, in novels and in plays, in painting and in sculpture.

Because of their eagerness to be accepted as Americans or perhaps sometimes because of their fear, they have written no novels and plays about Denmark Vesey, Harriet Tubman or Schields Green who went with John Brown. They have accepted supinely as heroes the Negroes whom white people have given us and told us to revere. Even today they run from DuBois and Paul Robeson.

In view of the Negro's history, the Negro intellectual and artist had a special opportunity and special responsibility. The process by which the Negroes were captured and enslaved in the United States stripped them of their African culture and destroyed their personality. Under the slavery regime and for nearly a century since emancipation everything in American society has stamped the Negro as subhuman, as a member of an inferior race that had not achieved even the first steps in civilization.

There is no parallel in human history where a people have been subjected to similar mutilation of body and soul. Even the Christian religion was given them in a form only to degrade them. The African intellectual recognizes what colonialism has done to the African and he sets as his first task the mental, moral, and spiritual rehabilitation of the African.

But the American Negro intellectual, seduced by dreams of final assimilation, has never regarded this as his primary task.

I am aware that he has carried on all sorts of arguments in defense of the Negro but they were mainly designed to protect his own status and soothe his hurt self-esteem.

I am talking about something entirely different. I am referring to his failure to dig down into the experience of the Negro and bring about a transvaluation of that experience so that the Negro could have a new self-image or new conception of himself.

It was the responsibility of the Negro intellectual to provide a positive identification through history, literature, art, music and the drama.

The truth of the matter is that for most Negro intellectuals, the integration of the Negro means just the opposite, the emptying of his life of meaningful content and ridding him of all Negro identification. For them, integration and eventual assimilation means the annihilation of the Negro—physically, culturally, and spiritually.

Guy Johnson has written that in the next twenty-five years there will be more integration but far less than the Negro hopes for, and as a consequence there will be much frustration. Moreover, as Park once wrote, the Negro will be treated as a racial minority rather than a racial caste.

I am inclined to agree on the whole with this prediction, especially for the South. But even in the North where Negroes will achieve greater integration, I can not envision any assimilation in the foreseeable future. The best evidence of this is the manner in which the centennial of the Civil War is being celebrated. The important fact about the Civil War is the emancipation of the Negro and Lincoln's achievement of worldwide immortality as the Emancipator

—not as the savior of the Union, which was a local political event.

Yet, the nation has ignored and repudiated the central fact which is the most important element in the boasted moral idealism of the United States. The Negro is left out of the celebration both physically and as a part of the heritage of America.

The Civil War is supposed to have been the result of a misunderstanding of two brothers, white brothers, of course, and the Emancipation of the Negro is forgotten.

Confronted with this fact, the Negro intellectual should not be consumed by his frustrations. He must rid himself of his obsession with assimilation. He must come to realize that integration should not mean annihilation—self-effacement, the escaping from his identification.

In a chapter entitled, "What can the American Negro Contribute to the Social and Economic Life of Africa" in the book, *Africa Seen by American Negroes*, I pointed out that the American Negro had little to contribute to Africa but that Africa, in achieving freedom, would probably save the soul of the American Negro in providing him with a new identification, a new self-image, and a new sense of personal dignity.

I want to emphasize this by pointing out that if the Negro is ever assimilated into American society his heritage should become a part of the American heritage, and it should be recognized as the contribution of the Negro as one recognizes the contributions of the English, Irish, Germans and other people.

But this can be achieved only if the Negro intellectual and artist frees himself from his desire to conform and only if he overcomes his inferiority complex.

It may turn out that in the distant future Negroes will disappear physically from American society. If this is our fate, let us disappear with dignity and let us leave a worthwhile memorial—in science, in art, in literature, in sculpture, in music—of our having been here.

Nathan Hare

The Challenge of
a Black Scholar

Nathan Hare, who was attracted to Howard University by
E. Franklin Frazier, represents the next generation of Black
sociologists. Frazier explicated the problems and failures of the
Negro intellectual; and Hare, building on the Frazierian tradition, set forth a plan of *action—a challenge.*

In offering this challenge, Hare asks Black scholars in general, and sociologists in particular, to release themselves from
the "sterile repetition" which Frazier so vividly described.

The first black scholar I ever knew was a professor at a
small Negro college in Oklahoma, at the same time mayor
of the town (all-Negro) and poet laureate of Liberia
(Africa). Though he had only a bachelor's degree, he
easily was the superior of his Ph.D. colleagues in debate
and discussion (whenever he could corner them) and used
to wind up on occasion telling them that they needed to
go back to school.

A scholar is a man who contributes original ideas, new
insights and information to the existing fund of knowledge

—whether or not he has a string of academic degrees or executes his scholarly activities in a manner appropriate to the traditions and conventions of the existing world of scholarship.

But a scholar is even more than that and a black scholar is still another species apart. It will be an irony of recorded history, we have hypothesized, though almost an axiomatic one, that black scholars will provide the catalysts not only for black liberation but perhaps for the ultimate resolution of America's pathology now infecting, in some form or fashion, the entire world.

On the shoulders of the black scholar falls an enormous task. He must de-colonize his mind so that he may effectively guide other intellectuals and students in their search for liberation.

The white ruler not only distorted and destroyed the educational development of blacks and colonial peoples but also miseducated himself. Thus the society he dominates is increasingly corrupt and bloody with no clear future. The air is filled with pollution and the land and forests are being destroyed as human alienation and conflict remain on the rise.

The connection between white colonialism and its scholarship has always been apparent to blacks and other victims of it. However, an examination of this relationship is in order.

Thorstein Veblen's observations on white scholarship in such books as *The Theory of the Leisure Class* and *The Higher Learning in America*, though decades old, remain quite applicable today. Veblen described the leisure-class mentality of the wealthy class who sought to conspicuously display their apartness from the manual worker through the attachment of prestige to non-productive endeavor. Thus education, which was largely private at the time and afforded only by the well-to-do, emphasized the abstract as over against the practical. Much time was spent on such matters as syntax, footnotes (implying the leisure to spend on the reading of many books), and the mastery of lofty jargon which, being incomprehensible, could be taken as profound. Even today a student can pass all of his courses with A's but fail to graduate because he flunks the French test though he may never see Paris and would not know enough to communicate well even if he did. Black scholars today, obeying the dictates of scholarly ritualistic tradition, are compelled to footnote, when writing, say, about the slavery era during which their ancestors were forbidden by law and custom to learn to read and write. They must footnote the white slavemasters or historians acceptable to a society which condoned black slavery.

The forces of production which eventually led to over-urbanization and industrialization have produced a concomitant specialization of learning, and a rise of gadgeteering, but the leisure-class legacy has nevertheless remained.

Neither leisure-class education nor specialized education is sufficient to transform black consciousness—or white consciousness for that matter—into a revolutionary, creative instrument for dynamic change. Leisure-class education creates dilettantes; specialized education creates pragmatists and moral zombies devoid of imagination or compassion in the exercise of their skills.

Black scholars too, members of the "black bourgeoisie" described by the late E. Franklin Frazier, have failed in their roles up to now. Aside from a disproportionate number of "house niggers" descendants among them, most received their early training at Negro colleges where the perfunctory trivia of white academia are mimicked and exaggerated. When I taught at Howard University, for example, there were an average of ten mandatory academic (or cap & gown) processionals yearly.

Now there has developed, out of the black studies call for black professors, a mass migration of many such individuals to the staid milieu of the white college faculty, but mainly what they bring there is their Ph.D. degrees and their social fraternity pins, with the same old style of teaching and attitudes toward matters intellectual. They remain isolated and alienated fundamentally from their non-professional fellows, as well as their students, perhaps to an even greater degree than is characteristic of the white professor. Thus whatever scholarly endeavors they execute are prone to be separated and in discord with the needs of their people's struggle. They pant after professional elevation, conforming to the criteria set forth by white racist administrators, while their people pursue liberation without benefit of a viable ideology or theory.

In the late spring of 1962, E. Franklin Frazier, who had been largely responsible for attracting me to Howard University just before his death, delivered an address at Atlanta University on "The Failure of the Negro Intellectual." This had followed by three decades Carter G. Woodson's *The Miseducation of the American Negro* (based on his experiences in acquiring the master's degree at the University of Chicago and the Ph.D. at Harvard). An expanded and refined version of these two indictments, *The Crisis of the Negro Intellectual*, was published by Harold Cruse. The paradox is that only Cruse, who was not college-trained, has been able, in this era, to write such a book.

Such criticisms have been both well taken and well made, but now is the time to take up the work of DuBois, who actually sought decades earlier to launch a program of black research and scholarship. In an essay entitled, "Science and Empire," DuBois told how, when he went to Atlanta University around the turn of the century, he encountered grave problems which not only obstructed his efforts but eventually led to his firing.

Social thinkers were engaged in vague statements and were seeking to lay down the methods by which, in some distant future, social law analogous to physical law would be discovered. . . . But turning my gaze from fruitless word-twisting and facing the facts of my own social situation and racial world, I determined to put science into sociology through a study of the conditions and problems of my own group. . . . I entered this primarily with the utilitarian object of reform and uplift; in contrast to Herbert Spencer who had issued ten volumes using biological analyses and the trappings of science but without true scientific results, but nevertheless, I wanted to do the work with scientific accuracy. . . . I did not have any clear conception or grasp of the meaning of that industrial imperialism which was beginning to grip the world. . . .

I tried to isolate myself in the ivory tower of race. I wanted to explain the difficulties of race and the ways in which these difficulties caused political and economic troubles. It was this concentration of thought and action and effort that really, in the end, saved my scientific accuracy and search for truth. . . . continually I was forced to consider the economic aspects of world movements as they were developing at the time. Chiefly this was because the group in which I was interested were workers, earners of wages, owners of small bits of land, servants. The labor strikes interested and puzzled me. They were for the most part strikes of workers led by organizations to which Negroes were not admitted.[1]

Eventually, after much persecution from blacks and whites, DuBois came to the conclusion that knowledge is not enough, that people know pretty much what needs to be done, if they would only act. And so, he switched, in his own words, from science to propaganda. Thus we lost the inestimable value of his scientific inquiry with regard to the way in which we should act and how to move other men to action.

[1]W. E. B. DuBois, *Dusk of Dawn*, New York: Harcourt, Brace and World, 1940 (Schocken Books Edition, 1968), pp. 50–54.

The importance of the intellectual in the struggle for national liberation has always been apparent. In a book titled *Black Intellectuals Come to Power*, for instance, the author told how, in Trinidad,

When the People's Educational Movement in 1956 became the People's National Movement, more was changed than just one word in the name of the organization, but much in the way of policy and key personnel had already emerged. The period of pre-party activity not only established the dominant themes on which the party platform would be based, but had also been a time in which the norms of leadership and influence within the organization took shape.[2]

The black scholar must recognize and study this and other movements, their successes and failures, as well as the nature of the oppressor and his ways. To date, there has been a tendency to be preoccupied with the study of his own group alone, influenced in part no doubt by the Establishment-sponsored white research to study the victim, as if to say that his own shortcomings, not the policy of oppression, bring on his problems. Thus there are shelves and shelves of books on blacks. Recently, I received a book called *Black On Blue*, and there are studies of "Negroes and Cotton-Picking in South Georgia," "The Correlation Between Negro Unemployment and the Price of Coons in Creek County, Oklahoma" without an increase in insight and understanding of what is necessary for black liberation. A wealthy foundation not long ago gave $10 million to a group of white scholars to study "the Negro." We black scholars at last have recognized that they have been studying the wrong man. We want $10 million, at the least, to study the white man.

The black scholar suffers from the problem of economic

[2] Ivar Oxaal, *Black Intellectuals Come to Power*, Cambridge: Schenkman Publishing Company, 1967, p. 137.

dependency and the Establishment's increasing monopoly on the world of grants as well as the publication and dissemination of materials. The black scholar must break free from this dependency as well as his fundamental enslavement to Western concepts of scholarship.

Let's examine a few of those concepts. One case in point is the taboo against taking a stand on matters of right and wrong.[3] Objectivity, or its facade, has been made synonymous with neutrality, allowing the scholar to remain ostensibly impartial while catering actually to the wishes of the status quo. Objectivity and impartiality are neither synonymous nor mutually inclusive. As a matter of fact, if a scholar is biased against bias he is possessed by a bias. The belief in neutrality is itself a value-judgment.

On the question of objectivity, the late Louis Wirth, in his prefatory remarks to Karl Mannheim's *Ideology and Utopia*, has written:

It would be naive to suppose that our ideas are entirely shaped by the objects of our contemplation which lie outside of us or that our wishes and our fears have nothing whatever to do with what we perceive or with what will happen. . . . The most important thing, therefore, that we can know about a man is what he takes for granted, and the most elemental and important facts about a society are those that are seldom debated and generally regarded as settled.[4]

The black scholar must look beneath the surface of things and, wherever necessary and appropriate, take a stand against the bias of white scholarship. He must be

[3] C. Wright Mills, *The Sociological Imagination*, New York: Oxford University Press, 1959, *passim*. See also Pitirim A. Sorokin, *Fads and Foibles in Sociology and Related Sciences*, Chicago: Henry Regnery Company, 1965, *passim*.

[4] Karl Mannheim, *Ideology and Utopia:* An Introduction to the Sociology of Knowledge, New York: Harcourt, Brace and World, 1936, pp. xxii, xxiii.

biased against white bias, must be an iconoclast, rallying to the call to arms of all the black intelligentsia, to destroy obsolescent norms and values and create new ones to take their place.

. . . the defetishization of "values," "ethical judgments," and the like, the identification of the social, economic, psychic causes of their emergence, change, and disappearance, as well as the uncovering of the specific interests which they serve at any particular time, represent the greatest single contribution that an intellectual can make to the cause of human advancement.[5]

The black scholar can no longer afford to ape the allegedly "value-free" approach of white scholarship. He must reject absolutely the notion that it is "not professional" ever to become emotional, that it is somehow improper to be "bitter" as a black man, that emotion and reason are mutually exclusive. Anna Freud, in *The Ego and Its Mechanisms of Defense*, suggests that it is, on the contrary, normal to be bitter in a bitter situation. If someone sticks a pin in you or a certain portion of your anatomy and you do not yell out, then there is probably something wrong with you or that portion of your anatomy. Emotion and reason may not only go together but may in fact be stimulants to each other. If one is truly cognizant of adverse circumstances, he would be expected, through the process of reason, to experience some emotional response.

To paraphrase racist Rudyard Kipling, if you can keep calm while all around you is chaos, maybe you don't fully understand the situation. If someone points a pistol at you and threatens to gun you down at the count of five (having shot your brother at the count of five, and your mother at

[5] Paul M. Sweezy and Leo Huberman, eds., *Paul A. Baran: A Collective Portrait,* New York: Monthly Review Press, 1965, p. 6.

the count of five), then gets to three and a half on you and you do not get emotional you probably are guilty of being unreasonable.

In any case, the "ideological fog" of the black scholar, which prevents his endeavors from leading to a central body of knowledge, stems in part from this very aping of pseudo-white scholarship camouflaged by grandiosity.

Scholarship is not realized in the individual in synthesis alone, but also in analysis. No true historical analysis is possible without the constant interpretation of meaning. In order to begin an analysis, there must already be a synthesis present in the mind. A conception of ordered coherence is an indispensable precondition even to the preliminary labor of digging and hewing.[6]

Let us look at an example of the way in which one's perspective or ideology influences interpretation. In the Moynihan Report on the black American family, where a correlation was illustrated between black unemployment and illegitimacy, ideology determines whether one concludes that it is the employment factor which must be changed in order to stabilize the family or, as Moynihan concluded, the family must be stabilized as a prerequisite to economic stability. Ideology enabled him to overlook the fact, though he had the figures showing, that there are thirty-three extra non-white females for every one hundred non-white males between the ages of 25 and 40 in New York City and that that demographic condition itself hampers family stability so long as blacks are impelled to adhere to white Western ideals (practiced only superficially) of monogamy and fidelity. Monogamous fidelity assumes a one-to-one sex ratio else the alternatives of celibacy or infidelity regardless of "moral" ideals.

[6] John Huizinga, *Men and Ideas*, New York: Meridian Books, 1968 edition, p. 25.

Therefore, I decided to develop a Hare Report in response to the Moynihan Report. I sought to make a simple study of marital happiness with the methodological notion of planting tape recorders in the bedrooms of relatives and neighbors. A professor said in horror that that would be both unethical (ideology) and crude (methodology). He instructed me to utilize a scale of intensity under which respondents would be asked if they were very happy, somewhat happy, somewhat unhappy, or very unhappy.

I discovered that some women would say that they were very happy but, should their husbands leave the room, would switch to say that, as a matter of fact, they actually were not happy. When told of this, the professor said that I would have to be methodologically more sophisticated, that people sometimes did not know their own true feelings and also might be reluctant under certain circumstances to tell an interviewer the truth. I must then, he said, construct an index to measure happiness by indirection. He suggested kissing as an indicator of marital happiness (as I thought of Judas), and respondents were asked how many times they kissed their spouses per day. Those who kissed their spouses five times or less a day were regarded as very unhappy; from six to 10 times a day, somewhat unhappy; from 11 to 15 times a day, somewhat happy; and those who kissed their spouses 16 or more times a day were—I felt certain—very tired at the end of the day.

The black scholar must develop new and appropriate norms and values, new institutional structures, and in order to be effective in this regard, he must also develop and be guided by a new ideology. Out of this new ideology will evolve new methodology, though in some regards it will subsume and overlap existing norms of scholarly endeavor.

He must understand the social function of knowledge in

general; he must re-assess the traditions, values and mores of Western European scholarship; and finally he must achieve a black perspective of all his training and experience, so that his scholarly tools can become effective instruments for black liberation.

The black scholar must not only develop a new ideology with appropriate methodology, but he must raise new and serious questions even when he cannot immediately find the answers. For "where no clear question is put, no knowledge will give response. Where the question is vague, the answer will be at least as vague."[7]

In Algiers last summer I happened to raise the question to Stokely Carmichael (as a teacher realizing that I could learn from a former student) what he thought the role of a black scholar should be. Stokely replied:

That is not an easy role, because what the black scholar must now do is to begin to find values that are anti-racist and anti-colonial. That means that the scholars must find a way to promulgate the idea of community where black people are, without actually saying that. Because that's the job of the black scholar, to give black people values very subtly because values people accept most are the most subtle values.

Black scholars must be culture carriers, recognizing that the Europeans living in America are not going to allow them to do that, are going to fight them in every way.

Which all boils down to what Paul A. Baran was speaking of when he observed that a genuine intellectual possesses at least two characteristics—the desire to tell the truth and the courage to do so.

As such he becomes the conscience of society and the spokesman of such progressive forces at it contains in any given period of history. And as such he is inevitably considered

---

[7] *Ibid.*, p. 26.

a "troublemaker" and a "nuisance" by the ruling class seeking to preserve the status quo, as well as by the intellect workers in its service who accuse the intellectual of being utopian or metaphysical, at best, subversive or seditious at worst.[8]

To conclude, then, the black scholar's main task is to cleanse his mind—and the minds of his people—of the white colonial attitudes toward scholarship and people as well. This includes the icons of objectivity, amoral knowledge and its methodology, and the total demolition of the antisocial attitudes of Ivory-Towerism. Such is the challenge facing the black scholar.

[8] Sweezy and Huberman, *op. cit.*, p. 10.

PART II

The Sociological Victimization of Black Americans: A Critique

Ralph Ellison

An American Dilemma:
A Review

Almost thirty years ago the Black writer Ralph Ellison reviewed Gunnar Myrdal's classic study of the United States race problem, *An American Dilemma*, a review which was not published until some years later. Ellison's insightful comments are as relevant today in our understanding of some of the age-old biases in American sociology and its treatment of Blacks as they were in the forties. His review of *An American Dilemma* is more than a book review. He goes to the core of some of the basic contradictions and "dilemmas" in American sociology. His later critical observations have continued to raise challenges to modern-day sociologists, and he never passes the opportunity to raise the provocative sociological questions.

Gunnar Myrdal's *An American Dilemma* is not an easy book for an American Negro to review. Not because he might be overawed by its broad comprehensiveness; nor because of the sense of alienation and embarrassment that the book might arouse by reminding him that it is necessary

81

in our democracy for a European scientist to affirm the American Negro's humanity; not even because it is an implied criticism of his own Negro social scientists' failure to define the problem as clearly. Instead, it is difficult because the book—as a study of a social ambiguity—is itself so nearly ambiguous that in order to appreciate it fully and yet protect his own humanity, the Negro must, while joining in the chorus of "Yeas" which the book has so deservedly evoked, utter a lusty and simultaneous "Nay."

In our society it is not unusual for a Negro to experience a sensation that he does not exist in the real world at all. He seems rather to exist in the nightmarish fantasy of the white American mind as a phantom that the white mind seeks unceasingly, by means both crude and subtle, to lay. Myrdal proves this no idle Negro fancy. He locates the Negro problem "in the heart of the [white] American . . . the conflict between his moral valuations on various levels of consciousness and generality." Indeed, the main virtue of *An American Dilemma* lies in its demonstration of how the mechanism of prejudice operates to disguise the moral conflict in the minds of whites produced by the clash on the social level between the American Creed and anti-Negro practices. There is, however, a danger in this very virtue.

For the solution of the problem of the American Negro and democracy lies only partially in the white man's free will. Its full solution will lie in the creation of a democracy in which the Negro will be free to define himself for what he is and, within the large framework of that democracy, for what he desires to be. Let this not be misunderstood. For one is apt, in welcoming *An American Dilemma*'s democratic contribution, to forget that all great democratic documents—and there is a certain greatness here—contain a strong charge of anti-democratic elements. Perhaps the wisest attitude for democrats is not to deplore the ambiguous element of democratic writings but to seek to understand them. For it is by making use of the positive contributions of such documents and rejecting their negative elements that democracy can be kept dynamic.

Since its inception, American social science has been closely bound with American Negro destiny. Even before the Civil War the Southern ruling class had inspired a pseudo-scientific literature attempting to prove the Negro inhuman and thus beyond any moral objections to human slavery. Sociology did not become closely concerned with the Negro, however, until after Emancipation gave the slaves the status—on paper at least—of nominal citizens. And if the end of the slave system created for this science the pragmatic problem of adjusting our society to include the new citizens, the compromise between the Northern and Southern ruling classes created the moral problem which Myrdal terms the American Dilemma.

This was a period, the 1870s, wherein scientific method, with its supposed objectivity and neutrality to values, was thought to be the answer to all problems. There is no better example of the confusion and opportunism springing from this false assumption than the relation of American social science to the Negro problem. And let us make no easy distinctions here between Northern and Southern social scientists; both groups used their graphs, charts and other paraphernalia to prove the Negro's biological, psychological, intellectual and moral inferiority; one group to justify the South's exploitation of Negroes and the other to justify the North's refusal to do anything basic about it.

Here was a science whose role, beneath its illusionary non-concern with values, was to reconcile the practical morality of American capitalism with the ideal morality of the American Creed.

Now, the task of reconciling moralities is usually the function of religion and philosophy, of art and psycho-analysis—all of which find myth-making indispensable. And in this, American sociological literature rivals all three: its myth-making consisting of its "scientific" justification of

anti-democratic and unscientific racial attitudes and practices. If Myrdal has done nothing else, he has used his
science to discredit all of the vicious non-scientific nonsense
that has cluttered our sociological literature. He has, in
short, shorn it of its mythology.

It is rewarding to trace the connection between social
science and the Negro a bit further. Usually when the
condition of Negroes is discussed we get a Morality Play
explanation in which the North is given the role of Good
and the South that of Evil. This oversimplifies a complex
matter. For at the end of the Civil War, the North lost
interest in the Negro. The conditions for the growth of
industrial capitalism had been won and the Negro "stood
in the way of a return to national solidarity and a development of trade relations" between the North and the South.
This problem was not easy to solve. Groups of Negroes
had discovered the effectiveness of protest and what Myrdal shows to be the Negro's strongest weapon in pressing
his claims: his hold upon the moral consciousness of Northern whites.

In order to deal with this problem the North did four
things: it promoted Negro education in the South; it controlled his economic and political destiny, or allowed the
South to do so; it built Booker T. Washington into a
national spokesman of Negroes with Tuskegee Institute as
his seat of power; and it organized social science as an
instrumentality to sanction its methods.

It might be said that this explanation sounds too cynical,
that much of the North's interest in Negro education grew
out of a philanthropic impulse, and that it ignores the real
contribution to the understanding of Negroes made by
social science. But philanthropy on the psychological level
is often guilt-motivated—even when most unconscious. And
here, again, we have the moral conflict. When we look at
the connection between Tuskegee and our most influential

school of sociology, the University of Chicago, we are inclined to see more than an unconscious connection between economic interests and philanthropy, Negroes and social science.

But if on the black side of the color line Washington's "Tuskegee Machine" served to deflect Negro energy away from direct political action, on the white side of the line the moral problem nevertheless remained. It does not, therefore, seem quite accidental that the man responsible for inflating Tuskegee into a national symbol, and who is sometimes spoken of as the "power behind Washington's throne," was none other than Dr. Robert E. Park, co-founder of the University of Chicago School of Sociology.

The positive contributions of Dr. Park and those men connected with him are well established. American Negroes have benefited greatly from their research; and some of the most brilliant of Negro scholars have been connected with them. Perhaps the most just charge to be made against them is that of timidity. They have been, in the negative sense, victims of the imposed limitations of bourgeois science. Because certainly their recent works have moved closer and closer toward the conclusions made by Myrdal. Indeed, without their active participation, *An American Dilemma* would have been far less effective. Nevertheless, it was Myrdal who made the most of their findings. Perhaps it took the rise of fascism to free American social science of its timidity. Certainly it was necessary to clear it of some of the anti-Negro assumptions with which it started.

Dr. Robert E. Park was both a greater scientist and, in his attitude toward Negroes, a greater democrat than William Graham Sumner. (It will perhaps pain many to see these names in juxtaposition.) In our world, however, extremes quickly meet. Sumner believed it "the greatest folly of which men can be capable to sit down with a slate and pencil and plan out a new social world"; a point of view containing little hope for the underdog. But for all his good works, some of Park's assumptions were little better. The Negro, he felt, "has always been interested rather in expression than in action; interested in life itself rather than in its reconstruction or reformation. The Negro is, by natural disposition, neither an intellectual nor an idealist, like the Jew; nor a brooding introspective, like the East Indian; nor a pioneer and frontiersman, like the Anglo-Saxon. He is primarily an artist, loving life for its own sake. His *métier* is expression rather than action. He is, so to speak, the lady among the races."

Park's descriptive metaphor is so pregnant with mixed motives as to birth a thousand compromises and indecisions. Imagine the effect such teachings have had upon Negro students alone! Thus what started as part of a democratic attitude, ends not only uncomfortably close to the preachings of Sumner, but to those of Dr. Goebbels as well.

One becomes impatient with those critics who accuse American capitalism of neglecting social planning. Actually its planning lay in having the loosest plan possible. And when it was economically expedient to change plans it has been able to do so. During the Abolitionist period the moral nature of the Negro problem was generally recognized. But with the passing of the Reconstruction the moral aspect was forced out of consciousness. Significantly, Booker T. Washington wrote a biography in which he deliberately gave the *coup de grâce* to the memory of Frederick Douglass, the Negro leader who, in his aggressive career, united the moral and political factions for the anti-slavery struggle.

Following World War I, under the war-stimulated revival of democracy, there was a brief moment when the moral nature of the problem threatened to come alive in the minds of white Americans. This time it was rationalized by projecting into popular fiction the stereotype of the

Negro as an exotic primitive; while social science, under the pressure of war production needs, was devoted to proving that Negroes were not so inferior as a few decades before. It was during this period that some of the most scientifically valid concepts for understanding the Negro were advanced. But social science did not have the courage of its own research. Following its vital Jamesian influence it began to discover the questionable values it supported and, until Myrdal arrived, timidly held its breath.

Why, then, should Myrdal be brought into the country in 1937 by the Carnegie Foundation to prepare this study and not before? Why this sudden junking of ideological fixtures?

According to F. P. Keppel, who writes the Foreword for the trustees of the Carnegie Corporation: "The underlying purpose of these studies is to contribute to the general advancement and diffusion of knowledge and understanding." There was, Mr. Keppel admits, another reason, namely, "the need of the foundation itself for fuller light in the formulation and development of its own program." Former Secretary of War, Newton D. Baker, target of much Negro discontent over the treatment of Negro soldiers during the last war, suggested the study; and the board agreed with him that "more knowledge and better organized and interrelated knowledge [of the Negro problem] were essential before the Corporation could intelligently distribute its own funds." And that "the gathering and digestion of the material might well have a usefulness far beyond our own needs."

These, we must admit, are all good reasons, although a bit vague. One thing, however, is clear: a need was felt for a new ideological approach to the Negro problem. This need was general, and if we look for a moment at those two groups—the left-wing parties and the New Deal—that showed the greatest concern with the Negro problem during the period between the Depression and the outbreak of the war, we are able to see how the need expressed itself.

Both the Left and the New Deal showed a far less restrained approach to the Negro than any groups since the Abolitionists. The Left brought the world-view of Marxism into the Negro community, introduced new techniques of organization and struggle, and included the Negro in its program on a basis of equality. Within its far more rigid framework the New Deal moved in the same democratic direction. Nevertheless, for all their activity, both groups neglected sharp ideological planning where the Negro was concerned. Both, it might be said, went about solving the Negro problem without defining the nature of the problem beyond its economic and narrowly political aspects. Which is not unusual for politicians—only here both groups consistently professed and demonstrated far more social vision than the average political party.

The most striking example of this failure is to be seen in the New Deal Administration's perpetuation of a Jim Crow Army, and the shamefaced support of it given by the Communists. It would be easy—on the basis of some of the slogans attributed to Negro people by the Communists, from time to time, and the New Deal's frequent retreats on Negro issues—to question the sincerity of these two groups. Or, in the case of the New Deal, attribute its failure to its desire to hold power in a concrete political situation; while the failure of the Communists could be laid to "Red perfidy." But this would be silly. Sincerity is not a quality that one expects of political parties, not even revolutionary ones. To question their sincerity makes room for the old idea of paternalism, and the corny notion that these groups have an obligation to "do something *for* the Negro."

The only sincerity to be expected of political parties is that flexible variety whereby they are enabled to put their own programs into effect. Regardless of their long-range intentions, on the practical level they are guided not by humanism so much as by expediencies of power. Thus if there is any insincerity here, it lies in the failure of these groups to make the best of their own interests by basing their alliances with Negroes upon a more scientific knowledge of the subtleties of Negro—White relations.

Dismissing the New Deal point of view as the eclectic creation of a capitalism in momentary retreat, what was influencing the Communists who emphasized the unity of theory and practice? This, we believe, sprang from their inheritance of the American Dilemma (which, incidentally disproves the red-baiters' charge that left-wingers are alien). Despite its projection of a morality based upon Marxist internationalism, it had inherited the moral problem centering upon the Negro which Myrdal finds in the very tissue of American thinking. And while we disagree with Myrdal's assumption that the psychological barrier between black and white workers is relatively rigid—their cooperation in unions and war plants disproves this—he has done the Left a service in pointing out that there *is* a psychological problem which, in this country, requires special attention.

For in our culture the problem of the irrational, that blind spot in our knowledge of society where Marx cries out for Freud and Freud for Marx, but where approaching, both grow wary and shout insults lest they actually meet, has taken the form of the Negro problem.

In Europe it was the fascists who made the manipulation of myth and symbol a vital part of their political technology. But here at home, as we have shown, it was only the Southern ruling class that showed a similar skill for psychology and ideological manipulation. By contrast, the planning of the Northern ruling groups in relation to the South and the Negro has always presented itself as non-planning and philanthropy on the surface, and as sociological theory underneath. Until the Depression the industrial and social isolationism of the South was felt to offer the broadest possibility for business exploitation. But attempts at national economic recovery proved this idea outdated; Northern capital could no longer turn its head while the Southern ruling group went its regressive way. Hence the New Deal's assault upon the ignorance and backwardness of the Southern "one-third of a nation." There was a vague recognition that the necessity of the economic base of American capitalism had become dislocated from its ideological superstructure. However, the nation, so technologically advanced and scientifically alert, showed itself amazingly backward in creating or borrowing techniques to bring these two aspects of social reality into focus. Not that the nature of the problem was not understood. Writers ranging from Earl Browder, through Max Lerner, to the New Deal Braintrusters had a lot to say about it. And Lerner especially emphasized the technological and psychological nature of the problem, stressed the neutrality of techniques and suggested learning even from the Nazi, if necessary. But for the most part, both New Deal and the official Left concentrated more upon the economic aspects of the problem—important though they were—rather than upon those points where economic and psychological pressures conflicted.

There is a certain ironic fittingness about the fact that these volumes, prepared with the streamlined thoroughness of a *Fortune* Magazine survey, and offering the most detailed documentation of the American Negro's humanity yet to appear, should come sponsored by a leading capitalist group. I say this grudgingly, for here the profit motive of the Right—clothed it is true in the guilt-dress of philanthropy—has proven more resourceful, imaginative and aware of its own best interests than the overcautious socialism of the Left. Not that we expect the Left to have recourse to the funds—some $300,000—that went into the preparation of this elaborate study. But that it has failed even to *state* the problem in such broadly human terms, or with that cultural sophistication and social insight springing from Marxist theory, which, backed by passion and courage, has allowed the Left in other countries to deal more creatively with reality than the Right, and to overcome the Right's advantages of institutionalized power and erudition.

The reviewers have made much of Dr. Myrdal's being a foreigner, imported to do the study as one who had no emotional stake in the American Dilemma. And while this had undoubtedly aided his objectivity, the extent of it is apt to be overplayed.

The whole setting is dramatic. A young scholar-scientist of international reputation, a banker, economic adviser to the Swedish Government and a member of the Swedish Senate, is invited by one of the wealthiest groups in the United States to come in and publicly air its soiled democratic linen. Bearing this set of circumstances in mind while we consider the writing problem faced by Myrdal, we can see how the various social and economic factors which we have discussed come to bear upon his book.

First, Myrdal had to delve into those areas of the American mind most charged with emotion; he had to question his hosts' motivation and present his findings in such a way that his hosts would not be too offended. He had also to tell the South some unpleasant things about itself; he had to present facts unacceptable to certain reactionary sections of the capitalist class; and, in the words of Mr. Keppel, he had, "since the emotional factor affects Negroes no less than whites," to present his material in such a manner as not to "lessen the confidence of the Negroes in the United States."

And when we consider the great ideological struggle raging since the Depression, between the Left and the Right, we see an even further problem for the author: a problem of style—which fades over into a problem of interpretation. It also points to the real motivation for the work: An American Dilemma *is the blueprint for a more effective exploitation of the South's natural, industrial and human resources.* We use the term "exploitation" in both the positive and negative sense. In the positive sense it is the key to a more democratic and fruitful usage of the South's natural and human resources; and in the negative, it is the plan for a more efficient and subtle manipulation of black and white relations—especially in the South.

In interpreting the results of this five-year study, Myrdal found it confirming many of the social and economic assumptions of the Left, and throughout the book he has felt it necessary to carry on a running battle with Marxism. Especially irritating to him has been the concept of class struggle and the economic motivation of anti-Negro prejudice which to an increasing number of Negro intellectuals correctly analyzes their situation:

As we look upon the problem of dynamic social causation, this approach is unrealistic and narrow. We do not, of course, deny that the conditions under which Negroes are allowed to earn a living are tremendously important for their welfare. But these conditions are closely interrelated to all other conditions of Negro life. When studying the variegated causes of discrimination in the labor market, it is, indeed, difficult to perceive what precisely is meant by "the economic factor. . . ." In an interdependent system of dynamic causation there is no "primary cause" but everything is cause *to* everything else.

To which one might answer "only if you throw out the class struggle." All this, of course, avoids the question of power *and* the question of who manipulates that power. Which to us seems more of a stylistic maneuver than a scientific judgment.

For those concepts Myrdal substitutes what he terms a "cumulative principle" or "vicious circle." And like

Ezekiel's wheels in the Negro spiritual, one of which ran "by faith" and the other "by the grace of God," this vicious circle has no earthly prime mover. It "just turns."

L. D. Reddick has pointed out that Myrdal tends to use history simply as background and not as a functioning force in current society. And we see this as one with Myrdal's refusal to locate the American *ethos* in terms of its material manifestations, or to point out how it is manipulated—although he makes it the basis of his stylistic appeal. It is unlikely in this mechanist-minded culture that such a powerful force would go "unused."

Myrdal's stylistic method is admirable. In presenting his findings he uses the American *ethos* brilliantly to disarm all American social groupings, by appealing to their stake in the American Creed, and to locate the psychological barriers between them. But he also uses it to deny the existence of an American class struggle, and with facile economy it allows him to avoid admitting that actually there exist *two* American moralities, kept in balance by social science.

The limitations of Myrdal's vision of American democracy do not lie vague and misty beyond the horizon of history. They can be easily discerned through the Negro perspective.

Myrdal's study of the Negro is, in comparison with others, microscopic. Here, to name only a few aspects, we find analyses of Negro institutions, class groupings, family organization, economic problems, race theories and prejudices, the Negro press, church and leadership. Some of the insights are brilliant, especially those through which he demonstrated how many Negro personality traits, said to be "innate," are socially conditioned—even to types of Negro laughter and vocal intonation. But with all this he can only conclude that "the Negro's entire life and, consequently, also his opinions on the Negro problem are, in the main, to be considered as secondary reactions to more primary pressures from the side of the dominant white majority."

But can a people (its faith in an idealized American Creed notwithstanding) live and develop for over three hundred years simply by *reacting?* Are American Negroes simply the creation of white men, or have they at least helped to create themselves out of what they found around them? Men have made a way of life in caves and upon cliffs, why cannot Negroes have made a life upon the horns of the white man's dilemma?

Myrdal sees Negro culture and personality simply as the product of a "social pathology." Thus he assumes that "it is to the advantage of American Negroes as individuals and as a group to become assimilated into American culture, to acquire the traits held in esteem by the dominant white Americans." This, he admits, contains the value premise that "*here in America,* American culture is 'highest' in the pragmatic sense. . . ." Which aside from implying that Negro culture is not also American, assumes the Negroes should desire nothing better than what whites consider highest. But in the "pragmatic sense" lynching and Hollywood, fadism and radio advertising are products of the "higher" culture, and the Negro might ask, "Why, if my culture is pathological, must I exchange it for these?"

It does not occur to Myrdal that many of the Negro cultural manifestations which he considers merely reflective might also embody a *rejection* of what he considers "higher values." There is a delusion at work here. It is only partially true that Negroes turn away from white patterns because they are refused participation. There is nothing like distance to create objectivity, and exclusion gives rise to counter values. Men, as Dostoievsky observed, cannot live in revolt. Nor can they live in a state of "reacting." It will take a deeper science than Myrdal's— deep as that might be—to analyze what is happening among the masses of Negroes. Much of it is inarticulate, and Negro scholars have, for the most part, ignored it through clinging, as does Myrdal, to the sterile concept of "race."

Much of Negro culture might be negative, but there is also much of great value, of richness, which, because it has been secreted by living and has made their lives more meaningful, Negroes will not willingly disregard.

What is needed in our country is not an exchange of pathologies, but a change of the basis of society. This is a job which both Negroes and whites must perform together. In Negro culture there is much of value for America as a whole. What is needed are Negroes to take it and create of it "the uncreated consciousness of their race." In doing so they will do far more, they'll help create a more human American.

Certainly it would be unfair to expect Dr. Myrdal to see what Negro scholars and most American social scientists have failed to see. After all, like most of its predecessors, *An American Dilemma* has a special role. And while we do not quarrel with it on these grounds necessarily, let us see it clearly for what it is. Its positive contribution is certainly greater at this time than those negative elements—hence its uncritical reception: The time element is important. For this period of democratic resurgence created by the war, *An American Dilemma* justifies the desire of many groups to see a more democratic approach to the Negro. The military phase of the war will not, however, last forever. It is then that this study might be used for less democratic purposes. Fortunately its facts are to an extent neutral. This is a cue for liberal intellectuals to get busy to see that *An American Dilemma* does not become an instrument of an American tragedy.

Albert Murray

White Norms,
Black Deviation

Albert Murray, noted author and social critic, has emerged as
one of the most outspoken critics of American sociology. Although not formally trained in the discipline, he has provided
his readers with gripping, everyday insights into the fallacies
of many social science theories and a great deal of the research
done in sociology. A special concern of Murray's is the way
in which the concept of social deviance has been attached to
Black behavior, a methodological bias that he describes in
this essay.

White Anglo-Saxon Protestants do in fact dominate the
power mechanisms of the United States. Nevertheless, no
American whose involvement with the question of identity
goes beyond the sterile category of race can afford to
overlook another fact that is no less essential to his fundamental sense of nationality no matter how much white
folklore is concocted to obscure it: Identity is best defined
in terms of culture, and the culture of the nation over

which the white Anglo-Saxon power elite exercises such exclusive political, economic, and social control is not all-white by any measurement ever devised. *American culture, even in its most rigidly segregated precincts, is patently and irrevocably composite. It is, regardless of all the hysterical protestations of those who would have it otherwise, incontestably mulatto.* Indeed, for all their traditional antagonisms and obvious differences, the so-called black and so-called white people of the United States resemble nobody else in the world so much as they resemble each other. And what is more, even their most extreme and violent polarities represent nothing so much as the natural history of pluralism in an open society.

No other inhabitants of the United States have ever been subjected to the economic, social, legal, and political outrages that have been and continue to be committed against Negroes. Not even the Indians have been more casually exploited and more shamelessly excluded from many of the benefits of the material wealth of the nation. The over-all social status of Negroes is such that even though the overwhelming majority are native born to multi-generation American parents, they do not enjoy many of the public services, normal considerations, and common privileges that are taken for granted not only by the most lowly of immigrants even before they become eligible for naturalization but also by the most questionable foreign visitors, even those from enemy countries.

The average law-abiding Negro citizen is constantly being denied such legal safeguards as are readily extended to the most notorious criminals, not to mention prisoners of war. It is a fact, for example, that Negro pilots of the 332nd Fighter Group who were captured during World War II preferred the treatment they received from the Nazis to that which they had endured at the hands of their fellow countrymen in Alabama, whose solicitude of German internees was beyond reproach! Qualified citizens of no other democratic nation in the world encounter more deviousness or nearly as much outright antagonism and violence when they attempt to participate in the routine process of local, state, and federal government.

Nor do Americans who are guilty of such atrocious behavior hesitate to add insult to injury. The very opposite is the rule. They hasten to *exaggerate* the damage they have perpetrated in the images of black depravity they advertise on every possible occasion and through every available medium. These images—which naive Negro spokesmen given to mortal outcry seize upon as evidence of the need for reform—are all too obvious extensions of the process of degradation by other means, and have always functioned as an indispensable element in the vicious cycle that perpetuates white supremacy through the systematic exploitation of black people.

The negative image, for example, now permits decent white people to find satisfaction in the so-called norms—which would not exist but for the exploitation and exclusion of black people. These creatures, the logic-tight cycle begins, being nonwhite (the *negative* of white) are *less* than white, and being less than white are less than *normal* as human beings and are therefore exploitable; and having been rendered *even less* human as a result of exploitation, are thus *further* exploitable because less than human, and so on. (It is not at all unusual for some arrivistes to make casual references to Negroes as being unassimilable.)

The cycle is no less vicious because philanthropy sometimes blurs its machinations. Indeed, American welfare programs for Negroes (and often for others too) increase the debasement they are supposed to ameliorate. Except in extremely unusual instances, the assistance afforded Negroes by philanthropic and governmental rehabilitation programs alike is not much more than a choice between contemptuous oppression and condescending benevolence. Not since the Reconstruction have there been any significant rehabilitation measures designed to accelerate the movement of Negroes toward equality. (The Reconstruction, of course, ultimately became the biggest betrayal in the history of the nation, but even so, no subsequent programs have approached, for one example, the achievements of the Freedmen's Bureau.) In fact, even the best of the programs now in operation are more slapdash substitutions for justice and equality than anything else—and at worse, they are downright insidious.

The point is not simply rhetorical. In New York City, for example, the HARYOU-Act Program was ostensibly initiated as a measure to accelerate the movement of Harlem youth into the mainstream of national activity. But what its built-in racism has actually stimulated is a greater sense of alienation. HARYOU is a so-called community development program that bunches young Negroes even closer together in Harlem and provides even less contact with other areas of the city than they *normally* have. It also encourages them to think not like the many-generation Americans—which they are—who have as great a stake in this country as anybody else, but like Afro-Americans. As a consequence of such programs, many Negroes who once proceeded in terms of the very concrete and immediate problem of coming to grips with themselves as native-born Americans, now seem to feel that because they are black (which most are not!), they must begin by establishing some symbolic identification with Africa, mistaking a continent for a nation as native-born "Africans" seldom do. But the riots across the nation since the summer of 1964 suggest that the self-segregation that seems so implicit in black racism is far less likely to lead to voluntary separatism than to a compression of resentment that explodes in violent rebellion.

The operating monograph for HARYOU, Kenneth Clark's *Youth in the Ghetto, A Study in the Consequences of Powerlessness and a Blueprint for Change* is a monument to social science nonsense and nonsensibility. It demon-strates again that other Americans, including most Amer-ican social scientists, don't mind one bit what unfounded conclusions you draw about U.S. Negroes, or how flimsy and questionable your statistics, or how wild your con-jectures, so long as they reflect degradation. And anybody who thinks this statement is too strong, should try giving *positive* reasons for, say, Andrew Brimmer, General Davis, Carl Stokes, John Johnson, and see if most social scientists don't insist on *negative* ones, nor will their insistence be based on any celebration of the dynamics of antagonistic cooperation.

Another kind of "help" provided Negroes is exemplified in most of the plans and programs for the rehabilitation of places like Harlem and Watts. Such efforts begin with studies that find such places are "ghettos" which suffer, as a result of being somehow blocked away from the rest of New York and Los Angeles. Every failing of man and beast is attributed to the inhabitants of such places; *and then the programs promptly institute measures that could only have been designed to lock the inhabitants even further away from the center of things.* Suddenly, pro-graming experts begin discussing ways to make Harlem and Watts *self-sufficient.* Nobody ever explains why Harlem should be self-sufficient but Inwood not. In concocting such plans, no social scientists seem to remember anything at all about the natural principles of centralization that underlie the existence of garment districts, financial districts, theater districts, shopping districts, manufacturing complexes, and so on. For some reason, when it comes to Negroes, the planners seem to forget all about the desirability of keeping residential areas free of commercial congestion.

But ill-conceived and condescending benevolence seems to be the way of American welfare-ism when dealing with Negroes. It is all of a piece with the exasperating convolu-tions of an immense number of social science theorists and survey technicians who, consciously or not, proceed on assumptions equivalent to those which underlie the rationalizations of intentional white supremacy and black subjugation. Moreover, not only are the so-called findings of most social science surveyors of Negro life almost always compatible with the allegations of the outright segregationist—that is, to those who regard Negroes as human *assets* so long as they are kept in subservience—they are also completely consistent with the conceptions of the technicians who regard Negroes as *liabilities* that must be reduced, not in accordance with any profound and compelling commitment to equal opportunities for human fulfillment but rather in the interest of domestic tranquility.

The statistics and profiles of most contemporary social science surveys also serve to confirm the negative impressions about Negroes that the great mass of "uninvolved" white people have formed from folklore and the mass media.

What such universal concurrence actually reflects, however, is far less indicative of the alleged objectivity, comprehensiveness, validity, and reliability of the methodology employed than of its preoccupation with the documentation of black shortcomings. There are, to be sure, many social science theorists who question and reject the motives of the segregationist. But few seem to find it necessary to register any insistent dissent to his assessment of Negroes as being generally backward—except perhaps to disavow any suggestion that such backwardness is inherent in black racial origins. (Of course no contemporary American social science theorist and technician of any professional standing would endorse racism in any form!) And yet no other survey makers in the world seem to have a greater compulsion to catalogue human behavior in terms of racial categories.

The widely publicized document that became known as the Moynihan Report (*The Negro Family: A Case for National Action*) is a notorious example of the use of the social science survey as a propaganda vehicle to promote a negative image of Negro life in the United States. It has all the superficial trappings of an objective monograph of scientific research and has been readily accepted by far too many editors and teachers across the nation as if it were the final word on U.S. Negro behavior. Many white journalists and newspaper readers now presume to explain the conduct of Negroes in the United States in terms of the structure of Negro family life as described by Moynihan. And yet Moynihan did not initiate his research project as a comprehensive study of family life at all. He set out to compile such data as would advertise Negro family life in the worst possible light in order to make, as he insists even in his title, "A Case for National Action."

In these terms, the report certainly has not achieved its purpose. The sensational nationwide attention the report has generated has not been in response to the case it makes for action. Not even the most generous do-gooders have made very much of that. Some black wailing-wall polemicists have in their usual quasi-literate intellectual bankruptcy grab-bagged it as "useful to the cause." But to most white people, sympathetic and antagonistic alike, it has become the newest scientific explanation of white supremacy and thus the current justification of the status quo.

Moynihan insists that his intentions were the best, and perhaps they were. But the fact remains that at a time when Negroes were not only demanding *freedom now* as never before but were beginning to get it, Moynihan issued a quasi-scientific pamphlet that declares on the flimsiest evidence *that they are not yet ready for freedom!* At a time when Negroes are demanding freedom as a *constitutional right*, the Moynihan Report is saying, in effect, that those who have been exploiting Negroes for years should now, upon being shown his statistics, become *benevolent* enough to set up a nation-wide welfare program for them. *Not once does he cite any Negro assets that white people might find more attractive than black subservience.* Good intentions notwithstanding, Moynihan's arbitrary interpretations make a far stronger case for the Negro equivalent of Indian reservations than for Desegregation Now.

The source of this document, strange to say, was not the Department of Health, Education, and Welfare but the Department of Labor. Yet the report does not concern itself at all with any of the extremely urgent labor problems that Negroes are forever complaining about, and it includes no data on the extent of noncompliance with local, state, and federal policies and laws against racial exclusion in employment. What it cites are numerous figures on illegitimate Negro children, broken homes, lack of education, crime, narcotics addiction, and so on. It charts Negro unemployment, but not once does it suggest national action to crack down on discrimination against Negroes by labor unions. Instead, it insists that massive federal action must be initiated to correct the matriarchal structure of the Negro family!

Even if one takes this point at face value, nowhere does Moynihan explain what is innately detrimental about matriarchies. In point of fact, there is nothing anywhere in the report that indicates that Moynihan knows anything at all either about matriarchies in general or about the actual texture of Negro family relationships in particular. And if his sophomoric theories about father figures were not being applied to black people, they would no doubt be laughed out of any snap course in undergraduate psychology. They most certainly would be questioned by any reasonably alert student of history and literature. Was Elizabethan or Victorian England a matriarchy? What about the Israel of Golda Meir? No father figure ranks above that of epic hero, and yet how many epic heroes issue from conventional families?

As for Moynihan's glib but predictably popular notions about the emasculation of the Negro male, not only do they have all the earmarks of the white American male's well-known historical trait of castrating black males by any means but the report's own statistics on illegitimate births among Negroes would seem to contradict any neat theories about the cycle of black female dominance at the very outset. For if males are generally emasculated and the women are well-established matriarchs, it is very curious, to say the least, that it is the women who get stuck with the illegitimate children and most of the problems of raising them while the men run loose. There was a time when you could bag Negro males for being diseased rapists. Moynihan now represents them in terms of complete emasculation and, as his figures on child-birth show, prodigious promiscuity at the same time.

The fact of the matter is that Moynihan's figures provide for more evidence of male exploitation of females than of females henpecking males. Instead of the alleged cycle of illegitimacy-matriarchy and male emasculation by females, which adds up to further illegitimacy, the problem of Negro family instability might more accurately be defined as a cycle of illegitimacy, matriarchy, and female victimization by gallivanting males who refuse to or cannot assume the conventional domestic responsibilities of husbands and fathers. In any case, anybody who knows anything at all about Negro women knows very well that what they complain about is not the lack of masculine authority among Negro men either as husbands or as father figures but the lack of employment and the lack of interest in conventional domestic stability. *Black women, who seem to be more aware of the instability of the white family than apparently is Moynihan, are forever referring wistfully to the white woman's ability to make the white man pay and pay and pay!*

But then if Negro males were as thoroughly emasculated as the Moynihan consensus insists they are, there would be no current racial crisis. White people would not feel so hysterically insecure about the resentment of those whom they are convinced have lost their manhood. White men would not feel that they needed a lynch *mob* to take revenge on *one* uppity Negro. White policemen would not go berserk at the slightest sign of black resistance. White teachers in Harlem would be able to handle Negro pupils at least as well as the great majority of Negro teachers have always handled them elsewhere. Nor would white people ever have felt the need to enact or defend any laws against inter-racial marriages.

Further, though images of black masculinity may simply be invisible to Moynihan, it does not follow that they are also nonexistent for Negroes themselves. Thus, while white supremacists were responding to Uncle Toms, Old Black Joes, and Steppin' Fetchits, Negroes were celebrating John Henry, Stagolee, Jack Johnson, and Joe Louis. While white people promote wailing-wall spokesmen, black people are committed to numerous "unknown" local leaders. For all his rhetorical resonance, the late great Reverend Martin Luther King was much more highly regarded among Negroes when he *did* more and *talked* less, not that they didn't love the way he talked. The mass media provide unheard-of publicity for empty-handed black hot-air militants but the truth is that while Negroes obviously enjoy making white people nervous, they much prefer to keep them guessing.

The Moynihan Report is the stuff of which the folklore of white supremacy is made, and providing such stuff is the role that the social science technicians and theorists all too often play in the extension of black degradation through the systematic oversimplification of black tribulations. There was a time when the white supremacist ideologized his conduct in terms of the divine rightness of the status quo: "If the good Lord had intended all people to be equal, he would have made everybody the same." In the current age of liberal enlightenment, however, even some of the most reactionary segregationists gear their prejudices to the methodology of scientific research. The situation now is that the contemporary folklore of racism in the United States is derived from social science surveys in which white norms and black deviations are tantamount to white well being and black pathology.

That most social science technicians may be entirely unaware of the major role they play in the propagation of such folklore can be readily conceded. But the fact that they remain oblivious to the application of the material that they assemble neither reduces the degree of their involvement nor mitigates the distortion, oversimplification, and confusion that they aid and abet. As a matter of fact, their innocence, which is not altogether unlike that of certain ever so nonviolent munitions experts, allows them to function with a routine detachment that is even more deadly than deliberate underhanded manipulation of facts, figures, and interpretations. The forthright white supremacist, after all, must often contend with matters of conscience, if only to rationalize them away (which accounts for much of his need for the folklore in the first place). The unwitting survey technician has no such problem. Believing himself to be free of ulterior motives, he assumes that his studies are disinterested.

As even the most casual examination of his actual point of departure and his customary procedures will reveal, however, such a technician's innocence is not nearly so innocent as it is intellectually irresponsible. Nor should his lack of concern with consequences be mistaken for scientific objectivity. When the technician undertakes any research project without having become thoroughly familiar with its practical context and with the implications of his underlying thesis, his action does not represent the spirit of scientific inquiry at all. *It is the very embodiment of traditional piety.* And it permits him to substantiate the insidious speculations and malevolent preconceptions of the white status quo as readily as it allows him to do anything else.

Ordinarily American intellectuals, like those elsewhere, are profoundly preoccupied with the abnormally wretched predicament of contemporary Western man in general. Ideas derived from Karl Marx (who was convinced over a hundred years ago that modern white society was so hopelessly corrupt that its only cure was violent revolution) like those derived from Sigmund Freud (who came to view the personality structure of contemporary European man as a tangle of pathology) occupy a central position in all intellectual and cultural deliberations. Furthermore, almost every significant work of art of the twentieth century contains some explicit and often comprehensive indictment of the shortcomings of contemporary society and the inadequacies of contemporary man. There is very little indeed in the texture of the existence reflected in *The Wasteland, The Hollow Men, The Great Gatsby, The Sun Also Rises,* or *U.S.A.*, that anybody can interpret as a glorification of white excellence in the United States. And matters are hardly improved by including such masterworks of contemporary Europe as *Ulysses, The Magic Mountain,* and *The Castle.*

As soon as any issue involving Negroes arises, however, most American social science theorists and technicians, the majority of whom are nothing if not Marx-Freud oriented, seem compelled to proceed as if Negroes have only to conform more closely to the behavior norms of the self-same white American middle class that writers like Theodore Dreiser, Sinclair Lewis, and Sherwood Anderson had already dissected and rejected long before the left wing political establishment of the nineteen thirties made it fashionable for even the average undergraduate to do so. Somehow or other, the minute the social science technician becomes aware of Negroes having fun "stomping at the Savoy" and enjoying luxuries (of say, Cadillacs) in spite of bad housing and low incomes and injustice, he begins to insist that they should cut out the apathy and escapism and join the all-American rat race—blithely ignoring the fact that there are in almost every Negro community domestic servants and relatives and friends of domestic servants who often have infinitely more first-hand experience with and inside information concerning the social structure and existential texture of white "middle class" life in the United States than is likely to be represented in any survey. In fact, it may well be that few psychiatrists have either more intimate contact with or more functional understanding of the effects suffered by white people from trying to keep up with the Joneses—or with the whims of Madison Avenue.

Some of the omissions and self-contradictions of white norm/black deviation folklore reveal the most appalling intellectual hypocrisy. Whereas the rate of illegitimate births among Negroes is represented as being catastrophic, for instance, the implications of the fantastically lucrative abortion racket among white Americans is conveniently overlooked—as are the procedures that deliberately obscure the rate of white illegitimacy. When the "high rate of crime" among Negroes is featured as cause for alarm, the universally conceded anti-Negro double standards of most white police, judges, and juries somehow become irrelevant! At that point, they apply only a single standard. When problems of drug addiction are under consideration, the very same Harlem that otherwise is always assumed to be suffering from the most abject poverty immediately becomes the main market for the multi-million dollar international cash-and-carry trade in narcotics. (References to crime can hardly explain this last inconsistency—not even if surveys could show that one half of Harlem burglarized the other half every night.)

The Moynihan Report, which insists that Negro men are victims of a matriarchal family structure, makes no mention at all of the incontestable fact that aggressiveness of white American women is such that they are regarded as veritable amazons not only in the Orient but also by many Europeans and not a few people at home. But then the Moynihan Report also implies without so much as a blush that all of the repressions, frustrations, and neuroses of the white Organization Man add up to an enviable patriarchal father image rather than the frightened insomniac, boot-licking conformist, "The Square," which even those who are too illiterate to read the "Maggie and Jiggs" and "Dag-wood" comic strips can see in the movies and on television. Shades of father Jack Lemmon and Tony Randall.

Similarly those white Americans who express such urgent concern when the reading test scores of Harlem school children do not conform to white-established norms seem to forget that some Negroes know very well that all the banality and bad taste on television and the best-seller lists comes from and is produced for those same norm-cali-brated whites. But Sancho Panza was far from being the last man of the people who had to go along with the pedantic foolishness of cliché-nourished bookworms. No-body in his right mind would ever seriously recommend illiteracy as a protection against brainwashing, to be sure; but still and all it may well have been his illiterate immu-nity from the jargon of the fashion magazines that enabled the little boy in Grimms' fairytale to see that the emperor's fancy new clothes were nothing more than his birthday suit.

There may or may not be something to be said for being an unenthusiastic black sheep in a school system that em-phasizes conformity to the point of producing a nation of jargon-and-cliché-oriented white sheep. Nevertheless, one factor that is always either overlooked or obscured in all interpretations of the low academic performance of Negro pupils is the possibility of their *resistance* to the self-same white norms that they are being rated by. What some white teachers refer to as being the *apathy* of Negro pupils, com-petent black teachers are likely to describe as lack of interest and motivation. Black teachers know very well that *when there is genuine Negro interest there is seldom any complaint about Negro ability*. And yet most social science technicians persistently interpret low Negro test scores not in terms of the lack of incentive but in terms of a historic and comprehensive *cultural deprivation*.

But then nowhere are the omissions and contradictions of white norm/black deviation folklore more operative than in matters of formal education. Indeed, the establishment of the notion of a so-called "culture gap" seems to have been the ultimate function of norm lore from the outset. By ignoring the most fundamental definitions of anthropology and archaeology along with the most essential implications of the humanities, the contemporary American social science technician substitutes academic subject matter for culture. He then misrepresents deficiencies in formal technical training as cultural deprivation, a very neat trick indeed.

Such is the procedure that enables the folklore technician to provide statistical evidence as proof to show that Negroes are not like other Americans. But why is it that no widely publicized social science surveys ever measure conformity and deviation in terms of norms of citizenship, which are based on the national ideals as established by the Declaration of Independence and the Constitution? The Constitution not only expresses principles of conduct that are valid for mankind as a whole; *it is also the ultimate official source for definitions of desirable and undesirable American behavior*.

The major emphasis in the large surveys is never placed on the failure of white Americans to measure up to the standards of the Constitution. The primary attention repeatedly is focused on Negroes as victims. Again and again the assumption of the surveys is that slavery and oppression have made Negroes *inferior* to other Americans and hence less American. This is true even of such a relatively fair-minded study as *An American Dilemma*.

In point of fact, however, slavery and oppression may well have made black people more human and more American while it has made white people less human and less American. Anyway, Negroes have as much reason to think so as to think otherwise. It is the political behavior of black activists, not that of norm-calibrated Americans, that best represents the spirit of such constitutional norm-ideals as freedom, justice, equality, fair representation, and democratic processes. Black Americans, not Americans devoted to whiteness, exemplify the open disposition toward change, diversity, unsettled situations, new structures and experience, that are prerequisite to the highest level of citizenship. Black not white or even somewhat white Americans display the greatest willingness to adjust to the obvious consequences of those contemporary innovations in communication and transportation facilities whose networks have in effect shrunk the world to one pluralistic community in which the most diverse people are now neighbors. It is Negroes, not the median of the white population, who act as if the United States is such a world in miniature. It is the non-conforming Negro who now acts like the true descendant of the Founding Fathers—who cries, "Give me liberty or give me death," and who regards taxation without representation as tyranny. It is the norm-oriented white American who becomes the rednecked progeny of the Red Coats, and yells, "Disperse, ye rebels." It is the white American who, in the name of law and order, now sanctions measures (including the stockpiling of armor-piercing weapons to be used against American citizens) that are more in keeping with the objectives of a police state than those of an open society.

There is little reason why Negroes should not regard contemporary social science theory and technique with anything except the most unrelenting suspicion. There is, come to think of it, no truly compelling reason at all why Negroes should not regard the use of the social science statistical survey as the most elaborate fraud of modern times. In any event, they should never forget that the group in power is always likely to use every means at its disposal to create the impression that it deserves to be where it is. And it is not above suggesting that those who have been excluded have only themselves to blame.

It seems altogether likely that white people in the United States will continue to reassure themselves with black images derived from the folklore of white supremacy and the fakelore of black pathology so long as segregation enables them to ignore the actualities. They can afford such self-indulgence only because they carefully avoid circumstances that would require a confrontation with their own contradictions. Not having to suffer the normal consequences of sloppy thinking, they can blithely obscure any number of omissions and misinterpretations with no trouble at all. They can explain them away with terminology and statistical razzle-dazzle. They can treat the most ridiculous self-refutation as if it were a moot question; and of course they can simply shut off discussion by changing the subject.

The self-conception in terms of which most Negroes have actually lived and moved, and had their personal being for all these years, however, has always been, as they say, something else again. Perhaps self-indulgence causes white people to overlook the most obvious fact in the world: Negroes are neither figments of bigoted imaginations nor academic abstractions. They are flesh-and-blood organisms and not only do they possess consciousness, they also enjoy self-awareness. They are, that is to say, purposeful human beings whose existence is motivated by their own self-centered interests.

There are, no one should be surprised to find, a number of prominent Negro spokesmen and black ideologists of welfare-ism who employ, repeat, and even extend the imagery of white supremacy. In most instances, they appear to have been far more thoroughly victimized by the current popularity of social science than by the system of oppression itself. In any case, what they say about how Negroes have been damaged by slavery and oppression is almost always restricted by Marxian and Freudian dialectics. But what many of them do often evokes nothing so much as the irrepressible spirit of '76—without so much rag tag and bobtail to be sure: the Negro revolution is certainly one of the most fashion-conscious uprisings of all times. (Even the protest hair-dos, to the extent that they are protest, are geared to high fashion, often misguided, no doubt, and sometimes disastrous, but high fashion nonetheless.)

The nature of Negro moral outcry polemics, it should also be remembered, is now such that the most glibly self-confident and even the most smugly chauvinistic black spokesmen and leaders readily and frequently refer to themselves as being fear-ridden, emasculated, and without self-respect. No wonder white Americans continue to be so shocked and disoriented by the intensification of the civil rights struggle. Instead of relying on what is now known about the nature of social uprisings, white Americans keep allowing themselves to expect the theoretical Sambo promised, as it were, by Stanley M. Elkins in *Slavery: A Problem in American Institutional and Intellectual Life*, implicitly confirmed by the pronouncements of Kenneth Clark in *Dark Ghetto*, and conceded by so much self-deprecating rhetoric. But what these same white Americans keep running up against is such bewildering, outrageous, and (to some of them) terrifying behavior as the intransigent determination of leaders like Charles Evers in Mississippi; the mockery and high camp of media types like H. Rap Brown on all networks; and people like those in Watts, Newark, and Detroit, who respond to the murderous hysteria of white police and national guardsmen with a defiance that is often as derisive as it is deepseated.

Rhett S. Jones

Proving Blacks Inferior: The Sociology of Knowledge

Until around 1930, the main thrust of white scholarship viewed Blacks as innately inferior. Social Darwinism was one of the cornerstones of this approach in sociology. Modern-day theorists have sought to eliminate genetic fallacies from the various disciplines, but not with complete success. Black inferiority is a recurring theme and white scholars continue to debate the issue. Arthur Jensen's theories on Black intelligence have far-ranging social implications. Shockley's genetic "theories" have provoked serious discussion among white intellectuals whom one would ordinarily expect to dismiss them as ridiculous and scientifically unsound. In the following essay, Rhett S. Jones examines some of these basic assumptions and biases from a historical perspective.

Utilizing the "sociology of knowledge" model, Jones explores the key historical question: Why did Blacks of the 1930's have less confidence in themselves, less belief in themselves as dignified human beings, than did Blacks of the 1870's? In setting out to explain how white and Black scientists "proved" Blacks inferior in their research and writings, he reveals much about the methodology employed by sociologists, psychologists, and physiologists in the nineteenth and early twentieth centuries.

One of the problems that continues to bedevil Black scholars today is the negative attitudes Blacks appear to have held toward themselves. As one writer put it, "The real problem is not with Mr. Charlie, but what Mr. Charlie has done to your mind." Students of Black History at the turn of the century know that for a time *after* Reconstruction, a dynamic developing Black society existed. One need only glance at any of the issues of the *Negro Yearbook* between 1912 and 1918 to see this. Edited by Monroe Work, it chronicled black achievements in publishing, academia, the arts, colonization, politics, religion and science. For the most part these achievements eclipse those of Blacks of our own time. But somewhere in the period between 1870 and 1930, Blacks lost hope. Many seem to have lost confidence in themselves. Black folk are only now beginning to recover such confidence.

The key question is "Why?" Why did Blacks of the 1930's have less confidence in themselves, less belief in themselves as dignified human beings, than did the Blacks of the 1870's? The answer is that white "objective" scientists and a few Black scientists had in these 60 years "proved" Blacks inferior. This paper is concerned with the nature of this proof. This paper will attempt to show that even tests rooted in physical reality resulted in the conclusion that Blacks were inferior. Whites, who believed them to be so, naturally accepted the findings of their scientists. And large numbers of Blacks accepted the verdicts of whites. Objective studies supposedly proved Blacks to be a lesser people. This was a great additional burden for Blacks of the time to bear.

In addition to exposing the nature of the proof, this paper, hopefully, will also demonstrate the uses of the sociological approach in general, and the Sociology of Knowledge, in particular, to students of Black History. Because the vast majority of Black Americans did not leave written records and diaries, if the Black historian is to understand the lives of ordinary Black people, he must employ white sources to get at these lives.

This is much easier said than done. It requires a disciplined kind of research. It is easy to make Blacks of the past say what contemporary radicals want them to say. It is much more difficult to uncover what was actually said by utilizing white records. For some time, American historians have used these records to portray the Black man in an unflattering light. Black historians may now move to use these same sources to portray Blacks in a flattering light. But that would be too easy. And that would be Black propaganda (which has its uses) and not Black History. Sociological constructs can provide some insight into what actually took place in the past. This paper utilizes one such construct, the Sociology of Knowledge.[1] When such constructs are thrown up against the reality of past Black society they produce hypotheses. At the same time, it is necessary to note, they may also create certain blindspots. There is a danger in relying too heavily on a given conceptual schema. But the Sociology of Knowledge can provide considerable insight into what happened to Black people between 1870 and 1930, and how they were proved inferior.

[1] One of the best discussions of the Sociology of Knowledge is found in Merton, Robert, *Social Theory and Social Structure* (Glencoe, The Free Press, 1957), p. 439. See also, Walter, Benjamin, "The Sociology of Knowledge and the Problem of Objectivity" in Gross, Llewellyn (ed.), *Sociological Theory*: Inquiries and Paradigms (New York, Harper and Row, 1967), pp. 335 ff. Cf. Adler, Franz, "The Range of the Sociology of Knowledge" in Becker, Howard and Boskoff, Alvin (eds.), *Modern Sociological Theory in Continuity and Change* (New York, Holt, Rinehart and Winston, 1957), pp. 335 ff.

The basic assumption of the Sociology of Knowledge is that what a person knows is determined by the society of which he is a part. More specifically, the location of the individual within a certain society will determine his knowledge. Some theorists have argued that the word "determine" should be replaced by the word "influence." In either case, the nature of the society, and the location of the individual within it, will be related to the knowledge he possesses. Of course, the individual may change his knowledge. He may modify his assumptions about persons, things, processes, and groups. But even such change will take place within a societal framework. In short, most students of the Sociology of Knowledge would argue that individuals have the kind of ideas their society conditions them to have. During the period under consideration here, Blacks were generally believed to be an inferior people. Previously they had also been thought to be inferior, but had profited from the paternalistic efforts of some whites (North *and* South). After 1930 (as an arbitrary date), increasing numbers of social scientists began to insist that Blacks were (in many respects) the equals of whites. Only with what has come to be called the "Jensen report" has a significant proportion of the white scientific community come to argue otherwise. But in the period between the Civil War and 1930 the status of the Black man was a miserable one indeed. Rayford Logan has termed the period the "Nadir" of the Negro.[2] Other historians, such as C. Vann Woodward[3] and Lerone Bennett Jr.[4] would appear to agree.

This is not to say that some Blacks did not enjoy con-

---

[2] See his *The Negro in American Life and Thought: The Nadir, 1877–1901*, first published 1954 and revised in paperback as *The Betrayal of the Negro* (New York, Collier Books, 1965).

[3] Woodward, C. Vann, *The Stange Career of Jim Crow* (New York, Oxford University Press, 1955).

[4] Bennett, Lerone, *Before the Mayflower* (Chicago, Johnson Publishing Co., 1962), see especially chapter 9.

siderable success during this time. But as racist pressures made themselves felt, these persons had an increasingly difficult time in being proud of being Black, and in expecting Black progress. The reasons for white hostility and determination to thrust Blacks back into "their place" are not hard to find. Some, such as Southern bitterness over Reconstruction, Northern Capitalist interest in the South, the desire of the nation to "get back together," Social Darwinism, the rise of imperialism, the "red scare," and the fear of a militant Japan, have been discussed elsewhere. The important point, here, is that most whites came to increase their negative attitudes toward Blacks. The student of the Sociology of Knowledge would expect that these beliefs would determine, or influence, the scientific investigations of the time. The scientists of the period could not fail to be influenced by the society's definition of the Black man. Scientists, in spite of applying very different kinds of tests, usually reached the same kinds of conclusions. This paper is concerned with the kinds of "tests" these scientists attempted and the nature of the proofs advanced about the inferiority of Blacks. For the purposes of discussion we shall divide the approaches of the scientists into three ideal types: the sociological; the psychological; and the physiological. These are ideal types in the sense that a method labeled "psychological" may seem to have many "sociological" components. This is inevitable because society and personality are connected, and because most persons reading this paper will have insights into the relationships between culture and pysche that were unknown to the men of this time. Perhaps one last observation is in order. The term "scientist" does not coincide with the modern usage of the term. It should be recalled that the social sciences were in their infancy. Many of the men who considered themselves social scientists had actually had very little of what most persons today would call scientific training. Perhaps this is one reason for their obvious failures. Yet they believed themselves to be using rigorous scientific methods. In some cases they were. The methodology compares favorably with some of the things that are being done today. In other cases, however, the methodology was inadequate for the task. In either case, the Black man was proved to be inferior. The following sections are concerned with the ways in which this was done.

The Sociological Approach

"According to the law which they shall teach thee, and according to the judgement which they shall tell thee, thou shalt do; thou shalt not turn aside from the word which they shall declare unto thee, to the right hand, nor to the left."   —Deuteronomy 17:11

The sociological approach generally relied on observations and commentaries on social life. Most of these are naive according to contemporary canons, but they impressed thinking men of the time. These observations on society may be divided into three areas. First, a number of scientists sought to demonstrate that whites had a natural antipathy toward Blacks. This itself proved the inferiority of Blacks. For whites instinctively sought to have nothing to do with such inferior persons. It should be noted that the "instinct school" of sociology (and psychology) was an important one during most of this period. A second group of scientists proved Blacks inferior by citing the conditions of Black life. The way in which Blacks lived "proved" their inferiority to whites. A third group proved Blacks inferior by examination of personal characteristics and character traits. Scientists who proved Blacks inferior by one method did not eschew proving them inferior by another. Some undertook no tests. They merely reasoned from what they observed and the beliefs of the society.

Such reasonings, as suggested above, could not help but lead them to the conclusion that Blacks were inferior.

A number of men argued for the natural repugnance of whites for Blacks. A few of these men, for the sake of consistency, also argued that Blacks felt repugnance for whites. N. S. Shaler, a prolific writer and onetime dean at Harvard, argued in 1886 that even lower animals resisted being forced into any kind of relationship with animals different from themselves. He argued that this characteristic was probably even more highly developed in men. Shaler insisted that the only possible relationship between men of two different races was where one race enslaved the other. Then clearcut rules could be established governing the conduct of the two races, and the activities of each could be controlled. Under such a system it would be possible to work for the advancement of each race. According to the dean, human sympathy rested upon a likeness of kind. It could never develop between persons who differed in physical type. Said Shaler, "Race hatred [is] . . . the remnant of the old hatred against the antagonistic fellow man, when not modified by human sympathy."[5] Other examples of this kind are not difficult to find. U. G. Weatherly, who was at Indiana University, also argued that an aversion existed between persons of different races. This aversion was said to stem from differences in physical appearance.[6] In a 1913 article, John Mecklin, then of Lafayette College, and later of the University of Pittsburgh, asserted that there was "a natural antipathy which regulates the reactions of widely separated peoples."[7] In 1916, Alfred Holt Stone, a member of a committee set up by the

[5] Shaler, N. S., "Race Prejudice," Atlantic Monthly, v. 58, Oct. 1886, pp. 510 ff.

[6] Weatherly, U. G., "Race and Marriage," American Journal of Sociology, v. 15, Jan., 1910, pp. 433 ff.

[7] Mecklin, John M., "The Philosophy of the Color Line," American Journal of Sociology, v. 19, Sept., 1913, pp. 343 ff.

American Economic Association to investigate the conditions of Blacks in the United States, advanced a similar argument. Stone said that it would be impossible to raise the Black to the level of the white because the differences between the two races were so great that a natural aversion existed between them.[8]

This "proof" has been considered first because it is easiest to see the connection here between the societal conception of the Black man and the beliefs held by these scientists. They simply argued that the Black man was different. And that the aversion of the white man for the Black was the natural result of a superior creature's knowledge of his superiority. These arguments were dressed up in sociological clothing such as "consciousness of kind," but essentially they represented scientific explanations and justifications of social patterns of belief.

A second sociological method of proving Black inferiority was to chronicle the conditions of Black life. The squalor and filth into which many Black people had been driven was taken as proof and widely cited as demonstrating the inferiority of the race. John Van Evrie in 1870 was perhaps less subtle about such arguments than some of his later colleagues. Said Van Evrie, "The Negro isolated by himself, seems utterly incapable of transmitting anything whatsoever to the succeeding generation." He then went on to list the achievements of the human race. He noted the absence of Black contributions. The conditions under which Blacks (and mixed bloods) lived proved their inferiority according to this M.D. turned social scientist. The backwardness of Latin America as compared to the United States proved the dangers of racial intermixture and demonstrated that miscegenation with Blacks could

---

[8] Stone, Alfred Holt, "Is Race Friction between Whites and Blacks Growing and Inevitable?," American Journal of Sociology, v. 13, March, 1908, pp. 677 ff.

have disastrous consequences for whites.[9] These arguments
are repeated over and over in the 60 years following the
Van Evrie publication. A sample is to be found in an 1892
statement of Philip A. Bruce, then editor of the Richmond
Times. Bruce advanced the idea that the conditions under
which Blacks lived proved them different from whites.
Education could help whites, but not Blacks. When cut
off from white contact, Bruce insisted, the Black quickly
reverted to a native African type.[10] "African" here, of
course, is a synonym for savage and uncultured. In 1912,
Alzada P. Comstock, of the Chicago School of Civics and
Philanthropy, argued that one proof of the inferiority of
Blacks was that they did not attempt to become home-
owners. Comstock argued that most Blacks did not appear
to even consider such a goal. Many writers of the time insisted that Blacks had an especial affinity for the soil. But
Comstock denied this.[11] Alfred Holt Stone, in 1908, simply
said, "The Negro is one of the oldest races of which we
have knowledge, and that is why its very failure to develop itself in its own habitat, where the Caucasian, Mon-
golian, and others have gone forward, is in itself sufficient
proof of inferiority." Stone also dealt with those who
would argue that Blacks were the equal of whites, because
some Blacks lived in good homes and had made contributions to society. He insisted that all of these persons were
mulattoes.[12]

The strategy of denying Black achievement by insisting
that it was mulatto achievement was an important one in
this period. It served to convince many Blacks that only

[9] Van Evrie, John H., *White Supremacy and Negro Subordination*
(New York, Van Evrie, Horton and Co., 1870), Chapter III.

[10] Quoted in Harris, W. T., "The Education of the Negro," Atlantic
Monthly, v. 69, June, 1892, pp. 721 ff.

[11] Comstock, Alzada P., "Chicago Housing Conditions, VI: The
Problem of the Negro," American Journal of Sociology, v. 18, Sept.,
1912, pp. 241 ff.

[12] Stone, Alfred Holt, "The Mulatto Factor in the Race Problem,"
Atlantic Monthly, v. 102, Nov., 1908, pp. 658 ff.

those who had some white blood could expect to contribute anything to society (or race) or to improve himself. It was a particularly vicious and cruel argument for
it prevented Black persons from taking pride in the achievements of all people of color. It also helped to perpetuate
differences within the race that already existed. Whites
made this argument come true by rewarding and advancing light-skinned Blacks and by denying opportunities to
Blacks of darker skin. Some Black spokesmen, such as
Marcus Garvey, insisted that even Black protest organizations, such as the NAACP, staffed their offices with light-
skinned rather than dark-skinned Blacks.[13] The concept
of the mulatto, and the use of this concept by Blacks and
whites, deserves intensive study. Such study is already in
progress.[14] It is important, however, to understand the role
the concept played in the ideas of Blacks and whites between 1870 and 1930.

Edward B. Reuter, who spent most of his academic
career at the University of Iowa, but who for a short time
prior to his death was at Fisk University, was perhaps the
best-known advocate of the argument that all Black achievement was, in reality, mulatto achievement. In a number of
books and works on this theme, Reuter advanced his thesis.
He insisted that the mulatto occupied a middle position between Black and white. In *The Mulatto in the United
States*, first published in 1918, Reuter "proved" that those
Blacks who had achieved any success were, in fact, mulatto.[15] Even as renowned a friend of the Blacks as Robert
E. Park, in 1930, drew a distinction between Black and

[13] Garvey, of course, aimed many such attacks at mulattoes in general
and the arrogant W. E. B. DuBois, in particular. See, for example, "W. E.
Burghardt DuBois as a Hater of Dark People" in Garvey, Marcus,
Philosophy and Opinions of Marcus Garvey (New York, Marcus
Garvey, 1923), pp. 310 ff.

[14] Jones, Rhett S., "The Mulatto Thesis: A Functional Analysis of
the Destruction of Black Pride," MS in progress.

[15] Reuter, Edward Byron, *The Mulatto in the United States*, Boston,
Thomas Y. Crowell, 1918, p. 315.

mulatto.[16] The onetime assistant at Tuskegee described the Black as docile, tractable and unambitious. A source frequently drawn on in such a description was Alfred Holt Stone. On the other hand, said Park, the mulatto was aggressive, restless, enterprising and ambitious. The mulatto was more sensitive, and his intellectual capacity greater. The mulatto argument, although important, was not universally accepted. Some scientists talked of "mongrelization" and viewed the mulatto as inferior to both Black and white, and as having the worst characteristics of each.

The mulatto argument may be seen as a kind of counter-argument for those who insisted that some Blacks did obtain high position and make contributions to the society. Most of the scientists, however, concerned themselves with recording the conditions of Black life, and from these conditions proving Black inferiority. Howard Odum, of the University of Chicago, published a typical work in 1910. In it, he stated in a discussion of the Black home that: relations between husband and wife often set a poor example for the children; that Blacks liked to crowd together and were never content unless several were sleeping in one room; that the interior of the home was not kept in good repair; that disorder and filth were characteristic; that basic supplies and provisions were not purchased; and that there was an absence of literature in the home. Odum asserted that this was due to the inherent inability of most Blacks to grasp the basic principles of family and home life.[17] This argument was also made again and again.

A related sociological argument repeatedly advanced was based on an examination of the personal (and moral) traits of Blacks. If it could be proved that the Black's moral attitude was inferior to that of the white, then it might be

[16] Park, Robert E., "The Mentality of Racial Hybrids," American Journal of Sociology, v. 36, Jan., 1931, pp. 534 ff.

[17] Odum, Howard W., Social and Mental Traits of the Negro (New York, Longmans, Green and Co., 1910), Chapter 4.

safely assumed that the Black himself was inferior. It was generally argued during this period that Black morality (read: Black sexual conduct) was hopelessly unrestrained. It was also argued that Blacks (for all their difficulties) were at heart, cheerful, forgiving persons. This last assertion was especially important and widely repeated. It served three related functions. First, it served to support the belief that the Black was less than a man. For what man could remain cheerful and forgiving despite the insults and humiliations that had been thrust on him in America? Black cheerfulness in the face of Black degradation demonstrated that the Black man was not like the white. Second, this belief in the cheerful, forgiving nature of the Black man enabled social experimenters (and there were as many of them between 1870 and 1930 as there are today) to believe they had a free hand in their efforts to solve "the Negro problem." Even if such persons should make grievous errors, the carefree Black would not bear a grudge. Third, if the Black appeared happy and content, did this not prove that he was in his proper place? If people of color insisted they were happy, whites should accept their argument. A typical argument is that of Edward Wilson, who said in 1906 of the Black man, "He carries no revenges concealed in his bosom. He forgives his enemies easily. Do him a grievous injury, and a modicum of kindness removes resentment, therefore. . . . Negroes rejoice at being told by one leader that in a thousand years they will be able to partake of the things the Aryan now enjoys."[18] Said Alfred Holt Stone, "[the Black man] accepts the situation, bears no malice, cherishes no ill-will or resentment. . . ." Blacks would be content, he insisted, if only they could be protected from outside agitators.[19] U. G. Weatherly advanced a similar

[18] Wilson, Edward E., "Joys of Being a Negro," Atlantic Monthly, v. 97, Feb., 1906, p. 245.
[19] Stone, "Is Race Friction . . .," *op. cit.*

thesis. It was his contention that Blacks were not bitter over slavery and that most of the race conflict of the time resulted from the actions of misguided whites who actually knew little about the Black man.[20] Said the dean at Harvard, N. S. Shaler, in 1900, "Coons will get wild when there was a racket going on, but all they will need is the firm hand of the master race."[21] Mecklin said in a 1914 article, ". . . the Negro is hopelessly immoral."[22] Blacks were both content and immoral. Each trait proved their inferiority to whites.

The sociological method of proving Blacks inferior consisted for the most part of simple assertions based on the social perceptions of the society of the time. Blacks were seen as inferior because whites had antipathies toward them, because of the conditions of Black life, and because of Black moral and character traits. While each of these arguments may appear weak to the reader today, they all had an impact on the people of the time.

The Psychological Approach

"Is there such a thing as an impartial history? The written representation of past events. But what is an event? . . . It is a notable fact. Now, how is the historian to discriminate whether a fact is notable or no? He decides this arbitrarily, according to his character and idiosyncrasy, at his own taste and fancy. . . ."

—The Gardens of Epicurus

The psychological method of proving Blacks inferior was at the same time more and less complex than the

[20] Weatherly, *op. cit.*

[21] Shaler, N. S., "The Negro Since the Civil War," Popular Science Monthly, v. 57, May, 1900, p. 29.

[22] Quoted in Villard, Oswald Garrison, "The Race Problem," The Nation, v. 99, Dec. 24, 1914, p. 738.

sociological. It was more complex in that it relied heavily on the experimental method. The scientists who employed psychological techniques attempted to control variables, and in a few cases to establish control groups. It was less complex in that there was one dominant method of demonstrating the inferiority of Blacks: psychological "IQ" testing. An attempt was made to be impartial. Many of the scientists really believed that they approached the question of the intellectual capacities of Blacks from a neutral position. Of course, the student of the Sociology of Knowledge would see this was not the case. Those cases where the Blacks proved superior to the whites were explained away. It could not be otherwise. Despite the neutral position they attempted to assume, most of the scientists believed Blacks to be inferior to whites. Where their evidence appeared to contradict these beliefs, they sought to rationalize it away. For example, they argued that Blacks seemed to excel whites only in those tasks that did not really matter. Reuter, writing in 1917, summed up much of the belief of the social scientific community of the time when he said, "Popular assumption of a difference in the mental capacity in the races seems to be borne out in part, at least, by the results of such psychological and educational studies as have been undertaken."[23] A neater statement of the relationship of the beliefs of the society and the conclusions of its scientists would be hard to find.

Reuter referred to tests such as those conducted by Dr. Josiah Morse of the University of South Carolina, who administered the Binet tests to several hundred white and Black students in the public schools of South Carolina. Morse had taken for his hypothesis a principle advanced by the French theorist Gustav LeBon in his *Evolution psychologique des peuples*. In the work, LeBon argued that a mental gap existed between Black and white that could

---

[23] Reuter, Edward Byron, "Supremacy of the Mulatto," *American Journal of Sociology*, v. 23, July, 1917, p. 83.

never be bridged. According to LeBon, the Black was by far the inferior. In the testing of this hypothesis, Morse attempted to set up controls. He was aware of the segregated system of schools that existed in South Carolina at the time, and that some might argue that the different school systems, and not race, were the source of differences. In his work, then, he sought to demonstrate that the course of study in white and Black schools was essentially the same and that Blacks and whites studied the same subjects. Another set of controls revolved around class (though, of course, Morse did not use this term). He suggested that the Black children were well-dressed (read: middle-class), and that they did not seem "embarrassed" by the white test administrator. He did report, however, that Black children, in comparison to white, seemed more relaxed in the actual taking of the test than in engaging in small talk and personal contact with the administrator. Morse reported that nearly 30 percent of the Black children were more than one year behind in their studies. Only 10 percent of the white children were. Five percent of the white children were more than a year ahead in their study, but this figure was reduced to less than one percent for Blacks. In general, Morse found, Black children bettered whites in rote memory, making rhymes, naming words, and in time orientations. White children bettered Blacks in "esthetic judgment," observation, reading, motor control, logical memory, use of words, resistance to suggestion, and ". . . orientation or adjustment to the institutions and complexities of civilized society."[24] It is important to note that Morse reported areas in which Blacks scored higher than whites. Contemporary social scientists seldom do so.

Frank Bruner, of the University of Chicago, provided

[24] Morse, Josiah, "Comparison of White and Colored Children Measured by the Binet Scale of Intelligence," Popular Science Monthly, v. 84, Jan., 1914, pp. 75 ff.

in 1914 one of the best summaries of the psychological approach to race. He cited the 1912 efforts of Dr. H. E. Jordan. Jordan had conducted psychological tests on whites, mulattos, and Blacks. He concluded that the more the Black approached the white in skin color, the more he matched him in "mental and social alertness." It is easy to see that the mulatto argument influenced scientists outside of sociology. Bruner also recorded the experimental tests of M. T. Baldwin in a Pennsylvania reformatory for delinquent girls. Thirty-seven white and 30 Black girls, ranging in age from 13 to 21, were tested by Baldwin in 1913. The Pennsylvania researcher found that the Black girls were 62.4 percent of the white girls in intellectual ability. At the same time, they made more than 245.3 percent more errors than the whites. It is difficult to know how to interpret such figures. But the conclusion is clear. Blacks were inferior to whites. Bruner also quoted the studies of a Dr. Mayo in 1913. Mayo listed his findings in a percentage table. The percentage indicates those Blacks who were able to attain the median score of whites. For example, in "Modern Language" only 33 percent of the Blacks who took the test were able to obtain the median white scores, according to Dr. Mayo. In other subjects, the percentages were as follows:

Mathematics	32%
History	31
Science	29
Greek and Latin	27
English	22[25]

These figures are fascinating not only for the student of the Sociology of Knowledge, but for any person who has

[25] Bruner, Frank, "Racial Differences," Psychological Bulletin, v. 11, 1914, pp. 384 ff.

any knowledge of the psychological and educational theories of the present. It is possible to explain the figures away in light of such theories, but that is not the purpose of this paper. Indeed, it is possible to make nonsense of many of the arguments that have been advanced, here. But that is not the purpose of this paper, either. This paper has as its central purpose the exploration of the nature of the tests used to prove the inferiority of Blacks between 1870 and 1930.

Tests similar to those reported by Bruner were conducted by William Pyle of the University of Missouri and reported in 1915. Pyle's evidence indicated that Blacks had about two-thirds the intelligence of whites. A number of other social scientists arrived at similar percentages. A few argued that Blacks had four-fifths the intelligence of whites; but most seemed to arrive at the two-thirds figure. The fact that so many scientists, conducting independent tests, arrived at similar figures served to confirm their belief in the objectivity and neutrality of their approach. Pyle attempted to control for social class differences. He noted that the "better" class Blacks tested much better than the others ("Negro children of the better class almost approximate white standards.") To account for the difference among Blacks themselves, Pyle suggested two, alternative, hypotheses. First, the fact that middle-class Blacks did better on the test indicated that social environment and not race was the decisive factor. A second hypothesis was that Blacks of better biological stock had been able to work themselves into middle-class positions. Pyle defined better biological stock as a large proportion of white to black blood.[26] This is the mulatto argument in yet another form. Pyle was atypical in his willingness to even consider the explanation that Blacks scored as they did on psychological tests for social rather than racial reasons. The fact that he

[26] Pyle, William H., "The Mind of the Negro Child," School and Society, v. 1, March 6, 1915, pp. 357 ff.

ignored this hypothesis, because the society of his time had conditioned him to ignore it, is again meaningful for students of the Sociology of Knowledge.

In the years beyond 1912, the most widely circulated proof of Black inferiority were the Army "Alpha tests." These were administered to the thousands of inductees, white and Black, who were called up as a result of World War I. For years, the Alpha tests, conducted by "impartial" social scientists, served to convince many of the inferiority of the Blacks.

One such battery of tests was administered to white and Black troops at Camp Lee, Virginia. Dr. George Ferguson, Jr., of Colgate University evaluated the tests. He concluded that Black reasoning power was 75 percent of whites. He also stated that, while Blacks did 89 percent as well as whites in mechanical endeavors, they did only 30 percent as well in literary endeavors.[27] These results were typical of those reported by scientists conducting similar tests.

The psychological tests were more rigorously organized than the sociological ones. The conclusions, however, were the same. White psychologists, like the white sociologists, usually concluded that Blacks were lesser men than whites. They cited a battery of experiments to prove these arguments. Results to the contrary were argued away.

The Physiological Approach

"If men define situations as real, then they are real in their consequences."

—W. I. Thomas

No matter how concrete these results might appear, the beliefs of whites of the time compelled them to argue them

[27] Ferguson, George, Jr., "The Intelligence of Negroes at Camp Lee," School and Society, v. 9, June 14, 1919, pp. 721 ff.

away. This is perhaps most clear in the physiological approach. The methods of the social scientists utilizing this approach were simple. They engaged in various controlled experiments in measurement. The controls exercised not infrequently resulted in conclusions contrary to the beliefs of the time. The scientists, however, managed to explain such findings away. This was difficult to do. For the physiological data had to do with concrete, real, physical measurements. Unlike sociological data, its conclusions could not be easily refuted. Refutations were concocted, however, as a few examples below will indicate.

Robert Bennett Bean, Professor of Anatomy at the University of Michigan, conducted a number of experiments relating to brain size. It was commonly assumed at the time that brain size, or more correctly, skull size, was directly correlated with intelligence. That is, the larger the skull, the greater the intelligence. Bean reported, in 1906, the results of measurements on over 100 brains of whites and Blacks. He concluded that the weight of the Black brain was less than the white, that the volume of the brain was less than the white, and that the frontal lobes of Blacks were much smaller than those in whites. These conclusions were reached, said Bean, despite the fact that he had to work with abandoned or unclaimed bodies. This meant that the worse of the whites were being compared to the entire Black population. Bean argued that the lowest type of white person left a body unclaimed, while Blacks of all types and classes did so. Bean also called attention to the fact that when the brains were ranked in size, a pattern emerged. The largest brains were those of white males, then came white females, Black females and Black males in descending order. This ranking, he noted, agreed with similar rankings made by the psychologists as a result of intelligence tests.[28] The student of the Sociology of Knowl-

[28] Bean, Robert B., "Some Racial Peculiarities of the Negro Brain," *American Journal of Anatomy*, 1906, pp. 352 ff.

edge would expect such agreement. Both groups of scientists occupied pretty much the same position in the society and generally held the same beliefs about Blacks and whites, males and females. Bean's tests may be taken as typical. They were often repeated during this 60-year period, and with similar results.

Another example of an often repeated experiment is to be found in the work of R. Meade Brache, of the University of Pennsylvania. Brache sought to prove that Blacks were inferior to whites by testing the reaction time to electric stimuli of whites, Indians and Blacks. He theorized that because of his highly developed intellect, the white man would be greatly slowed down in such automatic responses. Nature, on the other hand, to compensate the Black man for his lack of intellectual abilities, had endowed him with remarkably fast reflexes. Indians were expected to fall in between the two groups. In order to demonstrate the validity of his methodology, Brache first tested white males and females. The fact that women had the faster reaction time, he wrote, proved the validity of his approach for it was common knowledge that men were the intellectual superior of women. His hypotheses were supported in part. Whites had the slowest reaction time of all. However, the Indians had faster reflexes than the Blacks. Brache argued that these findings in no way disproved his basic theories. The Indian had deliberately cultivated what natural quickness he had, while the lazy Black man had let his native abilities decline. Brache also suggested that the results may have been influenced by a number of mulattos among the Blacks.[29]

In a still different kind of approach conducted in 1921, M. G. Wilson and D. J. Edwards tested white and Black children with regard to the total amount of air that could

---

[29] Brache, R. Meade, "Reaction Time with Reference to Race," Psychological Review, v. 2, 1895, pp. 475 ff.

be exhaled at a particular time. The fact that Black children could not exhale as much air as whites, made it difficult for them to "equal western standards."[30]

There were numerous other physiological tests conducted in this 60-year period, but these are representative. No matter how rigorous the test utilized, white scientists still found Blacks to be inferior. They proved what the average man and they themselves believed.

Conclusion

"Every goal we formulate for our actions, every decision we make, be it trivial or momentous, involves assumptions about the universe of human beings. To my mind, any attempt to draw a sharp line between commonsense ideas and scientific concepts is not only impossible but unwise."
—James B. Conant

A vicious cycle operated here. Whites believed Blacks to be inferior. Therefore white scientists believed them inferior and their experiments "proved" them to be. The proof offered by these scientists reinforced the beliefs of the general white population, and so on it went. An unhappy by-product of this cycle was that a number of Blacks came to believe themselves inferior, too. To social prejudices had been added "impartial" scientific proofs. The concern of this paper has been with the nature of these proofs. They have been presented, without sarcastic commentary (although many cry out for it) and allowed to stand on their own. A second goal of the paper was to demonstrate to Black historians the uses of sociology, and the Sociology of Knowledge in particular, in the study of

[30] Wilson, M. G. and Edwards, D. J., "Vital Capacity of Lungs and Its Relation to Exercise Tolerance in Children with Heart Disease," American Journal of Diseases of Children, v. 22, 1921, p. 443.

Black people. The sociologist would expect these men to discover as truth the truth in which they already believed. Until the beliefs of the society change, the kind of discoveries made by scientists about Blacks will not change, either.

Sidney M. Willhelm

Equality:
America's Racist Ideology

Utilizing the theme of his earlier book entitled *Who Needs the Negro?* Sidney Willhelm explores the concept of "equality" and its broader implications for Black survival or non-survival. Liberal reformers have long advocated "equality" for Blacks. Willhelm argues that the equality doctrine is but another form of Black victimization and, in effect, perpetuates racial inequality.

America has been a racist society from its very beginnings—adopting, modifying, and dispensing with tactics extending from complete acceptance of ethnic aliens in the form of acculturation and amalgamation to liquidation. *Myths* of racism, however, are the rationales White America creates to enhance the racist tradition. To sanctify its racist commitment, White America exhorts justifications which alter in light of changing conditions. To dispose of an unwanted race, whites avoid the pangs of compunction simply by confessing to the submission of racism in accord with the absolutes in the myths of racism.

136

Initially, whites perceived the Indian and Negro in terms of the Christian myth; the two peoples were heathens. Both were repugnant to whites, and Christianity legitimized the repugnancy so that Negroes and Indians were viewed as nonhumans at best and beasts at worst. As heathens, Indians could be murderously slaughtered and Negroes mercilessly enslaved for beasts of burden. Extermination for the former and subjugation for the latter were acts of civilization progressing over soulless creatures. White men could follow the spirit and letter of Christian theology without fear of contradiction. The God of Salvation is most pleased by diligent, industrious, and energetic people; if God could not very well admire the lazy Indian and Negro, it would be too much to expect whites to admire what God Himself admonished.

Eventually, Christianity transformed both Negro and Indian from beasts to humans. But in spite of the conversion, whites still doomed the Indian to extermination and the Negro to enslavement by advancing the theory of the natural dominance of white.

In the thoughts of early American whites, no white man ever commands because he chooses to do so; it is not by his choice, but by the will of God or the act of Nature that he rises to the fore at the expense of "inferior" races. To rule is really to submit, in the first instance, as an obedient believer of God's command and, in the second instance, a helpless pawn abiding by Nature's laws governing the races of men. "The causes which the Almighty originates, when in their appointed time He wills that one race of men —as in races of lower animals—shall disappear off the face of the earth and give place to another race, and so on, in the great cycle traced by Himself, which may be seen," explained General James H. Carleton, when serving as commander of the military department of New Mexico in 1866, "but has reasons too deep to be fathomed by us. The races of the mammoths and mastodons, and the great sloths came and passed away: the red man of America is passing away!"[1] Were whites to ignore the obligation to rank supreme according to natural and supernatural laws, they would submit themselves to the possibility of becoming beasts like the Indian and Negro. It was God's will blessing the industrious white for the good sense of condemning the lazy Negro and Indian; it was Nature's doings that placed the white man on top, overseer of inferior people. The white man felt virtually helpless before both Nature and God. Could any man dare to dare Nature? If so, then his fate was sealed, doomed to elimination; if one did not rule by Nature's rule, he could not rule but would instead be the object of eradication and enslavement. And could any man dare defy God's own dictum of righteousness? If so, then he stood to suffer forever the fire of eternity's damnation.

The white man's problem for the better part of four hundred years has been the necessity to make racism palatable to himself. What social thought could be conceived to justify white rule over all other skin colors without degrading whites in the very process of belittling non-whites? The answer was to be found within the very system of control which regulated whites' own life chances, namely, "external forces."

As long as the white American lacked in technological development, he would, to that extent, perceive his fate as determined by some outside force. If his welfare were not within his own hands, then the white person placed his trust for his existence in an external determinant. Thus man employed his farm tools within the bounds of utility, and when facing the wrath of Nature, such as during droughts or plagues, prayed to his Creator for better farming conditions. The Lord who could control Nature, and,

[1] Quoted by Henry Eugene Fritz, *Movement for Indian Assimilation* (Philadelphia: University of Pennsylvania Press, 1963), p. 124.

hence, so much of the white man's own success, must therefore possess control over all creatures. Surely, then, whites could not suppress blacks into slavery for expanding the agricultural economy through commercial crops as cotton, tobacco, and sugar cane unless God so willed; if human enslavement of blacks by whites offended the Lord of all, it would be expected for Him to intervene immediately and right any wrong. As whites linked their own fate with Nature's whims and God's command, they, in turn, extended the interpretation to account for the Negro's subordination.

With the expansion of industrialization social life replaced dependence upon Nature. With reduced obligation to Nature it would be inevitable that there would be less responsibility even to God. Such drastic changes would, of course, undermine the established myth of racism; the disentombment of the Negro appeared imminent. White America faced the prospects of removing all external reasons for restraining the Negro, unveiling to itself the reality of its racism without any recourse to exonerate whites. "It is neither God nor the physical universe the American [has come to] fear . . . since he sees himself as the associate of one and the master of the other. What he truly fears is his fellowman."[2] Unless whites could come through with some kind of omnipotent rationale as immutable as both Nature and God seemed to have been at first sight, then white hold over black stood to lose its legitimacy. Where could whites turn to sanctify their treatment of blacks?

Today, it is the highest Law of Man sustaining the Negro in disrepute. Constitutional law provides the external mandate to which all men must comply. It applies equally to all without favoritism or discrimination on the basis of skin

[2] Francis L. K. Han, quoted by Selma C. Hirsch, *The Fear Men Live By* (New York: Harper & Bros., 1955), p. 3.

pigmentation. Its equal provisions must be enforced with the same authority as God's will and Nature's dictums held sway in previous days. Immutable notions of parity burst forth with full assurance of righting the 350 years of wrongs committed against a dark-skinned minority. Numerous whites and blacks declare in unison a national commitment to the disappearance of racism through equality in the sincere belief of initiating the Negro into the freedoms enjoyed by whites.

Are Negroes advancing toward equality? No doubt about it, they are indeed. But where is the advancement leading them? As legal retributions seemingly remove racial segregation and discrimination in education, transportation, military service, housing, etc., whites turn to other measures to deprive the Negro people. The new efforts are designed not to subjugate, oppress, or exploit the black minority, but rather to separate the two races. *And this is more readily accomplished by treating any Negro the same as any white.* White America, by invoking the equality standard, reverses the maxim, "separate but equal" to "equal but separate." The placement of "equal" before rather than after the qualifying "but" accords with the present myth of racism—Constitutional equality—and assures the identical outcome as the pre–1954 Court-sanctioned "separate but equal" maxim: Negro removal. Today, the exclusion of black is intended for total isolation whereas yesterday the separation conveyed inferiority out of deference to whites. Unlike segregation, which prescribed an inferior status, separatism divides the American population according to race in order to inhibit racial contacts. Whites established segregation to keep the Negro in place; they now wish only to banish the Negro out of sight and beyond empathy or understanding. With three-quarters of the Negro population living in cities and 80 per cent of the black urban population settled upon ghetto-reservations, isolation solidifies still further the Negro's very life style, so much so that "the present generation of Negro youth growing up in the urban ghettos has probably less personal contact with the white world than any generation in the history of the Negro American."[3]

The racial imbalance in residential location invariably gives rise to racial imbalance throughout many other spheres. One of the most important consequences is reflected in the nation's classrooms. The inviolable equality principle sanctions the neighborhood for the fundamental criterion for assigning children to schools, since all races must be treated alike in a neighborhood. By enforcing uniform standards the nation fosters an educational system with distinct racial implications: 75 per cent of elementary Negro school students and 83 per cent of all white students attend schools made up predominantly of their respective races. More Negroes receive their education in isolation from whites than when the Supreme Court denounced, in 1954, the principle of segregation by law; de facto educational segregation is just as possible for racial separation as was the de jure educational segregation set aside by the courts. Even should Negroes receive the best education in the most advanced school facilities, designation of attendance by neighborhoods reinforces racial separation. In fact, however, no such improvement can be anticipated. A thorough review by the United States Commission on Civil Rights of the various compensatory programs in operation during 1965–1966 shows virtually all to be ineffectual in overcoming educational deficiencies among Negro school children.[4]

Universities may now open their doors to all persons

[3] United States Department of Labor, *The Negro Family* (Washington, D.C.: U.S. Government Printing Office, 1965), p. 44. This work is also known as *The Moynihan Report.*

[4] U.S. Commission on Civil Rights, *Racial Isolation in the Public Schools*, Vol. I (Washington, D.C.: U.S. Government Printing Office, 1967).

meeting established requirements regardless of race as required by Court orders because there will be few colored persons for mixed classrooms. Negro college enrollment remains low for integrated educated—less than two per cent—when judged by educational standards expected of whites.[5] Black students cannot compete against whites in great numbers; they face exclusion not strictly on account of skin pigmentation, but for the lack of college preparation. Major Northern universities accept fewer Negroes than their integrated Southern counterparts. It is no wonder Southern institutions try to match the educational standards of the North since "raising the standards" lowers the Negro percentage on campus.

Employment demands now far exceed Negro qualifications and capabilities, according to White America's economic values, such that blacks simply cannot successfully compete against aspiring whites. Inasmuch as 97 per cent of new openings fall within white-collar categories while three out of five Negroes, in contrast to three out of ten whites, qualify only up through semiskilled or unskilled blue-collar work, inequality barriers can be disregarded since the collapse will still assure the Negro will be discarded. As job requirements rise dramatically, equality in evaluating applicants apart from race excludes the Negro just as effectively as discrimination; by evaluating performance and abilities regardless of color, the Negro steps back not in deference to white but in compliance to white superiority in the form of exacting competition. Private business can project a faithful compliance to nondiscriminatory hiring practices because it need not worry that many Negroes will rush to apply. "We can show conclusively,"

[5] David E. Rosenbaum, "Study Finds State Universities Lag in Enrollment of Negroes," New York Times (June 18, 1969), p. 1. See also the chart containing college enrollments by race entitled, "Federal Survey of Negro Undergraduate Enrollments," The Chronicle of Higher Education 3 (April 21, 1969): 3–4.

a businessman informs us, "that there is a shortage of Negroes adequately trained to fill the positions that may be open from time to time."[6] Today, race is neither blatant nor always necessary for exclusion: industrialists simply dispose of jobs rather than Negroes. The denial of employment and promotion on the basis of equality reduces the Negro into economic servitude just as impressively as Southern sharecropping.

When the Negro dons the military uniform, equality keeps him out of reach of officer ranks for retention within combat units where his labor can be utilized upon the battlefields of Vietnam. The proportion in combat troops exceeds "20 per cent in the average infantry company," according to Joseph Alsop's May 25, 1966 column, simply because "Negro recruits, with a lower average of technical skills, are less likely to be assigned to one of the technical specialties." It is all a matter of assignment: the right man to the right job independent of race. The dedication to promotion free from racial dispositions rules out the Negro for all practical purposes beyond the enlisted ranks; about 2 per cent of the military officers are Negro. The higher one climbs in the military hierarchy, the higher will be the educational and training requirements, and therefore the less likelihood of Negroes being present. The military dispenses with prejudice and thereby dispenses with the Negro from higher advancements.

Real estate interests promote equality in light of Court decisions and still manage to exclude the Negro. Equal economic standards for loans and housing mortgages keep the Negro from new housing just as efficiently as restricted covenants so that suburbs are today 96 per cent white. Approximately .5 per cent of Federal Housing Authority

6 "Reports of Corporate Action" in Eli Ginzberg, ed., *The Negro Challenge to the Business Community* (New York: McGraw-Hill, 1964), p. 84.

loans extend to families with income of less than $4,000, thereby ruling out 60 per cent of Negroes without a trace of racial bias. Insurance agencies show considerable reluctance to cover Negro homeowners because of supposed high risks. It can be claimed that housing leading to racial separation is all a matter of the economics of equality, not race.

Extensive civil rights laws pass through the federal, state, and local governments, ruling out widespread discrimination. Such efforts stimulate white enthusiasm and receive nominal Southern resistance because little impact upon race relations can be expected by changing legal rights from white superiority to equality. Since economic forces of the market play an important part in excluding the Negro from suburbs and are so vital in determining where a person will go (rather than the laws providing the opportunity to go), only a small percentage of the minority can rub against the majority in eating out, flying about, and going out in general. Considerable white exclusiveness can be practiced by practicing economic exclusiveness without recourse to racial differentiation.

In 1960 there was a net gain of one Negro over the 1950 figure of 2,190 in the number of colored trade apprentices for the entire nation. But unions deny responsibility for discrimination; Negroes simply "fail" to qualify in meeting state and federal minimum requirements for certification beyond apprenticeship assignments. "We should try to help," announces George Meany, President of the AFL–CIO, with regard to accepting minority groups into the construction and building trade unions for the purpose of learning the skills. "But under no circumstances should we submit to a reduction of the standards for skilled workers."

Lacking qualifying standards the Negro fails to secure a job if employment can be attained; if employed, he receives the rather low compensations appropriate for his humble station in life. This reward system then preordains residence in low-income housing of massive black ghettos where the opportunities are so slim that neither advancement nor opportunity can be expected for an oncoming generation. Thus, with Negro unemployment persisting well beyond the 20 per cent in most metropolitan areas, whites have ample "proof" of Negro "worthlessness." To be jobless in a society begging for applicants is, in most whites' minds, substantial evidence for deliberate laziness. Whites cannot convince themselves of any reason other than that the Negro wantonly desires to do nothing. Those who do little deserve little! So keep the welfare rolls down and payments at a minimum—not to hamper the Negro, but to discourage the notion of getting something for nothing whether one be white or black.

Such instances of racial separation indicate the coming trend in race relations. *Racial discrimination has not been removed entirely. But as equality becomes a fact of life, we cannot avoid its concomitant of increasing racial separation!* Whites are more anxious than ever to introduce equality where equality introduces racial division within America. For the arrangement then allows for Negro removal from the affairs of White America in full compliance to an idealistic democratic precept, so vividly confirmed by the Supreme Court, rather than entrance into mainstream America. *Why discriminate when one can eliminate the Negro into nonexistence by practicing equality?*

What makes equality a racist contention? We find an explanation in these two accounts:

I do not doubt that my wants and feelings are fairly representative of those of most of my race [Ralph Bunche insisted in the early sixties]. I want to be a man on the same basis and level as any white citizen—I want to be as free as the whitest citizen. I want to exercise, and in full, the same rights as the white American. I want to be eligible for employment exclusively on the basis of my skills and employability, and for housing solely on my capacity to pay. I want to have the same privileges, the same treatment in public places as every other person.[7]

The American Negro [explains Kenneth C. Clark] is merely asking to share in whatever exists in America today, including its emptiness.[8]

What we discover in these typical illustrations bidding for equality is the clear statement in white terms: to be equal *according to standards set by whites.* The preference is explicitly devoted to characteristics emanating solely from whites; under the banner of equality, white expectations are to be replicated by blacks competing with whites. What could be more racist? And what better way to separate the races than by forcing blacks into competition with whites on terms assuring ultimate inferiority and division of life styles?

The apparition of Negro advancement comes forth by the actual bestowal of equality, and the fact of great strides toward equality serves to justify White America's mirage of improved relations between the two races. Just as the Christian faith sanctified enslavement and Darwinism blessed Negro inferiority following Emancipation, so too today, the enforcement of equality through Constitutional guarantees justifies dispensing with the Negro. Moreover, White America obtains a similar degree of self-righteousness from many social scientists just as the ideologues of yesterday buttressed the myths of racism through scholarly confirmation.

Sociologists profess emphatic concern for the Negro, yet, generally speaking, espouse theories supposedly obviating the necessity of racism but which, in fact, enhance the

[7] Ralph Johnson Bunche, "NAACP Convention Address," in Harvey Wish, ed., *The Negro Since Emancipation* (Englewood Cliffs, N.J.: Prentice-Hall, 1964), p. 140.

[8] Kenneth C. Clark, "The Negro in Turmoil," in Ginzberg, *Negro Challenge*, p. 64.

white myth of racism. Thoroughly convinced of no biological inferiority and imbued with an intense respect for all persons by expounding theories firmly committed to equality, most sociologists, nonetheless, dispense with the Negro by conjuring up inevitable social realities inherent within social forces. The most dominant and popular contemporary viewpoints in sociological writings blame external factors for affecting Negro-white relations; responsibility is established within particular external social forces or processes bearing their own racial imperatives.

Industrialization and urbanization are processes inevitably leading to parity among all races; they bring with them assurance of people made equal because they operate, as the Constitution itself, regardless of race. Persons must be judged by what they can do rather than by racial qualities, just as the Supreme Court now rules the law to be equal apart from color. Talcott Parsons, for example, maintains "the time is ripe for a major advance. The broad tendency of modern society, one in which America has played a rather special role, has been egalitarian in the sense of institutionalizing the basic rights of citizenship . . . so that universalistic norms of the society have applied more and more widely."[9] A society modernizing into an industrial, urban nation guarantees the ultimate realization of equality.

Migration, Philip Hauser assures us, must take its own course until it leads ultimately to parity among the races: the Negro is but another migrant who enters the city for assimilation, just as any other minority, into mainstream America.[10]

---

[9] Talcott Parsons, "Full Citizenship for the Negro American? A Sociological Problem," *Daedalus* 94 (Fall 1965): 1038–1039. "Because of the demand for labor in an expanding industrial society," E. Franklin Frazier informs us, "men can no longer be evaluated on the basis of their racial identity." E. Franklin Frazier, *The Negro in the United States* (New York: Macmillan, 1957), 2nd ed., p. 701.

[10] ". . . a demographic factor, internal migration, may be considered *the major factor in opening the door to integration.*" Philip M. Hauser,

Economic exploitation prevails as a mere reflection, we are told by the class-conscious scholar, of capitalism's stratification wherein the lower classes must be imbued with racism to turn upon one another rather than upon the ruling elite.[11]

Then there are two recent sociological pronouncements which must be declared blatantly anti-Negro in their formulations. The advocates of family disruption insist family life among Negroes to be *the* fundamental short-coming for ultimate acceptance; the disintegration of the family organization as an external life condition within the *black* community prevents integration through equality.[12] Since the prejudice of the family perspective has been so well established, it is not necessary to elaborate.[13]

What seldom receives criticism, however, is a much more serious denial of the Negro's abuse in White America, even though the orientation is well known and widely acclaimed, namely, relative deprivation. In the words of Thomas Pettigrew, "Thus after twenty years [i.e., from the 1940s to the present] of progress, particularly in certain areas, the Negro is nevertheless considerably more frustrated today than he was at the beginning of this period of change because, while his absolute standard has been going up, his

---

"Demographic Factors in the Integration of the Negro," *Daedalus* 94 (Fall 1965): 862. Emphasis supplied.

[11] E.g., Oliver C. Cox, *Caste, Class and Race: A Study in Social Dynamics* (Garden City, N.Y.: Doubleday, 1948).

[12] United States Department of Labor, *The Negro Family;* Daniel Patrick Moynihan, "Employment, Income, and the Ordeal of the Negro Family," *Daedalus* 94 (Fall 1965): 745–770; C. Eric Lincoln, "The Absent Father Haunts the Negro Family." *New York Times Magazine* (November 28, 1965), pp. 60 ff.

[13] For probably the best critique see William Ryan, "Savage Discovery: The Moynihan Report," *The Nation* 201 (November 22, 1965): 380–384. Also see Andrew Billingsley, *Black Families in White America* (Englewood Cliffs, N.J.: Prentice-Hall, 1968). A most inadequate defense amounting to a whitewash of the origins of the Moynihan family thesis is Lee Rainwater and William L. Yancey, eds., *The Moynihan Report and the Politics of Controversy* (Cambridge: M.I.T. Press, 1967).

aspiration level has been rising much faster. His relative deprivation, the differences between what he has and what he expects to have, and what he thinks is his right to have, is now probably greater than at any other time in American history."[14] The notion is widespread that rapid, objective accomplishments become the prime causes of spreading Negro discontent, that in proclaiming to protest against the snail's pace of their progress Negroes are misguided since advancement over the postwar years amounts to a virtual revolution.

The facts are distinctly and acutely otherwise: the supposed advancements in education, housing, income, integration, medical services, etc., are not supported; the Negro life situation deteriorates. Data to substantiate this statement cannot be presented here because of limited space, but the Kerner *Report* clearly shows the deterioration; my own detailed investigation of each area of erstwhile progress clearly shows the opposite;[15] studies of Negro riots clearly reveal uprisings occur not only in the most depressed housing areas, but in sections of the city where the black people experienced lowering of living standards.[16] Contrary to the claim put forward by relative deprivationists that the middle class is in the vanguard of racial strife, the Kerner *Report* presents the black middle class as the reactionary element, ". . . high levels of education and income not only prevent rioting but are more likely to lead to active, responsible [sic] opposition to rioting."[17]

[14] Thomas Pettigrew, "White-Negro Confrontations," in Ginzberg, *Negro Challenge*, p. 41. See also Thomas Pettigrew, *A Profile of the Negro American* (Princeton: D. Van Nostrand, 1964).

[15] Willhelm and Powell, *Who Needs the Negro?* Ch. V.

[16] For one of the best see the study of Cleveland's riot by Walter Williams, "Cleveland's Crisis Ghetto," *Trans-action* 4 (September 1967): 33-42. See the empirical data of the "typical" Negro rioter presented by the National Advisory Commission on Civil Disorders, *Report of the National Advisory Commission on Civil Disorders* (New York: Bantam Books, 1968), pp. 128-129.

[17] *Ibid.*, p. 132.

The theory of relative deprivation simply verbalizes, in scholarly fashion, what Southern racists have long expounded concerning black inferiority and white superiority. Ray Stannard Baker encountered, during his tour of the South at the turn of the century, remarks bearing more than just a casual resemblance to the explanation of black discontent in terms of relative deprivation: "If you educate the Negroes they won't stay where they belong; and you must consider them as a race," a Montgomery, Alabama lawyer told Baker, "because if you let a few rise it makes the others discontented."[18] Compare this to the statement by Leonard Broom and Norval Glenn: "With improved education come higher aspirations and increased discontent with inferior social status . . . education leads to unrest and troublesome ambitions."[19]

The major premises of relative deprivationists and Southern racists are the same. Both treat Negro demands as merely outcries of previous "gains." *There can be no factual justification for wants and fears.* Through this error in reasoning, the relative deprivation perspective not only distorts reality by supposing major progress, but provides a racist rationale for refusing further changes as well. White America can declare, in good faith, that progress for bettering the lot of Negroes in the aftermath of riots is absolutely self-defeating; amelioration simply brings rewards to the violent Negro and increases the level of frustration so that Negroes would then insist upon more rather than being grateful for the assistance.

Both perspectives refuse to credit the Negro with consciousness; neither can imagine the undercurrent of bitterness and hostility among Negroes in the history of this

[18] Ray Stannard Baker, *Following the Color Line* (New York: Harper & Row, 1964), p. 85. Originally published by Doubleday, Page and Co., 1908.

[19] Leonard Broom and Norval D. Glenn, *Transformation of the Negro American* (New York: Harper & Row, 1966), pp. 102–103.

nation. The Southerner's view of a happy-go-lucky, un-fettered, sensate, uninhibited Negro without a care in the world has its equivalent in the relativist's notion of the Negro suddenly breaking out of a docile acceptance of a subordinate position. Both express amazement and shock: the Southerner is astounded to learn of outrageous conduct from "his" Negroes, much as the supporter of relative deprivation sees intense black consciousness for a rather special quality in the "Revolt of 1963." For the Negro to live each day is a reminder of wrongs that must be borne and of feelings that must be suppressed.[20] There is no unique phenomenon—to be a Negro is to be aware of one's own inferiority in the eyes of White America; the very system White America perpetuates for subjugating Negroes is, at the same time, a major stimulus for creating awareness. If the Negro supposedly lacked the aspirations presently ascribed to him, what justifies legislation outlawing the right of slaves to be taught reading and writing, the op-portunity to become members of the Christian faith, the privilege to establish voluntary organizations, and so forth? There would have been no need for legal restrictions and constant white vigilance if the Negro were passive and content in bondage. Whites passed racial laws precisely because Negroes sought then what many seek today: opportunities to learn how to read and write, the chance to own property, equality before the law, etc. My own examination clearly shows that Negro aspirations have not, on the whole, departed from, but are rather, affirmations of the past. From the nation's very founding, during the Revolutionary War, Negroes called upon whites to abide by the precepts of life, liberty, and the pursuit of happiness.

The absence of an historical perspective by relative deprivationists leads to a fallacy common to the family

[20] See William H. Grier and Price M. Cobbs, *Black Rage* (New York: Basic Books, 1968).

thesis, namely, the Negro himself is blamed. The Negro supposedly phantoms an inner sense of deprivation when the external world alters drastically to accommodate. Though the advocates themselves do not always subscribe to their own notions of rapid gains, they nonetheless insist Negroes are exasperated because of marked gains.[21] To place blame for discontentment on the Negro minority while simul-

[21] Even though the factual state fails to support the insistence of Negro restiveness springing from vast improvements to unleash still greater desires for more drastic gains, the advocates disregard not only the virtual absence of evidence for their contention but also *their very own* assessment of Negro advancement. It would not seem unreasonable to expect proponents of relative-deprivation to convince at least themselves of rapid gains for American Negroes after giving emphatic declarations to tell others of the marked achievements responsible for the discontented Negro. It would seem they would subscribe to their own thesis. But, alas, such could not be. Indeed, there is the widespread inclination to insert a disclaimer to any thought of rapid gains; the adherer to the approach quickly disassociates himself from any possible interpretation that he believes the Negro to have made great amounts of progress. This is done in spite of page after page setting forth the advancement postulate. For all his efforts to bring out reams of data in an attempt to sustain rising expectations derived from substantial acquisitions in a relatively short period of time, Thomas F. Pettigrew inexplicably expounds, "The hard truth is that the Negro's recent progress does not begin to close *the gap between the two races*." (*A Profile of the Negro American*, p. 187; emphasis supplied.) As a consequence, he explains, "in each interrelated realm—health, employment, business, income, housing, voting and education—the absolute gains of the 1950's pale when contrasted with current standards." (*Ibid.*, p. 191.) And this is just the point! The measure for any achievement is not what one has relative to one's own past as the source for dissatisfaction, but rather the resources one has at his disposal to interact with others. As one's own position improves over a period of time but simultaneously suffers setbacks to deter the social relationships one intended to undertake all along, the person can hardly be accused of self-instilled frustration. It was the gap between the races which provided the initial incentive to challenge the social order of White America by Black America. Now that, as Pettigrew acknowledges, the gap expands, one should expect the expansion of protest as a direct result.

Still, others follow the same procedure of denying the very advancements they claim for explaining the discontent among Negroes over the last decade. Pierre van den Berghe admits in one sentence that "the objective situation has improved, to be sure, *but the change is im-*

taneously ignoring the white society of which this minority is a part is to deny reality and indict an already overly abused people. The perversion contributes to Negro misery and helps to absolve White America—particularly sociolo-

---

pressive only by conservative standards," but then proceeds to overlook this qualified statement by saying, in the very next sentence,

Recent developments seem to highlight two points. First, with the "revolution of rising expectations" on the part of Negro Americans, the gap between reality and aspirations has increased in spite of progress; consequently, the level of racial conflict, of frustration, and alienation has risen in the past few years. [*Race and Racism* (New York: John Wiley and Sons, 1967), pp. 92–93.]

Yet the viewpoint of the Negro who makes the same observation—"the change is impressive only by conservative standards"—to which van den Berghe so openly admits in order to avoid an association with conservative White America, are immediately taken for certain proof of relative deprivation. Van den Berghe will not allow the Negro to speak in the idiom that he himself feels so free to use. Neither the Negro nor van den Berghe wish to indicate the slightest notion of false progress by insisting that Negroes have made decisive gains in post-World War II America. Yet should the Negro declare that the pace is slow, van den Berghe and his school quickly dismiss the thought and substitute the ill-founded hypothesis of relative deprivation. The Negro is perceived in a state of frustration, but van den Berghe himself advances "objective" analysis and data.

J. W. Vander Zanden follows the identical pattern. He insists "the Negro protest is not so much a product of despair as a protest fed by rising expectations," only to deny any such possibility in an immediately-following disclaimer: "Yet Negroes face formidable obstacles and frus-trating barriers in realizing their aspirations. If Negroes are to satisfy their expectations, there must be a marked closing of the gap between Negroes and whites as well as large absolute gains. . . ." [*American Minority Relations* (New York: Ronald Press, 1966), 2nd ed., p. 415.] It is simply not possible to describe the Negro protest "fed by rising expectations" more so than "despair" and then immediately inform us of the "formidable obstacles and frustrating barriers." Could it not just be possible that black frustrations come from the "frustrating barriers"?

The declaration of sustained gains is a premonition resulting from a most improper adherence, on the part of the social scientist, to an un-substantiated theory of relative deprivation. We discover the strange contradiction of the relative deprivationists: Negroes make gains without any gains. But the gains account for "Negro restiveness" when all along, as admitted by the proponents themselves, there have been no outstanding gains for the dissident black within American society for the postwar years.

gists—of any guilt. Willfully or otherwise, advocates of relative deprivation promote racism by the elaboration of a theory which holds the Negro accountable for the expanding unrest among black Americans.

All the viewpoints we have mentioned here emphatically argue for an external compulsion *acting upon the Negro* without, save for the economic exploitation contention, any hint of racism; indeed, racism will simply fade as a by-product according to each train of thought rather than being a basis for white America's relationship to Negroes. Every explanation takes for granted equality will be achieved as the natural and inevitable outcome of its specific rationale, or, as in the case of the family thesis, equality will be attained by correcting an obvious wrong in Negro life. How strange, indeed, that contemporary scholarly discourses should just happen to lead to "equality"! This merely repeats Christian thought which just happened to lead to the liquidation of Indians and enslavement of Negroes; of evolutionary thought which just happened to lead to the liquidation of Indians and segregation of Negroes. The latest scholarly formulations present social thoughts invariably leading to equality for Negroes at just the moment White·America dooms the Negro to equality before the law!

The sustenance of racism in America is racism itself, nourished to the full extent possible by the economic resources existing at any given moment. It is an inner compulsion, not an external obligation. Racism in combination with economic motives constitutes a value system that dominates the nation's hold over a colored population. The nation's pattern of race relations flows out of this value system and cannot be considered but a mere reflection or continuation of one kind or another force ordained first by one kind and then another Superior Entity. Throughout its history, White America adjusts its expression of racism to accord with its economic imperatives and modifies its myths of racism to take into account the shifting economic circumstances. That is to say, racism remains a persistent value expression depending upon economic opportunities; White America generates a new ideology to sanction any fundamental alterations in race relations growing out of basic economic modifications. It has been the fate of ideologues, for the most part, to compose analyses in keeping with the myths of racism rather than to expose White America's racial motivation. By addressing explanations to the imageries of racism rather than exposing racism, sociologists embrace the very racism they pretend to explain and thus formulate intellectualized justifications for White America.

In the past, the Negro conceived his survival to be a matter of adjusting to changing economic conditions or forcing White America to bestow exclusively white privileges on blacks. Today, however, a growing number of Negroes stands in the vanguard, searching for solutions not only to racism but joblessness with the intrusion of technological displacement. As the Negro perceives the nation's unwillingness to undertake the task to compensate the dispossessed black laborer, he embarks upon a more radical program: increasingly, he advocates economic justice to restore all America. Just at the moment White America calls for *equality*, Black America demands *justice* to accord with Negro aspirations. Many Negroes want to develop into a creative minority endeavoring to found a radically different society for both white and black. Martin Luther King, for example, implored:

Let us . . . not think of our movement as one that seeks to integrate the Negro into all the existing values of American society. Let us be those creative dissenters who will call our beloved nation to a higher destiny, to a new plateau of compassion, to a more noble expression of humaneness.

. . . Giving our ultimate allegiance *to the empire of justice,* we must be that colony of dissenters seeking to imbue our nation with the idea of a higher and nobler order. . . .[22]

It is because equality according to white standards means the dismissal of blacks within American society that the radical Negro insists upon justice. By demanding justice, revolutionary blacks are able to formulate their own alternatives to remake rather than accept American values. The Negro leader, from Martin Luther King to Stokely Carmichael, shifts from the role of a mere critic to a radical figure—from an advocate of reform to a proponent of revolution—in seizing upon justice. Where he once contemplated the possibility of parity with whites by amending America to accommodate the Negro, he must now proclaim an inevitable necessity for altering the very fabric of White America; where he once sought acceptance as an equal, he must now overturn all America to win his sense of justice; where he could be content with integration, he must now express contempt; instead of being the subject of change, he must incite massive change. As White America implements economic repudiation of Negroes, Black America responds in kind, insisting upon a *new* America. There is something wrong *with* the system itself, not something *within* the system. The entire system is so corrupt in so many ways that it cannot be cured but rather must be discarded.[23]

Conclusion

America is a nation of white people marking time for a black people. After centuries of abuse, the white majority repudiates the black minority for the very qualities for

[22] Martin Luther King, Jr., *Where Do We Go From Here: Chaos or Community?* (New York: Harper & Row, 1967), pp. 133-134. Emphasis supplied.

[23] For a discussion of this point, see Willhelm, *Who Needs the Negro?*, Ch. 7.

which it must accept blame: poverty, ignorance, technical incompetence, family disruption, filth, crime, disease, substandard housing, etc. While assuring majestic prospects for acceptance, the nation removes the basic opportunities for achievement by enforcing the equality principle. Now that insurrections burst forth, whites reciprocate with more massive violence until resisting Negroes are fully suppressed. The white strategy reflects the nation's earlier history when "the ingenious plan evolved of first maddening the Indians into war, and then falling upon them with exterminating punishment," all along branding the latter with the charge of aggression.[24]

The bonds of unity collapsed in mid-nineteenth-century America when the economic and racial imperatives dictated the transition of the Negro from slavery into serfdom; the nation came to terms through a civil war. Disunity now afflicts mid-twentieth-century America as economic and racial imperatives necessitate Negro removal to an invisible existence upon the ghettoized reservation. White America's newest technological configuration provides a reformulated Manifest Destiny—to see to it that economic efficiency receives full expression in the form of automated production and mechanized agriculture. The enthronement of White America by a virtuous commitment to equality could not have been successful without an economy that makes labor less and less essential to production.

It is because the Negro moves more decisively in the direction of becoming an Indian ward at best that great despair spreads throughout the black ghetto. The ghetto riot in a carnival mood of gayety is expressive conduct by a collectivity in the initial stage of being doomed to an unwanted reservation existence; in time, it may very well turn, as was true for the American Indian, into a concerted effort to engage in warfare against White America.

---

[24] Helen Hunt Jackson, *A Century of Dishonor*, new ed., enlarged (Boston: Roberts Brothers, 1885), p. 40.

PART III

Black Sociology: Toward a Definition of Theory

Robert Staples

What Is
Black Sociology?
Toward a Sociology
of Black Liberation

Proposing that two of the basic tenets of sociology are humanism and value neutrality, Robert Staples illustrates how these
have been ignored by white sociologists, who have substituted
strong racist and class biases and a form of antihumanism.
Examining the works of classical European and American
sociologists, including Auguste Comte, Herbert Spencer, Charles
Darwin, Frank Giddings and William Graham Sumner, he
shows how these biases permeated their works. Turning to the
alternative model, he suggests that Black sociology can benefit
from the tradition set by Karl Marx, Karl Mannheim and
C. Wright Mills, and outlines the specific functions of the
Black sociologist.

To understand the meaning of Black sociology it is
necessary to have some knowledge of sociology in general
and white sociology in particular. The field of sociology is
generally concerned with the way human beings interact
with other human beings; the customs that grow out of
this interaction; the institutions that crystallize about human

needs; the changes that occur in these institutions; and the possibility of directing some of these changes in the ultimate interest of human welfare.[1]

White sociology refers to those aspects of sociology designed more for the justification of racist institutions and practices than objective analysis of human institutions and behavior. It is this body of theory and research that has been employed by the powers-that-be to sustain white racism and the instruments of its implementation. White sociology has provided not only the scientific covering for the exploitation of the Black masses, but the ideological rationale for the arrangement of power and the ascendancy of the powerful in human society.

While white sociology has by and large dominated general sociology, its practices have been antithetical to certain important tenets of the discipline: value neutrality and humanism. Sociology, as a discipline, is committed to the objective study of human relationships. The sociologist obtains the relevant data, classifies them, organizes a conceptual scheme, and subjects his hypotheses to empirical verification. Value judgments are not supposed to enter into the conclusions of his study.[2]

Humanism has traditionally served as an important part of sociology. The subject matter of sociology is man in his human relationships. Accordingly, the central concern of the sociologist should be an increased knowledge, appreciation and understanding of man as a human being. A function of sociology's humanistic function should be to foster democratic values in a society. White sociology has instead perpetuated the undemocratic and racist view that each individual belongs to a certain race, class, or other closed social group and that this membership ipso facto denies

[1] Frances Merrill, *Society and Culture* (Englewood Cliffs: Prentice-Hall, 1966), Chapter 1.

[2] William Kolb, "The Impingement of Moral Values on Sociology," *Social Problems*, 2 (October 1954), pp. 66–70.

him the opportunity to better himself in terms of his abilities.

Upon close examination, the two principles of humanism and value neutrality seem to be a contradiction. On the one hand, it is stated that no value judgments should be made, and on the other, that democratic values should be encouraged. This writer's view is that it is virtually impossible to exclude value judgments in sociology, and that to do so is not necessarily desirable. However, care must be taken to differentiate value judgments from statements of fact. In the case of white sociology, sociologists have not taken this precaution and express racist values as value-free, assuming an air of pontification in their judgments.

The uses to which white sociology has been put are manifest if one reviews the literature. What is equally important is why sociologists serve as ideological rationalists for racial and class oppression. One answer to this question is given by Gouldner:

> . . . The value-free doctrine is useful both to those who want to escape from the world and those who want to escape into it. It is useful to those young, or not so young, men who live off sociology rather than for it, and who think of sociology as a way of getting ahead in the world by providing them with neutral techniques that may be sold on the open market to any buyer. From such a standpoint, there is no reason why one cannot sell his knowledge to spread a disease just as freely as he can to fight it. Indeed, some sociologists have no hesitation about doing market research designed to sell more cigarettes, although well aware of the implications of recent cancer research. In brief, the value-free doctrine of social science was sometimes used to justify the sale of one's talents to the highest bidder and is, far from new, a contemporary version of the most ancient sophistry.[3]

[3] Alvin W. Gouldner, "Anti-Minotaur: The Myth of a Value-Free Sociology," *Social Problems*, 9 (August 1961), pp. 199–213.

Ideology, as a science of ideas used to legitimize institutions, is important to the elites that control American society. As C. Wright Mills states:

The demand for explicit ideological justifications has been greatly enlarged, if only because new institutions of enormous power have arisen but have not been legitimated, and because older powers have outrun their old sanction . . . Every interest and power, every passion and bias, every hatred and hope tends to acquire an ideological apparatus with which to compete with slogans and symbols the doctrines and appeals of other interests. As public communications are expanded and speeded up, their effectiveness is worn out by repetition, so there is a continuous demand for new slogans and beliefs and ideologies. In this situation of mass communication and intensive public relations, it would indeed be strange were the social studies immune from the demand for ideological communication, and stranger still were social researchers to fail to provide it.[4]

Historically, sociology and other social sciences have been used as instruments of racist ideology. In the South, there was a proliferation of studies that "objectively" reached the conclusion that Blacks were inherently inferior to whites. These research studies were employed to justify the subordination of Blacks through political disenfranchisement and racial segregation. Northern sociologists practiced a more subtle form of racism, studying Blacks and their cultural behavioral patterns as a form of pathology. Rarely did they challenge racism Northern-style by attacking job discrimination and housing segregation, or by approbation of interracial marriages.

The theories of some sociologists have in the past contained implicit racist assumptions. Even the founder of

[4] C. Wright Mills, *The Sociological Imagination* (New York: Grove Press, 1961), p. 31.

sociology, Auguste Comte, had a racist concept of society. Although Comte believed that the sociologist must turn to ordinary historical works for his data, it was possible for him to ignore the history of non-European peoples, because, he said, the sociologist is interested only in those people who have experienced social progress.[5] Apparently Comte felt he could eliminate the entire nonwhite world as not having experienced any degree of social progress. Even a very superficial knowledge of the historical achievements of the Chinese, Indian, and African civilizations would indicate that Comte's view is ethnocentric at best and racist at worst.

Another prominent sociologist, Herbert Spencer, is responsible for the social Darwinist theory: that nature is endowed with a potential tendency to get rid of the unfit and make room for the better. The unfit, according to Spencer, are those who lose their lives because of stupidity, vice or idleness. Because the sick and crippled are unfit, because of their inability to survive in society, they should not be protected by society. It takes little imagination to predict what Spencer's view would be concerning the higher rate of illness, substandard housing and unemployment in the Black community. He would probably say Blacks are unfit to compete in American society.[6]

Two prominent theories in sociology used to support racial segregation were provided by Franklin Giddings and William Graham Sumner. According to Giddings, social organization depends on a consciousness of kind. That is, a certain like-mindedness is found among different racial groups, and homogeneous populations are more stable social groupings. Thus, whites should be with whites, Blacks with

[5] Auguste Comte, *The Positive Philosophy* (New York: Calvin Blanchard, 1856).

[6] Herbert Spencer, *The Study of Sociology* (originated 1873; Ann Arbor: University of Michigan Press, 1961).

Blacks.[7] The Sumner doctrine is that the mores of a society can justify anything and prevent condemnation of anything. Since whites had certain customary ways of treating Blacks, no legislation or moral exhortations could change those practices.[8]

Contemporary sociological theory does not attempt to directly justify a blatantly racist social order. Yet one of the most popular conceptual models in sociology today provides an ideological base for the white racism extant in American society. This theoretical model, known as structural-functional analysis, sees society as composed of mutually dependent and harmonious elements. The main principle governing social relationships is that of homeostasis.[9]

According to the structural-functional model, society is based on collective tendencies toward consensus, not conflict as Marx predicted.[10] The proponents of this model see revolutions as unnecessary; what conflicts of interest exist can be resolved by mechanisms within the prevailing social system. A basic assumption of this theoretical framework is that individual members of the society share similar value orientations that undergird the normative structure.[11]

An example of this conceptual model's intellectual defense of the present social system is its explanation of the distribution of wealth in society. One of the major functional theorists asserts that there is a differential importance attached to the tasks that have to be executed in society.

[7] Franklin Giddings, *Principles of Sociology* (New York: Follett, 1935).

[8] William G. Sumner, *Folkways* (Boston: Ginn, 1966).

[9] Bernard Barber, "Structural-functional Analysis: Some Problems and Misunderstandings," *American Sociological Review* 21 (April 1956), pp. 129–135.

[10] Seymour Lipset, "Political Sociology," *Sociology Today*, Robert K. Merton et al., eds. (New York: Basic Books, 1959).

[11] Talcott Parsons, *The Social System* (Glencoe, Illinois: The Free Press, 1951), p. 262.

Therefore, to ensure that vital and difficult tasks are performed, it is necessary for society to reward the doers of such tasks more highly than those who perform less vital and less demanding jobs.[12] Such an explanation, of course, ignores the fact that the upper classes in this country are a parasitic group living off the labor of others. In reference to Black people, it assumes that they provide no vital services for the society, since they are located in the less rewarded positions of the society.

The ideological content of structural-functional theory lends itself easily to legitimation of the prevailing form of racial domination.[13] Any conceptual model that makes sacrosanct the present social system is antithetical to the needs of Black people. As Gerald McWorter states: "Anybody who's concerned with the status quo has basically defined Black people out because this is a racist country defined as being totally against Black people."[14]

It must be acknowledged that many white sociologists do not consciously purvey white sociology. The problem is that the white sociologist must study something of which he is an intimate part. He is a member of a racist society, participates in racist institutions, and develops a view of Black people partially derived from these relationships, along with his racist socialization. In the words of the existentialist philosopher Albert Camus, "Men cannot condemn themselves. Therefore, we must do it for them."

[12] Kingsley Davis and Wilbert Moore, "Some Principles of Stratification," *American Sociological Review*, 10 (May 1945), pp. 242–249.

[13] C. Wright Mills, *op. cit.*, pp. 42–49.

[14] Gerald McWorter, "Deck the Ivy Racist Halls: The Case of Black Studies," *Black Studies in the University*, Armstead Robinson et al., eds. (New Haven: Yale University Press, 1969), p. 59.

Black Sociology

Black sociology is based on the premise that Black and white peoples have never shared, to any great degree, the same physical environment or social experiences. People in different positions relate to each other and to their physical environment differently. The result is a different behavior pattern, a configuration that should be analyzed from the view of the oppressed—not the oppressor. Such an analysis is Black sociology. If white sociology is the science of oppression, Black sociology must be the science of liberation.

The task of Black sociology is to provide the legitimation of Black institutions and behavior that have evolved to meet the needs of the Black masses. Moreover, it must subject to social analysis and criticism those Black institutions and behavioral patterns that not only do not meet the needs of Black people, but serve as impediments to unifying the Black community.

Not only should Black sociology provide an elaboration of the "Black is beautiful" theme, it should explain that white is not necessarily ugly. In order to do this, the process of how people in a society come to place positive or negative valuations on racial traits should be examined, and the role of political and economic factors in influencing those valuations considered.

Black sociology will take from general sociology the method of historical analysis. The historical events that shape the Black condition will be examined for regularities so that we can determine at what stage of history Black people are, what is the level of political consciousness of the Black masses, what is the present course of racism, and what means are necessary to proceed to the next phase of the Black liberation struggle.

White sociologists such as C. Wright Mills[15] and Karl Mannheim[16] provide much of the theoretical framework for Black sociology. Mills, in particular, emphasized the use of classical social analysis unencumbered by vested interests, which have a material stake in things as they are. The central feature of classical social analysis is the focus on historical social structures to understand present-day conditions. In his own work, Mills used the historical method, and in the process made clear the elements involved in the social problems and issues of today.[17]

As a discipline, Black sociology continues in the tradition of E. Franklin Frazier, Oliver Cox and Nathan Hare.[18] These men not only laid bare the historical events that led to the Black condition, but analyzed the political and economic forces of historical epochs as they generated, or influenced, the character of Black deprivation. Not only did they indict the brutal system of white racism by their social analysis, they turned their attention to elements in the Black community which had abdicated responsibility for the Black masses. Frazier, for instance, criticized the Black middle class for living in a world of make-believe, imitating poorly the members of the white middle class, and not joining with the Black working class to seek their mutual liberation.[19]

Another of the tasks of the Black sociologist is to outline the intricately structured racist system of mind and social control; to show how constructing a countervailing

---

[15] Mills, op. cit.

[16] Karl Mannheim, Essays on the Sociology of Knowledge (New York: Oxford University Press, 1952).

[17] Cf. C. Wright Mills, The Marxists (New York: Dell, 1962).

[18] E. Franklin Frazier, Race and Culture Contacts in the Modern World (New York: Alfred A. Knopf, 1957); Oliver Cox, Caste, Class and Race (Garden City, New York: Doubleday, 1948); Nathan Hare, The Black Anglo-Saxons (New York: Marzani and Munsell, 1965).

[19] E. F. Frazier, The Black Bourgeoisie (New York: The Free Press, 1957).

racial mythology involving Black rhetoric, natural hair-
styles, dashikis, will not diminish the political and economic
oppression of Black Americans; and to use historical analysis in conjunction with the means necessary to achieve
Black liberation.[20]

In subject areas like the family, Black sociology should
demonstrate that the Western European form of family
organization is not necessarily superior to other types of
family organization.[21] Instead of denigrating the female-
headed households in our midst, it might celebrate these
for carrying many of us through the travail of the past four
hundred years. Children should be valued as potential
fighters in the Black liberation struggle, not as handicaps
that prevent the purchase of appurtenances of comfort.
The legitimacy of their conception should be irrelevant.
The sexual norms of the Black community should be revealed and accepted, with gratitude that Blacks avoid the
sexual neuroses of White America.

A social analysis of wars would reveal that a nation which
keeps its Black citizens in a colonial status will not expend
its resources on freeing an alien colored people ten thousand
miles from its shores. The task of Black sociology is to
show the underlying economic causes of wars and how
the interests of American Blacks are linked with the colonial peoples abroad fighting for national liberation.

Black sociology should also explain the problems of poverty and hunger. For example, hunger is allowed to exist
in American society in part because white racism permits a
callous and vindictive attitude toward poverty-stricken
people, who, to a large extent, are Black, Mexican-American or native Americans. In addition, the victims of poverty compose a reserve labor supply that can be hired

---

[20] Earl Ofari, *Black Liberation, Cultural and Revolutionary Nationalism,* Radical Education Project, June 1970.

[21] Robert Staples, "Towards a Sociology of the Black Family," *Journal
of Marriage and the Family,* 33 (February 1971), pp. 119–138.

when needed at the lowest wages. Thus the captains of industry benefit from having a large pool of hungry Black labor. Having an adequate food supply, they believe, would make this pool of labor "uppity."

Black sociology must define all Blacks in the nation's penal institutions as political prisoners. They are political prisoners because their incarceration derives from the racist conditions under which Black people are compelled to live. As Chrisman has noted, "a Black prisoner's crime may or may not have been a political action against the state, but the state's action against him is always political."[22] He elaborates on this analysis by stating that

The Black offender is not tried and judged by the Black community itself but by the machinery of the white community, which is least affected by his actions and whose interests are served by the systematic subjugation of all Black people. Thus, the trial or conviction of a Black prisoner regardless of his offense, his guilt or his innocence, cannot be a democratic judgment of him by his peers, but a political action against him by his oppressors.[23]

A Black criminology will reveal how crime is defined along racial and class lines. So-called white-collar crimes committed by the wealthy against the working-class citizenry are either ignored or lightly punished and are a negligible part of our crime statistics. Blacks face a double jeopardy in achieving justice: race and class. Being poor, they are more likely than members of the patrician group to be apprehended, convicted and sentenced to jail for crimes which involve little money or danger to the public interest. As Black people in White America, they will probably receive higher sentences for the same crime than their white counterparts, even at the same class level.

22 Robert Chrisman, "Black Prisoner White Law," *The Black Scholar*, 2 (April–May 1971), p. 45.
23 *Ibid.*, p. 46.

Finally, the role of the Black sociologist should be as both theorist and activist. Not only must he develop the theories embodied in the discipline of Black sociology, he must also man the barricades. The gulf between the Black academic community and the Black masses must be closed. By making Black sociology relevant to the needs of the Black community, the promise of Black sociology may be fulfilled; it may bring about a requiem for white racism and create a community of man where justice and peace once again prevail.

Abd-l Hakimu Ibn Alkalimat
(Gerald McWorter)

The Ideology of
Black Social Science

Increasing numbers of Black social scientists are seeking to find ways to infuse a Black ideology into the social sciences. The notion of a value-free discipline is strongly rejected, and proponents argue that the new role of the social sciences must be that of *creating an ideology* for the Black masses. In this chapter, Abd-l Alkalimat states that "Science is inevitably a handservant of ideology, a tool for people to shape, if not create reality." He analyzes the traditional role that white ideology has played in subjugating Blacks, in maintaining the status quo.

Our search for understanding through social analysis is conditioned by how we resolve several long-standing controversies, not the least of which is the relationship between ideology and science. In the case of Africans captured in the West, particularly in the United States of America, this has all too often been resolved by black intellectuals acquiescing to a white social science. This has meant swallowing the most favorable white positions without piercing

173

through to the implicit ideological assumptions really used to guide history with white interests. Many black social scientists seemingly have not really known the extent to which science is inevitably a handservant to ideology, a tool for people to shape, if not create, reality. This article is an attempt to clarify how the ideology-science controversy might be dealt with in a new way, a way serving black interests in our struggle for liberation.

There are two questions that we shall attempt to clarify and begin to resolve:

1—What is the necessary connection between ideology and social analysis for the Black Liberation Struggle?

2—How can black people begin to construct revolutionary thought based on an analysis that leads to a commitment to struggle for liberation?

Social Science involves two levels of analysis, empirical and theoretical. One level deals with organizing a set of systematically collected indicators of what's happening (like answers to a set of questions), while the other is an attempt to develop propositions explaining as wide a range of empirical relationships as is possible. An ideology incorporates these two components of social science under two aspects peculiar to its own makeup. Ideology involves the prophetic vision of an ought as well as the action orientation of a moral commitment to serve. Thus, ideology combines an interpretation of the social world with a moral commitment to change it.

Consider for a moment the notion of social class as a dynamic historical concept that reflected both the fundamental structure of society as well as the basic components of conflict and change. One's class position has a total relationship to power and its function, specifically the ownership and control of the economy. The concept, social class, in the United States is a sterile classificatory term used to merely suggest a hierarchical ordering of individuals by some social measure like education, income, or occupation. Marx is often ruled out as an ideologue, whereas science is at best used for classification. But upon further examination, it becomes clear that what appears to be science in the United States is at best a set of sophisticated tools used in the interests of a quite developed and comprehensive set of ideological beliefs.

Given this distinction, one can easily see that most of our analysis has served a white ideology, while black ideologies have lacked the support of a systematic social analysis. This observation is supported by Harold Cruse as he develops a critical history of contemporary black culture:

> . . . the black American as part of an ethnic group has no definite social theory relative to his status, presence, or impact on American society. . . . Coming at a moment of racial crisis in America, there has been no school of social theory prepared in advance for black power that could channel the concept along the lines of positive, radical, and constructive social change.[1]

White social science has dealt with black people on the basis of two theoretical models, one based on attitudes, the other on behavior. The attitudinal approach focuses on prejudice, the use of generalizations prejudging a group of people or institutions in guiding actions toward them. The behavioral approach is based on discrimination, differential treatment of people who belong to certain identifiable groups. Empirical research in the last 50 years has produced data that on the lowest level of theory can be organized under one of these two concepts. And this covers most of what passes for social analysis of race problems in the United States.

But these two approaches are really two different profiles of the same face, the hideous face of white racism. If

---

[1] Harold Cruse, *Rebellion or Revolution*, pp. 202–203.

one were to examine the social analysis of race before the empirical studies at the University of Chicago (Robert Park, Ernest Burgess, Louis Wirth, etc.), one would find more honest theoretical discussions expressed in the world of white racism. Empirical research has resulted in progress toward having access to more incidents of social reality, but has also resulted in the falsification of our understanding. The challenge of organizing vast amounts of social data under manageable theory has resulted in low-level theory like the concepts of prejudice and discrimination. We have been looking at the trees and ignoring the essential nature of the forest.

The fact is that black people have been oppressed by a system unified on the basis of white racism. Racism is a concept that speaks to the total system, the essential nature of the social order as perceived by black people. While the concepts prejudice and discrimination are helpful on an analytical level of theory because they are so easily operationalized and quantified, racism is the more appropriate theoretical description of the problem precisely because it captures the qualitative character of the oppression. It's only recently (since Malcolm and the Kerner Commission Report on Civil Disorders) that the concept of racism has become fashionable, and that our understanding of the problem has escaped the static descriptive theory of prejudice and discrimination.

Another important aspect of this set of two theoretical models (prejudice and discrimination) is the underlying ideological assumptions. Both prejudice and discrimination are normally conceived as continuous dynamic phenomena. Once one is able to discover strong correlations between indicators of prejudice and/or discrimination and other social data, it is possible to devise programs to structure reality as one wishes. So the most positive white approach has increasingly been strengthened because even social science supports certain programs for solutions to racial problems. For example, if educational achievement is a strong inverse correlate of prejudice (as one gets more racially integrated quality education, one gets less prejudiced), then it follows that placing a strong investment in education is a good integrationist policy. But those black people of the hip world know that everything is everything, and that the whole is not the sum of the relationships between its parts.

Take Robert Park as an example of the white liberal position. He used a sociological frame of reference including five major concepts—contact, competition, conflict, accommodation, and assimilation. His work was based on the optimal outcome of assimilation whereby the black man would be totally transformed from an African into an American, just another cat walkin' and workin'. Moreover, he held that black nationalism (or what he called race consciousness) might well be a true expression of what some black people believed, but that assimilation was an inevitable outcome. His position was clearly stated:

> Now that Negroes are free and have become race, if not class, conscious, they are in a position to state their case in more articulate fashion. However, the authors of the Declaration of Independence and the United States Constitution have provided them with a ready made ideology.[2]

Now this was a white dude trying to trick us into diggin' what some slave owners developed about us (remember that they counted us as three-fifths of a man).

Robert Park was the man most responsible in the social sciences for developing a liberal white game to run on black people. He and his colleagues at the University of Chicago were more responsible than any other graduate school for

2 Robert Park, *Race and Culture*, p. 307.

training black social scientists; perhaps their most important student was E. Franklin Frazier, a brother who was strong enough to collect a lot of important data but fell victim to theory based on the racist, white liberal ideology. However, he wasn't totally a pawn of Park's theory; he was able to state in 1962 that:

> In view of the Negro's history, the Negro intellectual and artist had a special opportunity and special responsibility. The process by which the Negroes were captured and enslaved in the United States stripped them of their African culture and destroyed their personality. Under the slavery regime and for nearly a century since emancipation everything in American society has stamped the Negro as subhuman, as a member of an inferior race that had not achieved even the first steps in civilization.
>
> There is no parallel in human history where a people have been subjected to similar mutilation of body and soul. Even the Christian religion was given them in a form only to degrade them. The African intellectual recognizes what colonialism has done to the African and he sets as his first task the mental, moral, and spiritual rehabilitation of the African.
>
> But the American Negro intellectual, seduced by dreams of final assimilation, has never regarded this as his primary task.[3]

Assuming the challenge laid forth by Brother Frazier is indeed a primary task of black intellectuals today. We must develop a social theory consistent with a revolutionary black ideology so that what we know will be worth knowing. We must know that which makes us really see/experience the future/past because it gives us "identity, purpose and direction." As the Bird-Coltrane revolution has redefined spirit-emotion, we must set ourselves to the task of totally redefining our mind-action. As an initial move toward this, we will now attempt to survey a basic set of

---

[3] E. Franklin Frazier, "The Failure of the Negro Intellectual," *Negro Digest*, February, 1962.

concepts used in white social science (and quite familiar to all of us), and present an alternative set of concepts for social analysis based on a Revolutionary Pan-African Nationalist ideology.

Terms of White Social Science	*Terms of Black Social Science*
Negro (non-white)	African (black)
Segregation	Colonization
Tokenism	Neo-Colonialism
Integration	Liberation
Equality	Freedom
Assimilation	Africanization

Social science has constructed a set of terms to explain black people and their experiences and, for the most part, these terms have suffered from being based on sterile analytical theory that attempts to *classify* social reality and not *explain* its essential nature. Perhaps the best illustration of this begins with the word-concept *Negro*. This term had practically no currency until 1880 when a group of middle-class black people rejected the terms African and colored; among them were Washington and W. E. B. DuBois. Horace Mann Bond quotes DuBois as saying "It was a short word; it was a strong word; I knew that it had been debased, but I thought it could be resuscitated, and given dignity!" However, when we test the word to see what it does or doesn't do, we find out how denigrating and freakish it makes people who use it to describe themselves.

What a people call themselves has meaning because it links them to their ancestors and refers to their role in human history. The only ancestors linked to the word Negro are people who were slaves to white people, people who were told they were inferior burdens to white people. Negroes were told they had no past and had never made significant contributions to human civilization. We were told that the Egyptians were white, and that only by having white blood could a black person develop enough to be somebody and make a contribution. In sum, the only people identifying themselves with the term Negro are people who have suffered the racist oppression of the white West. The Negro is held to be a creation of the West since slavery was supposed to have completely separated us from Africa, making all that we are what they have made us be. (See Arnold Toynbee, Gunnar Myrdal, William Faulkner, and Daniel P. Moynihan for illustrations of the above.)

Consistent with the term Negro is the use of *segregation* as the major concept to describe the U.S.A. race problem. Segregation means to keep separate, something that everybody believes in and disagrees with. Not many folks these days are against sexual segregation of public bathrooms, but most homes have communal toilets. Most sensible people agree that the segregationist laws applied to voting on the basis of age should be changed, but not so drastically as to include absolutely everyone regardless of age. The point is that when black folks have used this term we have meant something entirely different from the denotative meaning of the term. And rightly so, since our essential problem is not the result of being kept separate from white people (whether they do it, or we do it).

Following the term segregation is the concept *integration*. It's only logical that if the problem is segregation the two alternative solutions are integration or annihilation. The white liberal line is that by integrating black people with white people everything will work itself out. We have even been militant about this and declared that *desegregation* (essentially meaning the removal of segregationist barriers) was insufficient, as is the *tokenism* involved in allowing a very few blacks in where previously all blacks have been excluded. All of this is in large part based on the goal of *equality*, a near synonym for integration that means having the same life chances as white people. White people have been the standard for all of our goals, since the problem was that they kept us from them and what they had going for themselves.

Underlying the goals of integration and equality is the same belief expressed by Robert Park: "The race relations cycle which takes the form, to state it abstractly, of contacts, competition, accommodation, and eventual assimilation, is apparently progressive and irreversible."[4] *Assimilation* is the ultimate form of progress in the white liberal analysis, a process that more accurately should be called "*anglo-conformity*." Since the values and norms of white people are those served by the social coercion of institutions in this society, it is inevitable that if any changing is going to happen it will be all those people different from white folks becoming more like them. Even E. Franklin Frazier warned black people of this eventual outcome when he wrote:

In the final analysis, complete racial desegregation would mean the dissolution of the social organizations of the Negro community as Negroes are integrated as individuals into the institutional life of American society.

The theoretical orientation reflected in these terms is white and Negro. Black is not beautiful nor is it designed to survive. This is a theoretical orientation designed to wipe us out and convince us that our eventual disappearance from the scene is an inevitable outcome in the flow of human history. What we need is a theory of survival. Our understanding of the world must take full account of our past and propel us into the future with glorious possibilities.

[4] Robert Park, *Race and Culture*, p. 150.

Let us listen to the prophetic voice of the Mystic Oneda-ruth (who was called John Coltrane) sing Africa and get on with the work of constructing a social theory giving us the power and strategy to struggle toward capturing that spirit and bringing such a new revolutionary Africa into human history.

As listed in the right column in the chart, we will now present a set of concepts more consistent with a black frame of reference. Instead of using the terms Negro and non-white to describe who we are (as does the U.S.A.'s secular Bible, the census), a black social science would refer to us as black people, as African peoples. Black is prefer-able to non-white because it is positive and distinct, rather than negative and based on white as the standard. How-ever, the more significant name for black people is *African*. We should use African because it is our best link with our ancestors. It describes a continent in the world within which our forefathers built glorious civilizations and main-tained high standards of black cultural values. And as *African* ties us to a positive past, so it foretells of our future.

The major arguments against using the concept African include the following: (1) while we are "descendants" of African peoples, we are American Negroes because we were born here. Brother Malik Shabazz used to answer, "If a cat gave birth in an oven, she wouldn't have biscuits, she'd have kittens." (2) Robert Park and E. Franklin Frazier (and others) have demonstrated that slavery and the Middle Passage removed all of African culture from our way of life, and on the plantations of the Ante-Bellum South, we became Americans the best way we could.

The most obvious refutation of this is our music, our dancing, and the way most of us look. In addition, consider these facts: (1) Lorenzo Turner has found an overwhelm-ing number of African words and syntax patterns in our speech, as well as moving fraudulent white scholars who denied this by simply indicating that they had no knowledge of African languages; (2) Africans were brought to this country as recently as 100 years ago, so that many families can trace their lineage back (Alex Haley has recently done this for his own family by uncovering a wealth of factual information to be presented in a full length book as well as a feature movie); and (3) our basic religious beliefs and practices have never really changed (same of the middle-class mimicking of white folks), and so we have strong attachments to astrology, charms, emotional communion with the spiritual world, and an unshakable belief in the Gods (something white people have never really had integrated into their culture successfully).

So we are African peoples, black folks. Therefore, we can understand quite readily that the real problem is not our being segregated from white people in the West; the problem is our being in the West in the first place (and most regrettable of all, the U.S.A.). It follows, then, that the problem is *Colonization*. This concept of colonialism has definite meaning as a dynamic historical concept. It refers to the interaction of two whole communities of people by which one community attempts to colonize the other and make it subordinate. The concept refers to the oppressive group as colonizers, and the oppressed as the colonized. It implies that a society with this set of communities is bound together by coercion, and is in conflict under normal conditions. And the term suggests a history of before, during and after itself. Colonization is a total attempt at subordination, involving a people's values, beliefs, rituals, norms, institutions, myths, and its history.

Decolonization is a concept referring to attempts by the colonized to sound a total rejection of being colonized, a negation of the colonial oppressors and everything they have created resulting in colonial dependency. Since self-hate is instilled into the colonized, love of self is an important part of decolonization. In the U.S.A., black had always been negative until we were able to make it acceptable to black people; now "Black is Beautiful, and it's so beautiful to be black." Colonization made us distrust one another and only support white people. Now we are self-oriented and concerned about the internal development of our own community. Where once we went to get culture and good food, we now respect it because we know where we live. Soul is not only what's happening, but where it's happening as well.

The process of decolonization is more toward *liberation*, that process of becoming independent and completely positive about one's self and one's community. It also involves social structures, enabling the black community to have complete control over its destiny through all political, economic, and social institutions. Liberation is, however, necessarily conceived as a worldwide process. If the forces of racism are to be defeated, then it must be so everywhere, if it is to be so anywhere. Wherever you go to visit black brothers and sisters, you will find traces of concerns like Western white governments, Coca-Cola, Chase Manhattan Bank, United Fruit Company, the oil companies, and General Motors. These are institutional manifestations of white imperialistic colonial forces that must be contained and rendered helpless if we are to achieve liberation and self-determination.

The forces of oppression use several sophisticated schemes of subversion against us as we move toward liberation. Colonialism in it most illusory form is *neo-colonialism*, either the partial but not total control of the black community by black people (*i.e.*, having a black government but continued white control of the economy: Gary, Indiana or post-Nkrumah Ghana) or the use of Negroes to represent the covert interests of whites. Concerning African countries, Nkrumah writes:

The essence of neo-colonialism is that the State which is subject to it is, in theory, independent and has all the outward trappings of international sovereignty. In reality its economic system and thus, its political policy, is directed from outside.[5]

Within this framework of analysis, it is easy to see that programs like "Black Capitalism" are neo-colonialist tricks, because black people have no real capital of their own; besides, America has developed past small, entrepreneur capitalism into corporate, monopolistic capitalism. For example, Citizens Trust Bank, one of the oldest black banks in the country and located in affluent Atlanta, was forced to seek a loan from a major white bank in order to construct a new building.

Fanon speaks to this case through his analysis of Algeria: "True liberation is not that pseudo-independence in which . . . (there is) an economy dominated by the colonial past. Liberation is the total destruction of the colonial system. . . ."[6] To accept the idea of black capitalism is to accept the position of being a ward of the white man, a highly prized servant who is content with crumbs from the mildewed cake of whites rather than being about the business of baking a fresh black one with a black recipe to satisfy black appetites.

Of course, a major question is whether any reforms can occur that would not be neo-colonialistic. But this is a question that can only be answered once we have a clear set of goals in mind that will begin to give form to our liberation. Our essential goal must be one of *Freedom from white people and their oppressive, dying system, and not equality with them.* There can be no freedom in the present system; it must undergo fundamental changes or be replaced entirely. The only way for it to be changed is to have a new constitutional convention and reconstruct the basic political documents serving as the basis of the social order.

[5] Kwame Nkrumah, *Neo-Colonialism; the Last Stage of Imperialism,* p. ix.

[6] Frantz Fanon, *Toward the African Revolution,* p. 105.

We must have a new constitution, a new flag, new symbols, new songs, a new economy, a new way of relating to the rest of the world, a new commitment for peace and justice everywhere. The new society must be hip in the hippest sense of that beautiful word. We must be an answer to Frantz Fanon when he calls:

> Come, then, comrades; it would be as well to decide at once to change our ways. We must shake off the heavy darkness in which we were plunged, and leave it behind. The new day which is at hand must find us firm, prudent, and resolute . . . we must turn over a new leaf, we must work out new concepts, and try to set afoot a new man.[7]

And if anybody gets in our way trying to impede the marching progress of human history, to quote a brother, "we must strike them dead before God gets the word."

But if in our freedom we are responsible to ourselves and really move to "set afoot a new man," then we must begin to conceptualize what kind of positive action will give real meaning to our freedom. Inasmuch as we acknowledge that we are Africans in the Americas who have suffered the tortures of colonization, then it is appropriate that once free we will reorient ourselves to who we really are (and have always been). We must be committed to *Africanization* for, as Maulana Ron Karenga teaches: "To return to tradition is to take the first step forward." And for those who think of this as wishful romantic utopianism (especially in this highly technological industrial society), he would emphasize the role of cultural values:

> Cultural background transcends education. Having a scope is different from having a content.
>
> A value system has three functions: it gives some predictability of behavior, it is an ultimate authority and it serves as a means of security.

---

[7] Frantz Fanon, *The Wretched of the Earth*, pp. 252 and 255.

We stress culture because it gives identity, purpose and direction. It tells us who we are, what we must do, and how we can do it.[8]

So one real manifestation of Africanization is the re-orientation of our cultural values, a process utilizing all of ancient Africa both as the source of inspiration, as well as the source of truth by which our ultimate judgements are made concerning the present; indeed, Africa before the white man will be the cultural basis for our prophetic vision of Africa's children after the white man.

Africanization is essentially the same for black people in the United States of America just as it applies equally as a vision of our tomorrow for all African peoples colonized on the continent of Africa, or wherever we have wandered or been taken. The basis for our social, political, and economic systems can better be found among the communal traditions of our people rather than among those who have used their systems to oppress if not annihilate us. We must actively pursue concepts like the African Personality, Negritude, African Socialism, Ujamaa, and Pan-Africanism just as our kin folk on the African continent are doing. We must conjure up our ancestral spirits and let them guide us through inspiration.

While this has been simply an exploratory attempt at clarifying two alternative and opposing sets of concepts, it is still quite possible to summarize some of the major differences between the two perspectives. First, the conceptual approach of white social science is only useful on the analytical level of classification since for each term the social content must be specified. The concepts presented for a black social science clearly suggest a specific sociopolitical content to be understood as the race problem. Moreover, a second difference is that the white conceptual

[8] Maulana Ron Karenga, *The Quotable Karenga.*

orientation is quite local to the U.S.A., whereas the concepts for a black social science are related to an international analysis of African peoples wherever they are found. The model of colonialism is one which has currency among our brothers and sisters throughout the world, though up until now, we have at best thought of it as an analogue. Our understanding must be couched in concepts on the same level as the problems we attempt to understand.

The last major difference deals with models of society and notions concerning social change. The conceptual framework presented as white social science reflects an *equilibrium model* of society based on evolutionary change. All things happen in due course as the society evolves to a higher level based on more universalistic rational standards of operation. The concepts of a black social science reflect a *conflict model* of society bound together by coercion and changed by revolution. To put this in more pointed terms, the white concepts are based on the myth of salvation for the jailer, while the black concepts more directly speak to the reality of getting black folks out of the jail.

At the beginning of this discussion, we attempted to raise two general questions pointing the way toward a black theory of revolution. This is important because we need a revolutionary ideology that reflects the utility of a black social analysis, the inevitable correctness of African prophecy of black gods creating a new man and the immortality of communal love as the basis for a commitment to kill and die for the liberation of all black people. In other words, we need to get this shit on, and for that we need a revolutionary script for the terrible black drama of cosmic forces that we're about to rain down on these pitiful ofays.

Immamu Amiri Baraka teaches us:

. . . let Black People understand that they are the lovers and the sons of lovers and warriors and sons of warriors. . . .[9]

[9] Immamu Amiri Baraka, *Black Fire*, p. 303.

Ramos Mor teaches us:

Is now the heyday Mister John C tells of. . . .

And these whiteys are saying that if you get out of line U gonna get your asses kicked.

Now think about what you have just read in this paper and decide what the hell you're gonna do? We have to do? Africa. Revolution. Love. God. Family. YOU. Revolution. Africa.

Ronald W. Walters

Toward a Definition
of Black Social Science

In the midst of the Black challenge to make the social sciences more meaningful and practical to the Black condition, there has been an attempt by some Black scholars to develop a "Black social science." Ronald Walters, a political scientist whose approach to this subject is multidisciplinary, sets forth in this essay some of the basic premises of this new perspective, a basic methodological focus and an ideological direction.

Whether or not one believes in the possibility that there is a body of knowledge about Black life which can be disciplined and made useful in the survival and development of Black people depends upon many factors. Among them are a determination that such knowledge can be disciplined and a conviction that, in such a disciplined state, the knowledge will be useful when applied to actual problems the community faces.

For years both Black and white scholars denied that the "stuff" of Black life constituted a respectable enough body of knowledge to bother about recording it for posterity. Recently, however, there has been a recognition of this gross oversight and a grudging admission that perhaps there is such a thing as Black history (after all, a people have only to have existed to have a history). This is an important admission, because it was this small bit of intellectual awareness which, supported by Black students' protests, was a major factor in persuading university faculties to vote in favor of adopting Black Studies in the last few years. Once having established such programs, it was easy to see, from a perusal of some sample curricula, that the humanities were legitimate because Blacks have produced some of the most original art forms the country has had, and in some areas constitute the most dominant and dynamic forces existent today. But there is definitely no Black science as yet and no Black social science.

Another problem arises when those involved in Black education insist that the application of African history and culture is essential to Black progress. Most whites and Blacks still do not believe this! Standing in the residue of program after program to reconstruct the Black community by using white social science, these doubters know that something is wrong, but they refuse to believe that there is some efficacy in their own Black being, some Black power that, when added to other relevant factors, becomes the necessary ingredient for the solution. It is all the more confusing when solutions are not found because white social science has acquired a reputation for being oriented toward "social change" and for developing "intervention" strategies.

That the sum of white experiences (and therefore theorizing) does not add up to Black "fact" or reality can be seen in the following—I hesitate to call it an analysis— by an American sociologist.

[The Negroes] were without ancestral pride or family tradition. They had no distinctive language or religion. These, like their folkways and moral customs, were but recently acquired from the whites and furnished no nucleus for a racial unity. The group was without even a tradition of historic unity or of racial achievement. There were no historic names, no great achievements, no body of literature, no artistic productions. The whole record of the race was one of servile or barbarian status apparently without a point about which a sentimental complex could be formed.[1]

This study, published originally in 1927 (and re-issued recently in the wake of the panic publishing on Blacks) gives the impression of some authority, as the author cites thirty-three separate pieces of "consensus" for the "facts" in the chapter from which this quote was taken. Some of the pieces of evidence he cites are from white and Black authors, and no doubt today one could take the same sources and manage a "modern" interpretation of the nature of Black life. This suggests, at least to this writer, that the business of utilizing methods in arriving at a truth which appears to be objective (for Reuter had one of the best reputations of his day for objectivity) often do little more than yield to "vogueism" in the social sciences.

Black Social Science

Those concepts which discipline, or bring order to, the study of the history and culture of Black people constitute a working definition of the term.[2] Writing at the beginning of the development of Black Social Science, one can say

---

[1] Edward B. Reuter, *The American Race Problem* (New York: Thomas Y. Crowell, 1970), p. 365.

[2] It has been a traditional practice to define items not only by genus but also by function and application as the term "Black" fixed to the phenomenon "social science" implies. To wit, one would catch hell if he used a left-handed monkey wrench to turn a right-handed bolt, which would suggest the necessity to obtain the right tool in the first place!

only what it might become. This is suggested in the area of sociology in the writings of Robert Staples, Nathan Hare, Andrew Billingsley, and Joyce Ladner; in political sociology, in the work of Gerald McWorter and James Turner; in history, in the work of Harold Cruse, Lerone Bennett, Jr., John Clarke and Vincent Harding; in political economy, in the work of Robert Browne, Earl Ofari and James Boggs; in politics, in the work of Charles Hamilton. This list is not meant to be exhaustive; it is a subjective selection of the work of Black social scientists who have had the courage to criticize wrong-headed approaches whether from whites or Blacks, and the originality to try to create a Black framework for their analyses.

One should not rejoice prematurely, however, in this meager listing. The white scholar is still winning the race to the documents and to the publishing houses and thereby is still in a position to exercise a great deal of influence over what the younger Blacks read and think. Despite the beginning effort, there is very little internal intellectual Black ferment. For example, in Black history, there is very little consensus but no significant debate over periodization or the significance of various social, political and cultural movements; in sociology, no consensus and no debate over the structure and function of the Black social system; in economics, there is only a waning argument over the efficacy of "Black capitalism." There should be a great debate over the "isms" Black people have historically been sold, in order to clarify our choices. In general, Black intellectual energy at the present time seems to be concerned with a consideration of Pan Africanism (which is absolutely necessary), and we are, still to a considerable extent, in the finishing stages of having to react to the challenge to the legitimacy of Black social science by white and Black skeptics. We are also in the midst of developing embryonic organizations and settling their ideology and operations, hoping they will be the base of activities which will consistently feed attempts of Black social scientists to relate their craft to the struggles of Black people. The lack of volume in our activity may be attributed to many causes, but it may be, as a student of mine said recently, that in this period we are like the old mule who lashed out with his heels to kick the wagon and start it rolling, and who is simply rearing back to strike again.

What comes clearest at this point is that in the works that have been produced, the ideology is profoundly different from that of white social science. Perhaps it will suffice to take a few samples from the work of the authors listed above as evidence for this assertion. In discussing Black Nationalism, James Turner states that biased sociological studies have accepted the consensus model.

But while consensus models accept the core values of the dominant group as functional for society, some of these values may in fact be inimical to particular groups, who are thus increasingly led to question the legitimacy of the social system. Proper study of Black Nationalism employs a conflict perspective.[3]

Harold Cruse performs a valuable service, writing in the same issue of *Black World*, by pushing Black scholars toward social criticism:

I reiterate this critical assault on black social, political, and cultural thought was premeditated [speaking of his book *Crisis of the Negro Intellectual*]. It was my conviction that black social thought of all varieties was in dire need of some ultra-radical overhauling if it was to meet the comprehensive test imposed by the sixties. Now that the sixties are history, I am still convinced—even more so—that black social thought is in need of ultra-radical overhauling. In fact, the arrival of the

[3] "Black Nationalism, the Inevitable Response," *Black World* (January 1971), p. 9.

seventies revealed to me that I had underestimated the critical reassessing black social thought really needed.[4]

And he goes on to imply that our political theory needs to be seriously grounded in local conditions and perspectives, using the experiences of political events in other countries selectively. In his subsequent article (Part II) in *Black World*,[5] he chides the Black scholar for not having dealt critically with the revered Black historians of the past, and he is, oh so right.

John Henrik Clarke has a partial answer to what the role of the contemporary Black scholar in the struggle for Black liberation should be when he says that he must be a "scholar-activist" and adds (speaking of the formation of the African Heritage Studies Association)

We interpret African History from a Pan-Africanist perspective that defines all black people as African People. . . . Our program has as its objective the restoration of the cultural, economic, and political life of African people everywhere.[6]

In the realm of sociology, Andrew Billingsley points to the fact that "white social science" excludes consideration of the complexity and strength of the Black family as factors of prime importance.[7]

The ideas of Earl Ofari and James Boggs in political economy make a powerful argument as they analyze the reasons for the failure of Black economic life. In looking at the failure of Black business, Earl Ofari finds:

[4] "Black and White: Outlines of the Next Stage," *Black World* (January 1971), p. 9.

[5] "Black and White: Outlines of the Next Stage," Part II, *Black World* (March 1971), pp. 9–14.

[6] "The Meaning of Black History," *Black World* (February 1971).

[7] See Andrew Billingsley, "Black Families and White Social Science," this volume.

Examples abound throughout the voluminous reports and studies the mythmakers of black business have conducted. The blame for black business failure for a long time was laid on black people themselves. The main argument [citing E. Franklin Frazier's study, *The Negro in the United States*, p. 410] can be easily summarized: black proprietors are inefficient, lazy, lack education, have little business experience, are slow and discourteous. Black businesses fail because the very economic system in which they are trying to succeed is stacked against them.[8]

If this is true, then Boggs seems to point up the solution:

Any program for the development of the black community must be based on large-scale social ownership rather than on private individual enterprise. In this period of large-scale production and distribution, private individual enterprise [or small business] can only remain marginal and dependent, adding to the sense of hopelessness and powerlessness inside the black community.[9]

Central to this particular problem seems to be the discussion of whether or not racism in America is endemic to capitalism. This point was settled long ago by one of our most brilliant and neglected Black scholars, Oliver Cox, who listed racism as one of the features of capitalism.[10] But the debate over the form and substance of the system that will guarantee equality to Blacks proceeds from the perceived need to have radical change in the distribution of wealth. Thus far the center of this debate has been over the value of "Black capitalism," but as it begins to appear in

[8] Earl Ofari, *The Myth of Black Capitalism* (New York: Monthly Review Press, 1970), p. 77.

[9] James Boggs, *Racism and the Class Struggle* (New York: Monthly Review Press, 1970), p. 141.

[10] Oliver Cox, *Capitalism as a System* (New York: Monthly Review Press, 1964), pp. 32, 65–66.

social science literature there is a recognition of the need for new concepts as S. E. Anderson says:

Paradoxically, black business education and most of the relatively few black economists have made the tragic mistake of embracing unequivocally the principles and practices of American Capitalism; the same system that white people manipulate and scheme to deny black people significant participation.[11]

He continues, in a fashion not dissimilar to Boggs, that if Black people are to be liberated under capitalism they must have the power to effect and control significant changes in their current status. The answers to Black economic development have not been found within the concepts of white social science because it assumes the ideology of the capitalist system.

This discussion has been based on the knowledge that there are questions inherent in the Black experience which have been approached incorrectly by the utilization of both the ideology and the methodology of white social science. But Black truth does not necessarily proceed in dialectical fashion because of the intimate juxtaposition of Black people to whites in the history and culture of America.

The black scholar must develop new and appropriate norms and values, new institutional structures, and in order to be effective in this regard, he must also develop and be guided by a new ideology. Out of this new ideology will evolve new methodology. Though in some regards it will subsume and overlap existing norms of scholarly endeavor.[12]

Black life has been distinctive and separate enough to constitute its own uniqueness, and it is on the basis of that uniqueness that the ideology and the methodology of Black social science rests.

11 *The Black Scholar*, Vol. 2, No. 2 (October 1970), p. 11.
12 See Nathan Hare, "The Challenge of a Black Scholar," this volume.

IDEOLOGY

In the works cited above it is possible to identify certain elements which contribute to an ideology for Black social science; they refer to radicalism and conflict theory as well as an infusion of the substances of Blackness—Africanism, nationalism, history, cultural style, self-determination and consciousness of racism. Elsewhere I have dealt with the problem of using Basil Matthews' term the "Unity and Order of Blackness."[13] I believe this term (which he is in the process of applying to research as the "Black knowledge process") to be comprehensive enough to include all aspects of a Black social-science ideology. Also, concepts of "unity" and "order" may be regarded as tools which, when applied to the data, help to discipline it. Here, it is useful to turn to the seminal works of Gerald McWorter[14] and Preston Wilcox.

Like McWorter, Preston Wilcox performs a transforming function on terms which, to him, are examples of the "rhetoric of oppression," by his use of a Black educational ideology and a taxonomy resulting from the comparison of scientific colonialism and scientific humanism.[15]

Urban Renewal	really means	Negro Removal
Model Cities	"	Model Colonies
Human Relations	"	Colonial Relations
Culturally Deprived	"	Illegally Deprived
Public Welfare	"	Public Starvation
Code Enforcement	"	Tenant Exploitation
School Decentraliza-tion	"	School Recentraliza-tion

[13] Ronald W. Walters, "The Discipline of Black Studies," *The Negro Education Review*, Vol. 21, No. 4 (October 1970), pp. 138–144.

[14] See Abd-l Hakimu Alkalimat, "The Ideology of Black Social Science," this volume.

[15] *Negro Digest*, Part III (March 1970), p. 83.

In each case the writer has "translated" from the white into the Black terminology, using his sense of Black consciousness as the cutting edge to redefine reality so that the Black terms which result are congruent with the objective Black situation.

Terms alone, however, do not make an ideology. If, therefore, we can distill the essential experience which these terms collectively represent, we come to the following figure:

A   B

Urban-Technological   *Classic-Colonialism*
(Institutionalized   (Economic, political
white racism)   and cultural
                       exploitation)

X

Black Oppression
(Individualized,
group)

Without going into the details of either A-to-X or B-to-X relationship (which would be beyond the scope of this paper and volumes in themselves), perhaps a comment on each would suffice to relate to the subject at hand what the reader must most assuredly know to be some of the facts.

Variable A. Many of the analyses, particularly in the historical, cultural and political realm, do not yet take into account the pervasiveness of technology as a weapon against us and an impediment to the full expression of our Blackness, or even of the ways in which technology can be utilized to enhance those elements of our culture we would like to emphasize, and how we can control such technology as might make this possible. The functioning of such technology in an urban environment has, we know, increased the effectiveness of institutionalized racism by expelling more Black people from institutions which would theoretically make them productive, and by using such institutions to objectively control our lives—one has only to mention the press, among other institutions, in this regard. The distorted picture of Black life presented in the national media will be changed only if Black people participate in the media in significant ways, and until that happens, the media will continue to contribute to the oppression of Black communities. Increasing levels of unemployment and the disparity between white and Black incomes and economic opportunities make the relationship of oppression starkly evident.

Variable B. The explosive work *Black Power* contains within it the colonial paradigm[16] that explains the connection between the white and Black communities with respect to power relationships and, thus, to all the attendant relationships which logically follow. Sociologist Robert Blauner applies this model to an analysis of the Black community in Los Angeles as a rationale for the rebellion of 1965.[17] The use of this model is no accident; the objective conditions of power prevailing between the groups, plus the fact of an easily identifiable Black group as the target, together with the geographical unity of most Black communities, give every evidence of the colonial characteristic. That such relationships deal in exploitation is a necessary corollary to the existence of the colonial condition, as is the fact that such exploitation is traditionally interpreted by the exploited as base oppression.

Both variables A and B interact with each other in the

[16] Stokely Carmichael and Charles Hamilton, *Black Power: The Politics of Liberation in America*, Chapter 1, "White Power: The Colonial Situation" (New York: Random House, 1967).

[17] Robert Blauner, "Internal Colonialism and Ghetto Revolt," *Social Problems*, Vol. 16, No. 4 (Spring 1969).

American context to produce circumstances of unique and unequaled social quality. Together they constitute a powerful source of Black oppression, that is, the consistent reality to which the Black scientist must address himself. Beyond the massive studies which document it and the models which explain it, the Black scientist, through the application of his skill to ideology and the willingness to act out the implications of his findings, must deal with his own oppression and the oppression of his people.

METHODOLOGICAL FOCUS

Liberation-oriented social science must have an explicit focus. Billingsley's suggestion that the existing disciplines need to be revitalized could begin with the construction of Black social science. For example, there is nothing new about the field of political sociology as one can readily see by reference to the studies compiled by McWorter,[18] but in the dichotomy between it and mere sociology is the realization that it is often necessary to include an operative ideology and, at the least, the recognition that it may be impossible to draw a hard, fast boundary between the fields. Perhaps a sociology rooted in Black social science would on balance emphasize the "end-use" as well as an analysis of the structure and function of Black social institutions. The result is that political sociology would be emphasized more than implicitly neutral sociology.

The same argument could, of course, be made for economics. Black social scientists should not only be concerned with the analysis of the economic system or the state of Black economy, but should seek to develop and utilize theories that lead to the production of economic

[18] Gerald A. McWorter, "The Political Sociology of the Negro" (New York: Anti-Defamation League of B'nai B'rith, August 1967), p. 31. Pamphlet.

resources. In this case, we could take a page from Chapter Seven of *Dusk of Dawn* by W. E. B. DuBois, where, as he often did, he made an analysis of the state of Black society, concluded that capitalism was antithetical to Black accumulation of wealth, and put forth a plan of action to radically change the situation. Both in the discipline of sociology and in economics, the focus should be the acquisition of influence (or control or power) over choices in each sector of society, and to that extent we should recognize the inherent political activity involved in the development and espousal of such concepts and their employment in real situations. Certainly, in the other disciplines of social science, the same suggestion could be made about focus, which does not in each case involve the use of the term political, but which recognizes what is involved in emphasizing the "end-use" dimension of the discipline.

TECHNIQUE

Many of the existing methodologies are valid for the analysis of Black life, but I would argue that the Black researcher's "field experience" in being Black gives him a better potential understanding of the techniques of analysis which are relevant in a given situation. In a way, such a position mirrors the older conflict between the traditionalist researcher who has the knowledge of substance, be it geographical or historical, and the technician who is skilled in the technique of his particular discipline at the expense of substance. My position is that a proper marriage, that is, a balance between substance and technique, is preferable, and that the deficiencies in white social science are revealed when, in dealing with Black life, the analyst comes prepared only with methodology. Studies that are produced in this way are in serious need of reinterpretation by Black scholars with a liberation orientation.

The question of achieving a proper balance, though important, can usually be assessed only after the results of the research are in, and therefore caution at the outset is a greater requirement. Nevertheless, it is possible to suggest that either extreme, using the traditional interpretation or overly quantitative approaches, is unsatisfactory for most questions that deal with any human life. And since the current quantitative fad is in full swing in academic life, perhaps a word should be said about it here.

The assumption upon which quantification is based is that there are units of analysis that stand for a given amount of social value, which, when manipulated mathematically, reveal aspects of social reality, either actual or theoretical. The wish of the user is to come as close to the real situation as possible and even perhaps be able to anticipate and plan for human responses to given situations or events. It strikes this writer as highly plausible that one of the fruits of a highly technological society, such as this one, is the notion of "precise value"—that is, there are many things produced and developed in a manner that makes them amenable to the quantitative approach; this is true from material goods to social services. Indeed, many problems in the field of administrating social services revolve around the necessity to monitor value precisely in quantitative terms, not necessarily for the sake of the user, but for the sake of the decision-maker who allocates resources. The writer is not at all sure, in fact is skeptical that either African or Afro-American culture is thus amenable to the quantitative approach. This is the subject of another discourse, but the problem suggests itself here: To what extent is the exercise of "Blackness" compatible with the vagaries of a Western technological situation? We should be aware that the material aspects of such a civilization have a powerful influence on the way in which we are able to perceive and to express our culture. One of the wonders of Black culture is the way in which it has survived and still flourishes, buffeted by strong historical events both quantitative and qualitative. But the question of compatibility is important on another level, because of the increased desire for analysts to learn and utilize the tools of systems analysis in the disposition of Black problems. The cost-benefit type of analysis has been adapted to "software" output only with questionable results.[19] If there are problems at that level of analysis, the utilization of such techniques on Black problems is even less effective. One has to cope with the effectiveness of the instrument itself, as well as with the fact that even now some of the most elementary facts about Black people, such as an accurate population count, are still in a questionable state, and such data are the life of the quantitative approach.

This leads me to challenge the assumptions upon which some developing graduate programs in Black Studies are founded. One basic assumption is that one should get a degree in an established discipline, while the subject of research for the dissertation may be in the area of Black life. Graduate students need substantive as well as methodological training if such work is to be accurate as well as profitable. *Treating the substance of Black life as something secondhand, which can be "picked-up" at will, or as something "we already know" which does not need systematic and constant elucidation, clarification and development is an insult to the quality and complexity of the Black experi-*

[19] President Johnson directed the Bureau of the Budget to install PPBS analysis throughout the government in 1966. In 1968 this writer was conducting interviews in the Department of State pursuant to a doctoral dissertation, and he discovered that many bureaus had written negative appraisals of the extent to which the new system had been successful. Some had, in fact, recommended that it not be further used, which points up the vulnerability of this method of analysis when used on products such as foreign policy which are difficult to quantify. See also "The Politics of the Budgetary Process," James Oliver, Ph.D. dissertation, American University, 1970, unpublished, for some of the difficulties involved.

*ence and perpetuates the graduate schools' racist attitude
toward the value of the study of Black life in general.*

The caution urged here is in the use of extremes of
theory and methodology, and in substantive areas. What
the Black social scientist should seek is the balance between
efficiency and humanism that puts technique in its proper
role as servant rather than lord.

Now that we have explored, and I must say at its fringes,
the concept of Black social science, it is necessary to point
to the possible "end-use" of the discipline in suggesting
the need for a Black research strategy.

Black Research Strategy

Chester Pierce, a Black psychiatrist at Harvard University,
in a recent article entitled "Offensive Mechanisms" discusses
what it means for Black people to think strategically and
for the development of what he calls "street therapists" to
know and teach "offensive and defensive tactics" to Black
people for their own survival.

In order for black individuals to both analyze and project
propaganda (that is, understanding what is in one's own best
interest, which would, of course, include domestic tranquility
and good international relations), the applied knowledge of
how to defense offensive maneuvers is obligatory.[20]

This knowledge also applies to the Black social scientist,
who should also be a "street therapist." He must develop
an offensive strategy around the collection, analysis, pack-
aging, dissemination and use of knowledge about Black
people in order to properly defend himself against the lead
that white social science has established in all of these areas.

[20] In *The Black Seventies*, edited by Floyd Barbour (Boston: Porter
Sargent, 1970), p. 281.

THE CHALLENGE TO WHITE SOCIAL SCIENCE

One of the clearest duties of the Black social scientist is to vigorously challenge the very foundation of white social science and its effects upon the Black community. In this regard, Nathan Hare says,

The black scholar must look beneath the surface of things and, wherever necessary and appropriate, take a stand against the bias of white scholarship. He must be biased against white bias, must be an iconoclast, rallying to the call to arms of all the black intelligentsia, to destroy obsolete norms and values and create new ones to take their place.[21]

The best mechanism I have yet seen for providing Black people with a defense against the encroachments of white social science is a new Black institution which has been recently established in Boston called the Community Research Review Committee. The Committee is composed of a primary group of Black social scientists who are accountable to the community through the Black United Front. Its function is to detect the kind of research planned and in progress that relates to the Black community, to screen actual research proposals and otherwise to evaluate the project and, finally, to provide the results to the community, which decides whether or not it would be advisable for the study to be carried out there. If the community decides the study is needed—cool. But if it decides that it is either unnecessary or harmful, then, in the age-old manner, it takes care of business. The Black social scientist must participate in a process which says, in effect, we will no longer participate by passiveness in the destruction and dehumanization of our communities through white social science research. But in order to participate, we need to

[21] Hare, *op. cit.*, p. 61.

pay much closer attention to the kind of research that is funded, who does the funding, who carries out the research, what the findings are, who is responsible for dissemination of the findings, and how they are used, and be willing to intervene at any stage of the process. This is one type of viable defensive strategy which also has offensive connotations.

THE CHALLENGE TO OURSELVES

One obvious bit of offense is to begin to build the institutions that will redress the imbalance in expertise, and to support those already in existence, such as the Black World Foundation, the Institute of the Black World, or the many research institutes developing on college campuses across the nation so that we can do the work ourselves. The obvious retort is that this takes money, and so it does; it has been interesting to note that, despite the generally widespread interest in Black Studies, massive funding is nowhere yet in sight. Contrast this picture with the funds which became available to universities and independent agencies to do research on Africa in the early 1960's (one such center with which I am familiar at one point had close to $600,000), or to the figures in the press recently which show the magnitude of financial support for Chinese studies.[22] Many would say that funding was available because both of these areas had strategic or security implications of international significance. But it is equally true that the managers of these funds in Chinese and African

[22] In discussing the funding of China scholarship since 1959, James Reston, editor for *The New York Times*, says, "Since then, the Ford Foundation has contributed about $22 million to the China language and area studies, other foundations have added a little over $2 million, and the Government has put up about $15 million under the National Defense Education Act. Meanwhile, the Universities of the nation have contributed another $20 million to this effort over the same period of time." *The New York Times*, Wednesday, May 12, 1971, p. 39m.

studies, down through the bureaucracy into the universities, are essentially white (even in African studies!!), while the socio-academic system for Black studies is largely Black, at least at the working level.

This problem of support has been raised before, both publicly and privately, and one astonishing reply from conservative Blacks and whites has been that Black Studies must demonstrate their validity a priori—that is, in advance of the necessary support. This position is a new kind of Tomism and an old brand of racism; Blacks have always had to overprove themselves to get what whites have had only to ask for. How could anything of value be demonstrated in Black Studies or any other kind of studies without adequate support? Could it be because the payoffs we seek for Black social science are in the Black community? In any case, we must support our activities and institutions from our own meager funds, through forced savings if necessary. Perhaps the realization that we must do this is the price we must pay for our own self-determination. I cannot escape the notion that if the words "freedom" or "independence," both here and in the homeland, mean anything, it all finally comes down to the necessity to be self-reliant, in the words of the document, "Education for Self-Reliance," developed by the Tanzanian government.

RESEARCH PRIORITIES

The colonization of African history and culture is international in scope; it may not surprise you to learn that at the International Conference of African Historians in 1968, only four of the eighteen papers presented were by Africans, and that there was one paper presented by a non-African on the periodization of African History. Black social scientists cannot afford to spend a lifetime organizing while other people are deciding upon the very nature, the ebb and flow of our historic experience. In this section I would like to give some support to the increasing problem-solving orientation of Black social scientists by examining the rationale of some of the classic studies on Black life.

Martin Kilson, professor of government at Harvard University, said on one occasion that we who are now engaged in an analysis of Black life "stand on the shoulders of our ancestors" in this endeavor. But it may also be true that the theoretical questions with which they dealt are different in this day and age. The central question which seems to have guided, for example, *The Philadelphia Negro*, *Black Metropolis* and *An American Dilemma* was "What is the nature of Black life?" The Black man had been defined as a problem in American society, and since all of our investigators were trained in the Western tradition of scholarship, one had to pretend to be interested only in the nature of the problem. At the point one had discovered (researched) the nature of the problem to one's satisfaction, ethical neutrality took over, and the solutions or value questions (which were unobjective and which could not, therefore, be defended in the province of scholarship) were left to politicians and administrators.

W. E. B. DuBois says that the impetus for the study *The Philadelphia Negro* was the need for the white decision-makers of the city to have some data on the significant and largely corrupt Seventh Ward in order to plan a campaign of reforms.[23] So that it was in the nature of his study to emphasize the "nature of the problem"—Black people. DuBois himself says of this methodology:

The best available methods of sociological research are at present so liable to inaccuracies that the careful student discloses the results of individual research with diffidence; he knows that they are liable to error from the seemingly ineradicable faults of the statistical method; to even greater error from the methods of general observation; and, *above all,* he must ever tremble lest some personal bias, some moral

23 W. E. B. DuBois, *Dusk of Dawn* (New York: Schocken, 1968), p. 59.

conviction or some unconscious trend of thought due to previous training, has to a degree distorted the picture of his view.[24] [Emphasis mine]

In other words, DuBois himself confirms what a reviewer said of the study at the time: "In no respect does DuBois attempt to bend the facts so as to plead for his race."[25] DuBois performed his role well, and his objectivity was admirable, but an action program for dealing with the ills of the Seventh Ward would have not detracted from the value of his work. He could not do so, however, because of the political problem of the end-use of his product.

Another classic socioanthropological study, *Black Metropolis*, by St. Clair Drake and Horace Cayton started out to be an inquiry into the general social conditions which produced juvenile delinquency on Chicago's South Side, and was eventually enlarged to take into account the entire Black Community. Richard Wright and E. C. Hughes say in the Introduction:

The authors have not submitted a total program of action in this book; rather they have assumed the ultimate aspirations of the Negro, just as Negroes have always assumed them, and just as Whites assume theirs. Negroes feel that they are politically and culturally Americans. The job of the authors was not to quiet and soothe, but to *aid white people* in knowing the facts of urban Negro life.[26] [Emphasis mine]

In a way, Wright and Hughes are saying that this study, too, was not produced as a blueprint for Black survival, but as something which would provide an accurate picture of Black life of most benefit to the decision-makers in their management of resources in behalf of the Black community.

Finally, the massive study by Gunnar Myrdal, *An*

---

[24] *Ibid.*

[25] *Outlook*, Vol. 63, 1899, pp. 647–8.

[26] St. Clair Drake and Horace Cayton, *Black Metropolis* (New York: Harcourt, Brace and World, 1970), p. xxx.

American Dilemma, made with the assistance of numerous Black scholars and the funds of the Carnegie Foundation, is another example of the trend we are viewing here. The main objective of the Foundation, to gather data on the Black condition, is clear from its own description of the usual nature of such studies, "the primary purpose of studies of this character is the collection, analysis and interpretation of existing knowledge."[27] In fact, Myrdal himself at one point almost yielded to a temptation to engage in serious prognosis, as he reports after touring the United States preliminary to undertaking the study:

When I returned to New York I told Mr. Keppel of my deep worries. I should confess that I even suggested a retreat to him; that we should give up the purely scientific approach and instead deal with the problem as one of political compromise and expediency.[28]

However, from the author's Preface to the first edition it is clear that he held fast to tradition, making a "comprehensive study of the Negro in the United States, to be undertaken in a wholly objective and dispassionate way as a social phenomenon."[29]

We are, therefore, in a position to observe from the record above that the generation of hypotheses relating to the analysis of Black life which produced these well-known studies was remarkably similar, dealing with the "nature of the problem" which Black people presented to whites. To say this is not to demean the quality of these studies or the necessity for scholars to search for the objective truth at every opportunity, for, as Wright and Hughes said, no program of action could afford to ignore the validity of the work if it was to be viable. *But we need to recognize the difference in the purpose and context of*

[27] Gunnar Myrdal, *An American Dilemma* (New York: Harper and Row, 1969), Vol. 1, p. xlvii.
[28] *Ibid.,* p. xxv.
[29] *Ibid.,* p. li.

*those earlier studies and the needs of the Black community
now for a new generation of hypotheses.* Reducing the
theoretical question of this generation to the Unity and
the Order of Blackness, I would have to ask, How does
Black social science contribute to the survival and development of Black people in the United States and in the
Diaspora? And more specifically, now that in a few areas
we are beginning to accumulate important knowledge,
how do we begin to use what we know to create areas of
security and well-being which we can eventually establish
as a comprehensive fact (nationhood)?

There are no canons that will answer these questions,
but, in general, it is a beginning to know that the search
for Black Power has started a number of Black scientists
groping for the right methods to help institutionalize that
ethic. Doubtless, further questions will be developed in
each discipline, and especially between disciplines in interaction between the scientist and his community. In general,
however, each social scientist must recognize the need to
bend his efforts toward the creation of some form of community power, by whatever definition, and toward ensuring
that whatever power is created becomes systematized.
These two basic considerations underline the difficulty of
using Black social science in a world where white social
science dominates. This was the burden carried by DuBois,
who started his life believing that a scientific approach to
the analysis of racism would help to alleviate its poison—
as, indeed, it eventually has. But just as important was his
realization that he could go only so far with the tools of
social science, that at some point he had to act out the
moral and ethical implications of what his keen senses told
him to be true. This lesson for the Black social scientist is
fundamental; his tools are conservative tools, and he cannot
use them to define the whole truth, for there is always that
something extra that DuBois sensed, which, when added
to analysis, reveals the whole Black truth.

Dennis Forsythe

Radical Sociology
and Blacks

In 1969 the Union of Radical Sociologists was formed. Led by young white Marxist-oriented students and professionals, it attempted to force the mainstream, "bourgeois" sociologists of the American Sociological Association to confront such issues as the Vietnam war, radical politics, poverty and racism. With little success so far, the Union of Radical Sociologists and the Sociological Liberation Movement have continued to press their demands for a more relevant sociology. But what are the limitations of "radical sociology" for Blacks? Dennis Forsythe, in a perceptive analysis, tackles this question.

Nowadays two prevailing sets of attitudes may be found among Black students and activists toward sociology. Both embody degrees of messianism. On the one hand, many Black students see sociology as a discipline that offers the means by which valid information and analyses on race relations can be gathered and distributed, on the basis of which, it is believed, people will come to their senses and begin to interact in a "human" and meaningful way.

Prompted by various formulations of this liberal hope, one finds a proliferation of Black students registering in sociology courses and as sociology majors. On the other hand, there are those other students who, on the basis of some cynical, religious and absolutist impulse reject sociology as a "honky" discipline.[1] Along with other white bourgeois creations, they argue, sociology should be shoveled into the scrap-heap of history.

This paper argues for a middle road between these two positions. The writer sees value in sociology, but only sociology of a particular kind. Regarding the cynical view, the writer rejects the monolithic conception of sociology: What is needed is an analytic, not a religious or messianic, approach.

The best way to characterize mainstream sociology is by outlining its philosophy, for it is this which determines both its methodology and content. Basically, American sociology defines itself as scientific, purportedly extending the rational-bureaucratic ethos of modern capitalism to the sphere of intellectual life. Taking the natural sciences as its model, conventional sociology has committed itself to the ideal of "neutrality," "noncommitment" or "objectivity." Presumably the goal of this philosophical premise (itself meta-sociological) is a belief in a cumulative inventory of facts (reduced to generalities) which could then become the basis of a rational ordering of social life.

But European sociology had been sufficiently critical to reject the notion of "objectivity" which was to become the cornerstone of a new and vitalized American orthodoxy. In Europe one finds the notion of objectivity rejected on the ground that there are fundamental differences between the natural and the social worlds. While still emphasizing

---

[1] Among many Black students, I have noted on many occasions that the minute the term sociology is mentioned, a derisive scorn or cynical laughter or grin is evoked.

sociology's "scientific" ideal, European sociologists admit that the study of society requires a different theoretical model and different methods than those of the natural sciences. They point to such differences as the reflexive character of social laws, the difficulties of experimentation in the social sciences, the context-bound nature of social phenomena, and the uniqueness of each social phenomenon. By using this analytical set of arguments European sociologists of knowledge appear to have, from the start, debunked and rejected the rigid empiricist tradition which came to dominate North American sociology.[2]

The American stress on "objectivity" naturally led to a distinctive methodology and a determinate content. Later leaders in the field rejected the reforming zeal of the first generation of American sociologists (Ward, Ross, Summer), who had been influenced by Europe, and attempted to sever facts from values. To do this, they used a supposedly detached and rigorous methodology to test small and specific "problems." Statistics became crucial in verifying theoretical propositions. "Abstracted empiricism" was the defining mark. The "inverse method" became embedded as the effective way of determining the content of sociology: one concludes from the existence of ready documentary evidence, of statistical material, that social research is worthwhile. Says Mannheim: "This is nothing but an exactitude complex which canonizes every fact, every numerical certitude, just because they are factual and controllable."[3] Other traits follow, like "collective research," which means research that may be continued by anyone, since the area is splintered into simple tasks. American

[2] The following references give support to the content of this paragraph. K. R. Popper, *The Poverty of Historicism*, London, 1957; Peter Winch, *The Idea of a Social Science*, London, 1958; John Rex, *Key Problems in Sociological Theory*, London, 1961; Percy Cohen, *Modern Social Theory*, London, 1968.

[3] Karl Mannheim, "American Sociology," in M. Stein and A. Vidich, *Sociology on Trial*, New Jersey, 1963.

sociology, mainstream variety, became more and more mechanical and technical and less and less theoretical and intellectual.

Radical sociology questions first of all the basic underlying philosophy of conventional sociology. Its adherents claim that a value-free sociology is impossible; values are forced underground only to be smuggled back into the discipline by various methods. Values enter into the selection of subjects for study, into procedures of study, into the determination of content, into the identification of "facts," into the assessment of evidence and into policy recommendations.[4] Values may easily be detected, too, according to radical critics, in the many hidden assumptions that characterize the main theoretical approaches of mainstream sociology.

Evolutionary Theory, especially its Social Darwinistic version, is openly and unashamedly racist and capitalistic because, rather than seeing the present state of development of Blacks as a result of oppression and exploitation, it evokes a Natural Law to explain and justify their fixation at the lower levels of the evolutionary process.

Functionalism, a more refined and sophisticated version of Social Darwinism, is such a generally popular approach in sociology today that Kingsley Davis has gone to the point of designating all sociologists "functionalists." Yet this model or approach is overwhelmingly status-quo oriented; it stresses order, consensus, stability and integration. That this approach is static and ahistoric may be seen in Michael Banton's *Race Relations*, which has been one of the most authoritative sources in the field of race relations. Banton makes the statement that "when racial differences are used as a way of dividing up a population and different sets of rights and obligations (roles) are ascribed to the division, then the outward differences serve as signs telling

---

[4] L. Gross, *Symposium on Sociological Theory*, section on "Values in Sociology" (New York: Harper and Row, 1959).

others the sorts of privileges and facilities to which the person in question is conventionally entitled." But then Banton moves on to make the untenable functionalist assertion that "for sociological analysis it is the sign function of racial characteristics that is usually more important for study."[5] Even if this has been the case, it is wrong. What is equally, if not more, important is a sociohistorical analysis of the specific factors that gave rise to such role-allocations. This method of analysis at least offers the chance of devising methods to counter such factors. It is the functionalist framework that makes political sociology and political science biased toward routine politics rather than equally concerned with nonroutine political behavior, such as social and political movements. Functionalism not only accepts the system, but prescribes ways of achieving integration and order, as, for instance, through piecemeal engineering and through assimilation and socialization.

The *Pluralistic Model* established by Tocqueville and Durkheim, and now epitomized by Kornhauser, Lipset and Hoffer, is equally biased in that it attempts to salvage democracy from becoming a moribund doctrine.[6] These sociologists think that "democracy" is possible because of the supposedly overall consensus of system-parts (including Blacks) which are now more or less integrated. Since "ideology is dead," all groups can now bargain and compete with each other within the system, so as to make democracy meaningful.

The *Middle Range* theoretical approach of Merton[7] is no

---

[5] Michael Banton, *Race Relations* (London: Tavistock Publications, 1967).

[6] William Kornhauser, *Politics of Mass Society* (New York: The Free Press, 1959); Seymour Lipset, *Political Man* (Garden City, New York: Doubleday, 1960); Daniel Bell, *The End of Ideology* (New York: The Free Press, 1960).

[7] R. K. Merton, *Social Theory and Social Structure* (New York: The Free Press, 1949). By "middle-range" theories he means testable hypotheses, distinguishable from the grand theorizing and system-building of Talcott Parsons.

less replete with values, for it leads to a proliferation of small "problems" and "theories." When each sociologist seeks a partial answer to a partial "problem," there is greater possibility of conflicts of theories and less chance of seeing the generic linkages between the various areas and problems. Such concepts as "capitalism" are subdivided into so many sub-areas that each theorist or researcher loses sight of a system's perspective.

All of these critiques of sociological models go to support Alvin Gouldner's claim that the notion of "objectivity" is a myth. Just the sheer descriptions of different categories of people serve a purpose—that of "intervening (by descriptions) against some 'bad guys' in favor of some 'good guys.' Their findings are 'for' and 'against,' judgments as well as verdicts and, in their redefinitional effects, acts of legislation as well." Radical sociologists not only undermine the concept of ethical neutrality but advocate a decisive involvement in the world of the subject matter. Their philosophical stance is that of seeing people as beings with feelings, rather than merely reactive atoms. C. Wright Mills puts this succinctly: "But we, as social scientists, may not assume that we are dealing with objects that are so highly manipulable, and we may not assume that among men we are enlightened despots."

When we realize that "radical" is derived from "radix" (the Latin for "root"), we can understand why radical sociologists stress involvement with root-sources as crucial and necessary. They are equally nihilistic toward the statistical precedents of conventional sociology. Mills calls it "abstracted empiricism" and its applied counterpart, "liberal scatter and illiberal practicality." Critics point to the elaborate sophistry and cost endemic to these statistic strictures and the lack of any attempts to subsume them to any criterion of social relevance and priorities.

To know the exact percentage of Americans who eat regularly in restaurants and the independent variables underlying this behavior pattern certainly meets the formal requirements of the signs of sociology and allows for prediction, but while these generalizations qualify as interesting time-consuming exercises and conversation pieces, they do not fulfill the criterion of significance.

Radical sociologists also criticize conventional sociology textbooks which assume an "arrived" state of knowledge. Instead, they advocate the use of an ad hoc assemblage of means to communicate ideas—manifestoes, speeches, interviews, symposiums, poetry, rock lyrics and scenarios. The assumption here is that "young people perceive differently because they have been nurtured by singular foster parents: nuclear energy, computerized technology and mass media. Naturally they respond to the visual, the aural, the tactile and the kinetic more than the 'rationally' organized essay, based as it is on traditional attitudes which often do not seem especially relevant."

This unconventional approach to data collection and presentation is instructive because Black sociology has to draw overwhelmingly upon folk tales, songs, poems, epithets, biographical and autobiographical material. The biographies allow for many generalizing propositions, because the similarity in the treatment of Blacks under a caste system leads to a common patterning. One finds therefore that the usual biographies of Black Americans do not vary greatly from each other in content.

Radical sociologists are also opposed to the *content* of mainstream sociology, which is a logical consequence of its philosophy and method. In addition to the insignificant nature of the issues studied, they argue, researchers focus upon the "less fortunate" to the neglect of the "powerful ones" of the society. Hence Martin Nicolaus' quippish but telling definition of a sociologist as one whose observing eyes are always turned downward and pecuniary palms upward. All this leads naturally to a functionalist assessment of the conventional sociologist vis-à-vis the Establishment. Radicals unsparingly point to the control-function executed by sociologists on behalf of the Establishment. Martin Nicolaus outspokenly called them "spies" who

stand guard in the garrison and report to its masters on the movements of the occupied populace. The more adventurous sociologists don the disguise of the people and go out to mix with the peasants in the "field," returning with books and articles that break the protective secrecy in which a subjugated population wraps itself, and make it more accessible to manipulation and control.[8]

The Chicago School of sociologists functioned preeminently in this capacity as collectors of information on urban groups, a role which at best resulted in piecemeal social engineering rather than structural changes. It is also noticeable that while many studies have attempted to detail the effects of slavery upon Blacks, the effects of slavery upon the psychology of whites have been ignored. C. Wright Mills, in dealing with the consequences of institutionalizing the social sciences, agrees that "the new social sciences *have* come to serve whatever ends their bureaucratic clients may have in view. Those who promote and practice this style of research readily assume the political perspective of their bureaucratic clients and chieftains . . . In so far as such researches are effective in their declared practical aims, they serve to increase the efficiency and the reputation of bureaucratic forms of domination in modern society."

Despite their avowedly neutral stance, it is argued, sociologists have leaped into the ranks of those ordering society. In the areas of industry, race relations, social movements, etc., there is often more than a tinge of Eric Hoffer.[9]

[8] Address to the American Sociological Convention, *American Sociologist*, May 1969.

[9] Eric Hoffer, *The True Believer* (New York: Harper & Row, 1971). Through this book, and through his other three books and frequent TV appearances, he has become the spokesman of the prejudiced "silent" Americans.

For instance, E. Mayo, a leading industrial sociologist, believes that "management is capable, trained and objective. Management uses scientific knowledge for making decisions. Political issues are illusions created by evil men. Society's true problems are engineering problems."[10] The co-option of the sociologist is apparent not only in confessions of admiration of the "welfare state," but also in sociologists' willful involvement in such affairs as "Project Camelot," designed to "contain" revolutions in Latin America.

"Squares"—professionals—are thus cynically dismissed by the radicals as "house-servants in the corporate establishment, white intellectual Uncle Toms for the government and the ruling class." The whole organization of sociology makes it clear that "politricks" has become a main aspect of his profession.

Sociology must redeem itself from the fact that it rose "to its present prosperity and eminence on the blood and bones of the poor and oppressed; it owes its prestige in this society to its putative ability to give information and advice to the ruling class of the society about ways and means to keep people down." As an antidote, radical sociologists contend that social systems and social structures, rather than individualized defects, should take the blame for ills of a society. This "systems" approach would lead to sounder policies, for "if problems are seen simply as accidents—then one poses policies which leave the fundamental structure of the system intact." The system or equilibrium focus of "square" sociology seems to legitimize the handing out of orders and constraints to the individual, but not for handing out blame. Radical critics use the system frame of reference for the latter purpose. As another way of salvaging sociology from its morass, radicals propose to focus upon substantive and significant issues and problems in the society with the aim of alleviating them.

"Class," "Race," "Technology," "Wealth," "Power,"

10 E. Mayo, "The Fifth Columnists of Business," Harvard Business School *Alumni Bulletin*, Autumn 1941.

"Conflict," "Interests," "Ownership" and "Control" therefore become key areas of focus in trying to determine the nature of problems. C. Wright Mills blazed the trail to the extent that he primarily focused on power—the nature of power, the distribution of power, the uses and abuses of power, the man of power, the power of organizations, the myth of power, the evolution of power, the irrationality of power, and the means of observing and comprehending power in the vastness of modern society.

I have argued so far that radical sociology has demystified many bourgeois concepts and put forward alternative ideas about the method, content, focus and role of sociology. I have concurred with these on the ground that they are progressive changes. But never for a minute did I intend to imply that Blacks are just jumping on the bandwagon of white radical sociologists. On the contrary, Black radical sociology has existed for a very long time. All the above radical criticisms were made by Black "sociologists" operating outside of universities, whose work proved to be more descriptive, predictive and prescriptive of Black behavior than that of bourgeois social scientists. That they were not recognized as sociologists was due to the fact that they operated outside the validating framework of universities, and also because their approach was broader and more "subjective" than the statistical and specialistic approach of bourgeois social science. What white radical sociologists are saying now was said by Black radical sociologists a long time ago—by Frederick Douglass, W. E. B. Dubois, Richard Wright, Frantz Fanon, Ralph Ellison, Malcolm X, James Baldwin and Eldridge Cleaver. It was fashioned and nurtured in the streets, ghettos, prisons and movements, and not in universities (with the exception of DuBois).

In fact white radical sociology grew out of the crisis when conscientious white social scientists began to see the failure of its bourgeois counterpart in predicting the upheavals of the 1960's in the United States and in the Third

World. They therefore began to look around for crucial variables that had been neglected; they began to look for alternative bases for the omnipotence of social scientists in the light of their blatant failure to understand oppressed minorities. Perhaps all conventional social scientists had done was to legitimize the policies of the government by means of a social science mystique! Perhaps they were mere undercover agents for the Establishment, using the epithet or disguise of "neutrality." Had not Baldwin spoken of *The Fire Next Time?* And did not Richard Wright's *Native Son* say the same thing? Perhaps, after all, sociologists should listen more carefully to the cries of the oppressed! Bourgeois social science ceased to be revered; Black rebellion had called the bluff. Conscientious whites decided to become less institutionalized in order to understand oppressed peoples and their relationship to the system.

In concrete terms, this is how radical sociology, as a "movement," developed. At the August 1967 Convention of the American Sociology Association held in San Francisco, a small group of activists who had experience in the antiwar and civil rights movements sought to have the Association adopt a resolution which began:

As human beings, citizens of the U.S. and professional Sociologists, we deplore and condemn the war in Vietnam as an undertaking which is resulting in the killing of innocent people and the destruction of a country and its culture . . . The disparity between the enormous financial and personal resources committed to this military adventure and the meager resources devoted to the urban ghettos makes it impossible to deal effectively with the problems of poverty and race in American society.[11]

The executive council's response was unequivocal: "The A.S.A. should not as a scientific and professional organiza-

11 Jack Roach, "Radical Sociology Movement," *American Sociologist*, August 1970.

tion express an official policy statement on political issues."

Small groups of activists then began discussing radical sociology, an exercise encouraged and fostered by events in 1968 like the assassination of Martin Luther King, the confrontation at Columbia University, the prominence of sociologists in the French upheaval of May, the incipient failure of the McCarthy campaign, Black repression, and the continuing war in Vietnam. The Boston A.S.A. meeting in 1968 saw a larger number of radical sociologists who organized a number of workshops around the theme "Knowledge for Whom."

At the end of the Boston meeting, a steering committee was formed, but it proved ineffective. So by the spring of 1969 the Eastern and Western Unions of Radical Sociologists were formed. The 1969 annual meeting was scheduled to be held in San Francisco, and radical groups met in that city to hold counter sessions. Ho Chi Minh's death prompted the radicals to request a memorial for the revolutionary leader. This was refused. A scuffle broke out. The Union of Radical Sociologists was set up as the major vehicle for the coordination of radical sociologists. Just as bourgeois sociology had emerged in response to the crisis in "ancient" regimes induced by the Industrial, French and American revolutions and been kept alive by subsequent bouts of political and social unrest, radical sociology emerged in response to the crisis precipitated by the political upheavals of minorities in the 1960's.

From the Black perspective, radical sociology has one inherent limitation which stems from its general theoretical and deductive approach to Blacks. It sees Blacks as part of a universal category of the oppressed. This is apparent in the following statement by one of the well-known radical sociologists, Marlene Dixon:

. . . the phenomenon of male chauvinism can only be understood when it is perceived as a form of racism . . . The so-

called "black analogy" is no analogy at all; it is the same
process that is at work . . . The fact that "racism" has been
practiced against many groups other than blacks has been
pushed into the background . . . Now two groups remain,
neither of which has been assimilated according to the classical
American pattern: The "visibles"—blacks and women. It is
equally true for both: it won't wear off.[12]

At best this position defines in a formalistic and abstract way
the commonalities of inequalities, derived from the universalistic postulates of Marxism. Albert Memmi's *Dominated
Man* has, in fact, reduced the main types of oppression and
group conflicts to their commonalities, thereby tying Blacks
to a general category, and even the Black sociologist Oliver
Cox has viewed the Black problem as part of the general
problem of class oppression.[13] At best this analogy is a poor
and tasteless comparison because it denies the uniqueness of
the Black situation and Black experience. For Blacks, the
universalistic theme is absurd when they consider in what a
unique and particularistic way they have been victimized.

Whites are too far removed from Blacks to be able to
understand them as a unique category. To arrive at the
uniqueness of Blacks, the method of *verstehen* or empathetic
understanding should be employed, a position which bourgeois social scientists such as Dilthey, Max Weber and Peter
Winch have strongly advocated,[14] and which is endorsed
by the symbolic-interaction approach to sociology. These
theorists argue that involvement (rather than detachment)

[12] Marlene Dixon, "The Rise of Women's Liberation," in G. Gaviglio,
Society as It Is (New York: Macmillan, 1971).

[13] Albert Memmi, *Dominated Man* (Boston: Beacon Press, 1968);
Oliver Cox, *Caste, Class and Race* (New York: Monthly Review Press,
1970).

[14] Max Weber, *Methodology of the Social Science*, 1949 translation;
H. A. Hodges, *Wilhelm Dilthey, An Introduction*, London, 1944; Peter
Winch, *The Idea of Social Science*; R. G. Collingwood, *The Idea of
History*, Oxford, 1946.

is important, because the only way to learn about a culture or a people is to immerse oneself within that context in order to get the hang and "meaning" of the situation.

White radical sociologists cannot get this type of information, either because they do not know the "language" of Blacks, or because Blacks allow whites to see only what they want them to see. As one Black folk song says: "Got one mind for white folks, 'nother for what I know is me." Not even the frequent white practice of changing one's color or wearing "hip" outward symbols is sufficient to allay the Black suspicion of whites. Whites have just not paid their emotional dues![15] This does not mean that black-skinned sociologists can get any more valid information. Blackness is necessary, but not sufficient. To get to the people, involvement is required, which means participation and trust.

A related issue is the use that will be made of information gathered on Blacks. If the aim were merely to pile up stocks of information on Black communities, then Black sociology would be even more reactionary than bourgeois sociology, if only because it provides more accurate information, which could be used to control Blacks. Therefore, by definition, Black sociology should be as activist as possible, guarding against the sterile accumulation of information and ensuring that this information is used for Black community development.

Since white radical sociology emanates from Marxist social science, it might be well to illustrate some of the limitations of Marx's theory of revolution from the Black Third World perspective, by way of the theoretical reformulations of Fanon. Though purporting to be universalistic,

---

[15] This is not to deny the role of White radical sociologists. All I am saying is that their role within Black communities is circumscribed by virtue of who they are, and that their universalistic postulate does not deal adequately with the uniqueness of Blacks. They cannot and should not attempt to deal with the "feeling" or subjective aspects of Blacks.

Marxism has proved to be very ethnocentric. Fanon attempted to transcend the limitations of Marxism by taking account of the Black situation. In very brief synopsis we can summarize the polarities of both theorists, which illuminate the white radical and the Black radical (sociological) perspectives:

(i) Marx elevates the proletariat as the revolutionary class and underrates contemptuously the role of other classes and groups. Fanon, on the other hand, elevates the peasantry and the Lumpenproletariat;

(ii) Marx focused on urban areas, whereas Fanon stressed rural areas;

(iii) Marx regarded Europe as the stage on which the modern drama of conflict will be worked out; Fanon, in turn, pointed to the Third World;

(iv) Marx was only partially committed to the use of revolutionary violence. Fanon regarded violence as an absolute necessity in the revolutionary process;

(v) Marx stressed class allegiances and class conflict; Fanon stressed and reconciled class conflicts and "race" conflicts;

(vi) Marx denied nationalism for internationalism. Fanon saw nationalism as the necessary stepping stone toward internationalism;

(vii) While Marx commends the bourgeois class for its progressivism and "revolutionism" in Europe, Fanon regarded the bourgeoisie of the Third World as inept, imitative and worthless, a point which C. L. R. James, Franklin Frazier and Amilcar Cabral later stressed;

(viii) Marx held a quasitotalitarian conception of the immediate postrevolutionary situation. Fanon rejects this in favor of complete liberal communalism.[16]

---

[16] Of course, that there were agreements at many points cannot be denied. There was certainly greater convergence on the more methodological aspects of revolution like the notion of Dialectical Materialism and the Unity of Theory and Practice.

The contrasts between Marx and Fanon are very illustrative, because they show that, despite the universalistic posture of Marxist theory, it is ethnocentric at many points. In order, therefore, to highlight the possible ethnocentric pitfalls of white radical sociology, I will give a more detailed criticism of Marxism from the Black perspective, because many of the criticisms against Karl Marx carry over to his disciples—the radical sociologists.

To begin with, Marx held the Third World in contempt because it did not measure up to the West. In the *Communist Manifesto* Marx wrote that the bourgeoisie,

. . . draws all, even the most barbaric nation, into civilization . . . and has rescued a considerable part of the population from the idiocy of rural life. Just as it has made the country dependent on the towns, so it has made barbarian and semi-barbarian countries dependent on the civilized ones, nations of peasants on nations of Bourgeois, the East on the West.

Marx described Bengalese communities as "small barbarian, semi-civilized communities,"[17] and found it "amusing" that China was "the seat of primeval reaction and conservatism."[18] Later he referred to Chinese life as a "fossil of social life."[19] Commenting on the Sepoy rebellion in India, he noted that it has "developed all at once on the part of the Hindoo and Mohammedan barbarians, a ferocious and fanatical hatred of their Christian and civilized masters."[20] His views on the Moorish War were equally damning: "From the Moors we cannot expect anything but irregular fighting carried on with the bravery and cunning of semi-savages. But, even in this, they appear deficient."[21] This

[17] Karl Marx, "The British Rule in India . . .," the New York *Tribune*, June 25, 1853.
[18] Karl Marx, London, January 31, 1850.
[19] Karl Marx, *Die Presse*, July 7, 1862.
[20] Karl Marx, the New York *Tribune*, April 5, 1858.
[21] Karl Marx, the New York *Tribune*, February 8, 1860.

despicable stance of Marx was shared by Engels, who spoke of "Asiatic barbarity" and of the difficulties of training "orientals" because of their "ignorance, impatience, prejudice and vicissitudes" and discussed the "Chinese nationality with its overbearing prejudice, stupidity, learned ignorance and pedantic barbarism."[22]

As part of his ongoing onslaught on Third World peoples, Marx rejected any notion of genuine virtues in traditional communal systems in the Third World. Instead he writes:

We must not forget that these idyllic village communities . . . had always been solid foundation of Oriental despotism, that they restrained the human mind . . . making it an unresisting tool of superstition, enslaving it beneath traditional rules, depriving it of grandeur and historical energies . . . We must not forget that this indigenous, stagnatory and vegetative life, that this passive sort existence, evoked on the one part, in contradistinction, wild, aimless, unbound forces of destruction . . . We must not forget that these little communities were contaminated by distinctions of caste and by slavery, that they subjugated man to external circumstances instead of elevating man to be sovereign of circumstances.[23]

The Western European cultural bias comes out again when Marx wrote to Engels about the "idyllic republics" of northwestern India:

I do not think anyone could imagine a more solid foundation for stagnant Asiatic despotism. And however much the English may have hibernicized the country, the breaking up of those stereotyped primitive forms was the sine qua non for Europeanisation. Alone the tax-gatherer was not the man to achieve this.

22 Frederick Engels, the New York *Tribune*, June 5, 1857.
23 Karl Marx, "The British Rule in India," the New York *Tribune*, June 26, 1853.

The destruction of their archaic industry was necessary to deprive the villages of their self-supporting character.[24]

Engels, too, referred to state socialism in Java as a government in which "people are kept at the stage of primitive stupidity . . . It is proof of how today primitive communism furnishes there, as well as in India and Russia, the finest and broadest basis of exploitation and despotism (so long as it is not aroused by some element of modern communism)."[25]

The biases implicit in this train of reasoning lead naturally into a critique of the whole Marxian concept of dialectics as Marx applied it to the Third World. His basic assumption was that since these traditional societies lacked their own internal dynamics for development, some external factor was necessary. Conceiving British civilization to be superior to Hindu civilization, he thus argued that "England has to fulfil a double mission in India: one destructive, the other regenerative—the annihilation of old Asiatic society and the laying of the material foundations of Western society in Asia."[25]

Holding to this same axiomatic basis, Engels regarded the conquest of Algeria by the French as "an important and fortunate act for the progress of civilization." "And after all," he continued, "the modern bourgeois, with civilization, including industry, order, and at least relative enlightenment following him, is preferable to the feudal lord or the marauding robber, with the barbarian state of society to which they belong."[27]

It is interesting to note that this bias, endemic to Marx, puts him in the category of Walt Rostow, whose "entire

[24] Marx to Engels, June 14, 1853.
[25] Engels to Kautsky, February 16, 1884.
[26] Karl Marx, "The Future Results of the British Rule in India," the New York *Tribune*, August 8, 1885.
[27] Frederick Engels, *Northern Star*, January 22, 1848.

approach to economic development and cultural change attributes a history to the developed countries but denies all
history to the underdeveloped ones."[28]

This automatically denies the cultural autonomy and distinctiveness of Third World Peoples. Furthermore, it was
precisely the incorporation of foreign peoples into the
expanding bourgeois empire that initiated the cycle of their
underdevelopment. Fanon saw and recognized this important flaw in Marxist reasoning. Cabral, too, noted the
Marxian assumption which implies that these countries lived
without history or outside of history up to the time when
they were subjected to the yoke of imperialism. For this old
misguided position, Cabral, like Fanon, has substituted the
view that imperialism, by imposing itself from the outside,
interrupted the normal development of the productive
forces of the Third World and thus interrupted their history; therefore liberation implies freeing the productive
forces from foreign domination, which would mean a return to history. Nyerere has since voiced a Fanonian reservation toward Marxism. The orthodox Marxist framework,
he writes,

gives Capitalism a philosophical status which Capitalism neither
claims nor deserves. For it virtually says, "without Capitalism
and the conflict which Capitalism creates there can be no
Socialism." This glorification of Capitalism by doctrinaire
Socialists, I repeat, I find intolerable.[29]

In sum, therefore, neither Fanon nor his later comrades
could accept categorically the assumptions criticized above,
for they boil down to a denial of the cultures and histories

[28] Andre Gunder Frank, "Rostow's Stages of Economic Growth,"
Radical Education Project Publication. (A shorter version appeared in
Catalyst, No. 3, Summer 1967.)

[29] J. K. Nyerere, *Ujamaa* (New York: Oxford University Press, 1968),
p. 11.

of these societies before the exploitative presence of whites. Those Blacks who tried to stick to the Marxian model mechanically soon got into trouble, either because of the arrogance of white Communists who accepted the dictates of the model, or because of the intrinsic weakness of the model itself when applied to Third World situations.[30]

The case of Albert Memmi can be used to show the dangers of approaching the Black experience from a priori theoretical models, like that of orthodox Marxism. Memmi, a Paris-based author, established a radical reputation with the publication of *The Colonizer and the Colonized* and *Dominated Man*, among others. Yet in *The New York Times Book Review* on March 14, 1971, he showed his white European ethnocentric biases. Instead of fulfilling the purpose of the essay (reviewing two books on Fanon—Caute's and Geismar's), he took the occasion to deliver a scathing onslaught on Fanon. He reduced Fanon's development and his revolutionary role to a "private drama," an identity problem: "The specific nature of his undertaking is, ultimately, to have sought the solution to his personal drama in political action and philosophy."

For him, Fanon moved from being a "Frenchman" (Martiniquan phase), to being a French West Indian (metropolitan phase) and then to an Algerian (African phase). While for Blacks those metamorphoses are to be admired as progressive and healthy, Memmi, for some idiosyncratic reasons, chose to view them as Fanon's "three serious defeats." Memmi just could not understand that Fanon was evolving, that the man's true nature, his "idea," his "physis," was unfolding. Memmi failed to see this because he had surrendered to the a priori theoretical dictates

[30] See Harold Cruse, *Rebellion or Revolution* (New York: William Morrow & Co., Inc., 1968); Cruse, *Crisis of the Negro Intellectual* (New York: William Morrow & Co., Inc., 1967).

of Marxism, which is apparent in his frequent measurement
of Fanon by the yardstick of Marxism. Fanon in his mature
Africanist phase had asserted his independence from the
European Marxist model. This was unpalatable for Memmi.
He wrote: "[Fanon] underestimated the short term importance of the national bourgeoisie and the long term significance of the urban proletariat; he overestimated the
role of the peasants . . . ; his perception of African unity
is largely illusory . . . [and] even his theory of violence
being inevitable and above all purifying . . . distinguishes
him clearly from the Marxists." Because Memmi did not
understand Fanon from the perspective of his followers, he
saw as failure what they see as success.

In conclusion, then, white radical sociology performs the
necessary function of demystifying bourgeois social science,
but this does not give it the right or the necessary prerequisites to study Blacks; radical sociologists must guard against
making general statements about Blacks, especially about
the subjective aspect of the Black experience. It is the task of
Black sociology to stress the uniqueness of the Black experience and to see that knowledge collected on Blacks is used
for change rather than for control.

James Turner

The Sociology of
Black Nationalism

The 1960's witnessed an upsurge of Black nationalism. Scholars and masses alike articulated this ideology and sought to define it theoretically, and to create new strategies for its application. James Turner has emerged as one of the most articulate spokesmen of the Black nationalist theoretical perspective. Turner's attempt in this essay to systematize a theory of Black nationalism and to relate it to sociology represents the task that many Black social scientists have undertaken to give practical and intellectual legitimacy to those emergent areas which are facilitating the redefinition of Black life and culture.

The movement of black nationalist ideas is dominated by the collective consciousness of its adherents as members of a minority group, which is subordinated to another and more powerful group within the total political and social order. The ideological preoccupations of black nationalism revolve around this central problem, the black man's predicament of having been forced by historical circumstances into a state of dependence upon the white society considered the master society and the dominant culture. The essential

234

theme of black nationalism can be seen as a counter-movement away from subordination to independence, from alienation through refutation, to self-affirmation. In this respect, such a movement of ideas represents an effort to transcend the immediate conditions of an undesirable relationship by a process of reflection which creates a different (and opposing) constellation of symbols and assumptions. Black nationalism is thus at once an ideological movement of both social-psychological and political portent.

The theme of disgrace and subjugation is the point of departure of the whole ideological expression of black nationalism, which derives from the political and cultural uprooting of black people in general through colonial conquest and enslavement. The overwhelming sentiment that dominates in this connection is the belief that the group is being denied a "true" and unadulterated experience of its humanity as a result of being forced into a social system whose cultural values preclude an honorable accommodation. The black nationalist recognizes himself as belonging to an out-group, an alien in relation to the white society which controls the total universe in which he moves. This sentiment of belonging no longer to oneself but to another goes together with an awareness of being black, which becomes translated in social terms into a caste and class consciousness. The association between race and servitude is a constant theme in Afro-American literature. The economic exploitation and social discrimination which defines persons of African descent as a social category gives many of its members an avid sense of race consciousness as a consequence of mutual humiliation.

Becoming a black nationalist seems to involve a realization that persons of African descent are treated categorically by the dominant group. Subsequently, there develops the firm conviction that Afro-Americans must become transmuted into a conscious and cohesive group. The rationale is that a group giving a unitary response can more effectively and honorably confront the constraining domi-

nant group. Race, color, and mutual resistance to the oppression of the dominant group and its imposed assumptions and definitions about the minority, become the vehicles
for realizing conversion from category to group. Loyalty
to group cultural attributes and commitment to collective
goals provide the adhesive for the group. Black nationalists
argue for the exclusive right of members of the group to
define, establish, and maintain their own group boundaries.

The black man's principal role and meaning in Western
history has been as an economic tool.[1] This is what Aimé
Césaire, paraphrasing Marx, has called "the reduction of the
black-man into an object."[2] However, the prevailing preoccupation of the proponents of black nationalism is with
the black people primarily as a "race," and secondarily as a
class. They are concerned with the collective image of the
black man in American society and his human status in the
world. They are concerned about a white racial ideology
which defined the black man as inferior, and as a consequence a social relationship between black and white men
which acquired the moral values summarized by the writer,
Bloke Modisane:

White is right, and to be black is to be despised, dehumanized
. . . classed among the beasts, hounded and persecuted, discriminated against, segregated and oppressed by government
and by man's greed. White is the positive standard, black the
negative.[3]

The cultural and political ascendancy of white men over
black men, combined with the active denigration of black
men, has thus had the effect of vitiating the latter's self-
esteem, with the profound psychological consequences

[1] Eric Williams, *Capitalism and Slavery*, London: 2nd edn., 1964.
[2] Aimé Césaire, *Discourse on Colonialism*, Paris: 1955, p. 22.
[3] Bloke Modisane, "Why I Ran Away," in J. Langston Hughes (ed.),
An African Treasury, New York: 1960, p. 26.

which involve shame and self-hatred.* Black men throughout the world suffered this negation as human beings. This
is the external reality with which the ideology of black nationalism is concerned.

Historically, contact between black and white peoples
has been seriously influenced by certain cultural assumptions
and premises upon which social relations were predicated
and legitimized. Slavery and the colonial enterprise were
nationalized as a civilizing mission aimed at transforming the
black man by his assimilation of the ideals of Western civilization through education. This implied in most cases a dis-
sociation on the part of black men from the basic social patterns of their original ethnic and cultural environment. This
predicament of cultural infusion but systematic social re-
striction and isolation has been variously referred to as the
"dilemma of the marginal man," the "pathology of the up-
rooted man," and called by R. E. Park, the "cultural hy-
brid,"[4] a result of culture contact and acculturation, but
also of systematic social segregation and denial of human
consideration.

Black nationalism becomes, as a result, testimony to the
injustices of segregated rule and expression of the black
man's resistance and resentment.

In this respect, one of the most striking social-psychological innovations of black nationalism has to do with the
reversal of color association within a dominant and pervasive white-ideal cultural context. A reversal of white-

* The psychological implication of racial discrimination for the black
man in white society have produced numerous studies. This question
seems to have been summarized by John Dollard. "The upshot of the
matter seems to be that recognizing one's own Negro traits is bound to
be a process wounding to the basic sense of integrity of the individual
who comes into life with no such negative views of his own characteristics," in *Caste and Class in a Southern Town*, New York: 2nd edn.,
1949, p. 184.
   [4] Robert E. Park, *Race and Culture*, New York: Glencoe, The Free
Press, 1950, p. 356.

Western symbols implies as well as reversal of the concepts associated with them. Thus, black nationalism is a refusal of those white values which are regarded as oppressive constraints.

It can be noted that, in general, the theme of revolt in the ideology of black nationalism represents a reinforcement of the antagonism created by the caste situation between the white dominant group and the black subordinate minority. The refutation of white political and cultural domination in the ideology of black nationalism represents an attempt to sever the bonds that tie the black man to white definitions.

. . . The American Negro can no longer, nor will he be ever again, controlled by white America's image of him.[5]

It is an attempt at toppling what some young black intellectuals call "the dictatorship of definition." The corollary to this claim for freedom from white determination of black identity is a search for new values. Revolt involves not only a confrontation with an oppressive and undesirable social status, but is also an act of self-affirmation and a cogent expression of identity. The following passage is illustrative of this point:

Our concern for black power addresses itself directly to this problem, the necessity to reclaim our history and our identity from the cultural terrorism and depreciation of self-justifying white guilt. To do this we shall have to struggle for the right to create our own terms through which to define ourselves. This is the first necessity of a free people, and the first right that any oppressor must suspend.[6]

The quest for new values thus leads the black nationalist to the belief that self-definition and self-determination are

[5] James Baldwin quoted by Thomas F. Pettigrew in *Profile of the Negro American*, New Jersey: University of Princeton Press, 1964, p. 10.
[6] Stokely Carmichael, *The Massachusetts Review*, Autumn 1966, pp. 639–40.

one and the same, and his new self-perception must of necessity be predicated upon terms that are non-normative or divergent from white-Western values.

Indication of this concern was expressed by a group of black women who asked, "Is *Ebony* Killing the Black Woman," in the title of an article they wrote:

Ebony magazine stands today as a classic illustration of middle class negro (small *n* is indicative of general scorn for the term as well as the behavior of the class of people being referred to) attempts to assimilate themselves into the mainstream of white american (small *a* is for symbolic de-emphasis) life. *Ebony* has been a highly successful magazine because it has mirrored the values and standards of the larger, dominant white society . . . *Ebony* has sought to perpetuate the fallacy and old cliche, "if it's white it's all right." The latest in this long line of insults and abuses was the cover story of the February (1966) issue. Under an article entitled, "Are Negro Girls Getting Prettier," *Ebony* cleverly selected a carefully screened group of girls to represent what they claim is positive proof, that "negro" girls are indeed getting prettier. The great injustice here is that girls chosen by *Ebony* did not nearly reflect a full cross-section of all black folks.

The psychological effect—on our people—of a publication such as *Ebony*, with its skin bleaching cream and straight hair ads, is demoralizing and tends to reinforce the already evident inferiority and self-hatred complexes of the black community. As a race we have been taught by whites that black is ugly; for example to be "blacklisted," "blackmailed" or "blackballed"—everyday phrases—denotes exclusion or alienation. By the same token, the symbols used to extol the virtues of honesty, purity and truth are always white . . . Thus we come to realize the majority of the masses are moved to act or react by the symbolism of the language they speak. The ideas, thoughts and deeds the oppressor wants us to see and react to, are those ideas which strengthen, defend or assert the goals of the established order. When a supposedly black magazine comes forth with the same ideology as the oppressor, it indicates the extent to which the oppressor has used his symbols, through culture, to psychologically enslave black people. It

also indicates how successful the oppressor has been. . . .
Every race has its own standards of beauty. Every race maintains a loyalty to its cultural and historical roots. Why then
would a publication such as *Ebony* want us to lose our inherent
standards of beauty, and substitute in its place a European
Criteria? ? ?[7]

The issue of identity is inescapable, and pride in race is
playing a crucial part in the new identity; it no doubt will
lead—as it already has done—to a considerable degree of
racial self-consciousness. Many black men and women are
not struggling to become free, simply in order to disappear.
Which is contrary to the liberal argument "that the race
problem can be solved in this country only by total integration and complete assimilation and eventual miscegenation,"
but there are Afro-Americans who do not want to disappear
and desire to preserve specifically Afro-American values
and cultural traits.

Such sentiments are expressed by a female student in
Robert Penn Warren's book:

. . . The auditorium had been packed—mostly Negroes, but
with a scattering of white people. A young girl with pale skin,
dressed like any coed anywhere, in clothes for a public occasion, is on the rostrum. She is . . . speaking with a peculiar
vibrance in a strange irregular rhythm, out of some inner
excitement, some furious, taut élan, saying "—and I tell you I
have discovered a great truth. I have discovered a great joy.
I have discovered that I am black. I am black! You out there—
oh, yes, you may have black faces, but your hearts are white,
your minds are white, you have been white-washed!"[8]

This exclamation of a sense of new "discovered" identity
is a conscious experience of "an increased unity of the phys-

[7] Evelyn Rodgers, "Is Ebony Killing Black Women," *Liberator*, New
York: Vol. 6, No. 3, March 1965, pp. 12–13.
[8] Robert Penn Warren, *Who Speaks for the Negro?* New York:
Harcourt and Brace Co., 1965.

ical and mental, moral and sensual selves, and a oneness in the way one experiences oneself and the way others seem to experience us."[9]

Much of the academic research and analysis of the race relations situation during the past three decades seems to accept the liberal assumption of historian Kenneth M. Stampp that, "Negroes are, after all, only white men with black skins, nothing more, nothing less." But black men in America are not simply carbon duplicates of white men; to contend that they are is misleading. Differences in skin color, hair texture and physical features are fact. But the issues are not whether differences exist, but what they mean socially.

Identified as a Negro, treated as Negro, provided with Negro interests, forced, whether he wills or not, to live in Negro communities, to think, love, buy and breathe as a Negro, the Negro comes in time to see himself as a Negro . . . he comes, in time, to invent himself and to image creatively his face.[10]

The Afro-American subculture maintains a subterranean and private world of rituals, symbols, and motifs. Rupert Emerson and Martin Kilson in a discussion of black nationalism make the following observations.

. . . The Black Muslims still represent, at the level of the Negro's subterranean world, a force of ultimate significance. This is found in its influence upon the new stage in the Negro's self-definition. This stage, moreover, has been reinforced by the rise of more rational black nationalist concepts than those represented by the Black Muslims, and all of them have been affected by the Black Muslims, all of them have been affected by the debut of African nationalism on the international

[9] Erik H. Erikson, "The Concept of Identity in Race Relations" in *The Negro American*, ed. Talcott Parsons and Kenneth Clark, Boston: Houghton, Mifflin Co., 1966, p. 232.
[10] Lerone Bennett, *Negro Mood*, Chicago: Johnson Publishing Co., Inc., 1964, p. 49.

scene . . . There are, however, many other groups of this sort, and they are likely to have a more sustained influence upon the Negro's new thrust for self-realization . . . than the Black Muslims. Unlike the Black Muslims, these organizations are secular in orientation, intellectually capable of coping with the modern world; and they reject naive political goals . . .[11]

According to St. Clair Drake ". . . increased identification of educated Negroes with some aspects of the Negro subculture and with the cultural renaissance taking place in Africa may become the norm."[12] It is not unusual to find people in the larger urban ghettos, who were previously wary about identifying themselves with Africa, now proudly proclaiming their blackness and developing interest in African politics, art, poetry and literature. Among the educated, and not so educated, discussions of Negritude are becoming commonplace. Among many young people there is a certain reverence for the memory and image of such men as Patrice Lumumba, Kwame Nkrumah, Jomo Kenyatta and Malcolm X, to name a few. These men are looked up to as black heroes and idols and role models. It is interesting to note, in this regard, that the late Medgar Evers—slain NAACP civil rights field director for the state of Mississippi—had named one of his sons Kenyatta. Ordinary black men and women who a short time ago were processing their hair and using hair-straighteners and skin-bleaches are now wearing the new "Afro" and "natural" hair styles, as well as African-style clothing. A few are even taking African names and learning to speak an African language.

[11] Emerson and Kilson, "The American Dilemma in a Changing World, the Rise of Africa and the Negro American," in *The Negro American*, eds. Talcott Parsons and Kenneth Clark, Boston: Houghton Mifflin Co., 1966, pp. 640–41.

[12] St. Clair Drake, "The Social and Economic Status of the Negro in the United States" in *The Negro American*, eds. Talcott Parsons and Kenneth B. Clark, Boston: Houghton Mifflin Co., 1966, p. 35.

Erik H. Erikson explains such social-psychological phenomena as the development of a conscious identity: "Identity here is one aspect of the struggle for ethnic survival; one person's or group's identity may be relative to another's; and identity awareness may have to do with matters of an inner emancipation from a more dominant identity, such as the 'compact majority.' "[13] Writer John O. Killens comments on the function and value of the new identity: ". . . one of the main tasks of Black Consciousness is to affirm the beauty of our blackness, to see beauty in black skin and thick lips and broad nostrils and kinky hair; to rid our vocabulary of 'good hair' and 'high yaller' and our medicine cabinets of bleaching creams. To de-niggerize ourselves is a key task of Black Consciousness."[14]

Thus the black artist who embarks upon a search for new standards and values for his salvation must, among other things, discard the tools presented to him by the social order which has proved to be the number one enemy to his sensibility and conscience . . . if he is committed to his people [he] looks elsewhere for new standards and values, for new identification and allies.[15]

The fundamental question black nationalism raises is whether integration is really desired or, more specifically, whether Afro-Americans "should" want integration. "In the whole history of revolts and revolutions, 'integration' has never been the main slogan of a revolution. The oppressed's fight is to free himself from his oppressor, not to integrate with him."[16] Black nationalist ideology molds a new image of the dominant group. The essential concern becomes

13 Erikson, *op. cit.*, p. 230.
14 John O. Killens, "The Meaning and Measure of Black Power," in *Negro Digest*, Nov. 1966, p. 36.
15 William K. Kgositsile, "Has God Failed James Baldwin?" *Liberator*, Vol. 7, No. 1, Jan. 1967, p. 11.
16 Killens, *op. cit.*, p. 33.

"not free from what, but free for what?" There is a radical conception in process which has black men redefining themselves and, of necessity, re-evaluating "the white man." The objective of the process is to wrest the black man's image from white control; its concrete meaning is that white men should no longer tell black men who they are and where they should want to go. The proposition that obtains from such a conception is that black men must no longer be bound by the "white man's" definitions. This is a clear response to the control of communications media by the dominant white group.

In the past, some Negroes attempted to define themselves by becoming counter-contrast conceptions, by becoming, in short, opposite Negroes, opposite, that is, to what white men said Negroes were.[17]

In its crudest and simplest form black nationalism is the assertion that black is good. At its most intellectually sophisticated level of development, it is the affirmation of the validity of traditions and values of black people derived from their peculiar heritage and creativity. This process has been described by one sociologist, "as the backfire of the dynamics of American assimilation which gave rise to an increased sensitivity, on the part of black people, in reacting to the institutionalized nature of bigotry. Also, a subsequent development of a more positive regard for black culture and community, and a determination to reconstitute the basic processes of United States life as they affect black people." He further contends that "the most pervasive trend for today's young black intellectuals is their vigor and degree of self-consciousness about being black."[18]

Black nationalism seeks to achieve the diminution of "the

---

[17] Bennett, *op. cit.*, p. 55.
[18] Gerald WcWorter, "Negro Rights and the American Future," *Negro Digest*, Oct. 1966, p. 20.

white man"—that is the demise of the idea that because of a
certain color of skin one man (or group of men) is ordained
to determine the lives of other men because of their darker
skin color.

The basis for understanding black nationalism is in acknowledgement of the historical by-products of the slave
system.

The tragedy bequeathed by racist beliefs and practices has in
modern times been experienced by no other people, save for
the Jews who fell into Hitler's hand, so deeply as by the
Negro Americans.[19]

The African and his descendants were conquered, enslaved,
demeaned and then converted to accepting their low status.
Black men were told that they had no history, no culture,
no civilization; and it was, for them, often economically
rewarding and socially advantageous to repeat this litany.
Some individuals began to realize that this was nonsense
and sought to dissipate this lack of self-pride. There becomes an awareness of cultural dispossession, which becomes as equal a concern as the problems of material dispossession. Out of this context black nationalism arises.
There develops a pattern of looking inward to historical
and social traditions in order to overcome low status and
low prestige. Attempts are made to construct a new "vision"
predicated upon collective traits of social distinction. This
vision, because of the "artificial" character of its development and its cultural equivocation, is not merely ambiguous
or difficult, but is ambivalent and often looks irrational.

That black nationalism is based on a vehement racial consciousness can be imputed to racism that grew out of, and
which often came to underlie, white domination. Black
nationalism can in the final analysis be reduced to a challenge to white supremacy—a refutation of the racial ideol-

[19] Emerson and Kilson, *op. cit.*, p. 638.

ogy of slavery and segregation. In order to understand certain aspects of black nationalism and its peculiarities, it is important to consider the fact that slavery and segregated rule was not only a political and economic affair, but that it also imposed a specific social framework for the black man's experience both of the world and of "himself." The fact of political domination created contact between black and white men under conditions that constantly underscored racial and cultural differences. Black nationalism, by confronting white domination with its own racial protest and zealous partisanship of the "black race," does more than draw together sentiments and attitudes that go into a collective black reaction, but embodies them in a heightened form that moves in fact very distinctly towards a racial ideology.

. . . Anti-white sensibilities among black nationalists operate to supply a unifying ideology which transcends the experience of any single individual.

In point of fact, however, black nationalism is much more than a response to white outrages (although it is of course that too). In the hands of such a gifted exponent as Malcolm, black nationalism is a sophisticated and pervasive political ideology based on a generalized understanding of the history of the black man in the United States.[20]

Malcolm X explains himself: "When we Muslims had talked about 'the devil white man,' he had been relatively abstract, someone we Muslims rarely come into contact with . . ."[21] A frequently repeated statement in many of his speeches was that:

Unless we call one white man, by name, a "devil," we are not speaking of any "individual" white man. We are speaking

[20] Frank Kofsky, "Malcolm X," *Monthly Review*, New York: Sept. 1966, p. 44.
[21] Alex Haley, *The Autobiography of Malcolm X*, New York: Grove Press, 1965, pp. 242-43.

of the "collective" white man's historical record. We are speaking of the collective white man's cruelties, and evil, and greeds, that have seen him "act" like a devil toward the non-white man. Any intelligent, honest, objective person cannot fail to realize that his white man's slave trade, and his subsequent devilish actions, are directly responsible for not only the presence of this black man in America, but also for the condition in which we find this black man here . . .[22]

Undoubtedly, such a broadly general and inclusive ideology directed at the dominant group serves the function of polarizing feelings and inducing conflict in the relationship between the two groups. Lewis Coser* suggests that such external conflict establishes group boundaries and gives identity to the group and strengthens its internal cohesion.

An ideology, when it becomes explicit, is a kind of thinking aloud on the part of a society or a group within it. It is a direct response to the actual conditions of life and has a social function, either as a defensive system of beliefs and ideas which support and justify an established social structure, or as a rational project for the creation of a new order. The latter type of ideology, even when it includes a certain degree of idealism, also implies a reasoned program of collective action; it becomes the intellectual channel of social life.

The ideology of black nationalism is an illustration of the conflict model in intergroup interaction. Black nationalism springs from a desire to reverse an intolerable situation—its adherents view the basis of social life as competition between groups for social and economic power. It is a challenge to the legitimacy of the system which white dominance has imposed on black men, whose experience—dispersal, subjugation, humiliation—generates social strain

[22] George Breitman, ed., *Malcolm X Speaks*, New York: 1965, p. 269.
* Lewis Coser, *The Functions of Social Conflict*, New York: The Crowell-Collier Publishing Co., The Free Press of Glencoe, 1964, pp. 87–88.

and tension. A prominent ex-civil rights leader and former activist explains this experience.

> The evil of slavery—and to some degree Negroes are still enslaved—is in the way it permitted white men to handle Negroes: their bodies, their action, their opportunities, their very minds and thoughts. To the depths of their souls, Negroes feel handled, dealt with, ordered about, manipulated by white men. I cannot over-emphasize the tenacity and intensity of this feeling among Negroes and I believe any fair-minded person pondering the history of the Negro's enforced posture in a world of white power would concede the justice of the feeling.[23]

The black man's worth was low, indeed, not only in the eyes of his white overlord, but also as a consequence, in his own eyes. He was on the lowest rung of the racial hierarchy which Western civilization had established. As Aimé Césaire, the West Indian writer and initial conceiver of Negritude, observed ". . . at the top, the white man—the being, in the full sense of the term—at the bottom, the black man . . . the thing, as much as to say a nothing."[24] The black man retained an awareness of his racial differences and was forced to organize his life on a racial basis.

Against this background it is not difficult to understand that such development as Garvey's "Back to Africa" movement in particular was not simply, mere atavistic expression: it was presented not as an escape from America, but as a national return to an original home, as a positive rather than a negative gesture. Garvey appreciated the psychological needs of his adherents, realizing that what they needed in order to struggle for political freedom was "freedom from contempt."[25]

[23] James Farmer, "Mood Ebony," *Playboy*, May, 1966, p. 126.

[24] Aimé Césaire, "Toussaint L'Ouverture," *Présence Africaine*, Paris: 1963, p. 31.

[25] E. Franklin Frazier, *Race and Culture Contacts in the Modern World*, New York: Alfred A. Knopf, 1962, p. 363.

Garvey's revaluation of Africa had the precise function of abolishing the world order created by the white man in the minds of black men. Abram Kardiner and Lionel Ovesey say as much when they write: "Marcus Garvey saw one important truth: that the Negro was doomed as long as he took his ideals from the white man. He saw that this sealed his internal feeling of inferiority and self contempt."[26] Garvey was among the first to create a "New Vision," based on a revaluation of the African cultural heritage, as a source of inspiration to the blacks in America and in the world.

Two facts stand out clearly from a consideration of the progressive development of black nationalism, seen in broad historical perspective. The first is that it was a movement of reaction against the white cultural domination which is concomitant with political domination. Second, it seems perfectly clear, however, that without the pressure of segregation and the conflicts which it creates and without the historical and social factors which dominate the situation of the black man in America—that is, without the racial factor —the forms of reaction to culture contact among black people summarized here would have had a completely different character. In short, black nationalism is inspired by a wish for freedom from both domination and contempt.

James Farmer writes about the shift in emphasis from integration, which had been largely rooted in the black middle class, to emphasis on race and nationalism, which has been the traditional appeal to the black masses. He gives considerable insight as to motives of this movement:

Almost imperceptibly the demand for desegregation had shaded into a demand for black dispersal and assimilation. We were told, and for a while told ourselves, all Negro separation was inherently inferior, and some of us began to think that

[26]Abram Kardiner and Lionel Ovesey, *The Mark of Oppression*, New York: Alfred A. Knopf, 1962, p. 363.

Negroes couldn't be fully human in the presence of other Negroes. Well, we have since come to learn that all separation need not be inferior in all cases and in all places.

. . . We have learned that what is needed is not "invisibility" but a valid and legitimate visibility . . . We have found the cult of color-blindness not only quaintly irrelevant but seriously flawed. For we learned that America couldn't simply be color-blind. It would only become color-blind when we gave up our color. The white man, who presumably has no color, would have to give up only his prejudices, but we would have to give up our identities. Thus we would usher in the Great Day with an act of self-denial and self-abasement. We would achieve equality by conceding racism's charge: that our skins are an affliction; that our history is one long humiliation; that we are empty of distinctive traditions and any legitimate source of pride.[27]

He recalls a meeting to reconcile a serious strife between "nationalists" and "integrationists" in CORE chapters in the San Francisco Bay Area:

One fellow, a Negro, immediately said, "Brother Farmer, we've got to dig being black." He kept repeating it over and over again, and I knew exactly what he meant. He meant that blackness of the skin had been accepted as a deformity by Negroes, that it had to cease being that, and had to become a source of pride, and so did all the culture and memories that went with it . . . Some form of nationalism is necessary, even healthy though the willfully color-blind refuse to acknowledge this . . . The doctrinaire color-blind often fail to perceive that it is "ideally" necessary for the black man to be proudly black today . . . We have come to realize that we must live here and now rather than in eternity.

. . . The system of segregation was mounted and perpetuated for the purpose of keeping the black man down; that it was and is a conspiracy to instill in the Negro and the white a sense of Negro inferiority.

. . . In a free society many Negroes will choose to live and work separately, although not in total isolation. They will

[27] Farmer, *op. cit.*, pp. 126, 177.

cultivate that pride in themselves which comes in part from their effort to make this a free land . . . In helping themselves they will come to love themselves. And because they love themselves, they will be determined to help themselves.

. . . We will accept, in other words, Malcolm X's insight that segregation will become separation only with a separate effort of Negro heart and soul rejecting the notion of some of the older civil right organizations—that desegregation and integration "in itself" will accomplish miracles.

Perhaps "independence" is a better term than separation. We shall become independent men.[28]

The cultural position of the black man in America possesses its own specific characteristics; he lives in a symbiotic relationship with the white man and is held in subordinate position by the caste system. Furthermore, he is governed by the secondary institutions imposed or sanctioned by the white dominant group, especially in the areas of religion and social morality. The wish for independent expression finds a ready springboard in those elements of black subculture which segregation had helped to mold into something of a definite structure.

An ironic aspect of black popular movements is the way in which white (Western) elements act as catalysts in the emotional reactions which produce nationalist feelings. Christian egalitarian teaching, for example, helps to show up in the eyes of black converts the fundamental contradiction that separate white domination from the avowed humanitarian principles of Western culture, and to underline the rift between the objective practice and the declared values of white men. A powerful emotional inspiration of nationalism is thus a disaffection for the white man, just against his own principles.

It is apparent that as the black power movement gains more strength and becomes more aggressive and defines its objective in terms of specific Afro-American interest, and

[28] *Ibid.,* p. 178.

not on (white) liberal terms, and is controlled by an increasingly politicized Afro-American element, it will appear more threatening and separatist to the dominant group. It would be a mistake, however, to dismiss such development as a futile and sectarian obsession with self—a kind of black narcissism. In the larger context of Afro-American experience, it represents, for many, the ultimate and perhaps most stable of self-awareness.

In their search for identity, the adherents of black nationalism have to accept and explore to the full their particular situation. But, although preoccupied with a sectional and limited interest, they are inspired by a universal human need for fulfilment.

Thus, black nationalism can be objectively defined as:

(1) The desire of Afro-Americans to decide their own destiny through control of their own political organizations and the formation and preservation of their cultural, economic and social institutions.

(2) The determination to unite as a group, as a people, in a common community, to oppose white supremacy by striving for independence from white control.

(3) The resistance to subordinate status and demand for political freedoms, social justice and economic equality.

(4) The development of ethnic self-interest, racial pride and group consciousness, and opposition to and rejection of those normative and dominant ideas and values perceived to be incompatible with this objective.

(5) A revaluation of "self," and relationship with the dominant group and the social system in general, and a shifting frame of reference (Africa and "Blackism" become significant referents) and change in perspective.

These characteristic attributes of the social phenomena referred to as black nationalism do not represent discontinuous factors, but are intricately related elements which animate a particular process of interaction; which take the form of conscious cultivation of social and cultural pluralism and a movement toward political self-determination.

PART IV

Black Psychology: A New Perspective

Joseph White

Guidelines for Black Psychologists

Black psychologists have gone farther than Black sociologists in their attempts to legitimize a new perspective in their discipline. They have established an autonomous national organization and have begun to effect change through new policies and programs. In this essay, Joseph White sets forth the basic rules of thumb for Black psychologists.

At the present time, black psychologists are still operating with a lot of assumptions and machinery that have been developed by white psychologists primarily for white people. For us to begin to develop a viable black psychology, it is important that we first assess some of the premises of white psychology, its various schools, and how those premises operate when black people are the object of their scrutiny.

As an example, let us take the white educational psychologist looking at the black home. He might observe that many of the standard cultural trappings of the middle-

255

class white home are missing: the collected works of Shake-speare might not be there; James Brown will be there instead of Brahms; *Jet, Ebony* and maybe *Sepia* are there instead of *Harper's* or *The Atlantic Monthly*. Not seeing the familiar white cultural trappings and seeing some that he does not understand, the tendency of the psychologist has been to assume that the child is deprived in some way.

As a psychologist, he thus enters the observational net of the black home or client with a deficit or weakness hypothe-sis, so that his recommended programs are based upon some concept of enrichment for the child, family or client. It is enrichment defined by the dominant culture—from Head Start to Upward Bound, to language enrichment programs, etc. Somehow the analysis is always corrective; implied is always some deficit that the child brings to the situation from his home. This analysis has pre-psychological origins, and it is a clear carry-over from slavery and Reconstruction days—that there is something inferior about the black child, and therefore, the black man.

One psychologist, Jensen, just out and out states that it is a genetic thing, that blacks are inferior by birth. But the more liberated type of white psychologist wants to move under the cultural deprivation, cultural deficit, psychologi-cal deficit type of hypothesis. Besides the cognitive school of psychology, whose practice I outlined briefly, we have also many psychologists who have been touched by Freud-ian and psychoanalytic kinds of thinking.

Such psychologists observe the black home and conclude that there is not a male figure present with the same fre-quency that there is in the dominant culture's home. From this premise, the neo-Freudian begins to develop all kinds of theory about the atypical attachment of black youth—especially male children—to their mothers. There is central emphasis on the Oedipus complex. Psychologists' percep-tions of relationships between black males and black females lead them to conclude that we are a matriarchal culture and that, therefore, the mother must translate to the male child a kind of negation of the male role and also does this to the female child.

Such an analysis is just another more sophisticated example of the deprivation hypothesis: either there is something wrong with us cognitively (we don't develop right and therefore we need school enrichment) or at a depth level, we have psycho-sexual problems which we act out through our adult life, in the male-female relationship and in the parent-child relationship.

What black psychologists must try to do is enter a theory building net about black children that does not draw primarily from either the psychoanalytic hypothesis or the cognitive deprivation hypothesis. Instead, they must try to develop the kind of psychological model that accounts for the strengths in our children. Many children growing up in the black community learn a certain kind of mental toughness. They learn survival skills. They know how to deal with the credit man; they know how to deal with the cat at the corner market; they know how to deal with hypes and pimps. They know how to jive the school principal, and they show a lot of psychological cleverness and originality in the particular style they emerge with. But most institutions have not yet learned how to appreciate and capitalize upon this particular kind of style.

As black psychologists, we might establish this hypothesis: that the psychology the black child has developed is a very positive and a very healthy kind of thing. It shows his recognition that he exists in a complicated and hostile environment, that he has an objective awareness of this environment and makes behaviors in terms of that awareness. I would also continue to stress that as we analyze the psychological make-up of white institutions, we find that the institution itself tends to negate the authenticity of the black child's existence. For example, if he comes to school popping his fingers and talking about another youngster's mama or being loud, the institution begins to negate the style as improper, bad and otherwise worthless.

White psychologists further find it very difficult to understand the apparent contradictions in black culture, the fact that these apparent contradictions do not mean the same thing that they would mean in white culture. For example, I remember one white psychology student who wanted to interview and observe a black nationalist student club. The brothers wouldn't let him come inside, but they did allow him to view the meeting from a window. A particular brother that we both knew went to the black nationalist meeting, where the brothers laid down a typical 1968 type of black power set. The brother was a very active participant in the meeting: right on, the whole bit. Subsequently, this brother left the meeting and went kitty-corner across the street to a store-front type of church, grabbed a tambourine, entered the ceremony and rocked with the sisters for about an hour and shouted a bit. Then he left there and went down the street a block to a bar and began to drink a little gin and dig on Aretha Franklin.

So when the white boy interviewed him in the bar, he asked him, "Well, don't you see a contradiction between black nationalist ideology, the store-front church and you sitting in this bar drinking gin?" The brother said he didn't see any contradiction because he did it every Sunday and all the sets were part of him. He just dug on it.

While it might have represented for the white psychologist a logical contradiction, it meant nothing to the brother. Black people could see the church as a strength organ on the part of their community and an escapist movement at the same time and the two not negate each other.

Closely related to black ease with seeming contradictions is the fact that black people have a greater tolerance for ambiguity and ambivalence than the white culture, and the white psychologist does not recognize this fact sufficiently.

Instead, assuming that black people are lower-class, he therefore assumes that blacks are impulsive. One of the things impulsive people have is little tolerance for stress and contradiction. Seeing us as being more impulsive, the white psychologist assumes that we have less ability to handle contradictions. I would turn it the other way around.

Furthermore, as Price Cobbs points out, it is good for black people to have a "healthy paranoia." A black person who is not suspicious of this culture is tied up in using a lot of very pathological mechanisms, like the denial of certain basic realities. The sociologist E. Franklin Frazier touched on this very well in *Black Bourgeoisie*. Part of the objective situation of black persons in this society is a paranoid condition: there is a persecution, an irrational persecution, at that. Moreover, it is systematic. We have therefore developed a set of tools to deal with it.

On the other hand, if a white dude were to sit down and tell a psychologist that he's being persecuted, that he's got some people that have been systematically persecuting him from his front door to the White House, the psychologist might say, "Well man you'd better take a little ride down to Fairview and we'll help you out." Black psychologists and white psychologists who have dealings with black people must bear this distinction in mind—that what can be seen as illness for the white man can be health for the black man, attitudinally, as it bears on their relationships to the white power structure in this country.

Black and white people operate from different frames of reference. When black people confront white people, what they primarily want is, first, a legitimate acknowledgement of their point of view and needs, and second, the appropriate actions to be taken. But when a white person is pushed up against the wall, the worst thing he can do is admit that the party who pushed him up there has a valid point of view. So, in a conference situation, when black people escalate the tempo of their language and their gestural style and get into verbal fireworks, the white reaction is to feel angry, threatened and alienated. Were whites to drop their defensiveness and acknowledge the legitimacy of the black point of view, they might be able to go from there to a more cooperative relationship. But this culture is so deeply entrenched in the whole concept of sin and atonement and paying up for that sin, that it expects retaliation in the Old Testament style once it admits "sin"; it expects a retribution, a punishment.

The question of image and hero emerges here. This culture is steeped in the tradition of a white hero who is infallible and rigid, who scores his triumphs with inhuman skill and retires undefeated. The whole psychology of the hero in the black and white cultures is different. In the black culture, the hero is by and large the brother who messes with the system and gets away with it. Black people on the whole could care less about certain political figures going off to the Caribbean and spending a little dough. They can dig it and can identify with it. Whereas this same hero, to the white psychologists, appears to be the villain. This comes together in literature. In John O. Killens, *And Then We Heard the Thunder*, Solly, the so-called Noble Savage, is a black college graduate who has had Officer's Candidate School. He's got this goof-off in his outfit, this brother who battles the officers, etc. But finally, over the course of the book, it's the bad nigger that becomes the hero. Nowadays, the bad nigger is very much in vogue as the hero in the black community, and yet white people continue to perceive this person as the villain.

Such was true in the case of Eldridge Cleaver. Eldridge became a kind of culture hero in the United States; a lot of white people were disappointed because he didn't stand trial. He had let down his responsibilities to his people and he wasn't "a credit to his race." But anybody that had heard Eldridge or read his books or knew anything about his life knew where he had been and knew he wasn't going to go there again.

What we black psychologists are getting at is a set of objective or factual recognitions that might help black people recognize that psychology is social as well as personal and develop a social psychology of blackness. Most of the white psychological theory that we have is personal, either some kind of cognitive approach or psychoanalytic approach. It further assumes that there is a regular social order which is satisfactory, neither of which are valid, with respect to the needs of black people. If one looks at the work of black psychiatrist Frantz Fanon, for example, he finds the opposite emphasis: that black psychological strains have social origins and that the present social order is not satisfactory for blacks but oppressive.

One type of psychological theory that we can possibly modify and use is that of the Gestalt psychologists, such as Carl Rogers, who view people as having a frame of reference and an individual phenomenal field which is legitimate. In this theory, people come from certain experiential pools, and that experiential pool determines who they are. Its primary ingredients are, namely, the home, the family and the immediate neighborhood. We have got to work to make these frames legitimate and then allow our children extension of them, in role models that they can associate with.

It's very important that these role models be realistic. Again, white psychologists and educators tend to miss the boat here. For example, a couple of weeks ago, I was looking at some new children's books. Now all publishers have got the idea that you have to have something black in children's literature so that black youngsters can identify with the pictures. One of these had a story of some white boys playing baseball. At the beginning of the ball game a brother was standing at the side, just standing there. One of the players had to go home and then the white boys allowed the brother to play. Well, he hit four home runs and struck out six people in a row and saved the game. But what the book was projecting is an image of another Willie Mays, that "super-niggers" are okay in ones and twos. Whereas, the average everyday, typical white boy is projected *all over* the culture—radio, television, books, periodicals and films. So from the black psychological standpoint we have to work to make a kind of breakthrough that puts black children into typical situations rather than into omniscient and omnipotent kinds of roles. As individual people, we have to trust our own kind of perception and not absorb white expectations of black super-heroes and villains.

One very valuable thing about the black consciousness movement is that it begins to psychologically legitimatize being black. But we must not equate the imagery of that consciousness with the actualities of social progress. We cannot have a black and proud community with no jobs, no transportation, no way of feeding the kids, no control of the police force, and schools and other institutions. It must be a two-stage kind of operation, consciousness and action. Perhaps as we develop black cultural anthropologists or whatever would be the black equivalent, we can get some greater insights to guide us.

One of the very different kinds of things about the black culture and the black psyche of America is that it is an oral culture—the blues, the gospel songs, the heavy rap, the sermon and traditions are carried orally, and people are going to have to examine that oral expression in order to make new insights into the psychological functioning of black people. For example, in black idioms—what we call black English or whatever—we do things that are unique in terms of syntax. I think this might have had its roots in an oral existence which still has some Africanisms, but also in our social need to use language to reveal and to conceal simultaneously. Black language is very deep in subtle meaning and nuances. For example, if you take a poem like the "Signifying Monkey," there are a lot of psychological processes tied up in there and there is a heavy amount of deception. Or take the old song ". . . steal away, steal away, steal away, Jesus, steal away home . . . I ain't got long to stay here . . ." The slavemaster perceives in the ante-bellum South that the brothers were thinking about heaven and religion when the cats were really laying out a message that the Underground Railway is coming through and you better jump on board.

This would probably mean—and I don't know if we can ever develop the instruments to test this out—that people who grow up in the black community tend to be much more intuitive in terms of their response to signs and gestures than they are in relating to the concrete syntax. In the attempt to translate black English into the standard vernacular, some of its quality and meaning may be lost. For example, a youngster might say, "Well the cat was rappin' on my rib," and we try to translate it, "He was flirting with my girlfriend," or, "He was being unduly solicitous toward a young woman whom I was dating," and something is lost. It's amazing that this is only now being talked about because many of us have always recognized that things get lost when they are translated from one language or style into another. Yet it is a daily black experience.

A consideration of black sensitivity training is in order. I think we have to develop some kind of psychological process by which black change agents who are continuously on the firing line can blow their minds out from time to time —go through some inner cleansing. Because, I'm sensing around the country that a lot of brothers are beginning to suffer from some combat fatigue and entropy. It is very difficult in such a state of mind to see clearly both the goal that one is striving for and the relevance of the tactic to the particular goal in the immediate situation. In that frame of mind, one begins to use words in a very global kind of way. Words like revolution, liberation, offing, Tomming, and so on. We may need to identify a network of black psychologists who can help brothers in groups work through the renewal, self-regeneration process. And there are probably some things we can utilize through standard sensitivity models, but they would probably need certain alterations.

For while aggression, affection and sexuality may be the kinds of encounters that white people need to work through within themselves, I think that as I see brothers in 1970, we need to work out in our local situations a clarity of direction given where we are. We must work through the kinds of problems that we get into when we mix image and rhetoric with the process of change itself. We may need the kinds of sets that have brothers examine what they are really saying. I can perceive of a set where we put some brothers together for a couple of hours and let them rap as intensely as they want about where they are relative to change and use closed circuit television film. We could then have each of those brothers watch the set together and individually and see the whole process at work, and then try to get back together and tell each other what they thought they were saying, what they then observed about themselves and the group, and then what the difference was between the intended message and the actual message.

When we talk about black-white encounters, one of the things that fascinated me which I saw on television recently was the forcing of each group to take the role of the other, but not a typical role-playing session. The sensitivity trainers put white masks on the black people and black masks on the white people and forced them to interchange positions. If one talks about psychologists having difficulty because they enter the communication net with different frames of reference, one way of helping them learn the other frame of reference is by forcing them to act it through—not for a fifteen-minute period but over a long, 30-hour encounter.

A lot of sensitivity and T group work can be a useful thing for blacks who are involved in the movement and leadership roles, to clean out their pipes once in a while.

With such sessions, the trainer or psychologist should be a black from another location, who does not have any built-in emotional reaction and/or commitments to any member of the group. We could also interchange black personnel—some of the brothers from the East might come here and work with us and some of us might go back there and work with them.

Another value I see to the group process type of model is that with all that has happened in the Movement in the last ten years, there is a lot of confusion, as we move from one pattern to another, just in the people in the community itself. We may need some type of store front in the ghetto itself, where brothers can drop in in groups, rap about child rearing, rap about hash, and rap about the revolution and so on. For, we don't seem to have a vehicle through which the standard citizen can involve himself, except when we call a mass meeting. That mass meeting, more often than not, is related to a particular crisis in the community. We don't have a place where, like on Monday night, there will be certain trained black personnel available who will work with any group that drops in from 7 to 9.

Former group nets are being broken up. For example, the church used to involve itself in a lot of activities in groups. They may not have been sensitivity groups, but you could drop down, and on Tuesday night there was choir rehearsal, Wednesday night young people's meeting, but that's breaking up now. Brothers also don't play the bar set in the way that they used to, going out on Saturday night, taking a chick, meeting his boys certain places, dancing, carrying on. That set doesn't seem to be as prevalent any-more. Brothers don't have a place to go to plug in—even barber shops, even clubs and joints are fading out.

A good sensitivity model, then, could pick up the com-munication lag that has occurred as the churches, the barber shops, the bars, and the joints lose that sanction.

These are the concerns that black psychologists must address themselves to. We must begin to develop a model of black psychology which is free from the built-in assump-tions and values of the dominant culture. We cannot, by rote, employ the psychoanalytic model nor the cognitive model. Real gains might come from the model of Gestalt psychology, with its sense of experiential pools, of field and subject. We must develop a kind of psychological jiu-jitsu and recognize that what the dominant culture deems devi-ant or anti-social behavior might indeed be the functioning of a healthy black psyche which objectively recognizes the antagonisms of the white culture and develops machinery for coping with them.

We should also recognize that black people have a great tolerance for ambiguity and uncertainty, for living with seemingly contradictory alternatives. As practitioners, then, we must eliminate the tendency to think in either-or terms, with respect to the black experience. Finally, we need to de-velop dynamic models of a group nature, to help support and restore and refresh our leadership and to renew com-munication within all levels of the black community.

William E. Cross, Jr.

The Negro-to-Black
Conversion Experience

What are the various stages and levels of awareness that
Blacks experience as they traverse the road to "psychological
liberation under conditions of oppression"? A young Black
psychologist attempts to define these processes in his "phenomenological interpretation of the Negro-to-Black conversion experience."

In the September 1970 issue of *Ebony* magazine, Joseph
White, a Black psychologist, called for research and development of a Black psychology. Professor White stated
that the so-called neutral value paradigms currently being
used to evaluate and conceptualize the behavior of Black
Americans are in reality weighted towards the conditions
and values of white middle-class America. A Black psychology, according to White, would evolve from an understanding of the behavior of human beings within the context of Black America, *i.e.*, the psycho-social economic and
cultural setting of Black communities.

267

A sub-heading or component of a Black psychology might be the psychology of Black liberation. In fact, one of the first concerns of Black behavioral scientists should be the creation of developmental theories, personality constructs and Black life-styles that promote psychological liberation under conditions of oppression. You will note my emphasis on the wording—"psychological liberation under conditions of oppression"—for it is taken for granted that the model for *complete* freedom has been articulated by the late Frantz Fanon. But Fanon's model stipulates an important prerequisite to total freedom: an on-going war to off one's oppressor! In the military sense of the word, we are not at war with white America. War may become inevitable, but today Black people are not being freed by the Fanon model. Yet, Black people are experiencing individual and collective change. Many of us can state that we were anti-Black, brain-washed, or "colored" in our perspective a few years ago, while today we see ourselves as having become Afro-Americans, Pan-Africanists, or simply Black persons. Oppressive conditions remain a constant factor; in fact, oppression is greater today than, say, in 1965; however, we have been liberated, psychologically speaking, despite continued oppression. In a sense, we are less susceptible to psychological and ideological domination by the enemy and more receptive to thoughts, values and actions that have revolutionary implications. As we are not in physical (military) combat with the enemy we are not experiencing complete freedom, but it is obvious that some other process or "model" is at work transforming our minds as if to better prepare us for the "unknown" obligations of tomorrow (including the option of war).

Using phenomenological data, scattered interview material, and juxtaposing information obtained by simply interacting with Brothers and Sisters who were going through changes as a consequence of their participation in the modern Black movement, I have attempted to construct a model depicting the various stages persons traverse in becoming Black oriented. In its current form it might best be called a "phenomenological interpretation of the Negro-to-Black conversion experience."

Negro-to-Black Conversion Experience

"I don't want to think of myself as a Negro and it offends me to be called 'black.' If each of us would pay particular attention to self-refinement the degree of racial friction would be significantly decreased."

"Yea, it all started when they shot Brother King. Honkies planned that shit and it really shook me up so bad until I began to see what was really happening to Black people. For awhile I could no longer stand to be around white people. I hated all their guts and on some days I swear I wanted to kill the first honky I saw. You know what, I even began to feel that we were better than they were because we had so much soul and love. . . ."

"To walk around 125th and Lenox Avenue is a powerful thing, can you dig it? When I see so many beautiful Black folks trying to make it, doing everything just to stay alive, yet still being able to sing and dance in such a soulful manner, it just blows my mind and I sometimes want to cry tears of joy. Can you dig it? I'm a part of it all! I see Black, feel Black, oh how wonderful it is to be Black."

"Black power must be more than group therapy. To be effective it must be programmed."

These comments, or ones like them, are being made by Afro-Americans, the educated and the uneducated, well-to-do and the poor, the light-skinned or the dark-complexioned, as each is transformed from a "Negro" into a *Black American*. When each remark was made, the person felt, thought, and acted differently; yet each statement reflects the qualities of a particular stage for *one* process. All too frequently, analytical articles and commentaries focus on the Black militant, the Black middle-class, or the apathetic Black person, creating the impression that each state or condition is unrelated to the other. A closer look suggests that today's Black theoretician *was* a well-programmed conservative three years ago and an impulsive rhetorical revolutionary last year! Obviously, Blackness is a state of mind and, as such, is explained by dynamic rather than static paradigms. Malcolm X was a Muslim *before* he promoted the Organization of Afro-American Unity; Cleaver was immersed in the hatred of white people and his conversion to a humanist camp *required* the rape of white women; LeRoi Jones' struggle for a master's degree in philosophy preceded his quest for a Black identity. In becoming Black, or in being deniggerized, as Sister Barbara Ann Teer might say, an individual *must* pass through a series of well-defined stages; the Black experience is a process. As we analyze and comprehend the process, we will be moving toward the development of a psychology of Black liberation. The five stages of the process are: preencounter (pre-discovery) stage; encounter (discovery) stage; immersion-emersion stage; internalization stage; and finally the commitment stage.

STAGE ONE: PRE-ENCOUNTER

In the pre-encounter stage a person is programmed to view and think of the world as being non-Black, anti-Black, or the opposite of Black. The person's world-view is dominated by Euro-American determinants. The sociological, political, cultural, and psychological conditions that result from this world-view are the same for both lower- and middle-class Black people. That is to say, the *content* of the pre-liberation Black experience within the class system differs but the *context* is similar since both think, act and behave in a manner that *degrades* Blackness. Thus, putting lye on your hair as opposed to getting it cut in an "Ivy League" fashion (content) are different styles of Black degradation (context). To continue, the pre-encounter person's historical perspective distorts Black history. It is believed that Black people came from a strange, uncivilized, "dark" continent, and that the search for Black history begins in 1865—that slavery was a civilizing experience.

Brothers and Sisters from the ghetto functioning at the pre-encounter level assume they are more relevant than Black folks who live "outside" the ghetto; ghetto residents will justify and even romanticize hustling or exploiting other Black people as being "necessary for survival." For pre-encounter Negroes a white aesthetic transcends class lines. It is dramatized by deifying the white woman, and is also reflected in the content, themes, vehicles of emphasis, colorations, and mode of expressions in numerous cultural and academic preferences. Even in the ghetto, where purer forms of Black expressions can be found, one discovers the ghetto resident referring to the blues or jazz as something low, bad, or sexy (white cultural value system).

Pre-encounter Negroes are politically naive and are programmed to have faith in the Protestant ethic. There is an extreme dependency on white leadership, and the assimilation-integration paradigm is thought to be the *only* model for cohesive race relations. Under the dictates of the assimilation-integration paradigm the development of an "American" identity involves affirmation of "White-Anglo-Saxon-Protestant" characteristics, and negation, dilution, or even denial of non-WASP behavior. As Western standards are *inherently* anti-Black, the cruel paradox of the assimilated Negro is that, in becoming a good American, he has also become anti-Black and anti-African. The white man is viewed as intellectually superior and technically mystical; Negroes in the pre-encounter stage tend to become enveloped in the white man's rhetoric, confusing his words for his deeds. Emphasis is on the individual seeking to get "ahead"; the advancement of the race is gauged by how far "I" progress in the system as opposed to how the system relates to the "group." Pre-encounter Negroes typically distrust Black-controlled businesses or organizations and prefer to be called "Negro," "civilized," "colored," "human being," or "American citizen."

STAGE TWO: ENCOUNTER

What experience, information, or event causes a person functioning at the pre-encounter level to become interested in, or at least receptive to, material that will contest a number of his or her basic assumptions concerning Blacks? More simply, what motivates a person (in the pre-encounter world) to encounter or to become Black? A predictable answer is suggested by the word *encounter:* some experience that manages to slip by or even shatters the person's current feeling about himself and his interpretation of the condition of Blacks in America. The encounter is a verbal or visual event, rather than an "in-depth" intellectual experience. For example, the death of Martin Luther King, Jr., hurled thousands of pre-encounter Negroes into a search for a deeper understanding of the Black Power movement. Witnessing a friend being assaulted by the police, televised reports of racial incidents, or discussions with a friend or loved one who is further advanced into his or her Blackness may "turn a person on" to his own Blackness.

Encounter entails two steps: first, experiencing the encounter, and; second, beginning to reinterpret the world as a consequence of the encounter. The second part is a testing phase during which the individual cautiously and fearfully tries to validate his new perceptions. On the outside the person is generally very quiet, yet a storm is brewing inside. The person will go to meetings and simply listen as he tries to determine the validity of this ominous thing called "Blackness," "Black Power," or "Black History." "Maybe, just maybe, things are different than I thought them to be and if so, *I want* to find the truth."

Each individual asks himself very personal questions. The Black intellectual wonders: "Have I been unaware of the Black experience or was I programmed to be disgusted by it?" A ghetto youth asks: "Is it right to kill another Black person or prostitute my sisters?" And the Black college student says: "Do I date white girls, or am I avoiding Black women?"

The tentative answers are obvious, and the person quickly compares the implications of his new insights with the manner in which he had been living (pre-encounter stance). Previously hostile, or at best neutral, toward the Black movement, the encounter jolts the person into at least considering a different interpretation of the Black condition. His heart pounding, hands sweating, and eyes filled with tears, the person speaks the magic words for the first time in his life: "Black is beautiful." At this point *guilt* becomes a tremendous factor. The middle-class person feels guilty for having "left" the race; the lower-class person feels guilt for degrading his Blackness! At the same time the person becomes increasingly angry as it is realized that he or she has been "programmed or brain-washed" all these years—and the vicious enemy is the white man and all the white world! Black rage and guilt combine to fling the person into a frantic, determined, obsessive, extremely motivated search for Black identity. A "Negro" is dying and a "Black American" is being resurrected. We have reached the immersion-emersion stage.

STAGE THREE: IMMERSION-EMERSION

In this period the person immerses himself in the world of Blackness. The person attends political meeting, joins the Muslims, goes to rapping sessions, attends seminars, and art shows that focus on Blackness. Everything of value must be

Black or relevant to Blackness. The experience is an immersion into Blackness and a liberation from whiteness. Regardless of the opinions of others, the person actually feels that he is being drawn toward qualitatively different experiences as he is being torn from his former orientations. The immersion is a strong, powerful, dominating sensation constantly being energized by Black rage, guilt, and a third and new fuel, a developing sense of pride. As one brother put it, "I was swept along by a sea of Blackness." The white world, white culture, and white person are dehumanized ("honky," "pig," "white devil") and become *biologically* inferior, as the Black person and Black world are *deified*. Superhuman and supernatural expectations are conjured concerning anything Black. Everything that is Black is good and romantic. The person accepts his hair, his brown skin, his very being as now "beautiful." That a person exists and is Black is an inherently wonderful phenomenon. Black literature is passionately consumed; brothers and sisters who *never* had an interest in reading teach themselves to read and write. One spends a great deal of time developing an Afro hairstyle, and it becomes common to wear African-inspired clothing. Persons give themselves African names or drop the "American" name, as did Malcolm X; some babies are named after African heroes. Of course, an intense interest in "Mother Africa" develops. The word "Negro" is dropped and the person becomes an Afro-American, Black, Black-American, or even African.

During the immersion-emersion stage, the person has a creative burst, writing poetry, essays, plays, novels, or confessionals; a segment turns to the plastic arts or painting. People who never before sought or experienced creative activity discover they are able to express themselves in a totally new mode; witness the rebirth of LeRoi Jones (Immamu Amiri Baraka). Professional artists speak of profound and fundamental change in the quality of their work. In explaining the change, these artists state that although they were born in a Black situation, their training and the pressure from society made them look for substance and content outside the Black experience. For example, some wanted to be "pure" and "free," creating art for art's sake, or others admitted that their senses could only receive messages from Europe and white America. With the realization of their Blackness, the professional artist is awakened to a vast and new world of rich colors, powerful dramas, irony, rage, oppression, survival, and impossible dreams! And it is all there within reach; the artist (or scholar) has simply to look in the mirror.

There occurs a turning inward and a withdrawal from everything perceived as being or representing the white world. Yet, ironically there also develops a need to confront the "man" as a means of dramatizing, concretizing, or proving one's Blackness. The confrontation, especially for Black leaders, is a manhood (or womanhood) ritual—a baptismal or purification rite. Carried to its extreme, the impulse is to confront white people, generally the police, on a life-or-death basis. When this impulse is coupled with a revolutionary rhetoric and program, a Black Panther is born. No control or oppressive technique—including the threat of death—is feared. Fanon's thesis of complete freedom through the violent overthrow of one's oppressor comes into the picture at this point, only the circumstances in the United States force the oppressor's death to be thought about or dreamed of but not actually carried out. Consequently, Brothers and Sisters report *daydreams* and *rhetoric* involving physical combat with white people but few have turned their thoughts into reality.

At this juncture in the conversion experience, a common daydream or fantasy is the urge to rip-off the first white person one passes on a particular day! "Kill whitey" fantasies appear to be experienced by Black people regardless of age, sex, or class background. Persons who fixate or stagnate at this point in their development are said to have a "pseudo" Black identity because it is based on the hatred and negation of white people rather than on the affirmation of a pro-Black perspective which *includes* commitment to the destruction of racism, capitalism and Western dominance. When warlike fantasies are nurtured by participation in a Black para-military organization, the dreams are sometimes actualized in the execution of planned attacks on police. In most cases, however, Black para-military groups take on a *defensive,* provocative, ambivalent, "I dare you whitey" stance. That they never quite devote themselves to the Fanon model suggests that paradigm may not be adequate (practical) for inclusion in strategies for Afro-American liberation.

Confrontation, bluntness, directness, and an either/or mentality are the primary if not the only basis for communication with other people, Black or white. The much discussed "Blacker than thou" syndrome intoxicates the minds of many people at this juncture. Black people are classified into such neat groups or categories as "Uncle Tom," "militant," "together," "soulful," "middle-class," "intellectual snob," etc. Labeling others helps the person clarify his own identity, but this name-calling phase can produce disastrous results (California Panther versus "US" murders). Not only does this person stereotype people, but his view of cosmology is greatly simplified and tends to be racist. To repeat, the person is concerned that his Blackness be pure or acceptable, and the purification rites are energized by a mixture of guilt, rage and growing sense of pride.

Rhetorically, the person shifts preference from individualism to mutualism or collectivism. A constant theme of selflessness, dedication and commitment is evident; the person feels overwhelming attachment to all Black surroundings. His main focus in life becomes this feeling of "togetherness and soul." The zenith of the immersion-emersion stage is the crystallization of these events.

The first half of the third stage is immersion into Blackness; the second is emergence from the dead-end, either/or racist, oversimplified aspects of the immersion experience. The person begins to "level off" and control his experiences. In fact, the person cannot continue to handle such an intense and concentrated affect level and must find a plateau. The desire and need to level off is greatly facilitated by the direction of the movement as discussed by national and international Black heroes. Malcolm X's trip to Mecca or Cleaver's discussions in *Soul on Ice* swing the person away from a racist ideology. One is able to discard or seriously question the simplistic components of the "Black is beautiful" philosophy, especially the tendency toward reverse racism. Such terms as power, control of one's mind, educational process, economic systems, institutions, programs, and process are considered. The white man is humanized (painfully, white people are recognized as equal to Black people at birth), and synthesizing Black rage with reason becomes the emphasis. The individual is now at least receptive to the critical analysis of the Afro-American condition from a cultural, political and socioeconomic view. Accepted factors of the Black experience are *incorporated*, and the person focuses on, or at least he is highly receptive to, presentations and plans for action for the development (liberation) of the Black community or the necessary transformations of Black life-styles. The rage is still evident, however, but guilt sensations are being replaced by feelings of pride. Whereas the immersion period dominated the individual, during the emersion phase of the Black experience the individual begins to gain awareness and control of his behavior. When control, awareness and incorporation predominate, the person is progressing into the fourth stage.

STAGE FOUR: INTERNALIZATION

The fourth stage is the most difficult and complex to explain because the events that occur during the immersion-emersion stage may frustrate or inspire an individual. Consequently, the degree of a person's future (or certainly his immediate involvement) in the Black movement may be either negligible or significant. During the immersion-emersion stage, the individual develops an idealistic, super-human level of expectancy toward practically anything "Black," in which case minimal reinforcement may carry the person into continued involvement (evolution into the internalization stage). Yet prolonged or traumatic frustra-tion (and contestment) of these high expectancy levels may produce a Black person more deeply rooted in *nihilistic* ex-pectancies than witnessed in the behavior of individuals functioning at the pre-encounter level. A surface analysis suggests three nonproductive options for persons moving beyond the immersion-emersion state:

Disappointment and Rejection: Some persons have their expectations frustrated and they resort to a nihilistic, hope-less, even anti-people world-view, perhaps becoming more believers in the white man's "magic" and the Black man's inferiority.

Continuation and Fixation at Stage Three: Individuals who experience particularly painful perceptions and con-frontations will be overwhelmed with hate for white people and fixate at the third stage. An aware Brother or Sister from the ghetto will be more angry than those who can move in and out of the most oppressive Black conditions (college students, the middle-class, or Black researchers).

Internalization: Others internalize and incorporate aspects of the immersion-emersion experience into their self-con-cept. They achieve a feeling of inner security and are more satisfied with themselves. There is *receptivity* to discussions or plans of action; however, receptiveness is as far as it goes. The person is not committed to a plan of action. He or she becomes the "nice" Black person with an Afro hair style and an attachment to Black things. Thus, it is possible for a person to progress to a state of psychological Blackness and then stop developing! Fixation and stagnation at the internalization stage is reflected in the arrogant anti-intellectual attitudes of many Black high school and college students. These students seem to believe that having experienced the Negro-to-Black conversion is tantamount to having completed an intensive intellectual analysis of the Black experience! "I am Black so why should I study the Black experience . . ." or so the saying goes. Feeling "Black and beautiful" becomes an end in itself rather than the source of motivation for improving one's skills or for a deeper understanding of the Black condition. Furthermore, his world-view remains the same—still very American. Cosmologically the person is unchanged, yet psychologically and spiritually the person is significantly different. Generally, the self-concept modifications do make the person receptive to meaningful change in his world-view. In fact, Black revolutionary changes may only be possible *after* Black people have been exposed to a more positive perception of themselves.

The Black theorist, planner, or leader must comprehend that a person does not always experience modification of his political views concurrently with changes in his psychological state. Our audience is not automatically enlightened, but it is now captive.

STAGE FIVE: INTERNALIZATION-COMMITMENT

I would like to regress for a brief moment in order to introduce a concept that will prove valuable in discussing the qualities of a person functioning at the internalization-commitment stage. When a person first decides to change his identity from Negro-to-Black, he generally experiences frightening periods of anxiety that are related to his intense concern over whether or not he is "Black enough," according to his internal definition of the ideal "Black militant" and/or according to the definition of a "perfect" Black person he perceives his peers to hold. Let us refer to this anxiety as "Weusi Anxiety," or anxiety over Blackness (*weusi* is the Swahili word for Black). The degree of experienced Weusi Anxiety varies as a function of the internalization of positive Black attitudes.

In other words, when a person is in the early phases of his transformation, we would predict that his new identity has not been incorporated, in which case he will feel insecure with his new and different frame of reference. He is preoccupied with rejection of his old ideas, values and behavior while romanticizing and oversimplifying his new ideal self. His first encounter with Black pride is really based on the negation of his past and hatred of white people, along with a simplistic rigid code of Blackness *rather than* the affirmation of pro-Black ideas, values and actions. The person's uneasiness with the new frame of reference is demonstrated by the level of Weusi Anxiety, degree of anger and lack of control over anger toward white people, and the limited internalization of a Black perspective. All of these factors in part characterize a restricted withdrawn ego that is protecting itself while "inside" it tries to re-shape, redefine, and rebuild those personality components related to the ego-ideal.

Now let us turn to a description of the person who has reached the fifth stage, Internalization and Commitment. Assuming the person is able to continue his development, it follows that as a Brother or Sister begins to "live" in accordance with a new self-image, he or she will eventually *become* the new identity. The shift is from concern about how your friends see you (Weusi Anxiety) to confidence in one's personal standards of Blackness; from uncontrolled rage toward white people to controlled, felt and conscious anger toward oppressive and racist institutions; from symbolic rhetoric to quiet, dedicated, long-term commitment; from unrealistic urgency to a sense of destiny; from anxious, insecure, rigid, inferiority feelings to Black pride, self-love and a deep sense of Black communalism. As internalization and incorporation increase, attitudes toward white people become less hostile, or at least realistically contained, Weusi Anxiety diminishes, and pro-Black attitudes become more expansive, open, and less defensive. At this point, I am simply describing the stage four (internalization) person in greater detail. The individual functioning at the fifth stage differs from the person in the fourth stage in that he or she is committed to a plan. He is actively trying to change his community. His values, like the stage-four person, will probably still have a decidedly Western overtone. He is going beyond rhetoric and into action and he defines change in terms of the masses of Black people rather than the advancement of a few. Academically speaking, should the person develop a comparative referent (non-Western and Western insights) we have the "ideal" Black person.

The significance of non-Western insights is dramatized when considering the problem of liberating Black scholars. The "Negro" scholar hesitates to become involved in the Black experience because his perspective is distorted by the limitations of the philosophy and epistemology of Western science. At least six factors define the constraints that prevent the Black scholar from attaining personal liberation: (1) Western thought relies primarily on *intellectual* factors as it concomitantly suppresses affective inputs; (2) the behavioral sciences, which have evolved from the rational referent, also deify cognitive functions and minimize the value of emotionally energized behavior; (3) the Western science *rhetoric* suggests nonviolent, rational-intellectual solutions and emphatically rejects violent resolutions as irrational and even "immoral"; (4) racism permeates Western thought to the extent that the social sciences have maintained racism rather than produced models for Black liberation; (5) social scientists have traditionally been content with a statistical, categorical, static, descriptive analysis of the Black community with minimal time and effort spent on prescriptive analysis for rectifying the Black condition;

and (6) a Negro trained in a Western university sees the Black experience as a study in gross pathology or cultural deprivation.

In essence, the Negro Western scholar seeks continued sophistication of intellect as he prays for emotional impotence. Emphasis is on the negation of affect rather than the eruption, embracement and survival of emotion. It is not surprising, therefore, that so-called Negro scholars have not been capable of presenting models for Afro-American liberation, especially when Black liberation must involve two components: first, the discovery, eruption, embracement, and incorporation of affect (Black rage, guilt, and pride); and second, the synthesis of affect with reason. In liberating Black scholars, we should add a third requirement: exposure to non-Western thought.

A final note on stage-five behavior. One of the most striking qualities of many people who are into stage five is the compassion they exhibit toward folks who have not completed the process. They tend to watch over "new recruits," helping them conquer reactionary white hatred, showing them the pitfalls of Black pride without Black skills, prodding the potential Black scholar, artist, or community organizer to have faith in the Black perspective, or firmly but warmly urging the rhetorical scientific communistic anti-religious super-Black "revolutionary" to recapture his Black humanism (etc.). The compassionate stage-five Black person understands and accepts the necessity of all phases of the Negro-to-Black transition, including the rage, anger, and Weusi Anxiety. On the other hand, I have also met Brothers and Sisters who, upon completion of the conversion experience, turn right around and *deny* the necessity for all that "symbolism, ritualism, and rhetoric." This type of person is very arrogant and short-tempered with people who are into their "stage-three super-Black bag." My guess is that this is a form of intellectual arrogance that results from the conviction that reason, thought and unemotionalism represent the essence of the Negro-to-Black transformation. Note the issue is not controlled anger or the synthesis of affect (Black pride) with reason (a plan of action), but the tendency of stage-five intellectualizers to underestimate, or even deny, the importance of anger and rage in the development of Black consciousness.

In closing this section, I turn to the wisdom of Malcolm X, who never forgot or degraded the highly emotional experiences that were a part of his own rebirth. In terms of the five-stage model being discussed in this paper, Malcolm's encounters with stages two, three and four centered around his life as a Black Muslim. Having moved or developed in a different direction with the establishment of the Organization of Afro-American Unity, Malcolm demonstrated great insight into his own renaissance and profound compassion toward the significance of the Muslim movement when he stated . . . "I said I respected the Nation of Islam for its having been a psychologically revitalizing movement and a source of moral and social reform . . ." (p. 359, *Autobiography of Malcolm X*, by Malcolm X and Alex Haley, Grove Press, 1964).

Fate Versus Design

One cannot help noticing the crudity of the process that results because so much is left to chance and the unconscious. The process shows potential for creativity and destruction. It has created new legislation, elected Black officials, created Black Studies Programs, resurrected Black womanhood and manhood, increased the receptivity of the masses to their Black heritage, and cured dope addicts. Yet the process has also been responsible for allowing the death of Malcolm X, the superficial battles between nationalists and Panthers, and students turning against each other in

"Blacker than thou-ness." Perhaps the most dreadful irony is that thousands of Black people were "turned on" to the realities of Black life (their encounter phase) by the murder of Martin Luther King, Jr.

Until the Black community controls and directs the process, we must continue to rely on the jolting consequences of fortuitous events. The Muslims, Panthers and cultural nationalists have helped to lead the way, but each tends to go into a "Blacker-than-thou" bag. We need a program designed to awaken the masses of Black people and to provide a multitude of *options* for actualizing one's Blackness.

Implications of the Process

The contemporary Black experience is a tribute to the masses of Afro-Americans. *Without* the insight and support of a significant vanguard group, the Black masses have formulated and experimented with methods for liberating themselves! The oppressed Black scholar has been freed by the crude, stumbling, unrefined, global expressions of lowly Black folks. It is the challenge, if not the obligation, of Black scholars to study, amplify, and develop those processes which have created conditions of Black liberation, even if these conditions are not to be legitimized in the sacred halls of Western scholarship. The implications of the Black experience when viewed as a process are:

1. The process should be viewed as the *Afro-American model for self-actualization under conditions of oppression.* A relevant Black community will be aware that all stages are necessary, including the eruption of Black rage, guilt and pride.

2. The goals of Black self-actualization will be (a) awareness of the condition of the masses of Black people; (b) development of skills; (c) preparation for participating in the mass struggle of Black people. Change will be de-

fined as actions that affect the lives of large blocks of people (relevant reform). Achievement and reward will be correlated with activities related to the collective good of Black people.

3. Black scholars must understand Black rage as genuine human anger that is manifesting itself all over the world. Black rage, in combination with guilt and pride, is the *fuel* of the Black movement. Our efforts must not mute, distort, or suppress Black rage; rather, we must recognize it for what it is: a potentially creative, productive, and unifying force when programmed by circumstances that are under the conscious control of the Black community.

4. Although he embraces Black rage as a natural and welcome component of the process for discovering the Black referent, the Black scholar must create programs which synthesize affect with ideas that will lead to action.

5. The dynamics of the programs developed to integrate affect and reason must increase the *options* for participation in the Black movement. Either/or, "Blacker-than-thou," or Panther versus nationalist arguments *must* be superseded by paradigms that: (a) teach and define the Black referent (Black condition); (b) allow for the expression of genuine human outrage; (c) synthesize rage, guilt and pride with ideas that lead to productive, creative action; and (d) allow for participation in the struggle on various levels. Even under conditions of revolutionary warfare, not every "revolutionary" is carrying a gun. Therefore, whether we speak of relevant reform or preparation for revolution, the options for participation in the Black struggle must be increased.

This entire discussion has been appropriately titled, "Towards A Psychology of Black Liberation," for several reasons. In the first place, one person *cannot* capture the essence and spirit of the modern Black Revitalization Movement; thus, a definitive statement from the psychological perspective will result from collaboration with other Black psychologists and psychiatrists, such as William S. Hall, Thomas White and Alvin Poussaint. Furthermore, the conversion model is really an adult experience, while a completed psychology of Black liberation *must* also create socialization models and child-rearing techniques that will demonstrate to Black parents how to raise children in the image and likeness of Black heroes who resisted oppression. For these reasons the above five-stage model is a step toward the establishment of a psychology of Black liberation. A completed version will include a refined model that depicts the conversion of deracinated Negroes into Afro-Americans; articulation of socialization or identification models based on the lives of Malcolm, W. E. B. DuBois, Angela Davis, Marcus Garvey (etc.); and elucidation of child-rearing techniques which will facilitate the actualization of the militant socialization models.

Harambee and Love.

PART V

*Toward a Black
Perspective in
Social Research*

Joseph Scott

Black Science and Nation-Building

What is the relevance of the scientific method for Black research conducted on the Black experience? In what specific
ways can science be applied in sociology, psychology, political science and economics? What have been the limitations of
the application of the scientific method in the past when applied to Blacks? In the following essay, the author attempts
to answer these questions by analyzing several popular "white
experience" models, showing their irrelevance to Blacks and
proposing alternative models based on the Black experience.

Science has been defined both as a set of methods and
techniques, and as a body of facts, theories and models.[1]
In methodological terms, science is one of the ways man
can know about the real world and can change the conditions of the real world if he finds them unsatisfactory. What
makes scientific knowledge different from intuitive knowl-

[1] William J. Goode and Paul K. Hatt, *Methods in Social Research*
(New York: McGraw-Hill, 1952).

edge is that the values of science require that scientific knowledge be verifiable and empirical—experiential. This causes scientists to use sampling designs, experimentation and classification. The knowledge derived by these methods consists of verifiable observations and generalizations, which we call facts and theories respectively.

The use of science is mandatory for Black people if they are to get and keep control over the physical and social forces that determine their life-chances. Nation-building requires that they be able to control not only a national territory but also the natural resources, natural forces, economic forces, social forces, political forces, and psychological forces that make life possible or impossible. One of the first prerequisites of nation-building is knowledge. Black people will not be able to develop themselves as a people and develop their land (once they get it) into a productive, harmonious place to live and work without specialized knowledge.

Today as Blacks apply the existing theories and models in an attempt to make life more predictable and to get control over the external and internal forces that shape their lives, they are finding that the theories and models which were developed on whites do not apply well to Blacks. Scientific knowledge in the social sciences in this country is mostly a body of facts and generalizations about white experience. More specifically, it is about the white middle-class experience. In the behavioral sciences, for example, the attitude tests have been "validated" on white people. The intelligence tests have been "standardized" on white people. The statistical curves "represent" the response patterns of white people. The theories of society, of government, of economy, of education and of personality are descriptive of white people.

These observations should tell us something: either present practices are invalid, or it is scientifically valid to focus exclusively on one societal group and to generalize from this for all other societal groups. Scientific knowledge claims not to be culture-bound or race-bound, but the assertion of universality does not make it empirically so. Black social scientists must be extremely skeptical of any research, theories or models that come out of exclusively white experience. They must not be misled into believing that there is no difference between white experience and Black experience, for in America whites have not been slaves or peons for three hundred and fifty years as Blacks have been; whites have never been disenfranchised as Blacks have been; whites have never been chattels or property as Blacks have been; whites have never been subject to systematic exploitation by means of legislative and legal decrees. Thus the theories, models and generalizations about government, economy, education and personality cannot possibly be the same for white people as for Black people. The scientific concepts and categories may come close, but they can hardly be a "good fit." Some types of white experience may coincide with some patterns of the Black experience, and some psychological illnesses may be the same as those found in the Black communities, but they can hardly be derived from the same type of racial oppression.

To continue to equate white experience with Black experience is fraudulent behavior. Black social scientists of the future who have had these errors brought to their attention will not be able to claim that they are not being deceptive when they start trying to predict and to explain Black life by white-experience models and theories. They will simply be identified as unwilling or unable to use a Black perspective. Applicable theories and models must be those derived from the experiences of Blacks as perceived and reacted to by Blacks. For example, regardless of how much whites see the Vietnam war as a struggle to make the world "safe for democracy," for Blacks, the war is a nightmare, a struggle to make "democracy safe for the world," an imperialistic threat to the world.

Virtually everything that maximizes the benefits and profits of whites means more exploitation of Black peoples. So in observing the operation of social, economic, political and psychological forces in the empirical world, the vantage point must be that of Black peoples. The way to acquire the Black perspective is to see the impact these forces have on their lives.

As researches are conducted and interpreted from the viewpoint of Black experience, almost every contemporary theory in the behavioral sciences will require modification. Several Black scholars have already begun the call for a new orientation.

Robert Chrisman, editor of *The Black Scholar*, and professor of English, has suggested that "the vanguard of black intellectuals, artists and behavioral scientists"[2] address themselves to the development of revolutionary values and resources latent among Black Americans. The intellectuals, artists, and scientists must, he feels, develop standards for the fine arts, and develop techniques of behavioral science that fit the Black experience. He believes that the present cultural schemes, concepts, and theories (like functionalism) of the Anglo-American cannot answer the needs of Afro-Americans, for contemporary culture is largely the culture of oppressors, and its contents relate mostly to how to oppress others, not how to liberate others. The Anglo-American culture was in large part developed to enslave and subjugate Blacks, so what the intellectuals, artists and behavioral scientists must do, according to Chrisman, is to "analyze, in truth and depth, Black class structure, Black economic conditions, the psychology of Blackness, and translate that analysis into practical formulas for revolutionary action."[3] Further, we must develop a Black propa-

[2] Robert Chrisman, "The Formation of a Revolutionary Black Culture," *The Black Scholar*, 8 (June 1970), pp. 2–9.
[3] *Ibid.*, p. 8.

ganda system, a revolutionary esthetic and the mechanism for mutual criticism between the vanguard and the Black community.

James M. Jones, a Black social psychologist, discussing the Black perspective in the study of Black political behavior, writes: "Black politics is the art and science of moving black people from a present, objective reality which is oppressive to a new reality, which is the liberation from that oppression."[4] The "moving" of Black people requires knowledge of the oppressor and his conditions of oppression. Jones has concluded correctly that "knowledge is relevant because knowledge is control, and control is what we need, what we must have."[5]

Black political scientists, he adds, must be about the business of "Black culture, Black ideology, Black revolution." In a sense there is only one objective to Black politics— Black liberation. And Black political scientists should lead the way. Jones suggests that Black political scientists must be oriented toward "the liberation of Black people from the political control of an alien power."[6] They must help to "wrest control from the hands of the alien powers, and to control our own behavior and value systems."[7]

Joseph White,[8] a Black psychologist, writes: "Black psychologists are still operating with a lot of assumptions and machinery that have been developed by white psychologists primarily for white people." As an alternative, he suggests that Black psychologists start legitimizing Black experience and building psychological models based on that experience. The behavior of Black children, he adds, must be viewed as positive responses to a "complicated and hostile

[4] James M. Jones, "The Political Dimensions of Black Liberation," *The Black Scholar*, i (September 1971), pp. 67-75.
[5] *Ibid.*, p. 73.
[6] *Ibid.*, p. 67.
[7] *Ibid.*, p. 69.
[8] See "Guidelines for Black Psychologists," this volume.

environment" and evaluated from the point of view of "mental toughness," "survival skills," "cleverness and originality," rather than as pathological or deviant behavior. White concludes that Black psychologists "must begin to develop a model of Black psychology which is free from the built-in assumptions and values of the dominant culture."

Robert C. Vowels,[9] a Black economist, has charged that "In the real world where the political economy of American racism holds indisputable sway, nonblack decision-making within nonblack organizations poses a formidable barrier to black higher status employment opportunities and aspiration."[10] He adds that contemporary economics "tend to deemphasize racial economic discrimination as a factor in the economic problems of minority groups."[11] Yet all sorts of white agencies, corporations and organizations making economic decisions are using race as a factor in their decision-making, and the market result is that Blacks pay more for goods and services and receive less. Perhaps even more important, schools, housing, food and other goods and services are denied Blacks altogether, whether they can pay the unfair prices or not. Vowels sums it up nicely: "When everyone is poor, black people are even poorer. And when everyone is prosperous, black people are still poor."[12]

What Black economists must do, he feels, is to include the factor of racial discrimination in their economic analyses and models. If the dynamics of racial discrimination are included in the theories and models, a new economics might emerge with different types of supply-and-demand relationships. Since racial discrimination is such an important market force in the lives of Blacks, and since it is left out of all

[9] Robert C. Vowels, "The Political Economy of American Racism—Nonblack Decision-Making and Black Economic Status," *The Review of Black Political Economy*, 4 (Summer 1971), pp. 3–42.

[10] *Ibid.*, p. 28.

[11] *Ibid.*, p. 4.

[12] *Ibid.*, p. 24.

major economic theories and models, it is logical to conclude that these present theories and models do not apply to Blacks. Black economists thus have a major goal, according to Henry Coleman, "to find a solution to the color problem that you know exists."[13]

Examples of Inapplicable White Experience Models and Theories
An Assimilation Theory

Robert Park,[14] a white sociologist, believed that he had accurately represented the Black experience when he applied his white-derived model to Afro-Americans. He characterized U.S. race relations as a process of evolving through five stages, with assimilation the final stage. The processual model was:

Contact $\longrightarrow$ Competition $\longrightarrow$ Conflict $\longrightarrow$ Accommodation $\longrightarrow$ Assimilation. (Presumably assimilation refers to full integration into the organizations, agencies, corporations, and institutions of "the mainstream.")

This model, however, which is derived from white experience, reflects neither the range nor the quality nor the subtleties of the Black experience.

A Black experience model would be quite different from Park's and definitely different from the experience models of the Irish, the Germans, the Scandinavians and other white ethnic groups. A Black model would "tell it like it has been and like it is now." For example, it would reflect the fact that Afro-Americans have been a captive people

[13] Henry A. Coleman, "Student Symposium—Economics, With or Without Color?," *The Review of Black Political Economy*, 4 (Summer 1971), p. 142.

[14] Robert E. Park, *Race and Culture* (New York: Free Press, 1950).

who are still under a colonialistic system of domination and exploitation. It would reflect the despotic power still entrenched in the grasp of the white power elite, and it would reflect the struggle for liberation by Black people. From my study of cultural, legal and economic history, a processual model based on Afro-American experience would be as follows:

White Strategies	*Black Strategies*
Epoch 1. Despotism ......[1]→	[2]←...... Abolitionism
Epoch 2. Jim Crowism ......[3]→	[4]←...... Neo-Abolitionism
Epoch 3. Integrationism ...[5]→	[6]← Communal Separatism
Epoch 4. Containmentism ..[7]→	[8]←.. National Separatism

In short, from the beginning of time, the relationship has been one of overt and covert conflict. There is no period not dominated by conflict.

The Consumer Sovereignty Theory

A second white experience model is found in economics. One basic theory in economics is the Consumer Sovereignty Theory.[15] This theory posits first that the consumer can make highly rational distinctions between products and prices in the marketplace, and second that the producer-sellers have no individual control over consumer choices, product pricing and aggregate demand. The postulated process is that the consumer stimulates the producer-seller into producing saleable products, which are priced in terms of the costs of production and other competitors in the

[15] John Kenneth Galbraith, *The New Industrial State* (New York: The New American Library, Inc., 1967).

market, who are all supposed to be operating independently in such a way as to keep the prices of the products close to the costs of making the products. In sum, the transaction begins with the consumers suggesting products to the producer-sellers and determining the prices mostly by what they, the consumers, are supposedly willing to pay. Thus the consumer is the sovereign figure in the producer-seller-consumer exchange.

A model based on Black experience would suggest that the producer-sellers are sovereign. It would reflect the fact that the Black consumer is manipulated by the various participants[16] in the marketplace—peddlers, retailers, advertisers, bankers, financiers and salesmen; that the producer-sellers do not wait to be stimulated by the Black consumer but produce products at their own initiative which they "market" or "sell" by various mechanisms—"buy-now-pay-later arrangements," "revolving charge accounts" and so on. Finally, the model would reflect the fact that Black consumers are designated "high risk" creditors and are denied the usual low-interest credit and the usual high-quality products, which are accessible only through the regular retail outlets that accept only low-risk creditors. Forced into a dilemma, Black consumers must either do without what they need or pay exorbitantly high interest rates and service charges to retailers of questionable repute who sell low-quality goods at high-quality prices and use various mechanisms to induce perpetual indebtedness.

The Deferred Gratification Theory

White social psychologists have made much ado about the deferred-gratification pattern of middle-class white children, arguing that Black children have not usually de-

16 David Caplovitz, *The Poor Pay More* (New York: Free Press, 1967).

veloped this trait and are thus more impulsive and non-rational in their behavior. They claim that white children are taught to delay immediate gratification for greater future rewards; to be future-oriented rather than present-oriented, inhibited rather than hedonistic, but that Blacks (and other lower-class children), who have not been taught by their parents to delay immediate gratification, do not make the long-range plans required for socioeconomic advancement.

High aspirations and achievements supposedly require a future orientation, the ability to defer gratification. Non-deferred gratification is said to lead to impulsive behavior, which is often antisocial, nonutilitarian and nonproductive. Thus Black children show higher rates of detected deviance and low achievement than white children.

It is evident to anyone acquainted with the Black experience in America that lower racial status is tantamount to a life of forced menial labor and a scarcity of food, clothing, shelter and police protection. In short, a deferred gratification pattern as a perpetual way of life is not a matter of personal preference. Young Black children, because of the societal rationing of those things making up "the good life," learn to live with deprivation much better than white children. Black children learn to defer immediate gratification as a regular fact of life; to expect very little future reward for persistent hard work and self-denial. White children can reasonably expect a future reward from immediate investments in inhibition, but Blacks cannot. The only ways out for Blacks are to sanctify the impoverished life or to profane it. The profane behavior of Black children is often the *result* of an imposed deferred gratification pattern, rather than the result of a lack of experience with it. The Deferred Gratification Theory is obviously a white experience theory, based on the reasonable expectations inherent in middle-class white life, rather than on the reasonable expectations of future reward inherent in Black lower-status life. Thus it is inapplicable to Black children.

The Multidisciplinary Approach
to the Black Experience

The Black experience itself in the United States is in essence a multifaceted experience, neither primarily economic, nor primarily political, nor primarily psychological, nor primarily sociological. It is all of these and more; it is also historical. The white oppressor (and that is what he has been, with no racism implied) not only erected economic barriers to Black advancement and productivity, but erected social, political and psychological barriers as well.

To use a metaphor, the institutional barriers are like rows and rows of intertwined barbed-wire fences surrounding a Black population which is in the main young, eager, talented, idealistic and energetic. The first fence could be thought of as the judicial and legislative barriers; the second fence, as the economic barriers to commerce and labor; the third fence, as the psychological barriers, specifically educational barriers which keep Blacks from acquiring the knowledge and skill to be creative, self-sustaining and productive; the fourth fence, as racial barriers which deny equal access to public accommodations and to purely social areas. Finally, these various rows of barriers, which keep Blacks disabled, disadvantaged and dispossessed in the competition for life, liberty and property, are themselves interlaced and reenforced by wires of racism which tie them together in a mutually supportive way. Under these conditions, one barrier cannot be removed without severing all the racist ties as well. Together, these barriers create a very difficult set of conditions to break through, especially when there are supporting troops to repair any breaches that Blacks might make from time to time.

Given the multiplicity of barriers to Black progress, the approach to overcoming these conditions must obviously be manifold. Malcolm X came to realize this and advocated "all means necessary" to overturn the situation. Malcolm was hearing voices of the past, the voices of Garnet, Holly, Hall, Turner, Delaney, Trotter, DuBois, Garvey, Douglass, Washington, Randolph, King, Young, and he came to the conclusion that there are layers of barriers superimposed on one another, tied together by racism. Contrary to what many Blacks think, the barriers are not like a circular stockade of tree trunks, with each trunk representing a different barrier—economic, political, social, psychological, etc.—so that all Blacks have to do is knock over one trunk to break out. A more appropriate model, as we have said, is a series of barbed-wire fences intertwined one behind the other and tied together by reenforcing wires of racism. This means that litigation, legislation, emigration, demonstration, rebellion, destruction, assimilation, separation, education, commercialization and coalition, among other strategies, are all essential ways of breaking through the barriers that constrain and thwart Black people. All types of means were necessary in the past, and they are still necessary today.

The contemporary Black assault troops are manifold in their approach: The Black Panthers, The National Urban League, The National Association for the Advancement of Colored People, The Black Muslims, The Afro-American Repatriation Society, The Congress of Racial Equality, and The United Negro College Fund. Considering them all together, we have almost all the means that we need; judicial, legislative, economic, political and psychological movements operating to liberate Blacks.

Given the fact that there are a variety of liberation movements afoot among Blacks today—and that their various strategies have been refined over the past three hundred years—Black behavioral scientists must become multidisciplinary in their approach. They must be able to contribute analyses that include the interactional effects of the imposed economic, political, social and psychological barriers facing Black people. Their Black experience models must reflect the manifold reality. Their theories must focus on the interrelated strategies for overcoming all the barriers simultaneously, not just one barrier at a time.

From the Sociological Perspective

According to some recent studies, Afro-Americans are more residentially segregated now in major cities than they were a decade ago. The 1970 *Current Population Reports, Series P-23, No. 38,* indicate that three of every five Blacks in the United States live in a central city of a major metropolitan area, and the rate at which Blacks have been herded into the central cities has been increasing; the percentage has increased from 59 percent in 1950 to 74 percent in 1970.

From the *Bureau of Labor Statistics Bulletin 1699* of 1971 we learn: "Urban Blacks have been segregated, residentially, and indications are that their segregation has been increasing through the mid-1960's.[17] Residential segregation has many consequences. One of these is school segregation; Blacks have, since 1950, become increasingly segregated in schools, and it is now public knowledge that many Northern schools are more segregated than some schools in the South.

An incredible result of forced school segregation is subeducation. Black schools get less support, in terms of facilities and trained faculties, than white schools. The white-controlled school administrations have been known to manipulate the hiring of teachers and to concentrate the lowest-quality white teachers in schools for Black children. Rejected white teachers from white schools are commonly assigned to schools where there is a predominance of Black

[17] *Ibid.,* p. 14.

children. The better teachers are dissuaded from asking for assignments in schools that are predominantly Black. The net result is inferior instruction for Black children. The longer Black children remain in such schools, the less well prepared they become and the less well they perform on national achievement tests (which are in any case biased toward middle-class standards). The U.S. government found in its study that "The gap in achievement levels between Negro and white students widened between the sixth and twelfth grades."[18] According to national tests, at the end of the twelve years Blacks have received an average of only nine years of education.

White employers use the results of educational achievement tests to discriminate against Blacks in salaries. Often this discrimination goes beyond merely adjusting wages proportionate to the degree that their education does not measure up; Blacks may be offered a lower amount of money than whites with the same degree of education simply because they are powerless to negotiate for a higher salary. The difference has been estimated at about a thousand dollars per male. The Council of Economic Advisers reported in 1965: "If Negroes received the same average pay as whites having the same education, the personal income of Negroes and of the Nation would be $12.8 billion higher."[19] The final result is that "At each educational level, Black men have less income than white men. The disparity is greatest at the college level."[20]

---

[18] *Ibid.*, p. 86.
[19] Council of Economic Advisers, "The Economic Cost of Discrimination," in John F. Kain, *Race and Poverty: The Economics of Discrimination* (Englewood Cliffs, N.J.: Prentice-Hall), p. 58.
[20] *Ibid.*, p. 82.

From the Psychological Perspective

Behind racial discrimination are both a private set of attitudes and a tacit public consensus among whites that Blacks are to be kept unequal. Even nonprejudiced officials discriminate racially in attempts to satisfy the tacit agreement among whites to keep Blacks out of certain residential, occupational and educational spheres.

Social psychologists have recently studied the attitudes of white citizens on a national scale.[21] They have found that whites have no great inclination to bring Blacks home to dinner, to share the same residential areas with them, to intermarry or to extend any other private sectors of their lives to include Blacks. The whites in the South favor discrimination more than those in the North, and their attitudes against full participation by Blacks in all areas of society are stronger. The authors of the study conclude: "Certainly there is no evidence that the majority of American whites eagerly look forward to integration. Most are more comfortable in a segregated society, and they would prefer that the demonstrators slow down or go away while things are worked out more gradually."[22]

On an eight-point scale measuring pro-integration sentiment, the average score for white Americans was around 4.3. Full integration into the institutional life of the society in the minds of many Blacks means liberation. In the minds of many whites, too, full integration means the liberation of Blacks from social, political and economic shackles. The social-psychological data on the attitudes of whites clearly indicate that they are not enthusiastic about this. This negative attitude governs the making and implementing of

[21] Paul B. Sheatsley, "White Attitudes Toward the Negro," pp. 128–38.
[22] *Ibid.*, p. 138.

political and economic decisions resulting in residential, occupational and educational subordination in American society.

From the Political Perspective

From political scientists we learn that the subordination of
Blacks in the United States has been forced and financed
by the officials of the federal and state governments. For
example, in the area of residential segregation, the Federal
Housing Administration has practiced a policy of guaran-
teeing mortgages only in racially segregated areas. An FHA
manual stated: "If a neighborhood is to retain stability, it is
necessary that properties shall continue to be occupied by
the same society and race group." During the 1950's millions of homes built mostly in the suburban areas were, by
mortgage denials, closed to Blacks. The federal government
in effect financed the white exodus from the central cities
and forced the containment of Blacks there. The containment practice is still in effect, as sociologists have discovered.

Segregated education is a second example of government
facilitation of racial discrimination. As previously stated,
Black children are more segregated in schools today than
they were a decade ago; this is because the government
implementers of the School Desegregation Decision of 1954
have permitted the forces of segregation to continue to
operate almost unhindered. Government agencies like
HEW have adhered to a doctrine of gradualism. Officials
of the judicial and executive branches of the government
have implemented the decision in such a way that token
integration could satisfy the requirements of the law. They
have not required "racial balance," nor have they required
"representative proportions" in school desegregation plans.

Support of segregation by the federal government has

not stopped with the public education system; it has been practiced throughout the public manpower training programs as well. Herbert Hill of the NAACP has found that "Negroes, with some few exceptions, are being limited to programs that simply perpetuate the traditional concentration of Negroes in menial and unskilled jobs."[23] Hill also found: "The Department of Health, Education, and Welfare each year distributes fifty-five millions of dollars of federal funds for education under the Smith-Hughes Act; a very large part of this is given to vocational training programs in which Negroes are totally excluded or limited to unequal segregated facilities."[24] Instance after instance of governmental policy and implementation of policy resulting in the subeducation of Black Americans can be presented.

Finally, there is federal government facilitation of employment discrimination. Even though the federal government has had a fair-employment practices policy for decades, it has not stopped employers' discrimination practices. Employers have been able to conduct "business as usual." Gradualism has been the doctrine followed by the government in its attempt to force compliance with the nondiscrimination provisions of the various codes and contracts, and the result is that little change in Black employment patterns has occurred. Even the Equal Employment Opportunities Commission has not produced any significant changes. A key reason for this, we learn from the *Wall Street Journal* of July 22, 1969, is that the EEOC has decided against public hearings to question employers about their discriminatory hiring practices. The net result is that billions of dollars in government contracts have been awarded to corporations and universities that do not comply

[23] Herbert Hill, "Racial Inequality in Employment: The Patterns of Discrimination," in John F. Kain, *op. cit.*, p. 82.
[24] *Ibid.*, p. 83.

with fair employment practices standards. The government provision outlawing discrimination in employment by corporations and universities holding U.S. government contracts has not been enforced. It should not be surprising, therefore, that despite the laws, codes, executive orders and policies, Blacks are still by and large concentrated in the same sectors, paid the same low wages, as they were at the time of the Emancipation Proclamation.

From the Economic Perspective

As we have seen, segregation has a psychological, sociological and political side. Let us now look at the economic side. Economic researchers have found that "the incidence of substandard units is higher, at every income category, for owners as well as renter Negro families,[25] and that "the poor condition of Negro housing arises from discriminatory treatment in the housing market, so that the purchasing power of the dollar spent by nonwhites is less than that of the dollar spent by whites."[26] The data from several studies indicate that Blacks at all rental levels "show a higher proportion of substandard units than do whites."[27] Blacks not only receive less quality for the money they pay, they also "obtain smaller units than whites." One economist, after one such extensive study, has concluded that "the Negro who achieves middle-class status is rewarded in the housing market by an increasing burden of price and locational discrimination."[28] The pricing and supplying mechanisms for housing and residential areas clearly operate to deny the Black American his "just dues."

In the area of education, certain economic mechanisms

[25] Chester Rapkin, "Price Discrimination Against Negroes in the Rental Housing Market," in John F. Kain, *op. cit.*, p. 113.
[26] *Ibid.*, p. 113.
[27] *Ibid.*, p. 114.
[28] *Ibid.*, p. 121.

operate to keep Blacks subeducated. Investing less money in the development of a Black child than one invests in the development of a white is one such mechanism. Investments in human development in the form of education and training are essential for any society to maintain itself over time. Nevertheless economists have found that "the value of the stock of human capital embodied in the average male adult Negro is on the order of $10,000 smaller than the human capital embodied in the average white male."[29]

The Council of Economic Advisers has corroborated this finding in its own study, which concluded: "If Negroes also had the same educational attainments as white workers, and earned the same pay and experienced the same unemployment as whites, their personal income—and that of the nation—would be $20.6 billion higher."[30]

Some employment discrimination, too, is based on economic mechanisms. Because of the powerlessness of Blacks, whites have used them for capital accumulation. The fruits of Black labor have been siphoned off through various wage-price devices. By underpaying Blacks for over three hundred years, whites have drained Blacks to the point of near-bankruptcy.

A second mechanism is job allocation processes. The industrial managers of the economy have, over the past hundred years, successfully pushed Blacks from the central position as the main source of skilled labor, relegating them to the marginal parts of the economy. William Tabb, an economist, writes: "The economy provides work for the Black underclass, but not the chance for advancement. The labor market, in fact, functions to maintain Blacks in the role of exploited undifferentiated labor. Most Blacks are allowed only a marginal attachment to the labor force."[31]

[29] Barbara R. Bergmann, "Investment in the Human Resources of Negroes," in John F. Kain, *op. cit.*, p. 52.

[30] Council of Economic Advisers, in John F. Kain, *op. cit.*, p. 59.

[31] William K. Tabb, *The Political Economy of the Black Ghetto* (New York: W. W. Norton & Co., 1971), p. 106.

The Department of Labor confirms this: Black families earn only about 62 percent of what white families earn, and they are unemployed and underemployed two to three times more often.

The industrial executives, who "manage" the labor market in the United States, discriminate racially in the process of economic decision making. "In a slack labor market, employers can pick and choose, both in recruiting and in promoting. They exaggerate the skill, education, and experience requirements of their jobs. They use diplomas, or color, or personal histories as convenient screening devices. In a tight market, they are forced to be realistic, to tailor job specifications to the available supply, and to give on-the-job training."[32]

Economic decisions can be—and are—skewed racially by tacit collusion and informal agreement.

Conclusion

Based on what has been said, we may conclude that the methodological aims of Black researchers should be: First, to perceive, record and theorize about the external world from the viewpoint of Black people; second, to apply to Black people explanatory models and theories which are derived solely from Black rather than white experience; third, to reevaluate and expose the inapplicabilities of all white experience theories and models as they have been applied to Black behavior; fourth, to be ideologically nonconformist and technically innovative in setting about the tasks of problem selection, data gathering and concept

[32] James Tobin, "Improving the Economic Status of the Negro," in *The Negro American*, Talcott Parsons and Kenneth B. Clark, eds. (Boston: Houghton-Mifflin Co., 1966), p. 456.

building; fifth, to be Black value-oriented instead of value-free in the interpretation of data and in conclusions; sixth, to approach data interpretation from the standpoint of how the data contribute to Black liberation and Black nation-building.

Robert Blauner and David Wellman

Toward the Decolonization
of Social Research

The relationship of the researcher to his subject has been defined as being similar to that of the oppressor to the oppressed.
Two white social scientists, Robert Blauner and David Wellman, here use the colonial analogy to analyze the methods by
which social research conducted in the Black community may
be "decolonized," and, based on their actual experiences as
researchers on such a project, discuss some of the sensitivities
the researcher must have.

During the 1960's many assumptions of the academic
world were challenged by events both external and internal
to the campuses. There was a growing tendency for powerless and excluded social groups to view academics and their
activities politically, to criticize their relation to, and responsibility for, existing economic, social and ideological
arrangements. In Latin America as well as Europe and
North America, debates raged on the political commitments
of social science. Calls arose for a radical sociology and

new political sciences, histories and anthropologies that would identify with the interests of oppressed classes and groups.

The relationship of social research to ethnic and racial minorities came under particular attack. The idea of internal colonialism was advanced in Latin America as a framework for interpreting the subjugation of Indian populations, and in the United States it became an important paradigm with respect to the oppression of Blacks, Chicanos and other Third World people.[1] Though no one seriously questioned the positive contributions that past social science had made to the liberalized climate in which subjugated groups were presently intensifying their struggles, the new perspective indicated that social science research was itself caught up in the colonial relationship between white institutional power and the communities of people of color. As ethnic and racial consciousness exploded in the Black Power movement, the social scientist began to look like another agent of the white power structure. Like the policeman, storekeeper, teacher and welfare worker, he was usually a white outsider who entered ghettos and barrios to advance personal and institutional goals that

[1] It appears as if the Latin American and North American theories developed for the most part independently of one another. See Pablo Gonzalez Casanova, *Internal Colonialism and National Development* (St. Louis: Washington University Monograph Series, Studies in Comparative International Development, I, no. 4, 1965), and Rodolpho Stavenhagen, "Classes, Colonialism and Acculturation," *Studies in Comparative International Development*, I, No. 6 (1965). For a statement similar in outlook to the present essay, see Stavenhagen, "Decolonizing Applied Social Sciences," *Human Organization*, 30, No. 4 (Winter 1971), pp. 333-57. For discussions of internal colonialism in the United States, see Harold Cruse, *Rebellion or Revolution* (New York: William Morrow & Co., Inc., 1968); Stokely Carmichael and Charles Hamilton, *Black Power* (New York: Vintage Books, 1967); Robert Allen, *Black Awakening in Capitalist America* (Garden City, N.Y.: Doubleday, 1969); Robert Blauner, "Internal Colonialism and Ghetto Revolt," *Social Problems*, 16, No. 4 (Spring 1969); and Mario Barrera, Carlos Munoz, and Charles Ornelas, "The Barrio as Internal Colony," in Harlan Hahn, ed., *Urban Affairs Annual Review*, Vol. 6 (1972).

were determined outside of the community of study. His authority to diagnose group problems and interpret culture and life-styles conflicted with the demands for group self-definition and self-determination that were central to the new consciousness of the racially oppressed. From such a perspective, the fact that the major studies and analyses of Third World people in the United States have been carried out by whites took on new significance.[2]

Movements toward decolonization, which have shaken other areas of culture and politics, thus confronted social research. Social scientists studying race and poverty in the 1960's found that the norms of pure disinterested scientific investigation were no longer adequate. The "subjects" had changed from "passive objects" to active critics of the research process. The experiences of our own study, the subject of this paper, were profoundly influenced by this new dialogue between social scientists and the racially oppressed.

In 1965 when the senior author began work in the area of Black-white relations, he was impressed by an apparent centrality of what might be termed "manhood issues" for understanding both racism and the comparative position of Negroes in American society. His initial theoretical approach to the low status and problems of Black people was in terms of cultural and social determinants within the group, paralleling the sociologists' attempts to understand the relative mobility of various European and Asian ethnic groups in terms of distinctive group characteristics. He

---

[2] In the United States the most strategic expression of this clash took place in the community and academic response to the "Moynihan Report." In Latin America the pivotal case of research serving American imperialism was Project Camelot, a Defense Department financed study of internal conflict that was attacked as a counterinsurgency operation. On the relatively more complete research colonialism in the study of Mexican-Americans as compared to Afro-Americans, see "Chicano Writing," in Robert Blauner, *Racial Oppression in America* (New York: Harper and Row, 1972).

was struck by indications of strong tension between men and women in the Black community and by a variety of data which suggested that women tended to be relatively more resourceful, assertive and perhaps "less damaged" by the legacies of slavery and discrimination. An early hypothesis was that Black lower-class society had innovated a concept of manhood—a street or hustling ideal—that, while viable as a survival technique, actually functioned to impede the integration and success of individuals—and by aggregation, the group as a whole.

About this time Moynihan's report became public. His perspective overlapped with our own in many ways, though there were significant differences. For our work, the key point about *The Negro Family* was not any new facts or theories, but the dialogue opened up by this controversial document. The critical responses, both reasoned and emotional, from the Black community and its scholars as well as from white social scientists, were important "inputs" for the clarification of our theoretical position. The emergence of the Black Power perspective the following year, as well as our continuous involvement with groups and individuals in the ghetto, also sharpened our awareness of the complex theoretical and political issues of contemporary racism.

In addition, our own staff members who knew racial oppression from firsthand experience forced us to look more closely at the realities of race. We saw that such questions as manhood and male-female relations could not be isolated from the larger structural pattern of racial domination. To place the problem in its original fashion, no matter how sophisticated and sensitive our research, would have clear theoretical and political consequences. As Moynihan must know by now, *emphasis* is not just a matter of style. Emphasis has substantive implications. Our original one implied a denial of the historical and contemporary power of racism, of power and privilege, as first causes of our racial arrangements. We therefore transformed our

project's focus, giving primary interest to racism and institutional conflict, and reshaping within this larger context
our concerns with manhood and culture.

Important as theory is, it cannot by itself resolve the
contradictions inherent in studies of race relations and Third
World groups that are conceived and directed by white
social scientists. As our project progressed, we became
more and more aware of these built-in conflicts between
the colonial aspects of racial research and our identification
with decolonization movements, between the institutional
and professional context of social science and our critical
posture toward established theory and practice in sociology.
In this paper we attempt an understanding of these contradictions and at the same time discuss the attempts we
made—only partly successful—to move in the direction
of decolonization. We have organized our ideas around
three sources of the problem that seem the most critical:
first, the essentially inegalitarian character of the research
relationship; second, its specially oppressive relation to
people of color and their communities; and third, the intensification of these dynamics which stems from the structure of the university as setting and sponsor of social research.

Social Research as a Reflection of Social Inequality

SOURCES OF THE PROBLEM

Scientific research does not exist in a vacuum. Its theory
and practice reflect the structure and values of society. In
capitalist America, where massive inequalities in wealth
and power exist between classes and racial groups, the
processes of social research express both race and class op-

pression. The control, exploitation and privilege that are generic components of social oppression exist in the relation of researchers to researched, even though their manifestations may be subtle and masked by professional ideologies.[3]

The behavioral scientist's control over the research enterprise, including all the intergroup interaction which he sets in motion, is supported by the norms of professional autonomy and expertise. According to this view, only the social scientist can define a suitable problem for research because he or she alone knows enough about the theories of the field and the methods by which theories are tested. In this model of science there is no place for the community-of-those-studied to share in the determination of research objectives. The theories, the interests, and the very concepts with which we work respond to the dynamics of increasing knowledge within our individual disciplines and professions, as well as to fashions and status concerns. The life problems and needs of the communities-under-study affect the scholar only indirectly; they are rarely the starting point for theory and research. A similar imbalance in control exists at the point of research production: the administration of a test or questionnaire, the conducting of an interview, even the moment when a participant observer sees something in the field and makes a mental note for his diary. At every stage there is a gulf between the researcher's purposes and the subject's awareness of what the investigator and his research instrument is all about.

Consider the norm of the in-depth interview—the respondent is expected to spill his guts about various aspects of his personal life and his social or political beliefs; the interviewer is supposed to be a neutral recorder, revealing

---

[3] An upsurge of critical questioning of the social scientist's ethical and political role in the mid-1960's is indicated in the publication of *Ethics, Politics, and Social Research*, Gideon Sjoberg, ed. (Cambridge, Mass.: Schenkman Publishing Co., 1967).

nothing in return about his own life, feelings, or opinions—this might "bias" the data. The monopoly of control continues through the stages of analyzing and publishing the results of a study. The individual research subject's unique outlook and specific responses are typically lost in the aggregate of data which are subjected to standardized statistical summaries, ideal type classifications, or some other operation. Because behavioral scientists write for other scholars and "experts," those who are studied usually can't make head or tail of the research report toward which their own responses contributed. The communication gap between researcher and researched, which probably exceeds that between doctor and patient, serves to maintain the inequality of power between the two mutually interdependent parties and underlies the privileged status and elite outlook that social scientists enjoy in a class society.

Exploitation exists whenever there is a markedly unequal exchange between two parties, and when this inequality is *supported* by a discrepancy in social power. In social research, subjects give up some time, some energy and some trust, but in the typical case get almost nothing from the transaction. As social scientists, we get grants which pay our salaries; the research thesis legitimates our professional status, then publications advance us along in income and rank, further widening the material and status gaps between the subjects and ourselves. Thus many of us know ghetto residents who have said, partly boasting, partly complaining, that they have put a dozen people through graduate school, so studied have some Black communities been. Of course, once a study is completed, the chances are that no one in the community ever sees the researcher again. There may be less unhappiness at being used in this way by a budding scholar from one's own ethnic group—but this doesn't change the essentially exploitative character of the relationship, since minority social scientists are still groping toward the forms that would relate their careers to their communities of origin in a meaningful way. Thus there is a growing hostility to universities in many Black ghettos (such hostility and indifference has probably always existed among Chicanos).[4]

What keeps the behavioral scientist from perceiving the fact that his project uses people as objects, as things, as means only to his ends? Not ethical insensitivity primarily, though it is true that professional socialization is notoriously indifferent to such philosophical issues. It is the ideology of science that provides rationale and rationalization. For we have been taught that the development of a science is a slow and cumulative process—therefore no quick results should be expected. Only when our science gets it together will we have the theoretical knowledge to provide the basis for solutions to the social and human problems that poor and oppressed people face. Built into the deepest roots of the scientific attitude is the assumption that the accumulation and systematization of knowledge *must* be in the interest of the common good; in America social science gained justification through its concern for the common man. Some scholars, perhaps many, in our divided society retain this belief; perhaps it is defensible if one's view of science and society is sufficiently long-term. For the short run, the span of time in which people live their lives, it is seriously open to question.

The poor and the racially oppressed have been promised much from social science. Occasionally a study, a book, or a series of investigations do make a difference to a particular

[4] For searching insights into the dynamics of this situation, we recommend Albert Memni's *The Colonizer and the Colonized* (Boston: Beacon Press, 1967). Frantz Fanon's "Medicine and Colonialism" in *Studies in a Dying Colonialism* also speaks to the fundamental irrelevance of the manifest purpose and professional goals of the colonizer in the colonial situation. Even though the French doctor in Algeria was committed to the cure of his patient, the structural and cultural conflict made it inevitable that the colonized Arab would react to him as an alien and an enemy.

community, or even to national policy as a whole. The 1954 Supreme Court decision responded to briefs that depended heavily on sociological and psychological research. But in the overwhelming number of instances, there is no tangible change in the lives of the subjects—either short run or long run. The poor and the oppressed, with their pragmatic sense and sensitivity to phoniness, knew this long before many of us. The lack of payoff comes from at least two sources—first, the distance between our theoretical and empirical concerns and the life-problems and situations of those we study; second, and ultimately the more crucial, our lack of power to implement and influence change. In many, though not all, problem areas, there is already enough known to tell us what should be done—why, for example, undertake research into the causes of Black joblessness when it is clear that most unemployment and underemployment is due to the old-fashioned racial discrimination of employers and unions.

OUR ATTEMPTS AT REFORM

We began our research with the idea of building into our project a number of specific strategies that might permit us to transcend the one-sided and exploitative dynamics of the research process. A first principle was paying respondents for the time they spent talking with us. The funding agency budgeted $2,500 to enable us to allot five dollars per interview. We stressed that this money was a wage for labor-time, rather than a bribe for information. In some cases the five dollars made a difference and was appreciated; yet a surprising number of interviews took place freely without any request for compensation. There is growing agreement that funded research on low-income communities should include sizable grants to indigenous people or organizations. It is not clear however that ours was the best way to do this.

A second tactic was an attempt to be honest about the purposes of the research and the difference it would make. The approach was no bullshit. We did not promise to save the world; we did make it clear that we were dissatisfied with the way social scientists have approached race relations and described the experience of Black people in America. We hoped to do better, and if we were able to, it would be because we intended to elicit depictions of the realities as perceived by the principal actors, ordinary people, Black and white. Therefore we aimed for interviews as unstructured and spontaneous as possible, permitting our workers to converse and exchange ideas with respondents. The interview was conducted as a life history, organized around experiences with major institutions: family, school, work, police, politics, welfare, etc. We wanted to find out where the respondent was at, to get as full a picture of him or her as possible. The point was to be flexible: to get inside the person and evoke a sociological portrait in the respondent's own language. Since our goal in data collection was the lived experience of ordinary people, we had to deviate from conventional notions of the appropriate research staff.

"Science" is usually restricted to "experts" who are traditionally selected by "objective" criteria: formal education, degrees and research experience. Of course, these criteria effectively exclude people of color from actively participating in studies of their own communities. We decided to consider as "experts" those who had lived the lives we wanted to understand. Thus in selecting the original staff in 1967, degrees and research experience were hardly considered. Of the five Black research assistants in a group of seven, only one had a university degree. Three had no association with any college or university. More pertinent to us were their ties to diverse segments of the Black community. The five field workers and interviewers included a working longshoreman, a community worker in the schools, a Bohemian-oriented part-time musician, a Southern-born civil rights veteran, and a graduate student from a middle-class Berkeley background, the one woman in the group. Their informal education included such schools as street hustling, New Careers and other poverty programs, civil rights and nationalist movements.[5]

What impressed us about this original staff was an ability to talk about sensitive issues, to draw people out, and to understand the feelings of a variety of sectors of the Black community. Training a conventional research team is not easy. The problems are magnified when you begin with a group with minimal exposure to sociological thinking. The problem was compounded by a commitment to use the assistants in conceptualizing problems as well as for data collection. Weekly seminars, attended also by other social scientists interested in race relations, were the format for both training and generating intellectual contributions from the staff.

The seminars began with discussions of the aims and ideas of the project. These seminars accomplished a number of purposes. They allowed the staff to participate actively in the ongoing development of the study. They were also concerned with specific issues of data collection, staff members sharing with each other the various problems faced in their work. We also related current issues to our emerging framework. Although time-consuming, and often frustrating, the weekly seminars were successful. Besides developing a certain collective spirit, they served to formulate and reformulate the basic assumptions and concepts underlying our research. They gave all of us a better grasp of the complexities surrounding race in America.

[5] Of course there is nothing new in this critique of standard research qualifications. The idea of using "indigenous" community people in research is part of the widespread subprofessional or paraprofessional movement, sometimes formulated as "new careers for the poor."

Sociologists in the Black Community

As our study progressed, we exhausted our original contacts, and it became more difficult to get interviews. Potential respondents would systematically stand us up. People
raised questions about our motives. Some refused to have
anything to do with us. Others demanded that we offer
something besides money in exchange for their time. We
became painfully aware that social researchers were not
welcome in Black and brown communities.

All of us, Black as well as white, had to come to grips
with this situation. If we were going to make any headway,
we had to understand the bases of these anatagonisms. Discussions with reluctant respondents usually evoked two
initial questions. One was "What's in it for us?" The other
was "What's it going to be used for?" The dialogue didn't
end when we answered the first by saying "little" and the
second with examples of Ph.D. theses and books, for the
two questions were merely the tip of an iceberg. Beneath
was a hostility toward the university, toward research in
general, and toward sociologists in particular. Probing in
these areas revealed a sophisticated consciousness of social
processes that negates stereotypes of oppressed people as
uninformed, apathetic and apolitical.

Many people resented the fact that the University of
California had only recently begun active recruitment of
Third World students. They complained that they, like
everyone else, were paying taxes for the university, yet
were virtually denied access to its facilities. Like many
institutions, the University of California does not pay city
taxes. It owns land which would provide a great deal of
revenue if taxed. In short, many considered the University
a parasitic institution and wanted little to do with it.

Hostility toward research in general was double-edged.

A sentiment frequently expressed was "What good's another book gonna do us? We've been studied to death." Another respondent said, "Nothing is happening. I mean they got research after research and nothing is happening. They darn right exploiting people." Yet this concern took on another, more sophisticated form. Many people seemed to know the difference between theory testing and problem solving. The former was associated with university people, the latter, with people attached to poverty agencies: "You guys are just gonna say something we already know," or "Sociologists just get on my darn nerves. They really do. They take the little research they do and just chew it up and come up with the biggest lies and generalizations that you ever want to hear." Since we were affiliated with a university, we were immediately suspected of either documenting the obvious or of distorting the complex—and thus were a waste of time.

In the ghetto, there is hostility toward research for another reason which may appear to contradict the above. People knew that sociologists have been used by government agencies (for example, police and welfare departments) to develop more sophisticated techniques for the control of poor people. Many Blacks saw themselves in a life-and-death struggle with white America. They believed sociologists had taken sides with the enemy and were therefore to be avoided at all costs.

There was also strong resentment toward the labels which social scientists have attached to racial minorities. People resented being tagged "culturally deprived," "disadvantaged," with "matrifocal families." And our respondents knew that this has been primarily the work of sociologists. One thing "Black Power" seemed to mean was freedom to define oneself without interference by sociologists or any other outside group.

We began to realize that this widespread hostility, resentment and fear could not be eased by payments or other devices. The issues were too complicated and deepseated. It was the entire *relationship* between researcher and researched that was resented. In this relationship the objects of study saw themselves as *exploited*—because books are written but oppressive conditions remain; as *distorted* or *humiliated*—because they get put into invidious categorical bags such as "the culturally deprived"; and as *repressed*—because sociologists intentionally or unintentionally produce studies which are used to keep people in their place. The question that faced us was whether we could change this relationship.[6]

Staff members began to commit themselves in various ways to the people they wanted to interview. Community groups called upon them to work and give technical assistance, and to prepare research for these groups. They had to help out in other mundane ways: making phone calls, writing letters, driving people around to appointments. In short, they had to alter the exploitative relationship which research imposes. In order to gain cooperation from the community, the gap between research and action had to be bridged in the immediate present.

Working closely with community groups posed a challenge to our notions of "objectivity" and other scientific principles. It was not enough to say that information was confidential and informants anonymous. We also had to take positions and become partisan. Concerned about the uses to which sociology can be put, we decided that some data would have to be "classified."[7] We could not consider ourselves dispassionate scientists without responsibility for

[6] Some field workers adapted by disassociating themselves from whites, from the university, from sociology, and from organized research. They would identify themselves as being on their own, writing a book or a paper, for example. While this sometimes helped gain access it did not change the basic relationship and probably intensified the alienation between staff member and project.

[7] For example, some of our respondents had participated in riots in the Bay Area. When researchers arrived to study these events and wanted to look at our interviews, our staff decided against opening our interviews to them.

possible misuses of our knowledge. Our respondents saw to that.

Problems in the University Milieu

The structure of the university is another impediment to the decolonization of research. The barriers which the norms of science throw up are often duplicated by the bureaucratic rules and regulations which govern university operation. Administrative reactions to our staff included defensiveness, skepticism and outright hostility. Everyone hired for research administered by the university must meet university requirements. These criteria had little to do with the realities of our project. On the contrary, the possibility of recruiting ghetto people is limited by the practice of linking job titles and pay scales to formal educational criteria. Often hassled by petty bureaucrats who would not waive such requirements, we had to go to higher levels to hire many of our staff.[8]

The predominantly white, middle-class character of the university presents further problems for the involvement of Third World and community people in research. The institute which housed us had long been a leading liberal influence on the campus. But its race relations policies and hiring practices reflected the civil rights emphasis on integration and middle-class Negroes. Its personnel apparently had little experience with lower- and working-class Blacks. Our staff felt put off by the vibrations of the place. Secretaries did not always relate cordially to our Black field workers; academic associates did not appear to regard them as colleagues in research. Characteristic was a combination

[8] Since 1967 when we faced these problems the situation has probably improved with the campaigns to recruit minority people and the more recent HEW "affirmative action" policy.

of insensitivity and bureaucratic thinking, which, in relation to people of color, adds up to a kind of bureaucratic racism. The worst example of this was expressed by an institute staff functionary who informed one of our most capable assistants that he could not work on the project because his grade-point average was too low. This administrator did not consult with either the principal investigator, the project coordinator, or the Department of Sociology, which had just admitted the researcher to graduate school with a five-year fellowship. Instead she took it upon herself to begin terminating him because he did not meet university requirements. The matter was settled only at a higher level. But it contributed to a developing feeling that in the institute's eyes we were the wrong kind of people.

When the building was robbed—a frequent occurrence, due to its proximity to the high-crime area south of campus —the problem was compounded by the fact that our Black researchers tended to be invisible and anonymous people to other institute personnel. Since it was always a Black person who was "seen" leaving the building late at night, people were always "just asking" if one of "our people" had been in the night before. We couldn't tell whether the administrators were just checking out leads or actually suspecting us. Since these tensions in part reflected a clash of styles, the paranoia at times was a two-way stream.

Our staff posed other problems that had nothing to do with the milieu of the University, however. Some members viewed their job as a pretty good hustle. There was no clock to punch. People were independent, allowed to gather interviews as they pleased. The only demand was a certain number of interviews a week. Sometimes this autonomy—which we considered crucial to good research —was misused. Objective difficulties in arranging interviews became excuses to goof off. We would give someone a couple of weeks to produce, but if it became evident that he wasn't trying, we had to call him on it. In some instances we had to supervise people more closely than we desired. This produced a degree of antagonism within the staff.

This antagonism may have been fueled by resentment on the part of Blacks toward the project's white administration. The white coordinator's job of evaluating interviews made by Black staff appeared to epitomize larger patterns of racial domination and colonialism. Those who were graduate students felt a somewhat greater stake in the research; to some degree they could mediate this racial antagonism. They could also carve out a subproject within the whole, to pursue as they pleased. In this way feelings of exploitation were lessened—though not alleviated.

But for those who had no intention of becoming part of the university, the project was just a job. And often they handled it as such. Undoubtedly the expectation that staff members will have a commitment similar to that of the principal investigators reflects the paternalism endemic in both master-apprentice and white-Black relations. But beyond these factors there was a residue of resentment traceable to the reality that Blacks were being studied by whites. Ultimately this problem can be resolved only when research on the Black community is conducted by Black scholars rather than white ones.

Concluding Issues and Implications

It is not easy to give a balanced assessment of our project experience. Clearly there was some progress in the direction of decolonization. There was a dialogue with the subjects of our research. When the staff had time to develop real relationships, giving something in return, rapport as well as interviews followed. However, we were not totally successful in even these limited aims. In some instances we failed to overcome the barriers between those with and those without experience in social research. When some staff members did not work out and were let go, we felt uncomfortable; we were never sure we had tried hard enough to incorporate them. Assessing where our responsibility began and their inexperience left off was difficult. Moreover, we never completely eliminated the feeling of exploitation among the staff who remained. If you spoke with some of our staff, they would tell you they felt used. We don't always see it their way and don't fully understand to what degree specific actions on our part or the general context of the research resulted in these attitudes. Perhaps exploitation is inevitable if Third World people are not involved from beginning to end in planning, administration and intellectual leadership. For this to happen, however, more must change than individual projects such as our own. The priorities of universities and funding agencies must be reordered.

Our attempt at decolonization was only partly successful for essentially three reasons. First, our understanding of the ramifications of the researcher-researched relationship came too late in the game; we could not fully reshape our strategies and priorities—a total overhaul was necessary, yet some major transformations in theoretical focus and research techniques were the most we could accomplish. This was partly due to the second problem, the limitations of our resources in money, time and people. If research with communities of the poor and the racially oppressed is to approach reciprocity in exchange values, the cost will be great. This in turn relates to the third shortcoming: because of our limited resources our priority had to be data collection rather than social action and service to the community. In decolonized research these priorities have to be equalized, if not reversed.

What is needed is new organizational formats: centers or institutes that integrate social action, change and community assistance with the theoretical and empirical goals of the researchers: Such a center would begin with a commitment to the philosophy of serving the interests of oppressed communities, as seen by their citizens and local organizations. Academic research projects would have to be related to these interests and be understood, discussed and approved within the community. Collection of data and theory-testing would go hand in hand with the work of the center's staff in dealing directly with the needs of a community: problem-solving technical assistance, organizing, education and, of course, allocating money. Every research inquiry would be part of a team effort in which the action and service components would play an integral part—of course some people would be research specialists, others action men. But the research effort and its personnel would then be identified with a larger unit that was clearly committed to community development and already functioning on behalf of the people rather than against them. Such a concept would require vast financial resources. It is possible that in many states, universities may no longer be the most feasible homes for such centers; other alternatives such as independent foundation-supported entities might be considered.

A final question is the role of the white social scientist today in the field of race relations research. Many of our day-to-day problems derived from the fact that two white sociologists initiated a research project that included a study of Black people. The two of us, in effect, were the bosses. None of the Third World members of the staff had any official long-term responsibility. Thus even a project which focused on racism, and which had a primary commitment to eliminate it from our society, reflected in its structure and function the prevailing patterns of racial domination.

We do not argue that whites cannot study Blacks and other nonwhites today; our position is rather that, in most cases, it will be preferable for minority scholars to conceive and undertake research on their communities and group problems. The Third World sociologist will face some of the same dilemmas we faced and some unique ones of his own. There are certain aspects of racial phenomena, however, that are particularly difficult—if not impossible—for a member of the oppressing group to grasp empirically and formulate conceptually. These barriers are existential and methodological as well as political and ethical. We refer here to the nuances of culture and group ethos; to the meaning of oppression and especially psychic reactions; to what is called the Black, the Mexican-American, the Asian and the Indian *experience*. Social scientists realize the need for a series of deep and solid ethnographies of Black and other Third World communities, and for more penetrating analyses of the cultural dynamics, political movements and other contemporary realities of the oppressed racial groups. Today the best contribution that white scholars could make toward this end is not firsthand research but the facilitation of such studies by people of color. We must open up the graduate schools in every discipline to Black, Chicano, Puerto Rican and other minority people, particularly those with strong ties and loyalties to their ethnic communities. When such a sizable corps exists, presumably there will be scholars who will choose to carry out such work.

The white social scientist in the field of race and poverty might accept the fact that a racial division of research labor is the most feasible present-day solution. The "minority" scholar must have the freedom to approach the entire range of problems that intrigue him. But the white sociologist might well eschew focusing on Black and other Third World communities. We recommend instead investigating the ways that racist practices are embedded in particular institutions, and the permeation of assumptions of white superiority in American culture and personality as well as the special situation and problems of white ethnic groups and working-class people. Scholars from the dominant groups have a special obligation to confront these issues.

The efforts to decolonize our project described in this

paper were at best tokenistic, since we could do nothing about the overall structure of academic research, its relation to social policy, and the specific life-conditions of our respondents. This raises the question of whether it is possible to decolonize research concerned with oppressed racial and economic groups when the fundamental relationship between these groups and the overall society is a colonial one. Writ large, the answer is essentially no, which suggests, as some people argue, that the point is not to reinterpret oppression but to end it. Yet to the extent that social scientists are caught up in an enterprise that is part of a total structure of control and exploitation, fundamental changes in the carrying out of research and in the relations between academic centers and people of color can contribute to the larger anticolonial dynamic.

Jerome Harris and William D. McCullough

Quantitative Methods
and Black
Community Studies

The struggle for the liberation of Blacks can be greatly facilitated by using the technique of quantitative analysis. Focusing on the advantages of this technique for the collection and analysis of data in the Black communities, the authors of the following essay posit that quantitative methods will be useful to Blacks in the (1) determination of goals and objectives; (2) establishment of needs and priorities; (3) use of models; and (4) evaluation of programs.

A recurring theme in discussions of the component parts of the task of nation-building is that of skill development. Technical skills have been emphasized as primary needs by many of the key architects of our developing nations. For the social scientist, the techniques of quantitative analysis are essential technical tools. The analyst who has command of these basic tools possesses a potent weapon with which to reconstruct the past, evaluate the present and mold the future.

Black people today are engaged in a world-wide struggle

for liberation and self-determination. Using quantitative methods in studying our communities will not, of course, set us free, but it can help in lighting the way and allocating our resources most efficiently and effectively. The struggle for self-determination should bear heavily upon our use of quantitative methods in studying Black communities. In the pages that follow we address ourselves to some of the basic considerations important in Black community studies with regard to the past, the present and the future.

Quantitative Methods

Quantitative methods may be defined as the methods, techniques and procedures of mathematics, statistics and, more recently, computer science that are useful to other disciplines in research studies and investigations. They include the more elementary methods of statistical tabulations, such as population-distribution data or opinion-poll results, as well as the more complex methods of statistical and mathematical analysis, such as statistical correlation or prediction techniques. Although quantitative methods are easily associated with the physical sciences, they are equally useful to the social sciences and have had broadened applications in this area in recent years.

Quantitative analysis adds the dimension of measurement to an otherwise qualitative assessment. Measurement allows us to be more specific or precise about our findings and arms us with a stronger case for appropriately drawn conclusions. It enhances insight and perception, enables us to get a clearer understanding of the nature and extent of problems or conditions. It facilitates the correlation or relationship of one variable to another, frequently disclosing cause-and-effect relationships.

Quantitative methods can be used quite advantageously in Black community studies. They can also be used to the detriment of Black people, as they have been in many past studies of our community. Since their application to Black communities is by no means unique, what aspects of quantitative methods have particular significance in Black community studies? What should be our specific concerns? We should be concerned about the specific kinds of endeavors that will be most beneficial to us. We should be concerned that these studies are carried out by our own people. We should be concerned about the specific subject areas upon which to focus attention. And, above all, we should be concerned that the use of quantitative methodology is in our collective interest.

Black Community Studies

Quantitative analyses of Black people and their communities have been going on for some time. Just prior to the turn of the century, W. E. B. DuBois did a penetrating study of the Black community in *The Philadelphia Negro.* This in-depth quantitative analysis of the Negro condition in Philadelphia made use of considerable statistical data. As such, it was a pioneer sociological study.

Studies of Black communities have been carried out by Black and white social scientists. Historically, Black and white researchers have viewed and analyzed Black communities from the perspective of white norms and standards, and have generally drawn predictable conclusions from their analyses. On the basis of their quantitative studies, white researchers have generally concluded that Blacks in the U.S. are pathological and inferior. Typical of this position are the works of Daniel P. Moynihan in studying Black families, and Arthur Jensen's work pertaining to Black IQ's.

Black researches on the other hand have attempted to document the Black condition and to appropriately assign the inferior status of Blacks to a condition of white racism and oppression of Blacks. Such was the case in *The Philadelphia Negro* and in the 1945 study by St. Clair Drake and Horace Cayton, *Black Metropolis*. However, having been oriented to white norms and standards through the educational system of this country, Black researchers in many instances treated the Black populace as pathological. Even in these cases, the Black condition was not looked upon as the result of inherent behavior characteristics but rather as the mark of oppression. Although Blacks were viewed as maintaining an inferior existence, in no case did Black researchers attribute this to basic inferiority.

During the emergence of Black consciousness in the United States in the 1960's, Blacks began to think in terms of their own value system and consequently to view themselves from a totally different perspective. Black researchers and intellectuals were similarly affected, and we began to see many more studies that examined the behavior patterns of Black communities in the context of survival in a hostile society. Andrew Billingsley and Joyce Ladner, for example, in their respective books, *Black Families in White America*[1] and *Tomorrow's Tomorrow: The Black Woman*,[2] focus upon the abilities of Black families and young Black women to cope with and function in a hostile society.

In *The Strengths of Black Families*,[3] Robert Hill provides an excellent example of quantitative analysis of Black families, using criteria developed from a Black perspective. Hill utilizes some twenty-three tables of quantitative data obtained from the U.S. Bureau of the Census, pertaining to Black and white family characteristics, to demonstrate the

[1] Andrew Billingsley, *Black Families in White America* (Englewood Cliffs, N.J.: Prentice-Hall, 1968).

[2] Joyce Ladner, *Tomorrow's Tomorrow: The Black Woman* (Garden City, N.Y.: Doubleday, 1971).

[3] Robert Hill, *The Strengths of Black Families* (New York: Emerson-Hall, 1972).

positive aspects of Black families. This is the same data used by Moynihan to demonstrate weakness in the Black family structure. The strength of Hill's study is in his premise that Black and white norms differ in respect to family structure and behavior and that therefore it is appropriate to view Black families in the context of Black rather than white norms. Moynihan, on the other hand, examines the Black family structure in the context of white norms.

Hill acknowledges the fact that survival in a hostile society is a major factor in determining behavior patterns of Black families and proceeds from this perspective. He identifies the following characteristics which have been functional for the survival, development and stability of Black families: (1) strong kinship bonds; (2) strong work orientation; (3) adaptability of family roles; (4) strong achievement orientation; and (5) strong religious orientation. He notes:

Although these traits can be found among white families, they are manifested differently in the lives of black families because of the unique history of racial oppression experienced by blacks in America. In fact, the particular forms that these characteristics take among black families should be viewed as adaptations necessary for survival and advancement in a hostile environment.[4]

From his analysis of the quantitative data, Hill is able to demonstrate how strongly Black families exhibit each of the five characteristics above.

The difference in approach of Black and white social scientists in studying Black communities highlights the need for Black researchers in these studies. White researchers are biased toward their own norms and standards, and their objectivity is often influenced by their vested interests. From the point of view of perpetuating slavery and subsequently of establishing and maintaining a subservient

[4] *Ibid.*

working class for capitalist exploitation, for example, whites found it desirable and necessary to demean Blacks and assign them an inferior status.

It is interesting that in recent years whites have begun to prepare statistical studies demonstrating Black progress and achievements. Statistics are emerging showing Black progress in education, employment positions, income, etc. The irony of these studies is that they, too, are done in the interest of whites rather than Blacks. For it is only since Blacks have begun to assert themselves on a massive scale during the last decade that these statements of progress have emerged. Their real purpose has not been to show Black progress but to attempt to dampen Black fervor for change by implying that effective change is already taking place. It is ironic that while absolute gains are being made, the same data frequently reveal that relative ground is being lost. For example, in the last twenty years the median income for Black families rose from 54 percent to 64 percent of the median income for white families. At the same time the dollar gap was widening from $2500 to $3600. Thus, while we note a gain in one respect, we see an increasing gap in actual income, resulting in even greater economic deprivation for Black families.

Black communities must be studied by Black people for our own self-interest. We can not afford to be misled by the interpretations and conclusions of statistical studies done by whites who are interested in preserving the status quo. We must gather the data, analyze and interpret them for our own needs and purposes.

Future Directions

We have pointed out that quantitative methods should be used to our advantage in the struggle for Black liberation and self-determination. There are various ways in which this might be done. Efforts such as that of Hill in examining the strengths of Black families should be continued. Such efforts put Black sociological data in the proper perspective. This is important to the development and maintenance of the self-image and self-esteem of Black people. New norms, standards and evaluation criteria relevant to the Black experience and Black values are essential for studies of this type.

While the Hill type of study is important, we must at the same time begin to focus on the use of quantitative methods in developing new prescriptions and workable models for positive action in the interest of Black community development. It is necessary that we not only make use of quantitative analysis in exercises directed toward balancing attitudes in American society regarding Black people, but that we also use this instrument as a means of moving forward in pursuit of our own hopes and aspirations. We must direct our efforts toward positive actions, as opposed to simply reacting to what whites have said or done with regard to data pertaining to Black communities. We understand that our enemies have made use of quantitative data and manipulated them in such a manner as to justify the treatment accorded Blacks. Such treatment is likely to go on whether or not we repair the situation with our own quantitative analyses, and we cannot afford to make the mistake of spending too much time conducting quantitative studies in reacting to what whites have to say.

Quantitative methods will be useful to us in many ways, but we shall restrict our discussion here to four subjects: (1) determination of goals and objectives; (2) establishing needs and priorities; (3) use of models; and (4) evaluation programs. These areas provide a sufficient framework within which to examine the applications of quantitative analysis.

In our efforts for self-determination we want to gain control of our communities and resources, to develop them as we wish. But we must have certain objectives in mind and must pursue rather specific goals if we are to avoid sporadic and/or chaotic development. At times we must quantify these goals in order to have some standard for evaluating progress and in order to pursue realistic levels of achievement in specified time frames. Our timetable will also permit us to have consistent long-range and short-range goals and objectives. For example, we are committed to gaining political strength for Black people and to exhibiting that strength in national, state and local elections. One test of that strength will be in the number of public office-holders we are successful as a people in electing. We should establish specific year-by-year goals to elect certain numbers of officials. Such goals would not be arbitrarily arrived at but would be based upon sound quantitative analysis of what is reasonable within the limitations of our resources.

In many kinds of situations we must establish priorities which again can be facilitated through the use of quantitative methods. In the article "Mathematics and the Struggle for Black Liberation,"[5] S. E. Anderson cites a number of statistics reflecting the Black condition as it pertains to education. Included are the following: Black females graduating from high school outnumber Black males two to one; the average reading level of Black high school graduates is between the second and third grade; less than 2 percent of Black college graduates major in any of the sciences, medicine, agriculture and engineering; in 1969 there were less than a hundred graduating Black physicians. Such statistics speak for themselves in portraying deficiencies in the education of Black people. It is obvious that we need to improve the quality of education and to increase the numbers of those finishing college in various fields. But the question arises as to how we should counsel our Black youth. Should we merely point out that we need more people in the sciences, medicine and engineering and allow people to settle into the various programs as they are

[5] S. E. Anderson, "Mathematics and the Struggle for Black Liberation," *The Black Scholar* (September 1970).

naturally attracted to them? Or should we attempt to encourage, for example, twice as many students to enter the pure sciences as into medicine because in terms of achieving self-determination our needs are more critical in the former? That is, what priorities should we give to developing the various resources we need or to other programs competing for limited resources?

Questions such as these can be addressed through quantitative analysis. By doing so, we are likely to wind up with the best answers in the light of our objectives. Our goals are likely to be reached in a much more orderly and systematic manner and more rapidly than would otherwise be the case.

A good example of the potential for quantitative analysis in setting goals and establishing priorities is provided in Robert Browne's consideration of an economic plan, such as those put into effect by the Soviet Union and other countries, for Black people in America. He writes:

Although differing in some details, the heart of these economic plans is the setting forth of specific goals to be achieved by a certain date, and some plan for attaining these goals. Goals are likely to be such things as: achieving a certain level of industrial productivity in designated categories, a certain level of agricultural production, a certain volume of exports, a certain rise in per capita income, lowering illiteracy by "X" percent, training "X" number of teachers, graduating so many doctors, etc. Obviously such a plan must be internally consistent if it is to succeed, i.e., a large increase in agricultural production cannot be achieved unless plans are also made for producing (or importing) the necessary fertilizer, farm equipment, etc. Considerable research and data collection must precede the making of any economic development plan so that the goals will in fact be within the realm of possibility.[6]

[6] Robert S. Browne, "Toward an Overall Assessment of Our Alternatives," in *Black Business Enterprise* (New York: Basic Books, Inc., 1971).

In developing such a plan, quantitative analysis would be necessary to obtain the consistency within the plan and to determine what the "X"'s and "certain quantities" ought to be.

Models are a representation of reality. Mathematical or quantitative models represent that reality by mathematical formulae which describe the functional relationships of repetitious patterns. For example, population increase and distribution tend to follow patterns that can be described mathematically, thereby providing a mathematical model of population growth which can be used to predict future population. The population of the United States, which has increased by approximately two million people annually over the last decade, can be predicted for future years from the linear model

$$Pn = Po + 2.10^6.n$$

in which the population change over a period of n years is simply n times the annual increment of increase. Po is the population at a chosen table base time, and Pn is the population n years later. The general form of the model is

$$Pn = Po + b.n$$

in which "b" is the annual growth increment.

Mathematical or quantitative models are useful tools for planning to meet the needs of a community. They are also useful for understanding the dynamics of a community or of any situation in which the variables of that situation can be related to one another in some mathematical way.

The economic plan discussed by Browne is a good example of a situation amenable to quantitative modeling. Models would be used to determine the appropriate levels of each activity to ensure the internal consistency of the plan. Models might also be used to determine optimum patterns of resource development such that progress in the development of Black communities could be accelerated to the maximum extent.

The evaluation of the progress and effectiveness of programs undertaken in Black communities will continue to be an important use of quantitative methods. A critical element here is the selection of appropriate evaluation criteria. Such criteria must be related to the goals and objectives sought and must be measurable. Although measurable criteria may be readily defined, it is not always an easy task to determine which is most appropriate for use in a given situation.

We have seen that it is in some cases inappropriate to examine Black communities in the context of white norms. To do so would result in the drawing of erroneous conclusions about the Black condition. Consequently, it will be important to develop new norms and standards for Black community evaluation studies.

Underlying the application of quantitative methods is the acquisition of quantitative data. Much of the data available to us has been collected by whites. Such data may be faulty for various reasons, but basically we must be concerned about them because they are amassed to serve the interests of whites. Thus, the raw data may have serious omissions, and processed data may well be biased to serve the interests of whites.

The solution, of course, is to collect our own data whenever possible. However, we will have to continue to make use of some data generated by whites. Census data is a case in point. It is impractical for us at this point in time to duplicate the efforts of the Bureau of the Census. Therefore we must use available census data. However, we could make use of sampling techniques to collect data on localized communities which we would use to corroborate or dispute data obtained from suspect secondary sources.

The Black People's Topographical Research Center (re-

ferred to as Tops), with offices in several cities, is engaged
in one of the most comprehensive programs of data collection and analysis in the country. Tops is amassing readily
available data from such sources as the Bureau of the
Census, Rand McNally Commercial Atlas and Marketing
Guide, newspapers, government reports, congressional sub-
committee reports, etc. Information is being amassed as to
where Black people are and their conditions of immobility,
and from this data base the Center moves to an analysis of
spatial relations to the white community and its implications
for the program of genocide, widely regarded by Black
people as a reality of white programs for dealing with
Black people. The importance of Tops' work is in amassing data in a comprehensive form such that quantitative
analysis relevant to the Black community can be undertaken that otherwise would not be.

Development of Resources

The models for the growth and development of Black
communities must be developed by Black people. Quantitative analysis is an important aspect of these endeavors, and
to accomplish our objectives we must have a resource pool
of people trained in the use of quantitative methodology.

We have individuals trained in the use of quantitative
methods, but they are far too few. We have organizations
that make extensive use of quantitative methods, such as
the Research Department of the Urban League, which
sponsored Hill's study of Black family strengths; The Black
People's Topographical Research Center mentioned above;
and The Black Economic Research Center in Harlem.
There are others, but we need even more.

We must begin to train many more of our people in the
use of quantitative methods, particularly those engaged in
social science disciplines. Students entering the physical

sciences will of necessity become familiar with quantitative methods. Students entering the social sciences are frequently unaware of the potential of quantitative methods or carefully avoid them for one reason or another. These students must be made cognizant of the use of quantitative methods and encouraged (perhaps even coerced, for our collective benefit) into developing some expertise in this area.

There are barriers to developing these resources. Many students enter college ill-prepared in the area of mathematics. They also have a fear of mathematics stemming from impressions made upon them in their early training by teachers, counselors and parents alike. For this reason they studiously avoid courses with mathematical or statistical content in their college programs.

The manner in which mathematics and statistics courses are presented often itself alienates the student. All too often, the material is presented as a sterile subject which must be mastered for its own sake. This may be appropriate for students of mathematics or statistics, but it is often devastating to the social science student who cannot see the relationship to his field of endeavor. It will be necessary to make the subject matter more realistic and interesting to the student by continually espousing its usefulness to the student's discipline.

Another barrier to acceptance of quantitative methods is the misuse often made of them. Statistics can be manipulated and are frequently used to promote erroneous arguments. Black people are quite accustomed to the use of statistics by whites to debase them. This leads to suspicion not only of the researchers but of the techniques employed as well.

Great barriers confront us as we go about the task of nation-building. The essential fact is that these barriers can, must and will be overcome. The requirement is persistent effort.

Walter Stafford

Issues and Crosscurrents in the Study of Organizations and the Black Communities

With the tremendous growth of complex organizations, which now control almost every aspect of daily life, racism has become institutionalized and more difficult to identify than previously. In this essay, Walter Stafford suggests some new lines Black social scientists might follow in studying organizations and racism.

Introduction

The decades following World War II witnessed a tremendous growth of complex formal organizations in the social, economic and political spheres of the nation. Where, previously, business concerns established for owner-profits had represented the prototype for the study of complex organizations (e.g., DuPont, Standard Oil), increased urbanization after 1945 and the mushrooming of organizations needed to provide public and private services in a post-industrial society introduced a perplexing array of functional organizational types for analysis and study by social scientists, planners and public administrators.

The study of decision-making processes within organizations, of organizational design, and of the development of organizational planning mechanisms for coordination and control of scarce resources, gradually spread into every segment of the American system, not merely for scholarly and intellectual reasons, but also as a result of governmental concern with the lack of coordination between private and public interests in resolving basic questions of the use of scarce resources in a rapidly developing urban society.

Americans, notoriously resentful of centralized planning authority, witnessed the uncoordinated growth of large-scale complex organizations in every aspect of their personal lives, with little comprehension of the full importance of these developments. The rules and regulations of these organizations affected the Black welfare mother in New York City; the assembly-line worker at the Ford motor plant in Dearborn, Michigan; and even the corporate executive paid $250,000 a year. In fact, by the 1970's one could think of few areas or groups in American society not affected by them.

Significant Factors of Organizational Growth and the Black Community

The Black population was significantly affected by most of the aspects of organizational growth in the United States. The basic necessity of large-scale complex organizations to meet the needs of central cities, where Blacks were 21 percent of the population in 1970, has meant that new conceptions of social change in the Black community have become a pressing priority. A substantial segment of the Black population in urbanized society is not needed in the labor force, and the administrative rules and regulations of most organizations operate against any significant upward mobility.

The areas of concern most significantly affected by the goals and administrative procedures of complex organizations in the Black community have been:

1. *Economic Mobility and Security*—Blacks were more likely than whites to be unemployed in 1970 than they were in 1948.[1] The managerial class, an essential aspect of organizational growth in postindustrial capitalism, has not increased at a significant rate in the Black community.[2] In addition, unions—particularly craft unions—have denied Blacks participation, and service unions representing professionals in client-serving organizations (schools, hospitals, welfare, etc.) have often been the most adamant against changes in existing administrative hierarchies which would permit advancement by Black professionals.

2. *Participation and Decentralization of Organizational Structures*—A crucial aspect of the increased political sophistication of Blacks in urban areas has been the demand for participation and/or decentralization of organizations with territorial jurisdiction in Black communities. These demands have been most notable in regard to urban school systems, but they have also occurred in health and other service areas.

3. *Organizational Design of Racial- and Social-Change Agents*—The design of organizations and the setting of goals to achieve racial change have become basic requirements in Black communities. Social and racial change has increasingly meant altering the existing hierarchies of or-

[1] Robert Vowels, "The Political Economy of American Racism—Nonblack Decision-Making and Black Economic Status," *The Review of Black Political Economy* Vol. 1, No. 4 (1971), p. 23.
[2] *Ibid.*, p. 14.

ganizations which are considered racially discriminatory in their policies. In addition, concern for organizational change has become prevalent in those organizations already designed for social change, e.g., NAACP, Urban League, Muslims, Panthers, where the stated goals are often democratic in nature, but internal participation in decision-making is limited. Serious debates (and violence) have emerged in these organizations, since organizational goals, more frequently than not, are established by top administrators, without internal staff participation or community consultation.

4. *Services*—The entire realm of services to the Black community is inherently related to the "community accountability" of organizations in the public and/or private sphere. There are few services delivered to the Black community which do not involve the collaboration of private and public officials on all levels of government. These range from garbage collection to drug-addiction clinics. Since many of the decisions regarding the finances for such services are made by technicians with little comprehension of Black problems, conflict between the Black community and administrators of these organizations has grown in intensity.

5. *Accessibility to Political Power*—Political power is an essential criterion for decision-making in complex organizations, or for the effectuation of desired changes. The basic requirements are accessibility to power on every level of government, combined with adequate financial and staff resources. The state and federal grant-in-aid system on which lower-income Blacks are so dependent, requires that Blacks shape legislative guidelines, in state legislatures or Congress, before bills are enacted. Since substantial legislation is shaped (even written) by lobbyists for large-scale organizations, lack of accessibility to the political process by Blacks subsequently affects what benefits they receive.

This is particularly true in the areas of housing construction, welfare, job-training, and other vital concerns of the Black community, where large-scale organizations have a vested interest in maintaining the status quo.[3]

6. *Planning*—Organizations involved in city, regional and metropolitan planning since the 1960's have significantly increased. With increased participation, particularly by the federal government, in financial assistance to groups and communities, planning requirements for local services have become mandatory. Organizations responsible for planning have mushroomed on every level of government, and most of the planning decisions regarding the Black community are rarely known or disclosed until they are ready to be implemented.[4] Moreover, since Blacks lack substantial political power and the number of Black decision-makers in such organizations is generally small, planners are rarely required to justify their choice of priorities.

These six factors are not exclusive, but are meant merely to outline the impact of complex organizational growth on the Black community. The struggle to influence or control the rules, policies and priorities of complex organizations in order to formulate or reformulate goals that relate to Black problems rates as one of the major areas of future concern for the Black social scientist.

[3] See Harold Wolman, *Politics of Federal Housing* (New York: Dodd, Mead & Co., 1971), for an analysis of this process in DHUD lower-income housing programs; and Peter Woll, *American Bureaucracy* (New York: W. W. Norton and Co., 1963), for a basic discussion of the pattern in the American governmental framework.

[4] One of the more useful discussions of planning in the Black community is presented in *Planning in Black Communities* (Chicago: American Society of Planning Officials, 1971).

Dilemmas in the Study of Emerging and Future Trends of Organizational Change and the Black Community

In studying the Black community one finds that the strategies relating to the growth of complex organizations in the Black community are not simple; the forms are more frequently inconsistent than not, and *fundamentally all of the strategies and demands are only a reflection of the larger problem.* The primary problems relate to (1) the growth of bureaucracies; (2) resources in the Black community to effectively deal with exploitation or administrative negligence of organizations; (3) resolution of issues of efficiency and control of organizational rules and regulations; and (4) the design of parallel and/or community structures for change.

In respect to the first and second problems, it must be noted that the growth of complex organizations in American society has completely *overwhelmed the resources and capacity of traditional forms of organizations* in the Black community to cope with this organizational growth; and, even more important, the *recourse* for dealing with these organizations when exploitation or oppression has been the issue has meant going through procedures and regulations established by, or formulated with the assistance of, these organizations.

The third reason that the development of strategies to gain control and participation will not be simple for the Black community relates to the basic administrative issues of *efficiency* and *control.* In many respects, the dichotomy established in the Black community between these factors is superficial and mythical, particularly the tendency to associate "bureaucratization"[5] with inefficiency, red tape and

[5] The use of the term "bureaucracy" in the social sciences refers to administrative patterns and relationships in organizations.

cloistered technicians. This is largely a result of the failure to distinguish the *types* and *functions* of organizations and their goals. In many areas of an industrialized, urbanized society like the United States, the complex organization *is needed*, particularly in areas such as transportation, water supply, sewage, etc., and the problem does not stem exclusively from the fact that Blacks have no control, but rather from the fact that these organizational structures are frequently given status as special-service districts without *any* form of control by the public.[6] There is however a particular problem with Blacks, who may indeed be challenged by an emphasis on administrative control or decentralization in organizations in which they have gained status and upward mobility (schools are a classic example in localities where Black teachers are predominant).

In outlining some of the dilemmas associated with the growth of complex organizations, one must be constantly aware of the organizational structures designed specifically to be accountable to the Black community. The problem here is that, if the organization from which accountability, control or decentralization is demanded, structures its organizational mechanisms so that Blacks participate, the result is usually superficial, which is one of the criticisms of the anti-poverty programs and student participation in universities. On the other hand, if the organizational mechanisms are designed by the Black community, and the organization "legitimizes" change, there is no *guarantee* that the new structure will be responsive to the Black community, as the history of unionism has indicated.[7]

The analysis of strategies in the Black community should not be the only concern in future areas of study of organizational change. A basic study of organizational structures themselves is also needed. Organizational theory is at a

[6] See John C. Bollens and Henry J. Schmandt, *The Metropolis* (New York: Harper and Row, 1965) for a basic discussion of this problem.

[7] See Seymour M. Lipset, Martin Trow, James Coleman, *Union Democracy* (Garden City, N.Y.: Doubleday & Co., 1956).

crossroads in many respects. This may not mean abandoning remedies of organizational change, as some sociologists have suggested, but it does mean that a better theoretical base will be necessary in the future.[8] The fundamental problem with the study of theories of change of organizations has been that since Max Weber's works have been studied in this country,[9] American social scientists have been more interested in trying to help maintain organizational structures than in trying to change them. Put in another way, social scientists have been concerned with the survival of organizations. Even if one does not fully agree with Alvin Gouldner's analysis in *The Coming Crisis of Western Sociology*,[10] there is substantial merit to his assertion that social scientists are increasingly getting support to show "organizational management, through deliberate planning and governmental intervention [how they] can make things work better . . . [and] in response to this new pressure for deliberate and rational policy-making . . . there is now a rapid growth of new theories such as decision theory, cybernetics, and operations research, that seek to do this precisely."[11]

The point Gouldner does not make (it was not his main concern) is that the new group of organizational theorists do not actually develop theories; rather, they reedify the quasi-mathematical formulas that are already used in public administration, thereby giving the management of complex organizations new control mechanisms through the legitimization of the language of social science.[12]

8 See the introduction to Michel Crozier, *Bureaucratic Phenomenon* (Chicago: University of Chicago Press, 1964).

9 Max Weber, *The Theory of Social and Economic Organization*, A. M. Henderson and Talcott Parsons, eds. (Glencoe, Ill.: Free Press, 1947).

10 Alvin W. Gouldner, *The Coming Crisis of Western Sociology* (New York: Avon Books, 1971).

11 *Ibid.*, p. 346.

12 See Fremont J. Lyden and Ernest Miller, *Planning-Programming-Budgeting: A Systems Approach to Management* (Chicago: Markham Publishing Co., 1968), for a useful discussion of these approaches.

There are considerable pressures on Black social scientists to study and analyze complex organizations with territorial jurisdictions in the Black community and to formulate solutions to the problems they present. However, it bears repeating that this cannot be accomplished without a knowledge of the *functions* and *goals* of organizations, a detailed knowledge of the society and the Black community, and a willingness to observe and criticize organizational oppression. This fundamentally means that:

(a) The functions and goals of organizations must be analyzed not only as they function territorially in the Black community, but also as they interact in the decision-making process of other organizations on all levels of government, and frequently on the international level as well. One of the many consequences of the growth of complex organizations is that they are not spatially delimited or "place-bound" in their activities in decision-making.

(b) The form of "structured recourse" to complex organizations that are exploitative in either their delivery of services, profit orientation, governmental responsibilities, or that have societal responsibilities (e.g., prisons and hospitals), must become increasingly the task of Black social scientists who will analyze and design the liaison forms between these organizations and the community. This means that they should not be "reaction oriented," but they must be adamant about accessibility and liaison to organizations that have *any* boundaries in the Black community. For example, Black social scientists were almost totally without recourse to prisons until the Attica and the Soledad incidents, although as a "closed institution" prison and its organizational structures have been studied extensively.[13]

(c) The forms of administrative decentralization must be studied, and the manner of "participation" analyzed so

---

[13] Richard Cloward, *Theoretical Studies in Social Organization of the Prison* (New York: Social Science Research Council, 1960).

that these do not become "ritualistic" exercises conducted at the organizations' discretion. This applies particularly to the political demands of community control by Blacks in urban complexes.[14]

(d) The adoption of hierarchical forms of revolutionary organizations by Black radical organizations, particularly the cell structure (if one considers "gangs" such as Black Stone Rangers of Chicago and Pea Stone Rangers of Gary, Indiana, as organizations), should be studied to discover structures that may be applicable to the Black community.

(e) Finally, Black social scientists must take an entirely new interdisciplinary approach to organizational design and institutional building, not only in the United States but in Africa, an area previously left almost exclusively to white Western social scientists.

The Theoretical Transition: A Hypothetical Model

It is imperative that Black social scientists analyze and attempt to structure the control mechanisms of complex formal organizations, particularly as these mechanisms relate to the Black community. Fortunately, these issues are intricately related to poor and Black populations, so the theoretical transition of Black social scientists in all fields may be a smooth one.

Indeed, many of the studies since the 1960's have attempted to place institutionalized patterns of organizations in a broad framework and usually seek out previous analyses by social scientists who studied organizations in their embryonic stages. Thus, one finds in many respects the study of institutionalized patterns of racial exploitation

[14] See Bertram M. Gross, "Planning in an Era of Social Revolution," *Public Administration Review* (Washington, D.C.: American Society for Public Administration, May/June 1971), p. 288.

and control through organizations is *not novel* and was expressed precisely in the writings of Oliver C. Cox,[15] Robert C. Weaver,[16] and W. E. B. DuBois.[17]

The theories developed since the 1960's have obvious roots. They are *not* necessarily based on a greater understanding of organizations, but they are directed toward the study of organizations' institutionalized rules and priorities, with the aim of legitimizing benefits for the Black community (e.g., grants from governmental agencies, public utilities, insurance corporations). Although much of the theoretical discussion has tended to indicate that the individual racist is no longer the main offender because with the growth of complex organizations has gone the institutionalization of racism, the real significance of institutionalization is much greater than is generally realized.

Institutionalization minimizes to the greatest extent possible the personality differences afforded the individual racist and transforms informal or local group sentiments into a persistent formal structural aspect of the organizational network. This is justified, to the Black community and to the broader society, as a crucial part of organizations' professionalization, specialization and expertise, and thus legitimizes institutional racism.[18] In other words, professionalization transforms institutionalized racism into a legitimate form of decision-making which is hard to chal-

---

[15] Oliver C. Cox, *Caste, Class and Race* (Garden City, N.Y.: Doubleday & Co., 1948).

[16] Robert C. Weaver, "Federal Aid, Local Control, and Negro Participation," *Journal of Negro Education* (January 1942), pp. 47–59.

[17] See W. E. B. DuBois, "Does the Negro Need Separate Schools?," *Journal of Negro Education* (July 1935), reprinted in *W. E. B. DuBois: A Reader*, Meyer Weinberg, ed. (New York: Harper and Row, 1970), pp. 278–88.

[18] For a useful discussion of professionalization, see Neal Milner, "The Biases of Police Reform" in *Black Politics*, Edward Greenberg, Neal Milner and David Olson, eds. (New York: Holt, Rinehart and Winston, Inc., 1971), pp. 159–74.

lenge. Moreover, since professionalization and expertise are both *expected* and *accepted* considerations in making decisions through the overlapping network of organizations, the "moral" issue of Black oppression, in broad societal terms, loses much of its vitality. Thus one finds that the advocates of the school of thought formulated by Gunnar Myrdal in *An American Dilemma*,[19] that the "American Creed" is the crucial dimension of the race problem, ignore crucial aspects of decision-making in the political and economic sectors and the role of professionalization in the American system. Myrdal stated that:

From the point of view of the American Creed the status accorded the Negro in America represents nothing more and nothing less than a century-long lag of public morals. In principle the Negro problem was settled long ago; in practice the solution is not effectuated. The Negro in America has not yet been given the elemental civil and political rights of formal democracy, including a fair opportunity to earn his living, upon which a general accord was already won when the American Creed was first taking form. And this anachronism constitutes the contemporary "problem" both to Negroes and to whites.[20]

Myrdal's view of the Black problem in the United States, which has often been treated as *the* classic statement of race relations, restricts the analysis of the role of organizations and their patterns of institutional racism. Theoretical assumptions based on this premise also ignore the fact that there *is not* and *never has been* a unified "American Creed"

---

[19] Gunnar Myrdal, *An American Dilemma* (New York: Harper and Row, 1944). The intention here is not to add to the list of critics of Myrdal, except that many of the formulations are still perpetuated in textbooks. Additionally, his orientation toward social change in organizations is based on a similar moralistic framework. See Gunnar Myrdal, *Objectivity in Social Research* (New York: Pantheon Books, 1969).

[20] *Ibid.*, p. 24.

accepted by the public. And, as Oliver C. Cox indicated in *Caste, Class and Race*[21] (which is perhaps the best theoretical analysis of the race problem), Myrdal and his associates were not concerned with power—an undue emphasis was placed upon "regenerating the individual"—and ignored the fact that in a capitalistic system, morality is a function of the social and economic system. Therefore, only by changing the system does morality change.[22]

While Cox, a confirmed Marxist, based his analysis of the American system on capitalism, Robert Weaver, former Secretary of the Department of Housing and Urban Development, in an article published in 1942, "Federal Aid, Local Control, and Negro Participation,"[23] set the stage for future studies by analyzing the function of the American system of federalism in terms of the Black problem.

The American federal system is based on patterns of "sharing," or political "relationships" between groups and organizations on all levels of government.[24] The interactions between these levels are not definite or precise, nor are the loyalties or moral bindings of such interacting groups. Rather than a single or all-pervasive set of loyalties, there are many, i.e., to ethnic groups, city, state, etc. Thus, while consensus is reached on many problems, the problem of Blacks, which is an *intrinsic* problem of loyalties, is an area where solutions within the federalist framework are least viable. Moreover, *even when* consensus on "national" interest is established, the American system allows for considerable "subterfuge" on the state and local levels, so that the values and sentiments of groups with power and accessibility to the "sharing" in the political process are respected. The key to American federalism is *accessibility* to

[21] Cox, *op. cit.*
[22] *Ibid.*, pp. 509–38.
[23] Weaver, *op. cit.*
[24] See Morton Grodzins, *The American System*, Daniel Elazar, ed. (Chicago: Rand McNally Co., 1966).

the "sharing" so that group interests are recognized, particularly those of the local community. Since local autonomy and group interests are two of the most sacred values of federalism, Weaver explicitly indicated thirty years ago, long before the emphasis on local control, that "Fundamentally, participation by Negroes in any public program *approaches* adequacy as it is planned with and by Negroes rather than *for* them *by* others more or less acquainted with Negroes' needs and specific problems."[25]

What Cox stated theoretically, and Weaver more pragmatically, is that the denial of accessibility to economic and political organizations, not the lack of public morals, has been the critical problem of Blacks. When this is applied to organizations in the American system, the collaboration of organizations in the decision-making process in the political and economic spheres means that the theoretical transition to serious study of organizations and institutional racism is not without forerunners.

This discussion is not intended to be complete. At best it can only suggest relationships between the growth of formal organizations, the roles of professionalization and institutionalization, and the importance of collaborative decision-making as the key differential. Further research is needed in this area, particularly on professionalization as a means of institutionalization. A general summary seems to indicate that racism in complex organizations has meant that local or informal group racial sentiments have been more or less institutionalized into the organizational structure. This institutionalization is necessary to reduce the uncertainties in the decision-making process intrinsic to all organizations,[26] and to provide regulations and priorities

---

25 Weaver, *op. cit.*, pp. 58–9.

26 For a basic discussion of institutionalization in organizations and the necessity for reduction of "deviations" from the established system, see Philip Selznick, "Foundations of the Theory of Organization," *American Sociological Review*, 13 (1948), pp. 25–35.

which can be justified to the Black community and the larger society. The *maintenance* of the institutionalized patterns and professional standards comes from the ability of professional interests within the organizations to influence standards and procedures, and from the collaborative sharing of organizational interests in establishing or influencing policies and priorities for the entire system.

Some Research Methods in Studying Organizations and Racism

A basic and useful typology for the study of organizations is presented in Blau and Scott.[27] The research approach outlined by the authors can be utilized for much of the field research on organizations.

But although studies of organizational racism are increasing, there is still not a substantial body of literature from which to formulate hypotheses. Studies since the 1960's have focused on Blacks' lack of power by analyzing decision-makers, benefits to Blacks from federal, state and local agencies, and a few research hypotheses for the study of professionalization and incorporation of racism.

A basic research design for the study of Blacks in decision-making roles is presented in Harold Baron's "Black Powerlessness in Chicago."[28] This method requires that the researcher establish the number of decision-makers in a typology of organizations and determine the *number* and percentage of Blacks in these roles or positions. On the surface this may appear simple, but it is time-consuming and frequently expensive. However, the design can be modified

[27] Peter Blau and Richard W. Scott, *Formal Organizations: A Comparative Approach* (San Francisco: Chandler Publishing Co., 1962), pp. 258–60.

[28] Harold Baron, "Black Powerlessness in Chicago," *Trans-Action,* Vol. 6, No. 1 (November 1968), pp. 27–33.

to study many different aspects of organizational racism by simply analyzing the overlap of decision-makers in organizations, or attempting to determine whether organizations with large numbers of Blacks in decision-making roles perform differently than those in which they are absent.

To study benefits to the Black community (generally grants-in-aid) from local, state or federal agencies, one can refer to Jerry Miner, *Social and Economic Factors in Spending for Public Education*,[29] for a useful empirical model, and to Roy W. Bahl, "Studies on Determinations of Public Expenditures: A Review,"[30] for an excellent summary of previous studies and techniques.

The entire area of public expenditures and organizational racism is an open arena to Black social scientists, and it relates directly to the demands by Blacks for increased public spending in welfare, housing, etc., and indirectly to the emphasis on local control. The statistical techniques utilized to show relationships between Blacks and expenditures can range from simple correlations to more sophisticated regression-analyses. Simple ranking techniques can also be utilized to indicate status or geographical relationships. The most difficult problem with these approaches and techniques is not the expense of the studies, but obtaining data on expenditures on grants from agencies. Frequently, the agency has not put the data in a systematic form, or, to protect the organization, is unwilling to provide data. However, usually the information *is public*, and, once the data are obtained, one can indicate numerous relationships by careful selection of independent and dependent

[29] Jerry Miner, *Social and Economic Factors in Spending for Public Education* (Syracuse, N.Y.: Syracuse University, 1963), pp. 66–92. It is important to note that although the model is developed for education, it can easily be applied to other areas of interest.

[30] Roy W. Bahl, "Studies on Determinants of Public Expenditures: A Review," published in *Functional Federalism: Grants-in Aid and PPB Systems*, Selma Mushkin and John Cotton, eds. (Washington, D.C.: George Washington University, 1968), pp. 184–90.

variables. Moreover, this provides an opportunity to study how organizations allocate funds, professional biases, and the institutionalized rules and priorities for judging what the Black community received (it could also prove useful in studying the influence of the "collaborative" decision-making process in the federalist framework).

If the two approaches to research on organizations are combined, one can gather significant data on the exclusion of Blacks in decision-making roles and simultaneously the lack of benefits to the Black community (one should analyze the markets of ownership-profit organizations), and thereby test the numerous assumptions perpetuated about organizations in Black communities.

Finally, one should refer to the previously cited article by Neal Milner, "The Biases of Police Reform,"[31] for a useful discussion of professionalization and the incorporation of racial biases. Several of the hypotheses for the conflict between the demands of the Black community and increased professionalization or administrative consolidation in the police department can be developed for other organizations.

A significant amount of theoretical and empirical work needs to be completed in the study of complex organizations and the Black community. If Black social scientists do not face the task, it is extremely doubtful that this important aspect of Black oppression will be recognized. Further prospects depend on emerging conceptions of the Black problem in American society.

[31] Milner, *op. cit.*

Ethel Sawyer

Methodological Problems in Studying So-Called "Deviant" Communities

What are some of the more "human aspects of the problem of methodology"? What does the Black researcher who goes out to study "deviant" Black communities face? To what extent can the researcher maintain "distance" and "objectivity"? Ethel Sawyer, through a discussion of the actual mechanics of these problems and processes, posits that there is no easy solution to the difficulties that emerge.

This essay will attempt to deal with what I call the more human aspects of the problem of methodology. The social science researcher is a human being who deals with other human beings. Not only does his presence influence his respondents or a particular situation, but he himself is in turn influenced by the respondents and the situation, and indeed by his field work in general. I have chosen to discuss the problems that arise from this in the study of socially "deviant" communities. Although many of the problems are also encountered in the study of conventional populations, they are often highlighted and crystallized in the "deviant" settings. I am particularly concerned here with the problem of the Black researcher who studies Black populations.

The Deviant Perspective

One very problematic feature of conducting research in "deviant" communities or communities with "deviant" populations is the researcher's general orientation toward that population. Glazer and Strauss point out that one of the advantages of qualitative research as a methodology and in the discovery of substantive theory is that, in the course of conducting his inquiry, the researcher is able to change his orientation and redefine his hypotheses in the light of new findings.[1] However, if one is unable to see these data, one is unable to incorporate them into one's future orientation and thinking. In studying "deviant" communities in particular, there is a danger if the researcher operates out of the "deviant perspective," that is, if the researcher in his field work focuses almost exclusively on deviance to the virtual exclusion of conventionality.

The deviant perspective stems from a number of sources. One is the bias in sociology toward a mono-role or a unidimensional identity. Persons are regarded as either deviant or normal. The literature is so structured that if one wishes to learn about certain manifestations of deviance, one finds a whole cluster of books under the subheading "social deviance," or even "social problems." If one choses to study deviance one does not study *groups* whose members possess some deviant characteristic—that of delinquency, homosexuality or prison experience; rather, one studies *deviant groups* or *groups of deviants*—delinquents, homosexuals, exconvicts, etc.

[1] Barney Glazer and Anselm L. Strauss, "Discovery of Substantive Theory: A Basic Strategy Underlying Qualitative Research," *American Behavioral Scientist*, Vol. VIII, No. 6 (February 1965).

There is a tendency in psychology to focus on the individual and individual variations, and in sociology, to focus on such phenomena as ecological areas and groups. The effect of these theoretical stances is to establish distinctions between individuals and groups. One result of this is the deviant perspective.

Aided by these theoretical assumptions, the researcher is apt to acquire or perhaps to fall back on the perspectives operating in the larger society. People in general tend to think in terms of a set of abnormal deviant persons who possess certain characteristics that separate them from the normal members of society; and they are likely to perceive the entire lives of these persons or groups as centered around that deviance.

The field worker who is interested in populations where certain deviant manifestations exist is aided by the fact that the label *deviant* has already been provided by someone else and applied to that population. Thus, it is relatively easy for him to define for himself, in the beginning of his research, a population as deviant.

When the researcher who starts out to study deviant behavior enters a community or gains entrée into a particular group, he is often so conditioned toward the characteristic of deviance that has prompted him to study the group that he not only focuses on it but in a sense searches it out with a magnifying glass. If he fails to find what he is looking for, he has all kinds of excuses: I was not in the right place at the right time; rapport was not sufficient to allow me to observe this kind of behavior; my own particular characteristics and ethnic identity imposed certain restrictions on the behavior of the respondents, etc. All of these may indeed be legitimate, but not always. The deviance he is seeking may simply not be present, or at least not to the extent that the researcher believes it to be.

In his concern with deviance, the researcher often ignores more conventional forms of behavior. In standard methodological procedure we encounter the notion of unconscious selective observation and reporting. In the study of populations already labeled deviant, the risk that this selective gathering of data may run rampant is worth noting. When the researcher becomes attuned to focusing specifically and particularly on deviance, he is unable to see "ordinary" conventional behavior when it is present. It is probably a fact—and one that some contemporary students of deviance have recognized—that the greater part of the lives of persons or groups labeled deviant is spent in "normal," mundane, day-to-day living. In the researcher's focus on deviance, not only is he likely to overlook these more conventional phenomena, and thus become insensitive to them, but he may in the process overlook the very data that help to explain the deviance he is studying.

The acquisition of the deviant perspective also has a bearing on the interpretation of data at the conclusion of the field study. It is quite possible for the researcher or those responsible for writing up his data to draw accurate and adequate conclusions from his field notes and yet present a gross distortion of the lives of the people studied. This situation occurs because, as the researcher leaves the field after a day's work, he decides that "Nothing happened today, everything went along quite smoothly—no people were evicted from housing projects, the warring gangs did not fight today, the ex-cons went to work and then back home, the 'natives' were quiet." And he fails to record these, to him, uninteresting phenomena.[2]

For those who have accepted the notion of all-pervasive deviance, the matter does not present itself as a problem. But for those who have not, it is a profound shock to read over one's own data or the data of other researchers working in communities labeled deviant—the bias toward deviance is manifested in the comparative absence of specific

[2] Joyce Ladner in conversation raised the issue that this orientation also raises serious questions of the value of data collection versus basic values placed on human existence.

and detailed descriptions of "everyday normal living," a striking contrast to the vivid accounts of spectacular and eye-catching events.

Another risk the researcher runs is that often his respondents become aware that he is focusing on deviance and assume for themselves the deviant perspective. Methodology textbooks and courses stress the importance of establishing rapport with respondents, eliminating loaded questions and maintaining oneself in a manner that will facilitate the observation and reporting of "deviant" sentiments, behavior and activities. In other words, the researcher should not place the respondent in a position where he feels it necessary to give socially acceptable answers or to behave in socially acceptable ways. Much can be said for the reverse argument—that the researcher must handle himself, and his research tools, in such a way as not to impede observing and reporting conventional sentiments, behavior and activities. Sometimes, for example, in informing respondents that he is interested in a certain manifestation of deviance, the researcher runs the risk that respondents will "perform" for him, will supply him with that very deviance—real or imagined. Researchers have frequently discovered, days, weeks or months later, that they have been "taken for a ride." This raises the very important issue of what is pertinent and from *whose* frame of reference. Since persons are not deviant across the board, they probably do not acquire a pervasive deviant perspective toward themselves without prompting. Fred Davis, for example, discusses the attempts at normalization and the disavowal of deviance among persons who are, in one respect, manifestly deviant at all times—the visibly handicapped.[3]

The researcher's preoccupation with deviance may also

---

[3] Fred Davis, "Deviance Disavowal: The Management of Strained Interaction by the Visibly Handicapped," in *The Other Side*, Howard Becker (New York: The Free Press of Glencoe, 1963).

have implications for his overall orientation toward social life. The deviant perspective is a double-edged sword. Just as it can "splice the lives" of those studied, so it can at the same time be turned outward upon others—even the researcher himself. Surrounded and engulfed by his "data," the researcher may begin to assume that nothing "normal" really exists. It is all a conspiracy to defraud!

Focusing on deviance, one fails to discover what patterns continue to exist; what are the really basic things that persist in various social structures, no matter how "deviant."

There is, however, not only a deviant perspective but also a normality perspective—one that holds that there is little or no difference between and among groups of people. I think the challenge of the field worker who seeks to give an ethnographically accurate portrayal of those studied is to break through these two perspectives and see life as a whole, as an entity.

The Black Researcher

Other problems may arise in the study of groups and communities whose members are either perceived or labeled as deviant, and many of them stem from the prevailing tendency to view persons—in this case the researcher himself—as uni-dimensional or mono-role. A basic problem confronted by field workers in general is maintaining objectivity and a degree of distance from one's research subjects. Standard methodological procedure may, however, be of relatively little help when the researcher himself is "deviant" with respect to a particular characteristic that he has in common with those he is studying. In much research focusing on classical deviance, this is not a major concern. Delinquents do not carry out sociological studies on other delinquents, drug addicts on other addicts and homosexuals on other homosexuals.

But in the case of Black researchers studying Black populations, the problems of role and identity, objectivity and distance are crystallized and assume new importance. Black populations, regardless of other particular and specific characteristics, are a priori deviant when viewed through white middle-class eyes—be they the Black middle class, a warring gang or the Black lower class. The Black researcher, then, is also deviant with respect to that same characteristic—skin color—and all the other elements white America has seen fit to link to that color which together make up the status of Black people in American society. There is also a whole set of attitudes and feelings which Black people hold toward the dominant white society, whether or not they express them verbally. Therefore, the mere fact of being Black presents the researcher with a number of problems. These are compounded when the researcher studies populations that, in addition to being Black, are perceived as deviant with respect to a number of other characteristics—say, a population dominated by female-headed, welfare-dependent households, high rates of unemployment, high conventional crime rates, high rates of illegitimate children, etc.

One of the first problems that confront Black researchers who study Black populations is that of "withholding tendencies." More specifically and bluntly phrased, they question how much of what they see they should write up, report, or even bother to record. This applies to data which are present, which the researcher actually sees and observes and considers relevant to the particular phenomenon under study.

At one level, the tendency to consider withholding data may be viewed from the perspective of the ultimate effects of one's findings for the population studied. Rainwater and Pittman have dealt briefly with this issue and concluded that

[This] is a knotty issue, and one which perhaps can only be resolved by an act of faith. If you believe that in the long run truth makes men freer and more autonomous then you are willing to run the risk that some people will use the facts you turn up and the interpretation you make to fight a rearguard action. If you don't believe this, if you believe instead that truth may or may not free men depending on the situation, even in the long run, then perhaps it is better to avoid these kinds of research subjects. We say perhaps it is better because it seems to us that a watered down set of findings would violate other ethical standards, would have little chance of providing practical guides to action, and thus is hardly worth spending time and somebody else's money for.[4]

Thus for them the issue resolves itself. However, from the standpoint of the Black researcher, for whom "acts of faith" have not proved so rewarding in the past, the issue is more difficult. Even if he believes that ultimately truth makes men freer, the fact of group identification still exists at another level.

It is an accepted fact that researchers often empathize with their research subjects. A sizable portion of what is known as the *new perspective on deviance* attests to this. Howard Becker, for example, discusses the tendency of many researchers to begin more or less to identify with those they study. Although Becker warns against sentimentality, either conventional or unconventional, he concedes that if the collection of articles included in the book *The Other Side* errs in one direction, it is probably in the direction of unconventional sentimentality.[5]

While a certain amount of empathy is necessary if one wishes to understand fully the persons he studies, empathy,

---

[4] Lee Rainwater and David J. Pittman, "Ethical Problems in Studying Politically Sensitive and Deviant Communities," *Social Problems*, XIV, No. 4, Spring 1967.

[5] Howard Becker, in the introduction to *The Other Side*, Howard Becker, ed. (New York: The Free Press of Glencoe, 1963).

sympathy, sentimentality or whatever label one prefers sometimes presents itself as a stumbling block to researchers.

In addition to empathy, the Black researcher must contend with the problem of identification—group identification. In identifying with Black people, he is plagued with additional problems of exposing shared secrets, sentiments and values to the white world. The already angry researcher may ask himself certain questions: Should that which is distinctly ours be exposed? Should we let them know that we say that Black people seldom go any place on time and hence have concocted the notion of C.P. time? My data will inform others that Black people call each other "nigger" perhaps with much more frequency and regularity than the Southern white (although it is conceded that with the advent of Dick Gregory, "nigger" has come into its own). What about our own language, which has allowed Black people to converse in the presence of whites without their being in the least aware of what has really been said, and which has also provided an important basis for group solidarity?

At a more general level, perhaps any group one chooses to study has its back stages and front stages and is equally concerned with the possibility of exposure of shared secrets and values. However, at a more specific level, the group culture of the Black people is distinct in that a very large chunk of this culture has been devoted to ways of coping with whites, whether through argot, games, Uncle Tomism, or what have you. Will sharing this information through professional publications have detrimental consequences?

For some, these issues may present themselves only in terms of the researcher's honesty vs. dishonesty, though I think it cannot be so simply stated. Even the researcher may at times honestly be able to rationalize away phenomena on the ground that he has already reported enough of this kind of behavior, attitude or activity for his purposes; or, as a result of his initial concern, he may become so insensitive to certain kinds of data that he is unable to communicate them even if he sees them.

For others, these same issues may resolve themselves by an "act of faith," a belief that truth makes men freer, and by a disdain for violating ethical standards. However, the Black researcher may find that if he reports everything he sees, hears or knows to exist, he is violating certain other ethical standards which he holds.

Aside from the Black researcher's concern for the people he studies and the ultimate effects of his findings or his fear of violating a group code of ethics, he faces some of these same issues in his concern for himself. In one respect his position is much the same as that of the researcher who gets too close to or too involved with his data, particularly if the involvement is along lines of morality. The researcher who, for instance, indulges in sexual relations with some of his respondents may refrain from reporting these data. To do so would be to incriminate himself. Likewise, some of the data the Black researcher gathers, whether or not he records it, reports it, or publishes it, are likely at times to be viewed by him as self-incriminating.

This is not to say that the Black researcher deliberately sits back and hoards vast volumes of data. Part of his problem stems from his inability to see as significant or to grasp the significance of manifestations which to him may be so commonplace as to follow logically and "naturally" from a given situation. The Black researcher who may himself have come from a family of seven would in all probability not wonder about the fact that in a large family he is studying, towels, toys and other objects are not in their "proper" places, or that eating habits are somewhat irregular, or that the parents do not insist that all the children sit down and say grace together. He feels that he knows immediately, or perhaps takes for granted, what lies behind this. There is, he feels, no need to focus attention on these phenomena. There simply isn't enough room for all the rituals associated with eating and the placement of objects found in middle-class families. The Black researcher who may know certain things from previous experience is not so likely to focus on these phenomena during his field work. This is often manifested in the interactions between Black and white researchers working on the same project or conducting similar studies. One white researcher, for instance, discussed with this writer his initial hostility upon returning from the field with a new insight and receiving the response from his Black colleague, "Yes, well, I knew that all along" (a sort of "so what else is new?" response).

It has been argued that what a Black researcher is able to observe or consider relevant or problematic is a function of his socioeconomic status. There is a good deal to be said in favor of this argument. Oscar Lewis reports on the difficulty of getting middle-class Black interviewers and observers to go into some areas to study Black families. Their reactions were that they did not care to mix with these kinds of people, even for the purposes of gathering data.[6] One encounters similar reactions from some middle-class Black people, one or two generations removed from similar life-styles, in their constant amazement and concern that a researcher would go alone to a public-housing project, or indeed do research at all in such a place. However, I would argue that the mere fact of being Black, and thus of having emerged from a particular background and cultural heritage (whether it be one, two or four generations removed) inevitably leads one to regard certain things as commonplace when studying Black communities, whereas the white researcher is likely to view some of these same phenomena as problematic or even striking. To give an example, a white researcher was utterly astonished, upon visiting the home of

---

[6] Oscar Lewis, in a verbal statement to the "Conference on The Ecology of Migrant Peoples" sponsored by the International Biographical Program, Chicago, March 17–19, 1967.

a Black woman, to find her in the process of "doing her hair," something which most Black women did in 1965 and which all Black people knew that they did. However, for a considerable portion of the lives of most Black children, from birth to well into primary grades and often junior high school, their hair remained in its natural state. Since Blacks never really entered the mainstream of American society, the habits and life-styles of Black people have only recently been of interest to certain segments of the dominant American society, and common features of Black life, which Black people take for granted, are largely unknown to white Americans, even those who study them. This naïveté has its advantages in the white-dominated academic world. What the Black researcher overlooks and assumes as part of the environment, the white researcher sees as something to be explained. Even the seemingly irrelevant example given above, where the white researcher discovered for herself and for some others that Black people "do" [straighten] their hair, is significant when viewed in the same context of the new mood toward Black consciousness.

None of this is to say that the obstacles confronted by the Black researcher studying Black communities are insurmountable. And since this is not an essay on the advantages of hiring Black researchers or training Black sociologists, the merits of Black researchers will not be discussed. My aim is rather to highlight some problems encountered by the Black researcher in his field work. Granted that some of these problems—especially those centered around the future use of data and findings for purposes other than those intended—may also confront the liberal white sociologist, even these plague the Black researcher more and are not so easily resolved by "acts of faith." And, many problems I see as peculiar to the Black researcher who studies Black populations, particularly ones labeled deviant. They are problems that stem from his tendencies (forced or voluntary), to identify with Black people and his proneness to see certain things as commonplace which others view as problematic.

The significance of this, as I see it, is that the Black researcher is often confronted with what at times appear to be two conflicting roles—that of Black person and that of detached observer. As a result, he is prone to crises of identity and perhaps invariably at some point asks himself who he really is. What are his real motives? Is he prostituting himself for an education or for monetary gain? Is he in essence selling out? Does he really believe that truth in the end sets men free—and if so, how much truth and *truth for how long?* Finally, while he may recognize the importance of what he is doing and constantly attempt to redefine his role as a researcher or a sociologist in the light of being Black, I think that these redefinitions must ultimately allow him to live with himself.

It is, of course, possible that not all Black researchers studying Black populations are confronted by these problems. I have not taken an opinion sample of Black researchers, and my approach is in part subjective and personal. I think, however, that it is also more than that. If one, for instance, compares Frazier's *Black Bourgeoisie*[7] and his reflections on that piece of research[8] with Kenneth Clark's *Dark Ghetto* and his introduction to that book,[9] one needs little imagination to conclude that Frazier was, comparatively speaking, able to stand back and, it seems, to divorce himself from Black culture. Thus he was able to acquire an objective stance in comparison to Clark's somewhat impassioned view. In a conversation with one student

---

[7] E. Franklin Frazier, *Black Bourgeoisie* (Glencoe, Ill.: The Free Press, 1957).

[8] E. Franklin Frazier, "Black Bourgeoisie; Public and Academic Reactions," in *Reflections on Community Studies,* Vidich, Bensman and Stein, eds. (New York: Wiley, 1964).

[9] Kenneth Clark, *Dark Ghetto* (New York: Harper & Row, 1965).

of Black life, Frazier suggested that to view this phenomenon in its proper perspective one must consider how the
Black researcher should balance the concerns I have outlined with his career concerns vis-à-vis his white-dominated
professional colleagues.[10] It is possible that in an attempt
to establish themselves professionally, Black sociologists of
the thirties dealt themselves out.

It may well be that contemporary Black social scientists,
having to some *minor* extent established themselves, may
not deal themselves out so easily. One may conclude from
this that the perspectives of Black social scientists will
change with the times, and that the demands on them will
change with the changing social structure, as well as with
the social science demands of research.

Although I have in this section focused exclusively on the
Black researcher, I think the discussion has broader implications. People are often hired as researchers, field workers,
interviewers, because of their relative access to certain
kinds of data. Often they may have that access because of
some previous or still-existing contact with those they seek
to study. The discussion, then, is relevant in terms of how
any marginal person views his role, the conflicts he encounters, the effects of these factors on the kinds of data
he gathers, what he is able to see or wishes to see, and certainly what conclusions he is able to draw—whether he
be a Black studying Black people, a white sociologist studying the white middle class or a sociologist studying sociologists.

Role, Distance and Objectivity

The sociologist in his field work may be defined in a number of ways by his respondents: as a social worker, counselor, psychiatrist, etc., but very seldom as a sociologist.

[10] Lee Rainwater, in conversation.

While persons may have some vague notion as to what the job of a social worker or psychiatrist, welfare worker or community organizer consists of, it is probably safe to say that a very large portion of the population has not the slightest conception of the sociologist's task. Aside from or in addition to semiprofessional or professional roles, the researcher may be viewed in the light of a number of other categories. He may be "one of us," an informer for the police or some other authoritative agency, a soul brother, a white boy, an allright guy, etc. These categories denote the human qualities populations attribute to researchers; they are roles which place us in a certain position relative to those we study, a position with which we have to contend—in some instances to work within that framework and in others to attempt to alter it.

Therefore in the course of his research one may be approached to find jobs for mothers' sons, or have to listen day in and day out to problems and miseries of everyday existence, either because the respondents perceive that the researcher is in a position to offer some minimal aid, or because they simply wish to use him as a sounding board or sympathetic ear. One may sometimes be subjected against his will (depending upon the kind of research in which he engages and how easily accessible he has made himself to his subjects) to constant interruptions, and will get participation from his subject only by listening in semipsychotherapeutic sessions.

I have discussed to some extent the pitfalls of failure to maintain proper distance from one's subjects. In some instances, one might recognize that to express one's values in any form, through gesture, speech or otherwise, may inhibit the respondents, particularly if the researcher himself personally disapproves of a certain activity in process— say if the researcher is on premises where drugs are being mainlined. In some situations, distance may be not only desirable but necessary—say in a case where a man thrusts a gun, in the researcher's presence, into the face of a respondent. In this case one needs both emotional and geographical distance.

However, in many situations and with many respondents, one questions the feasibility and necessity of maintaining distance. Does distance, for instance, mean the refusal to help a semi-illiterate mother compose a letter to the welfare department for a son who badly needs glasses, because we do not wish to influence the situation? We might wish to discover how she handles situations of stress, or to return later to see who wrote the letter in order to study patterns of friendship. Eleanor Bowen in an anthropological novel[11] raises a similar issue of "cool" scientific objectivity versus nonprofessional but human intervention in the case of the impending death of one she had come to regard as a friend.

A field worker on one research project who did not intercede when he felt that one of his respondents, a very reluctant woman, who had very little food and furniture, was being duped into purchasing a three-hundred-dollar sewing machine, was heard months later to express his regrets. His initial concern with objectivity and distance prohibited his intervention, although later he felt that he would intercede if a similar occasion presented itself again. The finance company, incidentally, soon moved in to claim the woman's old but working machine in addition to reclaiming the new one.

One may logically claim that to intervene would be pointless in that ultimately the problem would present itself again—in other words, the woman would allow herself to be exploited sooner or later anyway. I think in some situations the question is not whether one should or should not intervene from a research stance, but is rather a question of one's own morals, how the researcher himself feels in a specific situation and in a particular role—what is

[11] Eleanor Bowen, *Return to Laughter* (Garden City, N.Y.: The Natural History Library, Doubleday & Co., Inc., 1964).

tolerable to him. In some instances, by using the scientific stance of objectivity and maintaining distance, one is able to defend oneself as a human being. But in others, it does not suffice. What then distinguishes the researcher from the social worker or the general "do-gooder"? Very probably scientific training has raised his tolerance level—his ability to restrain himself in a variety of situations, and his realization that his intervention is changing the course of events.

In many cases, distance will not do for either the researcher or the respondent. If a researcher has spent a considerable amount of time getting to know a family (as opposed to going in with a well-structured questionnaire for one occasion), he is more likely to react as a human being when something affects that family: "Yes, I do think it is terrible that you were cut off welfare and have nothing to eat. I do think it is wrong that they make you pay for windows your children didn't break." Indeed, the expression of sympathy may often prove to be the best weapon at one's disposal for gaining entrée to a respondent and establishing rapport. However, empathy and the expression of sympathy are not always tools for gaining rapport, or the result of sustained interaction and familiarity with respondents. Often they are merely manifestations of the basic human qualities of the field worker.

Sometimes respondents attempt to engage the researcher in lively debates or disputes on matters that do not immediately concern him, and the respondent is not always keyed to interpreting the replies and arguments in terms of how the researcher's own philosophical views apply to his personal situation. Probably very few active, energetic and thinking people, no matter what particular characteristics they possess that prompt others to study them, appreciate being in the presence of a machine that sits back in a corner, emerges sometimes to ask questions and invariably responds to the respondent's questions and arguments with "You tell me what you think." Rosalie Wax has discussed the reciprocities that are established between field worker and respondents, underlining the importance of these exchanges for both.[12]

Objectivity and distance cannot be built into every research design. If studies were entirely dependent on these qualities many field workers would fall on their faces. One's own values and biases inevitably slip through. One may unwittingly pass a cup to a respondent who prefers to drink alcohol directly from a bottle. The respondent may not always accept the cup, but may point out that he prefers to drink his liquor from the bottle. The respondent in a number of situations may remind the researcher of his own human frailties, his own biases and values, which he has brought to bear on the situation. People do not emerge from the womb full-blooded sociologists and social scientists, and respondents are not always—and perhaps not most of the time—fooled by one's proclamation of pure scientific objectivity—of oneself as the noncondemning scientist who neither holds nor expresses values.

To highlight this point I shall draw one final example from my own study of homosexual women. One of the common sentiments expressed by members of that subculture was "If you are as objective and noncondemning as you claim to be, then you should be willing to experiment with lesbianism in order to find out more about it." It seems that vague notions and proclamations of objectivity, far from solving the problems of researcher role, may in some instances create more. Although the researcher himself may be cognizant of certain values he holds and adheres to, it may be expedient and even necessary sometimes to make these values explicit to the population he is studying. Although his scientific training has taught him

[12] Rosalie H. Wax, "Reciprocity in Field Work," in *Human Organization Research*, Richard Adams and Jack Preiss, eds. (Homewood, Ill.: Dorsey Press, 1960).

the hazards of showing personal disapproval, the researcher may find himself in situations where he has to respond not so much as a scientist but as a person who might have a different set of values. The field worker does best when he feels comfortable in his role, and he should seek a role that as much as possible accommodates both his human qualities and the dictates of science.

I have attempted to discuss here some problems encountered by field workers in the study of populations labeled deviant. They are methodological problems in the sense that the researcher himself is an instrument and a tool of research. Whatever affects him also affects his perspective toward his data, his performance in the field, the kinds of data he gathers and the conclusions he draws from them. Rather than presenting solutions, I have raised questions—questions of how one thinks about human behavior and how the researcher comes to grips with people as human beings so that neither researcher nor respondent suffers in the process.

Charles Saunders

Assessing Race Relations Research

Research on racial attitudes has traditionally been done from a white perspective. This author examines the earlier attitudinal scales, including the Likert and "N" scales, and their relevancy for assessing white attitudes toward Blacks, proposing as an alternative the development of a four-dimensional scale that would measure the positive and negative attitudes that Blacks and whites have about themselves and each other with regard to race.

The purpose of this paper is to examine race attitudes research on the most popular areas for the development of measurement techniques. Through a brief description of the beginnings of this type of research, and an analysis of specific instruments that have been recently developed, evaluative conclusions will be made, from which suggestions will be offered that may help to make race attitudes research more relevant to the needs of the black community.

Initially, race attitudes studies were included as subscales of more comprehensive assessment instruments. An early example of this stage was Likert's work on the development of instruments to measure "Public Opinion." In an attempt to assess attitudes on the most controversial issues of his time, Likert and Murphy[1] devised a technique which included three divisions: an "Internationalism Scale," an "Imperialism Scale," and a "Negro Scale." For the purposes of this paper, the "Negro Scale" will be the object of concentration.

Likert divided his scales into two segments. The first was a paper and pencil test containing items such as, "Would you shake hands with a Negro," "Negro homes should be segregated from those of white people," and "If the same preparation is required, the Negro teacher should receive the same salary as the white." The second recorded reactions to two films, one showing a race riot (of the armed, race-war variety) and the other an attempted lynching (we are not told why the attempt fails). The scales had a high intercorrelation, which established their reliability, and seemed to adequately discriminate racists, moderates, and liberals on the "race question" at that time. "Liberals," I suppose, were whites who were willing to shake a black man's hand on Booker T. Washington Day, or supported equal pay for black teachers as long as they taught in "Abraham Lincoln" schools.

Likert's work was primarily concerned with questionnaire technique development; the social implications of his results were secondary. Later, however, a group of investigators became concerned about fascism; specifically how to develop an instrument sensitive to potential for fascism in American citizens. One of the variables to which the investigators attributed this potential was "ethnocentrism," which is really "prejudice!"

From this theoretical background, Levinson developed

---

[1] Gardner Murphy and Rensis Likert, *Public Opinion and the Individual*, New York: Harper, 1938.

the "E" scale.[2] Because the entire research was devoted to devising a means of rooting out potential Nazis, the main purpose of the "E" scale and associated studies was to investigate anti-Semitism. However, the "E" scale also contained a "Negro" subscale that was designed to measure white hostility toward black people. This strategy made sense. After all, in the words of a present-day U.S. fascist, "A nigger is nothing but a Jew turned inside out."[3]

Likert's method of item construction was used in the "E" scale; in fact, some of Levinson's Negro Scale items were borrowed from Likert's scale. Representative of Levinson's items on the "N" scale are: "There is something inherently primitive and uncivilized about the Negro, as shown in his music and extreme aggressiveness," and, "An occasional lynching in the South is a good thing because there is a large percentage of Negroes in many communities and they need a scare once in a while to prevent them from starting riots and disturbances." The major difference between the Likert and "N" scales was that the Likert items attempted to cover a range from pro to anti-black statements, while the "N" scale items were uniformly hostile to black people. As an instrument to measure attitudes toward minority groups, the "E" scale has proven to be relatively valid. Later studies on measuring race attitudes used the "E" scale as a validity measure.

Although the purposes of these two scales were different, their results had similar relevance to black people. As Julius Lester[4] puts it in his comments on white backlash, "Whitey hates niggers. So what else is new?" This research was a reflection of the general white attitude toward blacks

---

[2] J. W. Adorno, et al., *The Authoritarian Personality*, New York: Harper, 1950.

[3] Eric Norden, "The Paramilitary Right," *Playboy*, 1969, Volume 16, No. 6.

[4] Julius Lester, *Look Out, Whitey! Black Power's Gon' Get Your Momma!*

in that time period. The research, the development of scales, instruments, and techniques of measurement were paramount. The implications of lynching, race riots, the doctrine of cultural and biological inferiority, and all the rest on the lives of black people, were a secondary consideration, if they were considered at all.

This "set" persisted until the 1960's, when other social forces began to impose changes in the direction and purposes of race-attitudes research. Although the "pure-research" trend continues (and of course it has its intrinsic merits), a "social-action" component also appeared. One of the first of these "social action" studies was done by Greenberg in 1961.[5] Greenberg attempted to develop an "Integration Attitude Scale," which was concerned with "measuring problems which may arise in integration, per se—athletics, dances, dormitories, etc." This scale differs from the Likert and Levinson methods in two ways. First, while the Likert and "N" scales tended to concentrate on white feelings toward blacks, both individually and as a group, the Greenberg scale measured attitudes on a policy: integration. Second, Greenberg used black subjects as well as whites in his study. Methodologically, the inclusion of black subjects has revolutionary implications. Finally, it seems that the black viewpoint was considered worth studying. Outside of Clark's doll studies, this research was the first that I found in the literature that indicated an interest in assessing black racial attitudes.

Items on this Integration Attitudes scale were devised on a continuous basis between poles of positive and negative attitudes toward the "other race." Examples of the items are: "I would be willing to accept, as an equal, a member of another race into the club to which I belonged," and, "Regardless of what anyone else says, I believe that

[5] Herbert M. Greenberg, "Development of an Integration Attitude Scale," *Journal of Social Psychology*, 1961, No. 54, pp. 103–109.

my race is superior and should be accepted as such." The results show that blacks were more pro-integration than whites, and that the "I A" scale correlated well with the "E" scale. Greenberg saw promise in the scale as an instrument to measure attitudes in "specific areas of integration."

Why were the blacks more "pro-integration?" The discussion of the results didn't investigate this matter very thoroughly. Instead, Greenberg emphasized the white results, and didn't elaborate on possible further studies on the attitude of Afro-Americans toward the "other race." Again, we have an example of the subordination of black interests in race attitudes research.

As the Black Revolution increased in intensity, the interest in race-attitudes research increased concurrently. There are nearly twice as many reports on "Negroes" listed in 1961 as there were in 1950, and in 1968 there were four times as many studies as in 1960. With the increase in the volume of research, there was an increase in diversity of studies. Instead of exclusive concentration on white hostility toward blacks, there were studies of black attitudes towards whites, as well as black self-esteem or self-acceptance. In white attitude studies, different approaches were being developed.

Weiss'[6] study was an example of diversification in white attitude research. Rather than being confined to hostility or to integration opinions, Weiss' work explored "dimensions of attitudes." The study was composed of two parts. First was a stereotype measuring study, in which subjects were asked to select attributes which[7] indicated how blacks were different from other Americans,[8] characterized blacks most

[6] Walter Weiss, "An Examination of Attitudes Toward Negroes," *Journal of Social Psychology*, 1961 No. 55, pp. 3–31.

[7] Adorno, *op. cit.*

[8] James A. Bayton, Lettie J. Austin and Kay R. Burke, "Negro Perception of Negro and White Personality Traits," *Journal of Personality and Social Psychology*, 1965, Vol. I, No. 3, pp. 250–253.

accurately, and[9] most important attributes. Typical stereotypes of "flashy, musical, God-fearing, superstitious, happy-
go-lucky" resulted. However, a vast range of individual
differences led Weiss to believe that, "people do make a
distinction between the selection of traits for description
and for attitudinal significance." I suppose that means that
some whites dig "happy-go-lucky niggers" and others don't.
Nevertheless, these distinctions between descriptive and
attitudinal traits implied dimensionality of race attitudes.
The second part of the study, an "opinion questionnaire,"
was intended to measure this dimensionality. The questions
were of the following types:

Own Motive Pattern—"I would be willing to dance with
Negroes in public."

Social Motive Pattern—"I think it is an unjustifiable
policy for a business, hotel, or club to refuse to admit
Negroes."

Cognition—"Negroes are no different from white people
in any essential biological way."

Affect—"The idea of contact with the dark skin of a
Negro arouses unpleasant feelings in me."

These dimensional patterns of attitudes were significantly
correlated, and seemed to be a potentially more sensitive
method for assessing how a white respondent acts or thinks
he would act toward blacks both individually and as a
group.

The dimensional study of race attitudes among whites
was carried further by Woodmansee and Cook.[10] Under
the hypothesis that race attitudes are composed of three
main dimensions, "policy toward integration," "feelings of

[9] Kenneth R. Berg, "Ethnic Attitudes and Agreement with a Negro
Person," *Journal of Personality and Social Psychology*, 1966, Vol. 4,
No. 2.
[10] John J. Woodmansee and Stuart W. Cook, "Dimensions of Verbal
Racial Attitudes: Their Identification and Measurement," *Journal of
Personality and Social Psychology*, 1967, Vol. 7, No. 3, pp. 240–250.

racial superiority," and "nature of social relationships into which one is willing to accept Negroes," a three-phase study was conducted. Subjects were asked their opinion on statements that (1) indicated self-consciousness and un-comfortability regardless of race attitudes, and (2) assigned blacks certain attributes that would make them superior to whites. A factor analysis was done on the results to extract clusters of attitudes which would add further clarification of racial feelings. The following factors were yielded:

- integration-segregation policy
- acceptance of Negroes in close personal relationships
- Negro inferiority
- Negro superiority
- ease in interracial contacts
- derogatory belief
- local autonomy
- private rights
- acceptance in status-superior relationships
- gradualism
- sympathetic identification with the underdog.

Some of these factors are similar to Weiss' proposed dimensions, and others resemble factors implicit in question-naires as early as Likert's. Discriminability was high in several scales, but the validity of the results was question-able. However, this kind of approach should prove to be valuable because it seems to be sensitive to other aspects of race attitudes than simple anti-black hostility.

Another innovative approach to the problem of white racial attitudes was that of Sellitz, Edrich, and Cook.[11] Their purpose was to "test whether ratings of a new pool of items would be influenced by the rater's attitudes, and thus whether ratings might be used as an indicator of the rater's

---

[11] Claire Sellitz, Harold Edrich and Stuart W. Cook, "Ratings of Favorableness of Statements about a Social Group as an Indicator of Attitude Toward the Group," *Journal of Personality and Social Psychology*, 1965, Vol. 1, No. 3.

attitudes." In other words, the way a subject rates an item may be as *valid* a method of determining attitudes as whether or not he *agrees* with it. The criteria for "attitudes" were affiliation with organizations which are pro- or anti-black and answers to a self-report inventory. "New pool of items" referred to items which the authors thought were more reflective of contemporary moods than the Likert or "E" scale items. Their results showed consistent differences in ratings according to attitudes expressed in the self-report in unfavorable items. For example, anti-black subjects rated unfavorable items lower than pro-black subjects. However, the differences were less consistent in favorable items. Perhaps these results were biased by some "I'm not prejudiced, but I don't want any colored living in my block" type subjects.

In a followup study[12] the same researchers studied the effects of context on the above rating procedure. They found that "changing the context of the items lessened their usefulness." Also, it was found that "shortening the item range causes a shift in the direction in which it was shortened." If negative items were removed, for example, there was a compensatory shift to less favorable ratings of positive items. The authors suggested that "strongly biased items at either end may be necessary to provide a background conducive to variation in ratings of more moderate items." If this tendency proves consistent, it may cast doubt on the validity of the "E" scale. Since all the items on that scale were negative, there may have been a "compensatory shift" to rate negative items more positively. But the idea of rating statements as a method of assessing attitudes is worth further investigation.

Two final examples of new directions in white attitude

[12] Harold Edrich, Claire Sellitz and Stuart W. Cook, "The Effects of Context and Rater's Attitudes on Judgments of Favorableness of Statements About a Social Group," *Journal of Social Psychology*, 1966, No. 70, pp. 11–12.

studies are the work of Williams and Roberson[13] and Kinnick and Plattor.[14] In the Williams and Roberson study, a picture-comparison test was developed to measure race attitudes in preschool children. The test was divided into two parts. The first part consisted of black and white pictures of toys and animals, which were associated with paired adjectives such as "good-bad," or "clean-dirty." For the second part, the same procedure was applied to pictures of black and white people. The high correlation between the responses to pictures of toys, animals and people led the authors to suggest "concurrent development of racial attitudes and color meanings." These results reinforce what black people have known for a long time. Kids are no fools. They pick up on the Anglo-Saxon cultural derogation of the concept "black" at an early age, and they don't need to go to school to do it. When they become exposed to black people, the association is made, and "concurrent development of racial attitudes and color meanings" follows inevitably.

Kinnick and Plattor's contribution was a 30-item "D" or "desegregation" scale to measure "specific attitudes toward Negroes and public school desegregation." Due to high correlations with the "E" and "F" scales, this "D" scale was thought to be a "promising" indicator of white attitudes toward desegregation. If we change the word "integration" for "desegregation," we have Greenberg's "Integration Attitude" scale, which has already been discussed.

The validity of any kind of race attitude measure was attacked by Berg.[15] Using a social agreement procedure in

[13] John E. Williams and Karen J. Roberson, "A Method of Assessing Racial Attitudes in Preschool Children," *Educational and Psychological Measurement*, 1967, No. 27, pp. 671–89.

[14] Bernard C. Kinnick and Stanton D. Plattor, "Attitudinal Change Toward Negroes and School Desegregation Among Participants in a Summer Training Institute," *Journal of Social Psychology*, 1967, Vol. 28, No. 4, pp. 338–52.

[15] Berg, *op. cit.*

which subjects were to "give autokinetic judgments with
a Negro and a white confederate," Berg tested the hypothesis that, "prejudiced attitudes toward Negroes would
be directly to disagree with a Negro person, and the relationship between prejudiced attitudes and social disagree-
ments would be closer when the judgmental task was more
important." As verbal measures of attitudes, the "E" scale,
the "F" scale, and the Bogardus Social Distance scale were
utilized. The results indicated "no significant differences or
correlations between attitude scale results and agreements
with a Negro person," which led him to conclude that: (1)
"Verbal attitude scales may not be good predictors of
prejudiced behavior," or (2) "Autokinetic judgments may
not be a good task for expecting prejudiced behavior."
Berg's first conclusion may be justified. His study was
reported in 1966, but it used instruments that were at least
20 years old. Perhaps the use of instruments more sensitive
to the contemporary racial situation would have given
better data. At any rate, the idea of testing verbal attitude
scores against overt behavior provides a good possibility
for the validation of race attitude scales. For example, does
a white cop who scores high on prejudice scales bust more
soul brothers' heads than one who scores low?

Black self-esteem has been another relatively new area
of race-attitudes research. We can conceptualize black self-
esteem or self-acceptance in part as a reaction to white
attitudes toward blacks. Some blacks maintain positive
self-esteem regardless of what the white man thinks of
them. Others turn their anger at negative white attitudes
inward toward themselves and their ethnic group. There
have been some studies devoted to these and other aspects
of black self-esteem. Trent[16] hypothesized that "acceptance

---

[16] Richard D. Trent, "The Relation Between Expressed Self-Acceptance and Expressed Attitudes Toward Negroes and Whites among
Negro Children," *Journal of Genetic Psychology*, 1957, No. 91,
pp. 25–41.

of self is related to acceptance of others—self-accepting Negro children would have more positive attitudes toward both Negroes and whites than would Negro children who were less self-accepting." To measure self-acceptance, he used a sentence-completion test with Berger's ten criteria as a guide. Attitudes were assessed by an "Attitude Finder," which was based on Kramer's three dimensions of cognitive, emotional, and action components of attitudes. Trent's major finding was that "children who were most self-accepting expressed significantly more positive attitudes toward Negroes and whites than the least self-accepting children." Important questions raised by that result are what the basis of these black children's self-acceptance was, and whether the positive attitudes of self-accepting children were greater toward whites or blacks.

Gaier and Wambach[17] postulated that because of the constant social oppression that they undergo, "Negroes adopt masochist-like behavior patterns." To test this hypothesis, the authors used an open-ended test to "examine behavioral and personality facets considered to be most positive, and most negative by racially different college students which might reflect different social determinants." Subjects were asked to "list three each of what they considered to be their greatest assets and greatest liabilities." Assets were divided into "group behavior, character traits, and achievement," liabilities into "group behavior, character traits and personal." Black males showed significantly less achievement response than white males, which was expected under their hypothesis. However, there were no other significant differences reported between blacks and whites of either sex. Although the hypothesis has merit, the listing technique may not be adequate to measure "masochist-like" behavior.

[17] Eugene L. Gaier and Helen S. Wambach, "Self-Evaluation of Personality Assets and Liabilities of Southern White and Negro Students," *Journal of Social Psychology*, 1960, No. 51, pp. 135-143.

Another study of black self-esteem was that of Gregor and McPherson.[18] The Clark Doll Test, which involves color-trait choices between black and white dolls (and was one of the deciding factors in the 1954 Supreme Court decision) was given to a group of black and white Southern children. The results indicated that both black and white children tended to identify with their own ethnic group, and also that the more a black child is exposed to a white environment, the more he identifies with whites rather than blacks, and the more he tends to show aggression toward his own group. This study demonstrates the continuation of the historical tragedy of "integration" for black people. Again, the results tell us nothing new. Since the days of slavery, the "house nigger" has been "integrated," identified more with the white slavemaster, and had displaced his aggression and frustration at not being totally accepted by his masters onto his more vulnerable brothers in the field. Malcolm X eloquently expresses this truth in his autobiography.[19]

Bayton, Austin, and Burke[20] conducted a similar study using a different technique. Their premise was that "members of minority groups tend to have attitudes and stereotypes concerning their respective groups which are similar to those held by the white majority." The instrument used here was the Guilford-Zimmerman Temperament Survey. Black subjects were told to respond to the items as they thought Negroes and whites would. The authors found "three dimensions of racial personality: the trait being 'stereotyped,' sex of group being assessed, and the sex of the subject . . . for six of the ten traits, the means for

[18] James A. Gregor and Angus D. McPherson, "Racial Attitudes Among White and Negro Children in a Deep South Standard Metropolitan Area," *Journal of Social Psychology*, 1966, No. 68, pp. 95–106.

[19] Malcolm X, *The Autobiography of Malcolm X*, New York: Grove Press, 1965.

[20] Bayton, *op. cit.*

whites, in contrast to those of Negroes, were in the direction indicative of better personality development." Their speculations as to why whites seemed to be moving more toward "better personality development" than blacks were "tendency to idealize aggressor,"[21] and "tendency to incorporate the aggressor's negative views toward minority group."[22] These results may indicate the "masochist-like behavior" suggested by Gaier and Wambach. They also could indicate another dimension of the McGregor results; that this "idealization" of the oppressor and introjection of his views may be the reason for further identification with whites and aggression toward blacks as blacks move further into white environments.

The main emphasis in all the literature thus far is the measurement of white attitudes toward blacks and black self-esteem. Other than Greenberg's Integration Attitudes Scale, I found only one recent study that dealt exclusively with black attitudes toward whites. Jackson[23] developed a questionnaire to assess attitudes of black faculty at all—or predominantly black colleges. Specifically, the object of the test was to investigate the attitudes of black faculty toward the addition of white faculty at their schools. Favorable and unfavorable factors were built into the test, and the initial results showed that the tendency was to favor the addition of white faculty, but there was deep concern over differential treatment, effects on the black teacher market, and adverse effects on morale, salary, and power structure among black teachers. This study was termed by its author as a "pilot study," and she indicated scant reliability and validity information. But anyone who has attended or had contact with a black college knows what she's talking about. These professors don't want Whitey encroaching

21 Adorno, *op. cit.*

22 Bayton, *op. cit.*

23 Jacquelyn J. Jackson, "An Exploration of Attitudes Toward Faculty Desegregation in Negro Colleges," *Phylon*, 1967.

on their academic fiefdoms. Ralph Ellison's *Invisible Man*[24] provides an enlightening glimpse of the power that administrators and faculty of a black college can wield. But this is a digression. The point here is that I could find no other studies that attempted to measure black attitudes toward whites and nothing else.

In conclusion, I would say that there have been some advances in race-attitude measurement in terms of the development of new techniques in assessing white attitudes toward blacks, and in the problem of black self-esteem. However, two other components of black-white race attitudes have been neglected; in fact ignored. The lack of investigation of assessment instruments for black attitudes toward whites and white self-esteem vis-à-vis race attitudes is where the deficiencies lie. Why are these aspects important? It has been emphasized that race-attitudes research has often reflected the climate of the times in which it was conducted. Today, black awareness and consciousness are powerful forces in our society. But recent literature has either ignored or barely touched on this trend.

For example, a study by Pierce-Jones, Jackson, and King[25] showed that black juvenile delinquents scored high on the "negativism toward society" section of the Cooperation Youth Study Scales. Does "negativism toward society" mean anti-white race attitudes? Current research doesn't tell us. But these attitudes exist, and Grier and Cobbs express them well in *Black Rage:*[26]

Observe that the amount of rage the oppressed turns on his tormentor is a direct function of the depth of his grief, and

[24] Ralph Ellison, *Invisible Man*, New York: Random House, 1947.

[25] John Pierce-Jones, Reid B. Jackson, and F. J. King, "Adolescent Racial and Ethnic Group Differences in Social Attitude and Adjustment," *Psychological Reports*, 1959, Vol. 5, pp. 549–552.

[26] William H. Grier and Price M. Cobbs, *Black Rage*, New York: Basic Books, 1968.

consider the intensity of his grief. . . . Slip for a moment into the soul of a black girl whose womanhood is blighted, not because she is ugly, but because she is black, and by definition all blacks are ugly. . . . Become for a moment a black citizen of Birmingham, Alabama, and try to understand his grief and dismay when innocent children are slain while they worship, for no other reason than that they are black. . . . For a moment be any black person, anywhere, and you will feel the waves of hopelessness that engulfed black men and women when Martin Luther King was murdered. All black people understood the tide of anarchy that followed his death. . . . As a sapling bent low stores energy for a violent backswing, blacks bent double by oppression have stored energy which will be released in the form of rage—black rage, apocalyptic and final.

Such intensity of feeling can hardly be adequately described, or measured, by studies concerned with "integration attitudes," "attitudes of black faculty toward desegregation of their colleges," or "negativism toward society." If race-attitudes assessments can concentrate on the study of white hostility, then, to be legitimate, instruments must be developed that are sensitive to "black rage." This is a wide-open field for black psychologists to study, both for the benefit of our community and the "body of knowledge" of Black Psychology.

White self-esteem is the other major aspect of race attitudes that needs investigation. Dick Gregory's insight[27] illuminates this need:

The free man is the man with no fears. The strange truth in America today is that the Negro has become the psychological master, and the white man the psychological slave. . . . When a Negro family moves into an all-white neighborhood, white residents begin running. . . . Who is free? If I went on the Ed Sullivan show tonight and spoke in favor of integrated

[27] Dick Gregory, *The Shadow That Scares Me*, New York: Doubleday, 1968.

marriages, nothing would happen to me. If Ed Sullivan spoke in favor of the same thing, he would lose his rating and his job. Who is free? I was on a radio show not long ago. It was one of those talk shows which encouraged listeners to telephone in their opinions. A lady phoned to speak to me while I was on the air. She identified herself as being white and said, "I am sorry I can't give you my name. I just wanted you to know that I agree with you." She agreed with me; but her color and the reactions of her friends and neighbors who might be listening to the same program kept her from mentioning her name. Who is free? Only the psychological slave hides from his own name!

Even if Gregory's observations were exaggerated, their implications would still warrant the investigation of white self-esteem as part of the overall study of race attitudes. This kind of research would parallel the study of black self-esteem in terms of ego and race attitudes. Also, the data provided may help to clarify nebulous popular concepts such as "white guilt."

And so, we have an outline of the state of affairs in the field of race-attitudes research. I have concentrated on instruments which have been developed as an attempt to measure these attitudes because it is this aspect which will prove to be most useful to the black community. Although some progress has been made over the years in refining and diversifying existing measures, glaring deficiencies exist in the important areas of black attitudes toward whites, and white self-esteem.

What can be done to correct these deficiencies and create measures that are more than the "paper soul food," that have been masqueraded as "relevant action-oriented research?" I propose that a four-dimensional scale of race attitudes be developed. It can be hypothesized that black and white people have positive and negative attitudes about themselves and each other in terms of various issues that involve race.

An ideal instrument for the measurement of these attitudes would thus entail the following four dimensions: pro-white, anti-white, pro-black and anti-black. These dimensions could be divided into categories which reflected issues such as militance, bigotry, integration and separatism. Items would be balanced between extremely positive, moderate, and extremely negative connotations. Responses to these items could indicate how the subject feels about the other race as well as himself in terms of his own ethnic identification. For example, positive responses to pro-white items could be considered "positive racial self-esteem" for whites, and "positive feeling toward the oppressor" in blacks. An "anti-white" response could be scored as "poor self-esteem" for whites and "negative feeling for the oppressor" in blacks. A "pro-black" response could imply "positive self-esteem" for blacks or "sympathetic identification with the underdog" in whites. "Anti-black" responses could indicate "prejudice" in whites, and "love self-esteem" for blacks. The various combinations of these dimensions could provide a single multipurpose instrument for race-attitudes assessment in blacks and whites.

All this is fine theoretically, but what good does it do the black community? An objective race-attitudes measure could be very useful to us. For example, a Black Studies teacher who scored low on black self-esteem might be less effective than one who scored high. Ghetto school children are classified by a multitude of tests. A race-attitudes test could be used to classify ghetto *teachers*. High-scoring anti-black teachers could be removed from black schools. High-scoring anti-black policemen could be removed from duty in black areas. For research purposes, this kind of measure would provide a comprehensive basis for investigating the reasons for development of unhealthy race attitudes and for developing methods to forestall these attitudes from developing in the future. We would finally have a technique of both research and practical value in the black community as an objective measure of blackness.

PART VI

Subjective Sociological Research

Kenneth B. Clark

Introduction to an Epilogue

One of the more penetrating analyses of Black life in the contemporary urban setting is Kenneth B. Clark's *Dark Ghetto*. Published in 1965, it appeared at a time when many urban programs had been implemented to attempt to find "solutions" to the problems of the urban Black masses. The book is important for another reason as well. In it Clark departs markedly from the traditional "objective" analyses set forth in community studies. Describing himself as an "involved" observer, Clark observes that he "could never be fully detached as a scholar or participant." The following essay is taken from the introduction to *Dark Ghetto*.

It is difficult to know the source of a book. This book grows directly from the two years which the author spent as chief project consultant and chairman of the board of directors of the planning stage of Harlem Youth Opportunities Unlimited (Haryou). But, indirectly, its source is far more complex.

Haryou was financed by the President's Committee on

Juvenile Delinquency and by the Mayor of the City of New York. In June 1962 its responsibilities were to set up the offices and hire a staff to study the conditions of youth in Harlem as background for a comprehensive program for these young people, and to submit within two years a report and a proposal for the funds necessary to implement these plans. With the publication of the report *Youth in the Ghetto: A Study of the Consequences of Powerlessness and a Blueprint for Change*, Haryou concluded its planning responsibility. In April 1964, the report was officially presented to the review panel of the President's Committee on Juvenile Delinquency. The review panel, headed by Dr. Leonard S. Cottrell, recommended an initial allocation of $1 million to put this program into action. The City of New York then allocated $3.5 million from its Anti-Poverty Program funds for general programming and the Department of Labor of the federal government granted $0.5 million to begin the job training and placement part of the Haryou program. I resigned from Haryou during this transition period between planning and implementation.

The action phase of the program is to be conducted by the combined forces of Haryou and Associated Community Teams (Act), an action program for the youth of Harlem, also financed by the President's Committee on Juvenile Delinquency during the same period when planning operations of Haryou were begun. Haryou-Act Inc. the new combined group, is charged with the responsibility of implementing the Haryou plans through operation of the multi-million dollar Harlem Youth Development program.

Initially, it was thought that the 620-page report *Youth in the Ghetto* should be published for more general distribution than it was possible to do privately. The board of directors of Haryou therefore established a committee with authority to make the necessary arrangements for such publication. The author of the book was chairman of the committee and was empowered to make the appropriate revisions. However, as work proceeded on the revisions and as one observed developments and problems related to the early stages of Haryou-Act, it became clear that a condensation and revision alone could not present a full and clear picture of the plight of Harlem's youth within the ghetto community. The Haryou report had been written for the specific purpose of presenting a plan for Harlem's youth to those review panels and groups in the federal, state and city governments and private foundations to whom requests would come for funds for the Haryou program. A book for the general public had to be broader and deeper in scope and purpose. While the Haryou report emphasized the plight of youth in Harlem, the present book concentrates on the problems of ghetto communities everywhere and with all of the inhabitants of the ghettos, not with youth alone. *Youth in the Ghetto*, therefore, became merely a point of departure for *Dark Ghetto*.

My two years of intense involvement with the Haryou planning project led to reflections that resulted in this study of the total phenomena of the ghetto. My direct involvement with the young people associated with Haryou, the countless committee meetings, board meetings, staff meetings, the inevitable contacts and communication with the newspapers of the community and the daily metropolitan press, and the meetings with federal, state and city officials brought me into the vortex of the ghetto community and in touch with the lives, the feelings, the thoughts, the strengths and weaknesses of the people who lived in the ghetto. *Dark Ghetto* attempts to communicate the momentum of this dynamic and, at times, personally threatening involvement. During this period the Harlem community became a laboratory in which I sought, not always successfully, to play the role of an "involved observer." It was hoped this concentrated project, with its clear and specific goals, would sharpen insight into problems which tend to become obscured for those who live in the ghetto and are required to struggle for their existence there.

But I could never be fully detached as a scholar or

participant. More than forty years of my life had been lived in Harlem. I started school in the Harlem public schools. I first learned about people, about love, about cruelty, about sacrifice, about cowardice, about courage, about bombast in Harlem. For many years before I returned as an "involved observer," Harlem had been my home. My family moved from house to house, and from neighborhood to neighborhood within the walls of the ghetto in a desperate attempt to escape its creeping blight. In a very real sense, therefore, *Dark Ghetto* is a summation of my personal and lifelong experiences and observations as a prisoner within the ghetto long before I was aware that I was really a prisoner. To my knowledge, there is at present nothing in the vast literature of social science treatises and textbooks and nothing in the practical or field training of graduate students in social science to prepare them for the realities and complexities of this type of involvement in a real, dynamic, turbulent, and at times seemingly chaotic community. And what is more, nothing anywhere in the training of social scientists, teachers, or social workers now prepares them to understand, to cope with, or to change the normal chaos of ghetto communities. These are grave lacks which must be remedied soon if these disciplines are to become relevant to the stability and survival of our society.

The role and method of an "involved observer" is not an easy one to describe, but it is necessary to try. One owes an obligation to do so to one's colleagues who are also concerned with problems related to a systematic approach to the study of men in society. This role is particularly difficult to maintain when one is not only a participant in the community but when one brings to the attempt to use this method, with that degree of clarity and objectivity essential for social science accuracy, a personal history of association with and concern for many of the people in the very community one seeks to study. The method of study has much in common with the more traditional methods of a "participant observer" and the methods of the cultural anthropologist, who lives with primitive peoples in order to understand and describe their customs, their mores, and their total culture. All such methods require the observer to be a part of what is being observed, to join in the lives of the people while at the same time seeking to understand them and the forces which mold them and to which they respond. The role of the "involved observer," however, differs from the other two in that it demands participation not only in rituals and customs but in the social competition with the hierarchy in dealing with the problems of the people he is seeking to understand. While the observer of an alien group has the protection of the stranger to whom the group is required to show some degree of courtesy or hospitality, the "involved observer" runs the risk of joining in the competition for status and power and cannot escape the turbulence and conflict inherent in the struggle. He must be exposed at the same time that he seeks to protect himself and to protect his role of observer. He must run the risk of personal attacks, disappointments, personal hurts and frustrations, at the same time that he maintains a disciplined preoccupation with his primary goal of understanding. He must mobilize and use every personal resource, strength, and weakness in his struggle for clarity and perspective, though the personal and at times deeply subjective involvement would seem to work against achievement of clarity. Probably the most difficult assault to which he will be subjected is the questioning of his personal motives, the veiled and at times rather flagrant assertion that his concern with the problems of the community stem from a desire for personal power or material gain. In a ghetto community, where the material rewards are hard to come by, the motives of almost everyone are suspect. It is not easy for even the more intelligent or more sophisticated prisoners of the ghetto to believe that anyone could be motivated primarily, if not exclusively, by the desire to understand the depth of the human predicament. How much more difficult then for the scarred or hardened victims of the ghetto to believe that anyone could desire genuine social change or social justice. For the residents of the ghetto, who have learned from bitter experience, any form of altruism appears to be a ruse, a transparent disguise for the "hustle." The "hustle," the "cashing in," the smooth or crude exploiter, seem the realities.

Distortion of vision and confusion may harass the "involved observer," but the inevitable pressures of his role bring, also, gnawing self-doubt. It is the ultimate test of strength, which this observer did not always pass, as the pressures intensify and as the examples of equivocation and broken agreements accumulate, to discipline himself and attempt to control his defensiveness, his doubts concerning the adequacy of self, and above all, his desire to escape before the completion of his task. The only effective antidotes to this tropistic need to protect oneself in the face of engulfing pathology are a commitment to the quest for understanding and truth and a compulsion to persist in this quest in spite of personal hazards. In this regard the role of the "involved observer" is not unlike that of Bruno Bettelheim and Viktor E. Frankl, who used their skill and training to provide us with some understanding of the nature of the horror and the barbarity of the German concentration camps.* The circumstances of their initial observation were involuntary. The return of a former inhabitant to the Harlem ghetto appears to be a matter of personal choice, but who can say how free the choice really is. Can the prisoner ever fully escape the prison?

What are the possible antidotes to the deficiencies and

* Bruno Bettelheim, "Individual and Mass Behavior in Extreme Situations," *Journal of Abnormal and Social Psychology*, 1943, *38*, pp. 417–452; Viktor E. Frankl, *Man's Search for Meaning, An Introduction to Logotherapy.* (A newly revised and enlarged edition of *From Death-Camp to Existentialism.*) Boston, Beacon Press, 1962.

pitfalls of involved observations? One desirable counter-check would be made by a parallel person who would test the observations, insights, and conclusions of the primary observer. Such a person would have to be more detached than he but at the same time fully cognizant of the problems and processes of the situation. He must be of equal professional stature and capable of the same level of, if not more, penetrating insight and intelligence. He must be protected and removed from direct competitive involvement with the community and with the primary observer himself. He must be a person in whose competence, but even more important, in whose critical judgment and integrity, the observer has total confidence. In the Haryou planning operation I had the good fortune of having available a number of consultants, some of whom played this critical role most effectively. Furthermore, for me, Dr. Hylan Lewis, professor of sociology at Howard University and a consultant to Haryou from its inception, assumed the burdens of this role with enthusiasm and at times with awesome and prophetic insights. If I had not been able to consult with him as the many crises arose I could not have continued my responsibilities through to their conclusion. Hylan Lewis's counsel, advice, critical comments, and suggestions from the beginning of the Haryou process to the completion of the manuscript of *Dark Ghetto* were, in the most literal sense, invaluable.

During the planning stage of Haryou some of the traditional social science methods were used, including tape recordings of meetings and of group and individual interviews. All of the statements of Harlem residents presented in the first chapter, "Prologue: The Cry of the Ghetto," were obtained by Willie Jones, Haryou staff interviewer, who has the capacity not only to talk naturally with the people of Harlem but to elicit responses from them by blending into the style and adopting the idiom of the particular group or individual whose opinions he was seeking. It is of some methodological significance to note that the presence of a portable or stationary tape recorder and the inevitable microphone did not inhibit the responses of these subjects even when they were discussing drug addiction or police graft. On the contrary, it seemed that the starvation for serious attention and respect which characterizes so many of the forgotten people of the ghetto made the microphone a symbol of respect and status or a stimulus to vanity which encouraged free expression. This might not have been the case for more reserved middle-class people who might tend to view a microphone or tape recorder as invasion of their privacy and therefore to respond with appropriate protective defenses of repression, censoring, or distortion. Among the Haryou subjects, the posture of exaggeration, if not bombast, seemed more apparent than did inhibition. Intensity of feeling, anguish, and concern were freely and at times vehemently expressed. But even the most obvious hyperbole reflected a level of reality which can not be ignored if the complexities and potential explosiveness of the American ghettos are to be understood.

It became clear in the early stages of the Haryou study that while usual methods of data collection and analysis would contribute to an understanding of the demographic statistics of the community, the use of standardized questionnaires and interview procedures would result in stylized and superficial verbal responses or evasions. The outstanding finding at this time was that data obtained by these traditional methods did not plumb the depth or the complexities of the attitudes and anxieties, the many forms of irony and rage which form the truths of the lives of the people of Harlem. Methods which simplified these complex realities, subordinating the difficult and multifaceted realities to the constraints of the methods, could not be taken seriously without presenting and perpetuating a superficial and methodologically distorted social reality. The task confronting the Haryou research staff, then, was to discover and probe the dimensions of the ghetto with the most appropriate methods. It was hoped that the social phenomena would determine the methods instead of the methods distorting or determining the phenomena. It was necessary, therefore, to run risks, to establish as many contacts as possible with groups in the community; to organize groups of young people; to plan confrontations and conflicts among individuals within groups and between groups in order to draw forth deep feelings and ambivalences, and to see how these individuals responded to and interpreted and resolved those conflicts.

Probably the most distinctive fact about the Haryou process was the involving of hundreds of young people from various social, economic, and educational backgrounds in the research and planning. A group known as the Haryou Associates was formed by the young people themselves, who worked as volunteer research assistants and who pretested program ideas. Others, generally college students and the children of middle- or upper-class parents, found themselves able to establish only a peripheral or specifically limited relationship with the planning operation. They tended to see themselves more as "volunteers" or "missionaries" who would contribute as much time to Haryou as their other activities and demands would permit. Unlike the young people in Haryou Associates, they did not consider that they were directly involved in the goals of Haryou nor did they see any direct benefit to themselves. But all the youth associated with Haryou formed a valuable natural laboratory for direct observation and study of the human forces at work in the larger community. They were a microcosm of the Harlem community, though in a technical sense not totally representative of the people of Harlem. Through them it was possible to see more clearly the struggles and patterns of adjustment of the ghetto. Their problems, conflicts, defenses, and fantasies, their strengths and their weaknesses, their perspectives of themselves, their doubts and their aspirations, their defiance and their defeat or their affirmation and success were living experiences and more valuable than statistics.

Dark Ghetto attempts to go beyond the data gathered by Haryou. Though it relies in part upon material which formed a valuable factual basis for the report, it does so primarily as a point of departure. *Dark Ghetto* is, in a sense, no report at all, but rather the anguished cry of its author. But it is the cry of a social psychologist, controlled in part by the concepts and language of social science, and as such can never express the pure authenticity of folk spontaneity or the poetic symbolism of the artist. This book is and can be no wiser than its author. It is his interpretation of the meaning of the facts of the ghetto, the truths behind the delinquency, narcotics addiction, infant mortality, homicide and suicide statistics. In determining the value to be given to these impressions, the reader should know that the author is a Negro, a social psychologist, a college professor, and that he has long been revolted by those forces in American society which make for Harlems and by the fact of Harlem itself; and that he has not lived in Harlem in more than fifteen years. These and other facts do not make for absolute objectivity in judgment and they might lead a critical and exacting reader to suspect distortion and bias. Some form of subjective distortion seems inevitable whenever human beings dare to make judgments about any aspect of the human predicament.

Throughout my role as a student of the Harlem community, I was conscious of my biases and sought to correct them and test them against the biases and judgments of others with similar and different biases. A bias, used in this sense, is a starting hunch or hypothesis determined by a system of values with which one approaches and seeks to understand social reality. As Charles Beard said of himself and other social scientists in *The Discussion of Human*

*Affairs,** I found that there was no one without some bias and that those who pretended to be most unbiased either were indifferent or reflected an insidious form of bias. An important part of my creed as a social scientist is that on the grounds of absolute objectivity or on a posture of scientific detachment and indifference, a truly relevant and serious social science cannot ask to be taken seriously by a society desperately in need of moral and empirical guidance in human affairs. Nor can it support its claims to scientific purity or relevance by a preoccupation with methodology as an end and by innumerable articles in scientific journals devoted to escapist, even though quantifiable, trivia. I believe that to be taken seriously, to be viable, and to be relevant social science must dare to study the real problems of men and society, must use the real community, the market place, the arena of politics and power as its laboratories, and must confront and seek to understand the dynamics of social action and social change. The appropriate technology of serious and relevant social science would have as its prime goal helping society move toward humanity and justice with minimum irrationality, instability, and cruelty. If social science and social technology cannot help achieve these goals then they will be ignored or relegated to the level of irrelevance, while more serious men seek these goals through trial and error or through the crass exercise of power.

This study of the Negro ghetto is an attempt to understand the combined problems of the confined Negro and the problems of the slum. Some of the problems of the lower-status Negro are similar to and identical with the problems of poor people and slums in general. But in America, the white poor and slum dweller have the advantage of the social and psychological reality which is an essential aspect of American racism; that is, the belief that they can rise

---

* New York, Macmillan, 1936.

economically and escape from the slums. The Negro believes himself to be closely confined to the pervasive low status of the ghetto, and in fact usually is. This book's emphasis on the pathologies of American ghettos attempts to describe and interpret what happens to human beings who are confined to depressed areas and whose access to the normal channels of economic mobility and opportunity is blocked. This approach is not to be equated with assumptions of "inherent racial differences" or with the more subtly discriminatory "cultural deprivation" theories. It seeks answers to many questions, and among them are these: What are the personal and social consequences of the ghetto? What are the consequences of the victims' lack of power to change their status? What are the consequences of the inability or unwillingness of those with power to use it for constructive social change? The answers to these questions have implications beyond the important problems of American racial and economic ghettos, implications that may extend to an understanding of the chances of stability of relations between underdeveloped and developed nations of the world and that may hold the key to general international stability.

There have been a number of studies dealing with the American Negro and a number dealing with the American urban poor, but few concerned with the Negro ghetto itself. As a consequence, one finds meager data in other cities to compare with the Haryou studies of Harlem, hence the necessary reliance in *Dark Ghetto* on data relating to Harlem. For example, delinquency statistics may be available for a slum area of a given city or there may be national statistics for Negro unemployment, but little is available to describe the Negro ghetto itself, and certainly little has been done by social scientists to study the psychological— i.e., the human—significance of the ghetto.

A few years ago a highly respected friend, who is a psychiatrist, interrupted a humorous but somewhat serious discussion by observing that I would not permit "the facts to interfere with the truth." At the time we laughed in appreciation of the wit inherent in the seeming incongruity of the observation. Since then I have many times recalled that remark with increasing appreciation of its profound significance. Throughout my involvement in the study of the ghetto, in the collection of the data about Harlem, in my exposure to currents and cross currents of the community, it became increasingly clear to me that what are generally labeled as the *facts* of the ghetto are not necessarily synonymous with the *truth* of the ghetto. In fact, there are times when one feels that "facts" tend to obscure truth. *Dark Ghetto* seeks to move, as far as it can, beyond a narrow view of fact, beyond the facts that are quantifiable and are computable, and that distort the actual lives of individual human beings into rigid statistics. Probably such facts reflect or suggest some of the truth; delinquency and infant mortality rates do tell us that some people get in trouble with society and that others die early in life. But such facts do not relate the truths of the parents' emotions when confronted with the blight of defeat or death nor do they reveal the individual delinquent, his struggle for self-esteem, his pretense at indifference or defiance of his fate, his vulnerability to hurt, his sense of rejection, his fears, his angers, or his sense of aloneness. These are rejected as facts by most social scientists because they are not now quantifiable.

To obtain the truth of Harlem one must *interpret* the facts. Certain social truths can be more painful and disturbing than facts, and this truth may account in some measure for social science's seemingly endless preoccupation with statistics. Statistics may be manipulated and played with, analyzed and treated in a way calculated to lead to minimum pain or personal involvement. They are "manageable." Figures on the extent of malnutrition in Southern states or rural areas are impersonal and are not especially disturbing. Direct encounter with a starving child, on the other hand, is a truth which is personal; it remains personally disturbing until the child is fed. To face social truths seems to require empathy, social sensitivity, and a peculiar type of courage.

Another basis for the confusion between social facts and social truths is that one fact may lead to different truths or assumptions of truth. There may be differences in the degree of empathy on the part of the interpreter or differences in the extent of personal encounter or in the resorting to devices like denial, repression, and rationalization. But also, differences in the nature of the interpretation may be the result of individual point of view or philosophy. A good illustration of this is found in the story that Otto Klineberg used to tell: Two alcoholics looked at the same bottle of whiskey in which half the content had been consumed. The optimistic alcoholic was glad that the bottle was half full; his pessimistic companion was depressed that it was half empty.

Similarly, one social scientist looking at the delinquency statistics in Harlem could rejoice in the *facts* that show that the vast majority of young people in the ghetto— nearly 90 percent—do not come in conflict with the law. Another social scientist might concentrate on the fact of the 10 percent who do become delinquent.

Truth is more complex, multifaceted and value-determined than is the usual fact. Fact is empirical while truth is interpretative. Fact is, in itself, unrelated to value; it merely *is*. Truth, as the understanding—in the fullest sense —of fact, is related to value and, for that reason, more fully human.

Dark Ghetto attempts to use some of the facts of Harlem to ascertain some of the truths of human ghettos. Since truth is not easy to grasp or recognize—it remains more of a quest than an attainment—one is obliged to seek it through a continuous process of observation, speculation, refinement of hypothesis, and testing of those hypotheses which are at present testable. It is my hope that the attempt presented in this book will stimulate further research and study in quest of truth and social justice.

To understand Harlem, one must seek the truth and one must dare to accept and understand the truths one does find. One must understand its inconsistencies, its contradictions, its paradoxes, its ironies, its comic and its tragic face, its cruel and its self-destructive forces, and its desperate surge for life. And above all one must understand its humanity. The truth of the dark ghetto is not merely a truth about Negroes; it reflects the deeper torment and anguish of the total human predicament.

Joyce A. Ladner

Tomorrow's Tomorrow: The Black Woman

What problems face the sociologist who attempts to transcend the "liberal bourgeois" perspective in his analysis and substitute for it one that emerges from and is shaped by the Black experience? In this chapter, taken from the introduction to the anthology editor's work, *Tomorrow's Tomorrow: The Black Woman*, some basic assumptions regarding the necessity for reconceptualizing this topic are set forth.

It is very difficult to determine whether this work had its beginnings when I was growing up in rural Mississippi and experiencing all the tensions, conflicts, joys, sorrows, warmth, compassion and cruelty that was associated with *becoming a Black woman;* or whether it originated with my graduate school career when I became engaged in research for a doctoral dissertation. I *am* sure that the twenty years I spent being socialized by my family and the broader Black community prior to entering graduate school shaped my perception of life, defined my emotive responses to the world and enhanced my ability to survive in a society that has not made survival for Blacks easy. Therefore, when I decided to engage in research on what approaching womanhood meant to poor Black girls in the city, I brought with me these attitudes, values, beliefs and in effect, a Black perspective. Because of this cultural sensitivity I had to the life-styles of the over one hundred adolescent, preadolescent and adult females I "studied," I had to mediate tensions that existed from day to day between the *reality* and *validity* of their lives *and* the tendency to view it from the *deviant perspective* in accordance with my academic training.

Deviance is the invention of a group that uses its own standards as the *ideal* by which others are to be judged. Howard Becker states that

Social groups create deviance by making the rules whose infraction constitutes deviance, and by applying those rules to particular people and labeling them as outsiders. From this point of view, deviance is *not* a quality of the act the person commits, but rather a consequence of the application by others of rules and sanctions to an "offender." The deviant is one to whom that label has successfully been applied; deviant behavior is behavior that people so label.[1]

Other students of social problems have adhered to the same position.[2] Placing Black people in the context of the deviant perspective has been possible because Blacks have not had the necessary power to resist the labels. This power could have come only from the ability to provide the *definitions* of one's past, present and future. Since Blacks have

[1] Howard S. Becker, *The Outsiders*, New York, Free Press, 1963, p. 9.
[2] See the works of Edwin Lemert, *Social Pathology*, New York, McGraw-Hill, 1951; John Kituse, "Societal Reaction to Deviance: Problems of Theory and Method," *Social Problems*, Winter 1962, pp. 247–56; and Frank Tannenbaum, *Crime and the Community*, New York, Columbia University Press, 1938.

always, until recently, been defined by the majority group, that group's characterization was the one that was predominant.

The preoccupation with *deviancy*, as opposed to *normalcy*, encourages the researcher to limit his scope and ignore some of the most vital elements of the lives of the people he is studying. It has been noted by one sociologist that:

It is probably a fact and one of which some contemporary students of deviance have been cognizant—that the greater portion of the lives of deviant persons or groups is spent in normal, mundane, day-to-day living. In the researcher's focus on deviance and this acquisition of the deviant perspective, not only is he likely to overlook these more conventional phenomena, and thus become insensitive to them, but he may in the process overlook that very data which helps to explain that deviance he studies.[3]

Having been equipped with the *deviant perspective* in my academic training, yet lacking strong commitment to it because it conflicted with my objective knowledge and responses to the Black women I was studying, I went into the field equipped with a set of preconceived ideas and labels that I intended to apply to these women. This, of course, meant that I had gone there only to validate and elaborate on what was *alleged to exist*. If I had continued within this context, I would have concluded the same thing that most social scientists who study Black people conclude: that they are pathology-ridden.

However, this role was difficult, if not impossible, for me to play because all of my life experiences invalidated the deviant perspective. As I became more involved with the subjects of this research, I knew that I would not be able to

[3] See Ethel Sawyer, "Methodological Problems in Studying Socially Deviant Communities," this volume.

play the role of the dispassionate scientist, whose major objective was to extract certain data from them that would simply be used to *describe* and *theorize* about their conditions. I began to perceive my role as a Black person, with empathy and attachment, and, to a great extent, their day-to-day lives and future destinies became intricately interwoven with my own. This did not occur without a considerable amount of agonizing self-evaluation and conflict over "whose side I was on." On the one hand, I wanted to conduct a study that would allow me to fulfill certain academic requirements, i.e., a doctoral dissertation. On the other hand, I was highly influenced by my *Blackness*—by the fact that I, on many levels, was one of them and had to deal with their problems on a personal level. I was largely unable to resolve these strands, this "double consciousness," to which W. E. B. DuBois refers.[4] It is important to understand that Blacks are at a juncture in history that has been unprecedented for its necessity to grope with and clarify and *define* the status of our existence in American society. Thus, I was unable to resolve the dilemmas I faced as a Black social scientist because they only symbolized the larger questions, issues and dilemmas of our times.

Many books have been written about the Black community[5] but very few have really dealt with the intricate lives of the people who live there. By and large, they have attempted to analyze and describe the pathology which allegedly characterizes the lives of its inhabitants while at the same time making its residents responsible for its creation. The unhealthy conditions of the community such as drug addiction, poverty, crime, dilapidated housing, unem-

[4] W. E. B. DuBois, *Souls of Black Folk*, New York, Fawcett World Library, 1961.
[5] I am using the term "Black community" to refer to what is traditionally called the "ghetto." I am speaking largely of the low-income and working-class masses, who comprise the majority of the Black population in this country.

ployment and the multitude of problems which characterize it have caused social analysts to see these conditions as producing millions of "sick" people, many of whom are given few chances ever to overcome the wretchedness which clouds their existence. Few authorities on the Black community have written about the vast amount of strength and adaptability of the people. They have ignored the fact that this community is a force which not only acts upon its residents but which is also acted upon. Black people are involved in a dynamic relationship with their physical and cultural environment in that they both influence and are influenced by it. This reciprocal relationship allows them to exercise a considerable amount of power over their environs. This also means that they are able to exercise control over their futures, whereas writers have tended to view the low-income Black community as an all-pervasive force which is so devastating as to compel its powerless residents to succumb to its pressures. Their power to cope and adapt to a set of unhealthy conditions—not as stereotyped sick people but as normal ones—is a factor which few people seem to accept or even realize. The ways Blacks have adapted to poverty and racism, and yet emerged relatively unscarred, are a peculiar quality which Americans should commend.

The concept of social deviance is quite frequently applied to the values and behavior of Blacks because they represent a departure from the traditional white middle-class norm, along with criminals, homosexuals and prostitutes.

But these middle-class standards should not have been imposed because of the distinctiveness that characterizes the Black life-style, particularly that of the masses.

Most scholars have taken a dim view of any set of distinct life-styles shared by Blacks, and where they were acknowledged to exist, have of course maintained that these forces were negative adaptations to the larger society. There has never been an admission that the Black community is a product of American social policy, *not* the cause of it—the

structure of the American social system, through its practices of institutional racism, is designed to create the alleged
"pathology" of the community, to perpetuate the "social
disorganization" model of Black life. Recently, the Black
culture thesis has been granted some legitimization as an
explanatory variable for much of the distinctiveness of
Black life. As a result of this more positive attitude toward
understanding the strengths of life in the Black community,
many scholars, policy makers et al. are refocusing their attention and reinterpreting the many aspects of life that
comprise the complex existence of American Blacks.

There must be a strong concern with redefining the
problem. Instead of future studies being conducted on
problems of the Black community as represented by the
deviant perspective, there must be a redefinition of the
problem as being that of institutional racism. If the social
system is viewed as the *source* of the deviant perspective,
then future research must begin to analyze the nature of
oppression and the mechanisms by which institutionalized
forms of subjugation are initiated and act to maintain the
system intact. Thus, studies which have as their focal point
the alleged deviant *attitudes* and *behavior* of Blacks are
grounded within the racist assumptions and principles that
only render Blacks open to further exploitation.

The challenge to social scientists for a redefinition of the
basic *problem* has been raised in terms of the "colonial
analogy." It has been argued that the relationship between
the *researcher* and his *subjects*, by definition, resembles
that of the oppressor and the oppressed, because it is the
oppressor who defines the problem, the nature of the research and, to some extent, the quality of interaction between him and his subjects. This inability to understand
and research the fundamental problem—*neo-colonialism*—
prevents most social researchers from being able accurately
to observe and analyze Black life and culture and the impact racism and oppression have upon Blacks. Their inability
to understand the nature and effects of neo-colonialism in

the same manner as Black people is rooted in the inherent bias of the social sciences. The basic concepts and tools of white Western society are permeated by this partiality to the conceptual framework of the oppressor. It is simple enough to say that the difference between the two groups—the oppressor and the oppressed—prevents the former from adequately comprehending the essence of Black life and culture because of a fundamental difference in perceptions, based upon separate histories, life-styles and purposes for being. Simply put, the slave and his master do not view and respond to the world in the same way. The historian Lerone Bennett addresses this problem below:

George Washington and George Washington's slaves lived different realities. And if we extend that insight to all the dimensions of white American history we will realize that blacks lived at a different time and a different reality in this country. And the terrifying implications of all this is that there is another time, another reality, another America. . . .

Bennett states further that:

It is necessary for us to develop a new frame of reference which transcends the limits of white concepts. It is necessary for us to develop a total intellectual offensive against the false universality of white concepts whether they are expressed by William Styron or Daniel Patrick Moynihan. By and large, reality has been conceptualized in terms of the narrow point of view of the small minority of white men who live in Europe and North America. We must abandon the partial frame of reference of our oppressors and create new concepts which will release our reality, which is also the reality of the over-whelming majority of men and women on this globe. We must say to the white world that there are things in the world that are not dreamt of in your history and your sociology and your philosophy.[6]

[6] Lerone Bennett, *The Challenge of Blackness* (Chicago: Johnson Publishing Co., 1972).

Currently there are efforts underway to "de-colonize" social research on the *conceptual* and *methodological* levels.[7]

Although I attempted to maintain some degree of objectivity, I soon began to minimize and, very often, negate the importance of being "value-free," because the very selection of the topic itself reflected a bias, i.e., I studied Black women because of my strong interest in the subject.

I decided whose side I was on and resolved within myself that as a Black social scientist I must take a stand and that there could be no value-free sanctuary for me. The controversy over the question of values in social research is addressed by Gouldner:

If sociologists ought not express their personal values in the academic setting, how then are students to be safeguarded against the unwitting influence of these values which shape the sociologist's selection of problems, his preferences for certain hypotheses or conceptual schemes, and his neglect of others? For these are unavoidable and, in this sense, there is and can be no value-free sociology. The only choice is between an expression of one's values as open and honest as it can be, this side of the psychoanalytic couch, and a vain ritual of moral neutrality which, because it invites men to ignore the vulnerability of reason to bias, leaves it at the mercy of irrationality.[8]

I accepted this position as a guiding premise and proceeded to conduct my research with the full knowledge that I could not divorce myself from the problems of these women, nor should I become so engrossed in them that I would lose my original purpose for being in the community.

The words of Kenneth Clark, as he describes the tensions and conflicts he experienced while conducting the re-

[7] Refer to Robert Blauner, "Internal Colonialism and Ghetto Revolt," *Social Problems*, Vol. 16, No. 4, Spring 1969, pp. 393–408; and see Robert Blauner and David Wellman, "Toward the Decolonization of Social Research," in this collection.

[8] Alvin W. Gouldner, "Anti-Minotaur: The Myth of a Value-Free Sociology," *Social Problems*, Winter 1962, pp. 199–213.

search for his classic study of Harlem, *Dark Ghetto*, typify the problems I faced:

> I could never be fully detached as a scholar or participant. More than forty years of my life had been lived in Harlem. I started school in Harlem public schools. I first learned about people, about love, about cruelty, about sacrifice, about cowardice, about courage, about bombast in Harlem. For many years before I returned as an "involved observer," Harlem had been my home. My family moved from house to house, and from neighborhood to neighborhood within the walls of the ghetto in a desperate attempt to escape its creeping blight. In a very real sense, therefore, *Dark Ghetto* is a summation of my personal and lifelong experiences and observations as a prisoner within the ghetto long before I was aware that I was really a prisoner.[9]

The inability to be *objective* about analyzing poverty, racism, disease, self-destruction and the gamut of problems which faced these females only mirrored a broader problem in social research. That is, to what extent should any scientist—white or Black—consider it his duty to be a dispassionate observer and not intervene, when possible, to ameliorate many of the destructive conditions he studies. On many occasions I found myself acting as a counselor, big sister, etc. Certainly the question can be raised as to whether researchers can continue to gather data on impoverished Black communities without addressing these findings to the area of social policy.

This raises another important question, to which I will address myself. That is, many people will read this book because they are seeking answers to the dilemmas and problems facing Black people in general and Black women in particular. A great number of young Black women will expect to find forever-sought formulas to give them a new

[9] Kenneth Clark, *Dark Ghetto*, New York, Harper & Row, 1965, p. xv.

sense of direction as *Black women*. Some Black men will read this work because they are concerned about this new direction and want to become involved in the shaping of this process. Others, of course, will simply be curious to find out what a Black woman has to say about her peers. I expect traditional-type scholars to take great issue with my thesis and many of my formulations because I am consciously attempting to break away from the traditional way in which social science research has analyzed the attitudes and behavior patterns of Blacks. Finally, a small but growing group of scholars will find it refreshing to read a work on Black women which does not indict them for all kinds of alleged social problems, which, if they exist, they did not create.

All of these are problems and questions which I view as inescapable for one who decides to attempt to break that new ground and write about areas of human life in ways in which they are not ordinarily approached.

There are no standard answers for these dilemmas I faced, for they are simply microcosms of the larger Black community. Therefore, this work is not attempting to resolve the problems of Black womanhood but to shed light on them. More than anything else, I feel that it is attempting to depict what the Black woman's life has been like in the past, and what barriers she has had to overcome in order to survive, and how she is coping today under the most strenuous circumstances. Thus, I am simply saying, "This is what the Black woman was, this is how she has been solving her problems, and these are ways in which she is seeking to alter her roles." I am not trying to chart a course of action for her to follow. This will, in large measure, be dictated by, and interwoven with, the trends set in that vast Black American community. My primary concern here is with depicting the strength of the Black family and Black girls within the family structure. I will seek to depict the lives of Black people I knew who were utilizing their scant resources for survival purposes, but who on the whole were quite successful with making the necessary adaptive and creative responses to their oppressed circumstances. I am also dealing with the somewhat abstract white middle-class system of values as it affects Blacks. It is hoped that the problems I encountered with conducting such a study, as well as the positive approach I was eventually able to take toward this work, will enable others to be equally as effective in breaking away from an intellectual tradition which has existed far too long.

One of the primary preoccupations of every American adolescent girl, regardless of race and social class background, is that of eventually becoming a woman. Every girl looks forward to the time when she will discard the status of child and take on the role of adult, wife and possibly mother.

The official entry into womanhood is usually regarded as that time when she reaches the prescribed legal age (eighteen and sometimes twenty-one), when for the first time she is granted certain legal and other rights and privileges. These rights, such as being allowed to vote, to go to certain "for adults only" events, to join certain social clubs and to obtain certain types of employment, are accompanied by a type of informal understanding that very few privileges, either formal or informal, are to be denied her where age is the primary prerequisite for participation. Entry into womanhood is the point at which she is considered by older adults to be ready to join their ranks because she has gone through the necessary apprenticeship program—the period of adolescence. We can observe differences between racial and social class groups regarding, for instance, the time at which the female is considered to be ready to assume the duties and obligations of womanhood. Becoming a woman in the low-income Black community is somewhat different from the routes followed by the white middle-class girl. The poor Black girl reaches her status of womanhood at an earlier age because of the different prescriptions and expectations of her culture. There is no single set of criteria for becoming a woman in the Black community; each girl is conditioned by a diversity of factors depending primarily upon her opportunities, role models, psychological disposition and the influence of the values, customs and traditions of the Black community. It will be demonstrated that the resources which adolescent girls have at their disposal, combined with the cultural heritage of their communities, are crucial factors in determining what kind of women they become. Structural *and* psychological variables are important as focal points because neither alone is sufficient to explain the many factors involved with psychosocial development. Therefore, the concepts of motivation, roles and role model, identity and socialization, as well as family income, education, kin and peer group relations are important to consider in the analysis. These diverse factors have rarely been considered as crucial to an analysis of Black womanhood. This situation exists because previous studies have substituted simplistic notions for rigorous multivariate analysis. Here, however, these multiple factors and influences will be analyzed as a "Black cultural" framework which has its own autonomous system of values, behavior, attitudes, sentiments and beliefs.

Another significant dimension to be considered will be the extent to which Black girls are influenced by the distinct culture of their community. Certain historical as well as contemporary variables are very important when describing the young Black woman. Her cultural heritage, I feel, has played a stronger role than has previously been stated by most writers in shaping her into the entity she has become.

Life in the Black community has been conditioned by poverty, discrimination and institutional subordination. It has also been shaped by African cultural survivals. From slavery until the present, many of the African cultural survivals influenced the way Blacks lived, responded to others and, in general, related to their environment. Even after slavery many of these survivals have remained and act to forge a distinct and viable set of cultural adaptive mechanisms because discrimination acted as an agent to perpetuate instead of to destroy the culture.

I will illustrate, through depicting the lives of Black preadolescent and adolescent girls in a big-city slum, how distinct sociohistorical forces have shaped a very positive and practical way of dealing and coping with the world. The values, attitudes, beliefs and behavior emerge from a long tradition, much of which has characterized the Black community from its earliest beginnings in this country.

What is life like in the urban Black community for the "average" girl? How does she define her roles, behaviors, and from whom does she acquire her models for fulfilling what is expected of her? Is there any significant disparity between the resources she has with which to accomplish her goals in life and the stated aspirations? Is the typical world of the teen-ager in American society shared by the Black girl or does she stand somewhat alone in much of her day-to-day existence?

In an attempt to answer these and other questions, I went to such a community and sought out teen-agers whom I felt could provide me with some insights. I was a research assistant in 1964 on a study of an all-Black low-income housing project of over ten thousand residents in a slum area of St. Louis. (This study was supported by a grant from the National Institute of Mental Health, Grant No. MH-9189, "Social and Community Problems in Public Housing Areas.") It was geographically located near the downtown section of St. Louis, Missouri, and within one of the oldest slum areas of the city. The majority of the females were drawn from the Pruitt-Igoe housing project, although many resided outside the public housing project in substandard private housing.

At that time my curiosity was centered around the various activities in which the girls engaged that frequently produced harmful consequences. Specifically, I attempted to understand how such social problems as pregnancy, premarital sex, school dropout, etc. affected their life chances for success. I also felt, at the time, that a less destructible adaptation could be made to their impoverished environments. However, I was to understand later that perhaps a very healthy and successful adaptation, given their limited resources, had been made by all of these girls to a set of very unhealthy environmental conditions. Therefore, I soon changed my focus and attempted to apply a different perspective to the data.

I spent almost four years interviewing, testing (Thematic Apperception Test), observing and, in general, "hanging out" with these girls. I attempted to establish a strong rapport with all of them by spending a considerable amount of time in their homes with them and their families, at church, parties, dances, in the homes of their friends, shopping, at my apartment and in a variety of other situations. The sample consisted of several peer groups which over the years changed in number and composition. I always endeavored to interview their parents, and in some cases became close friends of their mothers. The field work carried me into the community at very unregulated hours —weekends, occasional evenings and during school hours (when I usually talked to their mothers). Although a great portion of the data collected is exploratory in nature, the majority of it is based on systematic open-ended interviews that related to (1) life histories and (2) attitudes and behavior that reflected approaching womanhood. During the last year and a half I randomly selected thirty girls between the ages of thirteen and eighteen and conducted a systematic investigation that was designed to test many of my preliminary conclusions drawn from the exploratory research. All of the interviews and observations were taped and transcribed. The great majority of the interviews were taped *live*, and will appear as direct quotations throughout this book. (All of the girls have been given pseudonyms.)

I feel that the data are broad in scope and are applicable to almost any group of low-income Black teen-age girls growing up in any American city. The economic, political, social and racial factors which have produced neo-colonialism on a national scale operate in Chicago, Roxbury, Detroit, Watts, Atlanta—and everywhere else.

The total misrepresentation of the Black community and the various myths which surround it can be seen in microcosm in the Black female adolescent. Her growing-up years reflect the basic quality and character of life in this environment, as well as anticipations for the future. Because she is in perhaps the most crucial stage of psychosocial development, one can capture these crucial forces —external and internal—which are acting upon her, and which, more than any other impact, will shape her life-long adult role. Thus, by understanding the nature and processes of her development, we can also comprehend the more intricate elements that characterize the day-to-day lives of the Black masses.

PART VII

Institutional Racism: Two Case Studies

Andrew Billingsley

Black Families and
White Social Science

The Black family has been one of the most neglected and controversial areas of Black life. An abundance of myths, distortions and stereotypes surround it, and most of the sociological research conducted in this area has viewed the Black family as a pathological entity, emphasizing its weaknesses instead of its strengths. In the following essay, the author surveys some of the major textbooks on the family to show how little attention is given to the Black family. He also examines some of the popular myths regarding the Black family, as discussed in the literature, and attempts to show how and why social science has failed to present a true picture.

Students of human behavior, policy makers, and citizens who look to the body of knowledge about the human condition which has been generated and reflected by American social scientists will find no area of American life more glaringly ignored, more distorted, or more systematically disvalued than black family life.

Thus, black families who have fared so ill historically in

white American society have fared no better in white
American social science, and largely for the same reasons.
For American social scientists are much more American
than social and much more social than scientific. They reflect all the prejudice, ignorance, and arrogance which
seems to be endemic to Americans of European descent.
Furthermore, because of their skills at communication and
their acceptance as authorities on race relations, social scientists do even greater damage to the understanding of
black family life than do ordinary citizens.

Still, black families, who have survived some of the most
severe oppression at the hands of white society, also show
signs of surviving the treatment they have received in social
science. Let us consider first some of the evidence for this
characterization about the status of black families in social
science, then some of the reasons for this state of affairs,
followed by some speculations on the consequences of this
situation, and finally some of the solutions to the problems.

The Treatment of Black Families
in White Social Science

In *Black Families in White America* (Billingsley, 1968),
we described four areas of social science scholarship which
have been presented with both the opportunity and the
necessity to describe, analyze, and explain the changing
status of black family life in America. These areas are: (1)
studies of the family, (2) studies of ethnic assimilation and
stratification, (3) studies of the experience of black people
in general, and (4) studies of social welfare problems and
programs. Other areas might be added to this list. It is
sufficient, however, to support the generalization we are
making. For in none of these major areas of scholarship,
where social science studies and theories abound, have black
families been subjected to the systematic attention their

presence and function in the world demands. An examination of the history of each of these areas of scholarship shows the manner in which black families have been mainly left out, and then distorted when considered.

TABLE 1
BLACK FAMILIES IN SELECTED FAMILY TEXTS

	NUMBER OF ARTICLES			
Author and Date	On Families	On Black Families	By Black Authors	References to Black Families
Nimkoff, 1965	18	0	0	1
Kephart, 1966	23	0	0	56
Sussman, 1959	62	1	0	0
Queen & Habenstein, 1967	25	1	0	6
Bell & Vogel, 1968	52	1	0	4

The evidence for this situation, summarized in Table 1, is almost overwhelming. Bell and Vogel's new, enlarged, revised edition of *A Modern Introduction to the Family* (1968), which contains 52 articles, 18 of them new since the 1960 edition, still finds room for only one article about black families. Further, the new edition substitutes an article about black families by Daniel P. Moynihan for the earlier article by E. Franklin Frazier, an action which is not an improvement but a net setback to the black presence in the family literature.

The concept "Negro" does not appear once in the index of Parsons and Bales' *Family, Socialization and Interaction Process* (1960). M. F. Nimkoff (1965) also ignores black families.

In a 600-page textbook on urban society, Gist and Fava (1964) devote one 20-page chapter to "Urban Family Life in Transition." This work devotes less than one page to the treatment of Puerto Rican families in New York, less than a page to studies of African families, but not a single page, line, or word to black families in the urban United States.

In William J. Goode's *Readings on the Family and Society* (1964), more space is given to discussion of black-white marriages than to black families. And black families are considered only in the extended discussions of illegitimacy. Both of these are curious phenomena when viewed from the perspective of the sociology of knowledge.

The Family, Society, and the Individual, by Kephart (1966), is a good example of the treatment of black families. Of the 23 chapters not one is devoted to black families. In a 34-page chapter on cross-cultural family patterns not a single reference is made to black families. In a 48-page chapter on "minority family types," the author devotes five pages and 40 references to the discussion of black families, considerably less than he devotes to Italian families and less than a fourth of the space which he devotes to Amish families. In a 23-page chapter on "Socio-Demographic Aspects of Divorce" he devotes 1/2 page to a discussion of class and racial factors with eight references to black families. In a 20-page chapter on "Premarital Moral Codes" the author devotes a half page including six references to premarital coitus among black females and two references to "illegitimacy."

Sourcebook in Marriage and the Family, edited by Marvin B. Sussman (1959), does no better by black families. Of the 62 articles, one is devoted to marriage between black and white persons. None is devoted to black couples. In an eleven-page article on "The Normal American Family," Parsons refers to black people six times as a condition, and not at all to black families; it is very representative of other articles in the book. In an eleven-page article on "Boom Babies," the author (Sussman) devotes one page to a discussion of fertility among "nonwhites" with four specific references to black women and none to black families.

The Family in Various Cultures, by Queen and Haben-stein (1967), devotes one of its 25 chapters to black families. The chapter is new for this third edition; it is also unique in that it includes generous references to the work of black scholars.

The Tangle of Pathology

THE "MOYNIHAN REPORT"—AN ERROR PERPETUATED

It is nearly five years since the "Moynihan Report" con-cluded that the structure of family life in the black com-munity constituted a "tangle of pathology . . . capable of perpetuating itself without assistance from the white world," and that "at the heart of the deterioration of the fabric of Negro society is the deterioration of the Negro family. It is the fundamental *source* of the weakness of the Negro community at the present time [Moynihan, 1965, italics added]." This was an incorrect analysis of the rela-tionship between black families and white society. It re-verses the true nature of the influence process at work. It is not weakness in the family which causes poverty and racism—the true tangle of pathology which afflicts black people; it is quite the other way around. The family is a creature of the society. And the greatest problems facing black families are problems which emanate from the white racist, militarist, materialistic society which places higher priority on putting white men on the moon than putting black men on their feet on this earth. Still this analysis, which placed the cause of black peoples' difficulties on the family unit, was eagerly received by the American reading public as the key to understanding black people. Its author has subsequently modified this interpretation. One of the unfortunate consequences of his earlier analysis, however, was that it gave rise to similar analyses by other white stu-dents of the black family.

ARROGANT ANALYSIS BY WHITE LIBERALS

Thus, nearly five years later, two white liberal social scientists—who call themselves "militant integrationists"— have published a book based on their observations during a nine-month sojourn in a black community (Etzkowitz & Schaflander, 1969). It includes a chapter titled "The Negro Ghetto Non-Family"; it perpetuates the incorrect analysis made so famous by Moynihan, and which has been thoroughly discredited by more careful social analyses (Herzog, 1967, 1970). The authors state very candidly their own view and evaluation of black people: "It is our own belief that there are practically no pluses in Negro ghetto culture. . . . We see nothing but bitterness and despair, nihilism, hopelessness, rootlessness, and all the symptoms of social disintegration in the poor speech, poor hygiene, poor education, and lack of security resulting from a non-family background in which the stabilizing paternal factor is absent and where there is no stable institution to substitute for the family [Etzkowitz & Schaflander, 1969, p. 14]." They go considerably beyond the Moynihan thesis of disintegrating family life as they assert without qualification, "the fact that love, warmth, hygiene, education and family stability are absent for most Negroes." And that, "Booze, gambling, drugs, and prostitution are the inevitable result of the absence of a stable family institution [p. 15]."

These men are as insensitive and arrogant as they are incorrect in their analysis. They insist that the line of causation runs from the family to the society. After describing in very negative terms what they consider "momism," represented by the "harassed, cranky, frustrated, churchgoing, overworked mothers" who dominate these "non-families" by "driving young children into fierce competition," these white liberal social scientists conclude that "the damage *resulting* from this *typical* non-family life often leads to young dropouts and unwed mothers, and to crime, violence, alcoholism and drug addiction [Etzkowitz & Schaflander, 1969, p. 15, italics added]."

Despite the incorrectness of their analysis of the relationship between black family life and the white society, their views reflect the views of many people, even some in the social work profession. The authentication of such views by social science scholarship, foundation grants, high university and government positions serves to perpetuate this erroneous thinking, thus preventing enlightened people from getting on with the task of analyzing and helping remove the crippling consequences of institutionalized racism to which the Kerner Commission Report so correctly attributes the most important cause of the difficulties black people face in this country and the most important cause of their outrage against oppression.

For scholars and students trying to understand family functioning in the black community, the chief fault of the above type of analysis is the attribution of an inverse cause and effect relationship between family and society, and the ignoring of the forces of institutionalized racism. For social planners an additional problem with this analysis is that it ignores the variety and complexity of black family and community life while concentrating on its negative features. Analyses such as these stem almost unchecked from the white Anglo-Conformity perspective which judges black people outside the context of their unique anchor in history, their treatment in this country, and their contemporary social conditions. More important, such analyses ignore the existence of a black subculture, and the strengths of the black community and the black family which have enabled black people to survive in a hostile environment for over 300 years.

Unfortunately, analyses of black families by well-educated, well-meaning, white liberal integrationists come more out of the perspectives which they bring with them to the

black community than out of the realities and complexities
of life in the black community. The continuation of the
white, middle-class, outsider, Anglo-Conformity perspective toward black people—born out of a combination of
ignorance and arrogance—not only obscures the realities
which our society needs so desperately to understand about
black family and community life, but performs a downright disservice to such understanding because of the status
of the propagators of this view and their access to the wider
society.

MOST BLACK FAMILIES ARE HEADED BY MEN

The plain fact is that in most communities of any size,
most black families meet the American test of stability.
Contrary to the impression generally circulated by white
students of the black family, most black families, even in
the ghetto, are headed by men. And in most of these families, even in the very poor ones, most of these men are still
married to their original wives. Furthermore, most of these
men and many of the women are employed full time, and
are still not able to pull their families out of poverty. What
we need to know more about is how these families manage.
How do they function? How do they manage to meet the
needs of their children? Our own experience and research,
supported by an increasing body of other studies, suggest
that even among the lower-class families in the black ghetto,
life is more varied than is generally communicated by gross
uniform characterizations.

In a new book, David A. Schulz (1969) presents the
reader with 146 pages of descriptions, theories, and con-
jectures about the sordidness of life for low-income families
in a public housing project before he opens his final chapter with the following observation: "It would be a serious
mistake to leave the impression that the problems of the
Negro lower class derive mainly from patterns of agonistic

sexual development and broken unstable families. Yet, this is one possible interpretation of the data thus far presented [p. 147]." This statement and the orientation it suggests might better have been stated at the beginning of the study and then reflected in the treatment of his data and the modesty of his generalizations. Further, it is difficult to see how his intensive analysis of the behaviors of five low-income black families living in a single public housing project could provide an adequate basis for his theoretical generalizations about a three-way typology of black family life. It is indeed doubtful that he would have been supported in making generalizations on the study of so few white families, despite the fact that his own background and experience provide him with much greater knowledge of white families than of black families.

There are four tendencies in the treatment of black families in social science scholarship. The first is the tendency to ignore black families altogether. The second is, when black families are considered, to focus almost exclusively on the lowest-income group of black families, that acute minority of families who live in public housing projects or who are supported by public welfare assistance. The third is to ignore the majority of black stable families even among this lowest-income group, to ignore the processes by which these families move from one equilibrium state to another, and to focus instead on the most unstable among these low-income families. A fourth tendency, which is more bizarre than all the others, is the tendency on the part of social scientists to view the black, low-income, unstable, problem-ridden family as the causal nexus for the difficulties their members experience in the wider society.

Why Social Science has Failed the Black Family

Why, then, are black families so badly mistreated in social science scholarship? The factors which account for this are many, varied, and complex. Some are historical and some contemporary. Among these factors, however, four stand out as being paramount.

THE FAMILY, AS AN INSTITUTION, HAS BEEN NEGLECTED

The family as an institution has not been given the systematic thought, study, and theoretical speculation such an important institution in society deserves. Much of the literature on families is produced by social scientists whose major interest and competence lies in other areas. They give passing attention to some aspects of family life on their way to studying something else considered more important. An examination of the towering elites in the family literature will reveal that few of these men have devoted their lifetime careers to a study of the family. An examination of men who have revealed that few of them are considered among the towering elites in social science scholarship. Thus, the most important social institution in all of social life is relegated to a type of second-class treatment. This is a most telling commentary on the nature, the values, the relevance, and the priority system of American social science. The situation is confounded by the fact that social science scholarship is so heavily dominated by men. In a course I took with Theodore Newcomb, I once heard him say that although he had spent a considerable portion of his career studying small groups, it had not occurred to him until recently that the family was a small group and an appropriate unit of analysis in this context.

BLACKS ARE BLACK, SOCIAL SCIENCE IS WHITE

Secondly, the reason black families have fared so much worse than white families in social science is that they are black and social science is white. For the plain and simple fact is that black people, as a people, have not been taken seriously by social scientists. Consequently, the institutional life of black people has been generally ignored. We have observed elsewhere that when black people have been the object of analysis by white social scientists, it has been mainly *race relations*, that is to say, the relations between white and black people rather than the nature of the life of black people which has been at the center of their interests. The ethnocentrism reflected in this behavior syndrome is as pervasive as it is regrettable.

Yet these social scientists have been victimized by their own Anglo-European history and culture. They have tended to view other cultures primarily as objects of assimilation. This accounts in part for the high degree of interest in interracial marriage and the high interest in color variations among black families.

It also helps to explain why any behavior pattern manifested among black families which differs in degree or kind from what is observed among white families is considered deviant. But more important, this Anglo-European perspective obscures the realities and the complexities of black family life in America. Few white scholars have overcome this bias. A number of black scholars have also been victimized by it.

This perspective is not something completely of the past. It is reflected, for example, in the kinds of questions which are asked on Ph.D. examinations in the leading graduate departments of social science. A study of such questions in sociology recently published in the *American Sociologist* (Mack, 1969) showed the considerable uniformity with which the black perspective and, particularly, black families are excluded from the important matters social science scholars are expected to deal with.

INFORMED OPINIONS OF BLACKS ARE IGNORED

A third reason for the mistreatment of black families in social science is the relative exclusion of black scholars from these disciplines and the mistreatment of those who do manage to enter. One searches the social science journals in vain, even in 1970, for a steady stream of contributions from black scholars. Even on matters of book reviews, for example, the white social science journals with their white editors are much more likely to ask a white expert on black people to review books by and about black people than to turn to black scholars for these assignments. The problem with this is not only that it helps to perpetuate the exclusion of black people from social science scholarship, it also perpetuates the "white people know best" tendency, and at the same time produces inferior scholarship on such an important aspect of American life as black families.

Furthermore, one searches the faculties of the major social science departments in the country in vain for a representation of black people there. Nor is the production of black doctorates yet a high priority item for many of these departments. The distressing aspect of this particular pattern of exclusion is that social scientists in the major universities have not been among the leaders in trying to correct the situation. White social scientists, particularly those of the liberal persuasion, are amazingly satisfied that they can adequately reflect the black experience as well as they can the white experience, and better than black scholars can—in part because black scholars are not well "qualified," and in part because they are likely to be "estranged from their own people." White social scientists are much more interested in providing guest lectureships for black militants who have not completed high school, than they are in providing regular appointments for black scholars, militant or otherwise, who have completed their Ph.D.s. It is particularly distressing to observe the smug satisfaction and arrogance reflected as white faculties consider and reject one black scholar after another for positions on these faculties, while continuing to hire white faculty of mediocre talent or worse.

OVER-RELIANCE ON STATISTICAL
TECHNIQUES AND SPECULATION

Finally, much of the mistreatment of black families in social science is due to the nature of the disciplines involved and the manner in which each of these disciplines has come to rely heavily on statistical techniques, large-scale surveys, and overarching theoretical speculations. Thus both the theoretical and the methodological interests and imperatives in social science have tended to take them away from a clarification of the nature of black family life in America. It may well be, then, that the established social science disciplines are already too old and rigid (like most other aging institutions in America) to give us the knowledge about black families which is needed without major renewal of these disciplines themselves.

Some Consequences

When we consider the consequences of the manner in which black families have been mistreated at the hands of white social science, we must ask: "Consequences for whom?" And we must look for both positive and negative consequences, as well as for latent and manifest functions.

NEGLECT OF BLACKS HAS ENHANCED
STATUS OF SOCIAL SCIENCE

Clearly one of the latent consequences for social science of this pattern of exclusion and distortion of black families has been positive, in the sense that social science has reached relatively high status and acceptance in American society in large measure because it has stayed in the mainstream of American society and has not been unduly involved in studies, explanations, and advocation of "disadvantaged," low-status, and "deviant" groups. It has helped to enhance the status of social science in the general community when social science studies and conclusions have been consistent with the general interests of that community. Thus the very distortions of black people sanctioned and perpetuated by social science scholarship have helped to enhance the status of such scholarship in the white racist society which is America.

ENCOURAGING IGNORANCE AND MISINFORMATION

Still another latent consequence which is quite negative has to do with the spread of ignorance among students and the general population. Many young graduate students at the university in which I teach come from some of the best undergraduate social science departments in the country and know almost nothing about black people as a people, and even less about black families; Others come to graduate school with the most crippling kind of misinformation. Many of our brightest graduate students from some of the best colleges with social science majors are convinced from their exposure to social science that black families are characterized by disorganization; that the matriarchal family form is dominant; that most black children grow up without fathers; that female-headed families produce girls who are masculine and boys who are feminine; that children from female-headed families do worse in school than children from two-parent families; and that most low-income female-headed black families are supported by welfare and live in public housing projects. It cannot be expected that these middle-class white students would have learned any better from their own experience in their families, their churches, synagogues, or their lower schools; it might be expected that they would have learned better in their social science classes in college. But unfortunately the ignorance they brought to college has often been confounded by the misinformation generated and perpetuated therein by social science.

MISGUIDING POLICY-MAKERS

And what about policymakers who depend on social science for guidance? The disasters surrounding the issuance of the Moynihan (1965) and the Coleman (1966) reports are two recent and painful examples of the dysfunctions of social science scholarship for policy development. The first of these reports convinced some important policymakers and a large number of ordinary citizens that the major problem which black people faced was weakness in the family structure, and if that matter was attended to, the nation would not need to exert extraordinary efforts to assure black people all the rights and privileges white people now enjoy—these matters could take care of themselves. The second report convinced policy-makers and educators that if every low-income black student could sit next to a middle-class white student in school, equality of educational opportunity and achievement would follow without extraordinary efforts to improve the quality of instruction, the educational facilities, and the rapprochement between the school and the community. These are exceptionally abbreviated commentaries on these reports, and they may be unintended consequences of them. But it is clear that neither the Moynihan Report nor the Coleman Report advanced the status of our knowledge about black families and their children sufficiently to guide the policy development of the major institutions of our society—whose responsibility is to meet their needs and who ought to be able to look to social science for enlightenment. The major problem is that both of these studies were conceived, executed, and reported out of the white middle-class perspective in social science, with no meaningful participation by black people.

PERPETUATING THE DEPRESSED STATUS OF BLACKS

The consequences for black people directly are more severe. It is only a slight exaggeration to suggest that social science has had no appreciable effect in the struggle to liberate black people from the oppression of the white racist society, nor has social science made any substantial contribution to the liberation of black people from their own sense of inferiority. Much of social science has had the opposite effect. The social scientists who describe black families in such a negative and distorted manner must bear some of the responsibility for this self-fulfilling prophecy.

Some Rays of Hope?

Is there no hope at all that American social science can clarify the nature of black family life in America? In my view, there is some hope, though not very much. Some white social scientists on their way to some other goal have managed to shed some light on important aspects of black family life. Elsewhere (Billingsley, 1968) we have remarked on the contributions Thomas Pettigrew (1964) has made to the clarification of the black experience in America. Elliot Liebow (1967) has done a very sensitive analysis of the life styles of black men who hang out on a particular street corner in Washington, D.C., an analysis which takes an important step in correcting the manner in which men are left out of black family studies. Jessie Bernard (1966) has amassed an impressive array of studies which help to clarify the "normalcy" of black families in America. Elizabeth Herzog (1967) has exploded much of the mythology about black families which has been generated and perpetuated by other social scientists. Robert Coles (1967) has shown the positive attributes of black families under crises. Gurin and Katz (1966) have shown the strength of black families in motivating their children to aspire to higher education and beyond. Finally, the field waits with a great deal of expectation for a new volume on black families by Lee Rainwater. There are others. But for more hope we must turn toward black social scientists, who can bring to the assignment not only the theories and methods they have learned from white social science, but major modifications and contributions to those theories and methods based on their own lifetime experience as black people in America and their commitment to the liberation of their people from all vestiges of oppression, including the oppression by white social science.

THE BEST STUDIES OF BLACKS ARE BY BLACK SCHOLARS

Already the best studies of black families have been done by black scholars, despite an assertion to the contrary by August Meier (1969) who thinks that the best studies of black families have been done by white men whom he knows. That is because he does not know the literature very well, or is not a very good judge of studies, or knows little about black family life, or some combination of all three. For, clearly, the works of E. Franklin Frazier (1932a, 1932b, 1948, 1962), Drake (1962), Hylan Lewis (1955, 1961), Camille Jeffers (1967), Lewis Watts (1964), Harry

Edwards (1968), Daniel C. Thompson (1963, and with
W. Thompson, 1960), Nathan Hare (1965), Charlotte
Dunmore (1967), Joyce Ladner (1967), William Grier and
Price Cobbs (1968) have contributed more to an understanding of black family life in America than have all the
white social scientists combined. Yet this is not very much.
The major function of the work they have done is to show
the necessity and the promise of having more black scholars
devoted to the task of clarifying the nature of the black
experience from the inside.

BUT BLACK CREATIVE WRITERS
PROVIDE EVEN GREATER INSIGHT

In the final analysis one must admit that neither white
nor black social scientists have yet provided the insight into
the structure and functioning of black family life that has
been provided by the more "creative" black writers—including novelists, poets, essayists, biographers, and lyricists.
I have just finished reading *Bloodline*, a collection of short
stories by Ernest J. Gains (1968). His portrayal of black
family life in the rural south is classic. It is at once subjective and objective. It is successful in capturing the realities
of black family life and at the same time provides the basis
for several ideal family types. It is so perceptive that it
moves beyond art toward science.

Or one could do a lot worse than reading the works of
James Baldwin, particularly *Go Tell It on the Mountain*
(1963).

Or the works of Langston Hughes. One brief excerpt
from one of his conversations with Simple will make the
point:

"I'm still hoping it will get here in time for Christmas," said
Simple.
"What?"

"My divorce. But I just got word from that lawyer in Baltimore that he had been held up until he got my money before completing the process. He also writ me concerning on what my wife bases our divorce, now that I have paid. And, don't you know, that woman claims I deserted *her*."

"Well, did you?"

"I did not. She put me out."

"In other words, you left under duress."

"Pressure," said Simple.

"Then why don't you refute her argument? Contest her claim?"

"That is just why we separated, we argued so much. I will not argue with Isabel now over no divorce. She writ that she did not want to contest. Neither do I. I never could win an argument with that woman. Only once in a wife-time did I win, and I did not win then with words."

"How did you win?"

"I just grabbed her and kissed her," said Simple.

"Why didn't you try that method more often?"

"Because as soon as I kissed her she stopped arguing and started loving. Sometimes it is not loving a man wants. He wants to win—especially when he knows he is right." [Hughes, 1961].

It would be hard indeed for the modern theories and techniques of white-oriented social science to capture or reproduce the essence of the behavior being described in this story.

The Remedies

What, then, are some of the remedies for the situation in which black families find themselves reflected in social science scholarship. Clearly, the social science disciplines like the American institutions they reflect are aging, rigid, and in need of renewal along a number of dimensions. Some of the suggestions being put forward by the Youth Caucus, the Black Caucus, and the Women's Caucus at professional meetings are indicative both of the rigidity and the need for change. The need is pressing for social scientists to move out of their ancient theories, their libraries, their methodological preoccupations and take a good look at the modern world and try to describe it. It is unlikely, however, that the present aging, white male leadership in the social science disciplines can provide that kind of innovative leadership. The first need, then, is for the overthrow of the present social scientific hierarchy.

A second need is for the family as a unit to be elevated in the value and priority system of social science scholarship. In the process, however, social science must develop a more flexible array of techniques, perhaps borrowing heavily from some of the "creative" disciplines in order to understand, describe, and explain black family life with the degree of sensitivity it deserves and requires.

A third need is for all the social science disciplines to incorporate within themselves a measure of the black perspective. White people cannot do the job alone. They must, in fact, increasingly follow the leadership of black scholars, whom they must help to produce, sustain, and free.

The standards for the recruitment of major faculty in the major universities which are designed and operate mainly to protect the vested interests of the existing white faculty must give way to more relevant criteria so that black faculty can be appointed at sufficient status and in sufficient numbers to provide the kind of corrective instruction and research needed by both white and black students and the existing white faculty.

But clearly the kind of leadership which is needed for a new series of studies of black family life in America is not likely to come from the white social science establishment. This leadership must come from black scholars. And, unfortunately, the initiative must be seized by black scholars. It is not likely to be abandoned or even shared gracefully by the existing white experts on black people.

Richard F. America

The Case of the Racist Researcher

In this essay the author suggests that large corporate research organizations pose certain problems for the Black community, and that they should be reformed and perhaps controlled by some regulatory agency. To prove his point he carefully examines one such organization, the Stanford Research Institute, providing a case study in the dynamics and operations of these groups and the impact they have on public policy affecting Blacks.

This article is intended to inform readers of research activities that vitally affect their interests. It should especially interest attorneys who can employ the law to safeguard those interests when they are threatened by hostile or biased research.

The article suggests that the Public Information Act can be employed to the fullest extent to insure systematic review of publicly funded non-classified research. Something like Nader's Raiders ought to be established to pay attention to research and research organizations that bear on the interests, however indirect, of black people. The Fair Employment Practices laws and the provisions of the Equal Employment Opportunity Act should be brought to bear on the research and consulting industry. Legislative hearings on individual firm practice and industry behavior may be in order. Black congressmen as a group and committees concerned with research policy should be asked to undertake congressional investigations leading to administrative and perhaps legislative reform. The new Consumer Affairs Section of the Antitrust Division of the Justice Department may be useful in investigating complaints.

Black mayors, city councilmen, state legislators and other state and local officials, many of whom are lawyers, should consider appropriate legislation, perhaps along the lines of New York City's proposed "Freedom of Information Law." This proposal would require full disclosure by the city of all statements, opinions, and documents that affect the public.[1]

And last, class action suits, including antitrust action, may be useful in limiting hostile research undertaken with public funds.

The uses to be made of these tools will depend on the creativity and ingenuity of lawyers who bring suits and who press for hearings and regulation. It should become a priority matter for the National Bar Association and the National Conference of Black Lawyers.

The black community in the United States, with a population, by some estimates, approaching 30 million, is making progress toward collective social, political, and economic security. (So are many independent black nations in Africa). The pace of progress varies by region in the United States. Many obstacles remain, but enough tools have been developed and tested successfully to provide some basis for optimism.

---

[1] See "Plan Given to End Consultant Issue," New York Times, December 21, 1970, p. 52.

The opposition of white society to black progress has also been varied, differing by age, class, region, religion and so forth. There have been, let us agree, white allies in the effort, some more or less steadfast. As black people have moved on various fronts, however, resistance has taken both blunt and subtle forms.

Indeed, the matter of white opposition is fairly complex. Some organized opposition is simple in its determination to maintain white supremacy. But the behavior of white American corporations, consulting firms, and white-dominated public agencies is generally less single-minded. Most white corporations, for example, have explicit policies and programs to assist black communities on the one hand, and covertly act to stifle black aspirations on the other.

Black progress has in the last decade depended to a significant extent on the organization and application of information and knowledge. This will undoubtedly be true to an even greater degree in the seventies and beyond.

Research and consulting will be of great importance in private and public policy and program development. In the last five years or so, black people have become increasingly sophisticated about the operations of government as it affects their lives at every level. This article aims to discuss some of the dangers posed to the black community by at least some, and probably many, white research and consulting organizations. It points to dangers to their professional standing and to society generally from misbehavior. And it suggests that reform and perhaps regulation is appropriate if an increase in the already dangerously high level of mutual racial mistrust, at least deriving from this source, is to be avoided.

The knowledge industry[2] includes many types of or-

---

[2] For background on the industry see: Amitai Etzioni, "*Knowledge and Power*," (Review of The Rand Corporation: Case Study of a Nonprofit Advisory Corporation, by Bruce L. R. Smith), The New York Times Book Review, July 31, 1966, p. 3; William Lazer and Arthur E. Warner, *The Knowledge Industry's Research Consultants in Perspec-*

ganizations including, of course, colleges and universities. Attention here is limited to research and consulting firms, profit and non-profit, because they are most engaged in applied as distinct from basic research in urban affairs and the social sciences. University research, however, is also capable of similar mischief and is not to be ignored. The same watchfulness should be exercised by both the black and concerned white community over all processes of social analysis.

Non-profit organizations[3] increasingly active in urban research include fairly well-known examples such as the Rand Corporation, Systems Development Corporation (SDC), Stanford Research Institute (SRI), and Batelle Memorial Institute (BMI).

There are also the profit-oriented firms such as Arthur D. Little, based in Cambridge, Massachusetts, Planning Research Associates in Los Angeles, and others.

The general consulting firms such as Booz, Allen, and Hamilton, McKinsey and Company, and Fry Consultants are also active in urban research nationally. A number of accounting firms like Arthur Andersen and Arthur Young are also engaged in applied social science research and urban consulting for private and public clients from time to time.

Planning consultants and economic consultants are well known for their efforts in the field. Lastly, heavy industrial companies, for example in metals, aerospace, and forest

---

tive. Bureau of Business and Economic Research, Graduate School of Business Administration, Michigan State University, Marketing and Transportation Paper no. 13; and James MacGregor, *Brains for Hire: Tax-Exempt Batelle Prospers as It Studies All Kinds of Problems*, Wall Street Journal, January 12, 1970, p. 1.

[3] See: James D. Grant, "*The Future of Nonprofit Research and Development Organizations*," California Management Review, Summer 1965, p. 81; Bruce L. R. Smith, "*The Future of the Not-for-Profit Corporations*," The Public Interest, No. 8, Summer 1967, p. 127; and Dean C. Coddington and J. Gordon Milliken, "*Future of Federal Contract Research Center*," Harvard Business Review, March-April 1970, p. 103.

products, such as Alcoa, Lockheed, and Boise Cascade have been similarly engaged.

The principal concern here is with the first two groups, especially those that propose to apply to social problems analysis techniques first developed for military purposes.

Although each organization is unique, a closer look at one with which I am reasonably familiar at first hand, may provide insights that will assist the public toward self-protection.

Stanford Research Institute is a 24-year-old not-for-profit research organization with headquarters outside San Francisco in Menlo Park, California. It was founded after World War II by a group of West Coast industrialists who foresaw the need for organized independent applied research in the sciences and in techno-economics in support of the economic development of the eleven western states. Its early years were spent on the campus of Stanford University. As it grew it acquired a separate physical plant three miles from Stanford. Its relations with the University have been legally complex and politically subtle, but it has been often described as an operationally independent subsidiary of Stanford. Until very recently the Board of Directors of SRI contained some of the same men as sat on the Board of Trustees of Stanford, and for most of the last twenty years the president of Stanford had been ex-officio chairman of the SRI Board.

In mid-1970 after a series of student confrontations over military and other controversial research, the Board of Trustees of the University, with faculty support and over some significant student opposition, voted to dispose of SRI.[4] The disposition is in process of completion after legal and financial problems were negotiated. The point remains however that SRI's behavior has been vigorously called into

4 John Noble Wilford, "*Researchers Cut Link to Stanford*," New York Times, Saturday, July 4, 1970.

question by concerned critics for moral and political reasons relating principally to Vietnam and other military research. Challenges of that sort to the activities of any organization that is also doing research in urban affairs should be noted with interest, and the organizational responses to such criticism more and more carefully analyzed for any potential racial implications.

Until recently SRI had a staff of about 3,200, 1,500 of them professionals. Layoffs and unreplaced resignations have left about 2,700 employees, 1,300 of them professionals. SRI at present does work in almost every scientific and social scientific discipline. It has offices and teams around the world and across the United States. In recent years it has done as much as $65 million of contract research annually.

The quality of work in an organization like SRI varies according to the individuals working on a project, and it is sometimes influenced by factors outside the control of the professional researcher, such as forced contract renegotiations arising from federal budget cuts (rare), or the imposition of unanticipated time constraints. In general, quality is good and throughout SRI there are a number of excellent professionals with national and international reputations. The same, I would guess, is true of most other large research and consulting organizations.

The management sciences division contains the Urban and Social Systems Department composed of groups specializing in Urban and Regional Economics, Manpower, Education, and so on. Management Sciences also includes a Transportation Department that has done considerable work in urban transportation. Each of these departments and groups has individual staff members who are professionally outstanding and socially aware and sensitive. Each group also, however, includes men usually, as it happens, senior professionals and managers, who are preoccupied with internal politicking, whose professional skills as researchers have atrophied, and probably of greatest importance to the concerned public, whose behavior often has a racist effect, and who seem to be concerned with maintaining white supremacy roughly as they have come to know it through their life experiences. Often they are heavily engaged in the cronyism of mutual protection, and are frequently evasive or uninformed when queried on professional matters of social significance.

Since this is the knowledge industry and all of these men are highly educated, their racism often takes the relatively subtle form blacks have come to recognize in certain types of corporate liberalism. That is to say, their utterances and behavior are not uniformly, consistently and blatantly bigoted. They profess concern for social problems, deplore racism and discrimination, and fervently hope "the problems will be solved." But black people have dealt with enough quasi-liberal school superintendents, city councilmen, corporate personnel officers, and welfare administrators to generally recognize the type I have referred to. The problem in this case is that the consultant and researcher who is a racist is also represented as an expert and a scientist, an objective and dispassionate analyst who presents findings and conclusions backed by data and evidence.

The problem is increasingly compounded by another fact. There are often, even usually, black researchers on the staff who, though constrained, have participated in the work, and who to the public's mind seem to bring additional authenticity and legitimacy to the final report.

Now most black professional researchers, as many white researchers, are probably vitally concerned with community welfare. But in an organization like SRI, these men, usually juniors, working on a large, say six-figure contract, led by a senior professional or manager, are not able to single-handedly review entire research efforts and point out bias. Large research efforts consequently are sometimes seriously contaminated, and when the results are accepted and applied, to the extent the application affects black or other minority people, the research organization has acted as a contaminating agent in the community. At SRI, younger white researchers, like educated young whites generally, are less likely to transmit bias in their work, but since the bigger the project the more senior the leadership, as a rule, concerned communities and their professional advocates should be especially alert to examine the method, the data, and the results of large publicly funded projects. Indeed, the award of large study contracts to research firms even suspected of significant racial bias will, I would expect, be subject to more and more public questioning by advocate organizations and concerned professional groups as they come to recognize the potential of harmful results of biased research.

Because of the increased sense of community vigilance developed over the last few years, and often because of the insistence of federal contracting officers, white firms have more and more found it wise to employ black consulting firms as subcontractors. (These black firms, as their expertise and muscle increase, are increasingly in the running for prime contracts, using white subs when necessary.) The use of black subs, like black staff of the prime contractor, tends to provide internal watchdogs on projects as they proceed. Black lawyers monitoring contract award procedures or acting as community advocates should be increasingly mindful of the need for black subs on large public contracts of all kinds including those that appear to be strictly technical, e.g., in transportation, water resources, and other engineering economic studies.

It is accepted practice that much work in applied social science research is done under some form of public contract, federal, state or local. Most of the key contracting officers in the relevant agencies are white and middle-aged, and given what we think we know about social conditioning and social dynamics, it is reasonable to assume that many are biased to some degree. Research firms such as SRI generally maintain a relatively high degree of professional integrity. But integrity, i.e., basic honesty, is not incompatible with racial bias in the conduct of research. There is such a thing as a reasonably honest bigot. But if his research concludes, for example, that a transport system is optimized by a freeway or other transit structure through black neighborhoods, his technical honesty is of little consolation to those adversely affected. Indeed, the structure may be an optimizing solution in a narrow technical sense, but if the final report neglects to fully discuss political and social implications, the community may be the loser.

Comprehensive attention to "non-economic" factors, psychological, social, cultural, political, and aesthetic, has increased in the last couple of years and such blatant or stubborn oversights are becoming fewer. Nevertheless, the black community and its representatives seem increasingly to be coming to believe that they ought not leave the matter entirely in the hands of the professional researcher and the contracting officer. (Research affecting the black community will be felt to be too important to be left entirely to researchers.) Surveillance increasingly is considered necessary throughout the study process. Progress reports to communities and full access to final reports and back-up data are more and more requested by representatives or advocates. Lawyers should be especially involved in this process, and should use such tools as the Public Information Act to gain access to research in progress.

Many studies for local public agencies are subject to public hearings before acceptance, although they are often "sanitized" with controversial or, to the client, unwelcome views or findings, softened or deleted before final presentation through preliminary review and negotiation. Most federal studies for HUD, DOT, DOL, HEW, and OEO are not, in practice, subject to much public scrutiny. Actually, dedicated researchers are often frustrated when their reports end up on a shelf or in a file and are never acted upon.

Concerned communities have a vital interest in examining every unclassified report done for every public agency that bears on community interests. There may on occasion be good reason for treating a report as confidential for a period of time. But in general that period should be brief. Disclosure of the existence of all domestic research, including that of the Defense Department, should be insisted upon, and the Public Information Act should be used to gain access to all reports of interest to these communities. Research of AID relating to black nations in Africa and the Caribbean will probably be similarly perused.

Such review should perhaps be undertaken on a regular and systematic basis by several review centers established both at black and predominantly white universities, at some of the emerging black and white activist think tanks, by advocate planning and research groups, and by national organizations like NAACP, Urban League, SCLC, or NAACP Legal Defense and Education Fund. Some pressure for disclosure could also be brought on research for private clients that bears on the welfare of concerned communities.

So far I have suggested that surveillance and examination of research are necessary because of the personal bias of significant numbers of senior professionals and managers in contract research organizations like SRI.

Many senior professional and managers are "good government" advocates whose principal criterion of good government is efficiency rather than equity, responsiveness, or openness. This concern leads to interest, for example, in metropolitan or regional government because of the expected realization of scale economies. Black people apparently are increasingly wary of regionalization when it means reduced political power and protection.

The concern of such researchers for efficiency is often related to a generally benevolent, paternalistic, or even "neo-colonialistic" stance toward the solution of social problems in which senior white professionals are presumed to know fairly well what is best for all social groups.

Many professional researchers following academics such as John Kain and David Birch are also intrigued by the possibilities of dispersal of the black population as a solution to some urban problems. Often this seems to be a racist reflex reaction to black concentration and political leverage, rather than the result of careful and responsible analysis of a range of policy choices.

Both "good government" and "dispersal" preferences often reflect general ignorance of, opposition to, or contempt for the political aspirations of the black community.

These men are often also relatively johnny-come-latelys to the field, having spent most of their careers in such fields as real estate, logistics research, military systems analysis, or the military itself. As a result they often bring professional habits and ideological baggage that are incompatible with what to concerned people is satisfactory social research (e.g., housing, transportation, education). Systems analysis can make important contributions to solutions of complex problems. When the systems analysts are turned loose on social problems, however, the results are sometimes ludicrous. They should almost always be led and constrained by thoroughly trained social scientists. Black lawyers should be alert to the dangers in current notions of retraining out-of-work aerospace professionals for an attack on "social problems." Many, if not most, of the scientists and engineers in this field should probably not be allowed to bring their views to bear, in a professional context, on matters directly affecting black people.

Black organizations, lay and professional, can take steps to protect themselves by inviting senior researchers and managers, including top managers, to speak or sit on panels. These men and women ought not be allowed to remain hidden from public scrutiny. Some of them hold views on race and urban affairs that cannot stand the light of day. Under careful questioning the basic racism in many will emerge. They can then be quarantined.

Commercial realities affecting research also are an influence that may concern minority communities. Many firms in the field are there out of a desire to diversify from military work, a respectable motive in some cases. But often, as pointed out, this leads to the use of military analysts whose social judgments may fairly be suspected, and whose concern for excessive scientific rigor and elegance is inappropriate to the problems at hand. Also firms are sometimes preoccupied with commercial survival and the "follow-on," or next and related contract, and are therefore willing to compromise the research by modifying the conclusions or recommendations in order to keep a client happy or at least unembarrassed.

Most of the men discussed here consider themselves objective and unbiased on questions of social research and policy. Most do not believe they should be "advocates." Apparently many black people, and increasing numbers of whites on the other hand, understand that all Americans, white and black, who work on these problems are advocates in one manner or another. Every middle-class American certainly has an interest and a stake of some kind in the outcome of the race conflict, and each advocates, however subtly, the status quo, small change, or major change in some direction. Most seniors at SRI, and I would guess elsewhere, seem to favor either the first or the second. Many, if not most, black people favor the third. It is unlikely that SRI's senior staff will come to view their interests much differently during the remainder of their career, but black people will probably be increasingly alert to the problems of advocacy or its denial, and of questionable objectivity in the conduct of research on the part of research and consulting firms generally.[5]

---

[5] See Gunnar Myrdal, *The Challenge of World Poverty* (Pantheon) 1970. In Chapter 1, "Cleansing the Approach from Biases," he addresses this problem in the context of research in developing countries. Professional researchers have been known to express disrespect for nationals of countries in which they were or had been working.

Now we can look briefly at a few other characteristics of SRI's organization that may be fairly general in the industry. These characteristics also suggest a need for wariness.

At SRI, in my opinion, there is a serious shortage of first-rate talent among the managers in the Urban Department and in the Institute's top management. Because of the economics of the industry, its competitive position in the management markets, and for other reasons of personal and organizational eccentricity, the Institute, at present, seems burdened with many managers who are incapable of successful innovation and dynamic leadership. Since research institutions like SRI can be a valuable national asset, it is to be hoped that when current problems are solved and the Institute is stable and independent, new managers and a new top management team will be brought in that will be capable of recommending more enlightened policies to the Board, and that will be able to accomplish important internal organizational and program reform.

Let us now look at four examples of problems in need of solution that will probably also concern the black community although perhaps not as much as unsatisfactory research.

As mentioned earlier, many white firms behave toward the black community in a positive manner on one hand and with hostility on the other. Consider some SRI policies and practices that may be viewed with concern by black people. First, the Institute in the past has done work for at least one U.S. corporation interested in opportunities in South Africa, and for Portuguese corporations with interests in Mozambique and Angola. What should be SRI and industry policy toward research in these areas for such clients (to say nothing of possible potential work for the South African government or corporations there)?

Second, SRI and others may have done (I do not have the facts) work in "riot control," including work for local and federal agencies interested in the problem popularly known as "law and order." Black people, and concerned whites of course, are generally interested in "law" and "order," but not in "law and order." More seriously, it is possible the Institute has or could undertake studies of a more general variety, examining the black community as it would a hostile entity and evaluating and preparing alternative suppressive strategic and tactical responses (a sort of "cold war" planning).

Some problems in South Africa or in internal security may be legitimate subjects of analysis under some circumstances by some researchers. But nonprofit corporations have a public nature, and the studies in question are contracted with public funds. To the extent they have been undertaken and are hostile to black people, the black community should take such legal measures as are available to prevent continuation of such work.

Of concern here is the issue, will an organization that with one division conducts studies in the "suppression" or "exploitation" of black people in the U.S. or Africa (i.e., studies seen by many as hostile), and with another, health, housing, transportation, education, and welfare, be allowed to study the latter in these communities? SRI, to my knowledge, has made no explicit policy statements concerning either its work in Southern Africa or Portugal, or its work in what is often called domestic counter-insurgency. No final judgment is possible here. The key question remains, however, will an organization that remains silent respecting its policies, one way or the other, in areas many black people feel are sensitive be allowed to send its researchers into black communities even to do what most black people can agree is socially useful work? Does the one hand contaminate the whole and hence the other? It would be entirely appropriate to put these questions to all organizations, profit and non-profit, that have multifaceted and far-flung research programs.

The matter of "academic freedom" is relevant here.

Most, if not all researchers and consultants, wherever they are, but especially in universities and non-profit organizations, seem to believe that they are or should be free to study anything that is researchable limited only by the availability of financial support. Morality is a consideration for some men, political reality for others, in determining areas for investigation. Academic freedom is an important issue, complex and delicate. Some research executives who use the term, however, are not really speaking of an important principle but are merely using the expression to defend immediately profitable work, however socially questionable.

It is reasonably clear that the historical merit of the concept of academic freedom has been principally the protection of iconoclastic or critical social analysis. It is further clear that research organizations can and do establish policies limiting research in a variety of ways, according to client, subject, size of contract, and so on. Indeed, few if any consulting research organizations would do work for, say, the Ku Klux Klan, even if the work were on a legitimate and researchable problem. The behavior of "respectable" clients though subtle on occasion can be as hostile to reasonable minority group interests as that of the Klan.

Third, the Board of Directors at SRI, a non-profit corporation active in public policy research, is entirely white. This situation is likely to be questioned, and changes will probably be brought about, but a hard rule on board composition will most likely remain elusive.

At last, what of research staffs generally? SRI, for example, has a handful of black professionals, fewer than 20 out of a staff of about 1,300. Its record is a bit better with non-professionals, but racially backward personnel policies can be inferred from an examination of the work force, and from discussions with the President, other principal officers, department and group managers, and black staff. There are no black professionals in the entire Economics Division.

The market for contract research is difficult just now; there have been layoffs at SRI, federal research budgets are tight; competition is keen, and so forth. Probably not much can be done about professional recruiting through 1971. But the question that will be raised in the black community is what are the real, as distinct from stated, personnel policy preferences of the management of such organizations? What legal remedy is available here?[6]

The concerned community, black and white, will probably begin to question SRI and similar organizations on all these policy issues. Those found wanting will tend to be viewed with suspicion as to their capacity to perform consistently reliable research that relates to the well-being of black people especially, and society in general. Those that do thorough, careful, and imaginative work will be rewarded. And those that refrain from engaging in offensive work probably will be relatively more favorably regarded.

SRI, The Hudson Institute, and a number of other research organizations are working on the problem of "the future." Teams of researchers are examining as carefully as they can, trends, projections, forecasts, and scenarios relating to U.S. and world development over the next three to five decades, the focus of work often pointed "toward the year 2000." The clients are often government agencies, such as the Office of Education in HEW, interested in "alternative futures." The idea, not a startling one, is that social change can be at least somewhat anticipated, and perhaps partially managed. In any case, it is hoped that surprises, especially unpleasant ones, can be avoided to some extent.

At present few people know about this research in the black community. Few, if any, blacks or browns monitor

----

[6] Dr. Melvin Humphrey, a black economist, has recently been appointed Director of Research for the U.S. Equal Employment Opportunity Commission. His work can be very helpful in this regard. SRI, for example, has been given a clean bill of health, by the EEOC. Deeper investigation might alter that.

it, or participate in developing scenarios or evaluating "alternative futures." What is desirable for minority groups in the year 2000? Black think tanks are looking ahead. But the work of white think tanks should not be allowed to go unquestioned or conducted quietly in private. These are public issues studied at public expense and it is the black future being anticipated as a part of that of the larger society. Inasmuch as this work will affect public policy, especially in education, the work should, to the extent feasible, be fully public every step of the way, and a variety of organizations concerned with black community welfare and security will likely begin to make direct inquiry and take steps to keep the work in the public eye through periodic reports of evaluations. Black lawyers concerned with these long-range studies might derive some benefit from examining the literature on "futurism."[7]

Much of this examination of the case of SRI as one example in the research and consulting industry of questionable practices and products may be likened in spirit to that of the growing consumerism movement generally. Ralph Nader and others have uncovered flagrant abuses by manufacturers of consumer items and providers of services. The professional research industry can perhaps stand some investigation, legal as well as technical. There is increasing concern about secrecy in government and science. George Bernard Shaw is said to have once claimed that "Every profession is a conspiracy against the public." That, of course, is arguable. But concerned people ought to be wary of the impact of the work of planners, researchers, and consultants. As a young American patriot pointed out about 200 years ago, in a different yet strangely similar context, eternal vigilance is the price of liberty.

[7] See: Daniel Bell: "*The Study of the Futures* v. *Can One Predict?* B. *The Oracle at Delphi*," The Public Interest, No. 1, Fall 1965, p. 119; and Otis Dudley Duncan, "*Social Forecasting—The State of the Art*," The Public Interest, No. 17, Fall 1969, p. 88.

Conclusion/Future Trends

Charles V. Hamilton

Black Social Scientists: Contributions and Problems

The history of Black social scientists has been characterized by inadequate institutional support, low salaries, poor working conditions and a general lack of recognition of their achievements by the established professions. Charles V. Hamilton briefly describes these problems against their historical backdrop and proposes that a new "Black" social science be created to undertake analyses of the conditions of Blacks with the aim of improving them. Outlining specific kinds of studies that need to be made, he challenges the Black social scientist to take them on.

Much of what is accurately known about social and political conditions of black Americans from the Civil War to World War II is a result of scholarly work done by black social scientists during those years. The work of Dr. W. E. B. DuBois from 1897 to 1910 at Atlanta University in a series of seminal studies of virtually every aspect of black American life still stands as a model for research activity, along with his monumental study, *The Philadelphia Negro*.

471

One could list Dr. Charles S. Johnson and his studies of black youth during that time; Professor E. Franklin Frazier's research on the black family, the scholarship of Dr. Ira De A. Reid, Dr. Horace Mann Bond on black education and several others still stand as authoritative materials for their subject.

No less important is that these black social scientists worked under financial conditions which were far from desirable. They had great insights, but little income; they had many research proposals, but few research facilities. But in spite of these handicaps, they produced a body of scholarship to be noted and quoted.

These earlier black social scientists brought to their work a set of values and experiences that contributed immeasurably to the quality of their work. They were concerned not only with methodology, but with meaning.

At one time, there was the rather widespread, but mistaken, belief that social science research could and should be "value-free," that the social scientist could and should be "objective." This view is still held by many white (and some black) academicians. It is a mistaken notion precisely because it is not possible for a human being to divorce himself so dispassionately from his subject of study, and especially so, when he is studying human society. When that society is his own, he has added subjective notions, whatever his race.

The black social scientist in this country is a member of a race that is subjected and oppressed. *He* is subjected and oppressed. It is impossible to be "objective" about that, any more than it is possible for a white social scientist, who has benefited directly or indirectly from racial oppression, to be "objective" about his position of preference, whether he admits it or not. Each brings insights from his own vantage point of reality to his work. Each brings preconceived value judgments.

For years, traditional (white) social science research—

especially on political life and organizations—told us how politically healthy and workable the society was, how all the groups in the society were pretty much getting their fair share, or moving certainly in that direction. There was a social scientific myth of consensus and progress developed. But those "objective" social scientists apparently did not read carefully (or at all) the accumulated literature of the earlier black social scientists.

They had to wait for the explosions of the mid-1960's to point out to them their own essentially mediocre work on social and political problems. It took loud, dramatic noises from the black community to tell them they were substantially wrong. And now, many of these traditional social scientists are busily setting up urban studies institutes, etc., trying in an instant, to "rush to relevancy."

No More Influence

Today, the black social scientist has no more certain influence or power with white decision-makers than his forefathers. And in most cases, he has very little more research funds. But this cannot be, any more than it was for the earlier black scholars, an excuse for not proceeding to do the hard and tough research necessary to present alternative solutions.

There are two major ongoing challenges facing the black social scientists today. The first is to continue the careful work of the earlier scholars. This is being done, and much more is needed. Already, there are new studies being published reexamining the black family, looking at the strengths of that institution for purposes of finding ways to build even more viable community organizations. There are new studies on the black woman.

The entire black-community social structure is being reexamined by black social scientists, focusing on extended kinship groups, the role of the church and other communal organizations. This is vital research. It is necessary in order to obtain a clear and accurate definition of black societal conditions that go beyond the clichés of traditional social science.

There is another, equally challenging role the black social scientists must assume. Not only must they examine the black community, but they must take their insights and their skills into a hard examination of the sociopolitical and economic nature of the total society in order to point out its contradictions and to chart viable alternative policies for change.

It is not sufficient, although crucial, to study only black people. White-dominated political and economic institutions that directly and indirectly oppress blacks must receive the immediate attention of black social scientists. The fact is, today, a black social scientist can get at least a little money to study blacks.

But watch what happens when the proposal is made to study the decision-making processes that affect, say, private employment policies on federally subsidized projects. Or the city planning process in New York City. Or to do a simulation study of the potential effects of revenue-sharing on ten selected northern or southern metropolitan areas heavily populated by blacks. These fields of inquiry are not normally seen as within the purview of the black social scientists.

But black social scientists must begin to deal with these and similar specific public policy issues. We must begin to study most carefully, for example, all the implications of the electoral college system. What new electoral mechanisms on the national and local levels are viable from a black political perspective?

It is precisely the function of the black social scientists to be directly engaged in research on new forms of government. Under what circumstances, and in what places does metropolitan government become dysfunctional? And when is it, if ever, useful for black people?

What new tax-bases must be developed to end retrogressive taxes and to move to progressive taxes? When new legislative and congressional boundary lines are drawn, where should they be drawn so as to provide the maximum benefit for black people?

Need No Apology

There is nothing "value-free" about this kind of social science research. But there need be no apology made for this. There is nothing "value-free" about the same science research of Rand-New York or any of the other numerous research agencies that now exist and feed into policy-making.

One should expect that this kind of work of the black social scientists will have immediate value to those black organizations whose function it is to organize and to push for change. The black social scientists should not expect that they will have ready access to the decision-making councils of city hall, the state capital or Washington, D.C. Or certainly not ready receptivity. This we would have assumed from the outset.

The black social scientists must include on their agendas not only those matters which are immediately indigenous to the black community. In other words, a study of "Harlem Politics" must be more than a study of black political groups in Harlem, how they organize, how they act, etc.

A study of Harlem Politics, of necessity, must include a study of the impact of private outside capital on the financing of economic ventures in that community. It must include a study of the decisions made outside Harlem which affect Harlem, the different networks of external influence. Black Americans and the black social scientists cannot afford to be trapped in the conclusion that says a hard, piercing, critical examination of white political and economic institutions is off limits to us.

If this society is to change in any viable way, black people will, of necessity, have to play a leading role. It will be, in large measure, the new values, new insights, and new alternatives proposed by black people that will have the considerable legitimacy. It will not be without intense political struggle, which, again, one assumes from the outset. And neither will it be without the kinds of hard work started by our giants of social science scholarship many decades ago.

AFTERWORD

Reflections on Ethics in Research:
The Death of White Sociology Twenty-Five Years Later

By Becky Thompson

In his article "Sociological Amnesia," sociologist Herbert Gans cautioned against a tendency of social scientists to design, seek funding for, conduct, and then write about research that, for all intents and purposes, has been done years ago.[1] He advised against this reinvention of the wheel, aware of its possible negative consequences for the field of sociology. What would sustain the field's honor, particularly in the public's eye, if it seemed that sociologists mainly spun our wheels intellectually—sometimes at the taxpayers' expense at that? His warning also had an ethical implication: In times of grave need for policies that will help ameliorate such issues as the spread of AIDS, poverty, police brutality, and breast cancer, can we afford to do even one thing that has already been done?

In a word, Gans cautioned against the effects of historical amnesia in the social sciences. As Adrienne Rich explained in her pioneering article "Resisting Amnesia: History and Personal Life," *historical amnesia* is "starvation of the imagination...leaving depression and emptiness in it wake."[2] Gans' concern—fueled by his experience in the field for more than 30 years—made me scrutinize the extent to which I was reinventing the wheel in my own thinking about ethics in conducting multiracial research. That question sent me careening back in search of studies and scholarship that had already made the wheel. For although there are some unprecedented ethical dilemmas, much of the groundwork needed in current debates has already been laid.

It is this quest that brought me to consider the ethics offered in *The Death of White Sociology*, which was first published in 1973 when volume editor Joyce Ladner was teaching at Hunter College. The issues it addresses continue to echo in many debates currently occurring on college campuses and among researchers.

I happened upon *The Death of White Sociology* accidentally in the second basement of a university library already four full years into graduate school, even though I had done my undergraduate and graduate work in departments with national reputations as "lefty hotbeds." This is one telling sign of the historical amnesia regarding the pioneering work of African American theorists.

Historical Context and Purpose

It might be said that *The Death of White Sociology* was to sociology in the 1970s what *This Bridge Called My Back* was to women's studies in the early 1980s or what Patricia Williams' *The Alchemy of Race and Rights* has been to legal scholarship in this decade. These books were "wake-up calls" that questioned—with passion and commitment—the most sacred tenets of mainstream academic traditions. In the terms of Thomas Kuhn, these books offered *paradigm shifts* requiring a reformulation of the very foundations of the disciplines in question.[3]

One purpose of *The Death of White Sociology,* according to contributor Robert Staples, was to expose white sociology as the "body of theory that has been employed by the powers-that-be to sustain white racism."[4] Although the anthology's title reveals its focus on the discipline of sociology, the inclusion of the prominent psychologist Kenneth Clark, writer Ralph Ellison, and political scientists Ronald Walters and Charles Hamilton along with several sociologists enabled critical analyses that had sweeping implications throughout the social sciences. The contributors documented how the social sciences have perpetuated destructive ideologies about African American people in the name of science and showed how these ideologies historically have been translated into social policy, economic planning, and education, and have influenced the hearts and minds of American people. The myth of the Black matriarch and the "culturelessness" or pathology of Black communities are two of the many ideologies used to justify the continued intellectual, political, and economic subjugation of African Americans. The contributors documented how white sociology—as an arm of the racial status quo—has been built on studies intended to perfect methods of controlling Black people under the pretense of governing them, while rationalizing poverty and inequality as inevitable by-products of so-called "cultural inferiority."

Although the anthology's agenda was necessarily reactive, it also has a proactive purpose to articulate the central tenets of African American social theory and the history of social scientific thought from a more inclusive perspective than had previously existed. Defiant and forthright in its tone, the anthology celebrated the contributions of Black theorists—W.E.B. DuBois and E. Franklin Frazier, to name just two—whose intellectual contributions are still largely unsung and underrepresented in social science texts and in the annals of historical sociology. Some essays by white theorists who were dedicated to the destruction of white sociology were also resurrected from the burial grounds of history with the publication of this anthology. The book also confronted race biases in graduate education and the effect of racism on research priorities. Essays also explored class and race issues in social scientific research, as well as the scientific process itself and other research that amounts to "non-scientific nonsense."[5]

Like the contributors of *The Politics of Anthropology* (1979) and *All the Women Are White, All the Blacks Are Men, But Some of us Are Brave* (1982), the authors of *The Death of White Sociology* seemed little concerned with choosing words and positions to promote their careers and gain recognition within the academy.[6] The mere fact that Joyce Ladner edited the book and decided to use the title *The Death of White Sociology* at the young age of twenty-eight speaks volumes to her political wisdom in consolidating the writings of key intellectuals in that particular historical moment. The tone of the anthology is neither assimilationist nor accommodating. In this way, the title does justice to the work, and is a telling reminder of its historical specificity and relation to the Black Power movement.

The anthology's publication in 1973 occurred at the end of what some historians refer to as *the turbulent era* in the United States—1961 to 1973.[7] This period was scarred by the deaths of Carole Robertson, Cynthia Wesley, Addie Mae Collins, and Denise McNair—four Black girls who were murdered at the Sixteenth Street Baptist Church in Birmingham, Alabama.[8] Witnesses of this era remember what came to be known as the "long hot summers," during which people protested poverty and segregation that continued despite the Civil Rights Act of 1964. These rebellions began with Watts in 1965, Newark and Detroit in 1967, and more than 150 cities and towns in 1968. Key leaders were assassinated—Malcolm X in 1965 and Martin Luther King in 1968. Others were jailed, as in the case of Angela Davis in 1970, American Indian Movement leader Leonard Peltier, and many others.[9] This was the time of the late great Marvin Gaye's "What's Going On," the Staple Singers' "Respect Yourself," and the Temptations' 1970 hit "Ball of Confusion—That's What the World is Today," all of which spoke to the anger, conviction, indignation, and pleas for racial justice characteristic of the late sixties and early seventies.

The Death of White Sociology captured much of the mood of

people who were literally "taking it to the streets" in protests against poverty, voting restrictions, the Vietnam War, and with the Stonewall Riot in Greenwich Village in 1969, harassment against gay men and lesbians. On university campuses, these protests laid the foundations for the first African American and women's studies programs, open admissions policies, and eventually affirmative action plans—all institutional struggles to which current commitments to multicultural education are absolutely indebted.

As a product of its time, it is hard to imagine such a book being published in the 1990s, despite the flourishing attention to multicultural education. And in many ways, it is no surprise that *The Death of White Sociology* was, until this republication, out-of-print. Its lack of availability for the time that it was out of print is no indication of the book's irrelevance or obsolescence; but paradoxically, it reflects the accuracy of the anthology's insights, which 25 years later remain too threatening to the status quo to be taken on in a serious way. And although a historical reading gives evidence to this threat, the book's ethical presuppositions are at the base of its challenge and are what pull it forward across time and historical circumstance.

Ethics

Reading the text for its ethical stances requires a clarification of the term *ethics* in general and *liberation ethics* in particular. The purpose of liberation ethics is to examine the ethical stances evidenced by oppressed people while exposing how these moral positions are masked in normative ethics scholarship.[10] According to social ethicist Katie G. Cannon, liberation ethics are founded on a commitment to disentangle and unmask dominant ideology and power relations and offer steps for change that support justice.[11] The most well-known work in liberation ethics has been developed by activists and scholars whose work centers on the liberation of oppressed people. Elie Wiesel, Nelson Mandela, Howard Thurman,

Paulo Freire, Cornel West, James Cone, C.S. Song, and Carter Heyward are among many who are either self-defined as liberation ethicist or whose work can be read as examples of liberation ethics. Despite the impressive diversity in generation, ethnicity, religious tradition, and the particular liberation struggles in which they are involved, a common theme in these people's work is that those facing oppression create ethical standards that go beyond the boundaries of normative, mainstream morality.

Cannon powerfully explicates the stretching of normative ethical boundaries in her scholarship on the Black woman's literary tradition.[12] Using African American women's writing as the basis of her analysis, Cannon delineated how ethical positions of subordinated people are not the same as, and thus cannot be measured by the same criteria as those of people spared injustice. Cannon wrote, "[Racism, gender discrimination, and economic exploitation...require the Black community to create and cultivate values and virtues in their own terms so that [Black people] can prevail against the odds with moral integrity."[13] Cannon explained, for example, that while dominant Christian ethics support being independent and saving money as desirable qualities that insure financial reward, these characteristics assume that wealth is available for all who seek it. Accepting the notion that all people have the resources to "pull themselves up by their bootstraps" renders invisible the impact of racism as a force that has denied most Black people jobs that make capital accumulation possible.

Like the Black women novelists discussed in Cannon's analysis, Black social scientists have pushed apart narrow ethical formulations. Being what Patricia Hill Collins refers to as an *outsider-within*—one who is viewed or treated as an outsider within a given institution—affords Black academics a critical perspective of both their disciplines and the academy's relation to society.[14] This outsider-within perspective has fueled controversies and the emergence of innovative methodologies and pedagogical styles throughout the academy. The creative potential this perspective engenders is currently evident in the explosion of research in critical race theory, feminist theory, cultural studies, gay and lesbian studies, and African American studies.

It is this outsider-within status that informs the ethics in *The Death of White Sociology* and contradicts the normative ethics in the field. At the core of this contested terrain lies the value placed on objectivity, which is the first principle in the current American Sociological Association (ASA) code of ethics, the officially endorsed ethics document for the discipline of sociology.[15] For many authors in *The Death of White Sociology,* this standard stands in the way of so-called objectivity rather than ensuring fairness.

Subjectivity

The contributors' opposition to objectivity is two-fold. On one level, they reason that there is no such thing as objectivity because all people come to whatever they do with subjectivity; that makes us human. Anthology contributor Kenneth Clark wrote, "there is no one without some bias and those who pretend to be most unbiased either were indifferent or reflected an insidious form of bias."[16] But the authors' opposition to proclamations of objectivity go deeper than simply acknowledging its impossibility. They also reject the concept because of the misuse of power that historically has occurred in the name of objectivity. This injustice has included promoting harmful and erroneous assumptions about Black people in scholarship and social policy (such as enduring ideology of the Black matriarch) while rendering irrelevant many questions that might illuminate the sources of victim blaming and scapegoating in research.

This commitment to what Cannon referred to as "demythologizing whole bodies of so-called social legitimacy" includes renaming commonly used sociological concepts that mask inequality.[17] Thus political scientist Ronald Walters clarifies that *urban renewal* is actually *Negro removal, model cities* is a normative term for *model colonies, human relations* is more accurately *colonial relations,* and those *considered culturally deprived* are actually *illegally denied.*[18] Such a renaming is not necessarily an issue of semantics, but rather a reaction against what Adrienne Rich and Janet Koenig refer to as *advertisements of the state.*[19] The English language is replete with such tools of obfuscation, such as, for example, the Reagan and Bush administrations' *vertical insertion*—a euphemism for the bombing and killing of human beings during the Gulf War. One task, then, is to identify when and how social scientists adopt these advertisements for the state and develop new terms that accurately reflect political realities.

The willingness to scrutinize commonly accepted sociological concepts comes from an ethical commitment to refuse to apply a framework that twists the reality of those whose lives are being studied. For example, Joyce Ladner's research on Black adolescent girls' self-perceptions led her to rethink her training as a sociologist, especially in relation to the deviance perspective. Instead of accepting deviance as a sign of inferiority and pathology, Ladner identified it as an "invention of a group that uses its own standards as the ideal by which others are to be judged."[20] By questioning the deviance framework, Ladner recognized Black girls' healthy self-esteem and explored how the messages they were taught about injustice and inequality helped them resist negative self-perceptions. Her identification of *Black resilience* was a far cry from the portrayal of Black socialization as deviant or pathological. Ladner's research also anticipated the limitations of feminist theories of female moral development, which focused primarily on white girls. In so doing, Ladner's work gives example to why theory that relies on false universalism is not only theoretically problematic, but also ethically so because it renders invisible many forms of resistance to oppression that need to be acknowledged.

Social Responsibility

The contributors to *The Death of White Sociology* were not the first to underscore how—in the name of objectivity—facts may be created at the expense of truth. However, they certainly have been leaders in drawing links between the methodological inadequacy of objectivity and the responsibility of social scientists to be activists in a society scarred by racial injustice. In fact, many of the contributors were both activists and scholars in the 1970s and have continued to be so since. Kenneth Clark explained that a social science built on a posture of objectivity "cannot ask to be taken seriously by a society desperately in need of moral and empirical guidance in human affairs."[21]

This commitment to a liberatory social science enabled the contributors to consider two interrelated questions as essential components for an ethical analysis. First, who is being served by the community he or she is studying? For Joyce Ladner, for example, it wasn't enough that she refused to apply sociological concepts that denied the adolescent girls' dignity. She also asked, what responsibilities do researchers have to the communities they study? During the four years of her research, Ladner not only interviewed the girls, their parents, and other adults around them, but also became a part of their lives. She visited the girls outside of scheduled interview sessions, opened her house to them as they had opened theirs to her, and conducted interviews around their schedules rather than her own.

Other contributors raised different questions about community accountability. For instance, Blauner and Wellman selected a research team that reflected the racial and ethnic composition of the people they were studying, and became closely involved in several community-initiated projects in order to "decolonize" the research process. Considering such questions of responsibility central to the research project often requires going beyond the ethical parameters supported by the discipline of sociology.[22] In fact, because those being studied were not included in the creation of ethical codes to begin with, the researchers had to develop ethical standards that the profession did not demand. For instance, despite a white bias in their original research plan, Blauner and Wellman had not breached any ASA ethical codes. Through a dialogue with Black staff members and their exposure to the Black power movement, these researchers granted authority to ethical standards that went far beyond their professional obligations.

The Epistemological Privilege

Along with upholding an ethic of accountability, the contributors to *The Death of White Sociology* also grappled with what liberation ethicists refer to as the *epistemological privilege*—the right and responsibility of those facing oppression to name the parameters of this oppression and develop strategies for change. Numerous theorists—Richard Hernnstein, Daniel Patrick Moynihan, and Charles Murray, among others—have espoused debilitating theories of the intellectual and cultural inferiority of Black people.[23] Support for an epistemological privilege was a protest call for Black intellectuals to take control of the scholarship and research previously dominated by white people. The application of this ethical principle to sociological research means accepting that Black people are the ones who have the experience and insight needed to understand Black reality and responses to injustice. This principle assumes that "concrete experience is a criterion for credibility" in the words of Patricia Hill Collins, and must be an essential building block for all research designs, policies, funding decisions, and hiring priorities having to do with Black life.[24]

While upholding this privilege, most of the contributors did not, however, support forms of essentialist determinism such as, "Nothing white people have contributed can be useful," "Black people are naturally able to understand and therefore study Black people," or "All scholarship by Black people is ethical and conversely that all conducted by white people is not." In fact, the contributors explicate—with finesse and sophistication—distinctions between essentialism and informed consciousness about race. The anti-essentialist position of the anthology contributors offered a template for an "informed consciousness" on race that fully twenty years later was still tragically missing in most discussions surrounding Clarence Thomas' nomination to the Supreme Court. In place of considering a candidate's race *and* his/her community commitments relevant for the nomination, George Bush, Strom Thurmond, and others cynically treated blackness as a sufficient qualification despite that Thomas was neither trusted by nor considered himself accountable to Black people.[25] Several authors also argue against the essentialist thinking that being Black naturally or inevitably affords insight and expertise in understanding Blackness.

In *The Death of White Sociology,* the contributors offered moral justification for an epistemological privilege as a means to ensure Black control over Black scholarship while they continued to ally themselves with antiracist white people. Put into practice, this epistemological privilege means accepting that Black and white researchers must often have differing research agendas.

The race of the people being studied must be reflected in the research team studying them. It is not enough that a team researching the lives of Black people include both white and Black researchers if principle investigators are white. There needs to be racial parity at all levels of a research project. Accepting what Blauner and Wellman refer to in this volume as racial division in research labor flies in the face of notions of individual choice and free agency; it remains a necessary reality given the continued existence of racism and other inequalities.

This methodological position remains instructive. It assumes that honoring an epistemological privilege requires that white people work in racially mixed teams when conducting research about communities of color. This not only upsets the balance of power at the level of the researcher and people being studied, but also shifts the racial power among the researchers.

Since the original publication of *The Death of White Sociology*, several projects have upheld this commitment to combining researchers of varied ethnicities to match those of the community. But while such studies are indeed models, team research projects are expensive and usually depend on acquiring substantial funds from outside of the academy. In addition, if a multiracial team collects the data, but has little or no power over how the material is, for instance, interpreted and disseminated, the value of diverse of voices and perspectives is minimized. This again underscores why including people of color at all levels of a research project is essential.

An increasing awareness of people's multiple identities also adds nuance and sophistication to debates about what is required to uphold an epistemological privilege in research designs. For example, the logic that Black people should study Black people gives privilege to race at the expense of other categories of identity, such as gender and sexual identity. Feminist and gay rights movements and their attendant scholarship have established that such ranking of identities (and oppressions) is neither a productive nor an accurate methodology. Given the complexity of multiple identities, race matching in interviews without gender matching, for instance, can compromise one's methodology. In addition, many people's multiple identities make establishing who is an "insider" or an "outsider" in a study quite complicated. As anthropologist Lynn Wilson asked, "How 'local' is the Black ethnographer from the rural South who goes to study an inner-city Black community in Denver? How 'indigenous' is an Indian ethnographer who travels 700 miles to study a group that lives in the same country, but in a different linguistic or religious region?"[26]

Despite the complexities of translating the epistemological privilege into practice, I propose that the crux of this ethic, as upheld in *The Death of White Sociology* and more recent model team-research projects, remains informative. At its base, this principle recognizes "experience" as a resource of power and substantiates why social inequalities must inevitably be taken into account when designing and implementing research plans. I also suggest that it is precisely careful analyses of how power inequalities have influenced research that illuminates how people of color are often marginalized in research designs. In order to avoid the false assumptions that Black people are "raced" and white people are not, that women are "gendered" and men are not, social scientists need to support research conducted by people of various social locations in studies that both explicitly focus on people of color and those that do not.

Democratic Representation

Three ethical principles offered in *The Death of White Sociology*—a valuing of subjectivity, an ethic of accountability, and an epistemological privilege—lay the groundwork for a fourth ethical guideline: an ethic of democratic representation. In addition to an epistemological privilege regarding research about Black people and other communities of color, we need an ethic that upholds democratic representation in studies that are not ostensibly about race. A study about white families and child care arrangements in Iowa, for example, might benefit from the involvement of a Black researcher raised in an extended family in South Carolina. A study of heterosexual bar culture might benefit from the input of a gay researcher. In both instances, these researchers may well have considerable expertise in documenting how "privilege" shapes these contexts in ways that a white researcher or a heterosexual researcher, respectively, might not.[27] In this way, recognizing the need for epistemological privilege on ethical grounds in research about traditionally subordinated communities becomes the building block for an ethic of democratic representation in other research projects as well. This step helps avoid the creation of research "ghettos" in which people of color are considered essential for certain research topics and yet unqualified for or uninterested in others. It also shifts the racial power in projects that historically have been the enclaves of white researchers.

Conclusion: "Inroads in Ethics"

The importance of these ethics invites us to think about what social scientific training aimed at supporting these ethics might look like. What will be required to ensure projects with research designs that sensitively account for people's multiple identities? Certainly, the empowered presence of people of color, lesbians and gay men, white women, and working class people at all levels of the academy is an absolute foundation of such a goal. At the same time, the tendency to consider "subjectivity," "identity," and one's relation to power as fixed and static entities must be countered. As researchers recognize the experience and insight made possible by those who are outsiders-within, we need to find ways to teach people who are not outsiders to see the world from the outsider's perspective. It is this agenda that may make it possible to design research studies that counter the exploitative relations that have marked so many studies, and it may save us from the hopeless and overwhelming relativism that can take place when such basic concepts as "objectivity" and "science" are questioned.

Historically, inroads in ethics have occurred in response to intense social protests against injustice. The atrocities of the Nazi medical researchers during World War II and of the U.S. Public Health Service during the Tuskegee syphilis experiment are just two examples of misconduct that led to direct change in scientific ethics. Likewise, the protests against poverty, racism, and militarism in the late 1960s were partly responsible for revised codes of ethics adopted by the American Anthropological Association and the American Sociological Association in 1971.[28] In the years since the first publication of *The Death of White Sociology*, much has happened politically that will urge sociologists to look at research ethics anew. The explosion of race-conscious, feminist scholarship in gay and lesbian studies, cultural studies, law, anthropology, and other disciplines will inevitably demand consideration of ethics that are in many ways different than those of twenty-five years ago. But certainly any accurate historical account underscores our debt to that work as well.

Becky Thompson teaches sociology and African American studies at Simmons College in Boston. She is the co-editor of Names We Call Home: Autobiography on Racial Identity.

Notes

An earlier version of this afterword was presented during the Race, Class and Gender Seminar at Memphis State University in 1993. I would like to thank Jacqueline Davis, Mary Gilfus, Gayle Pemberton, and Sangeeta Tyagi for their insightful suggestions on earlier drafts.

1. Herbert J. Gans, "Sociological Amnesia: The Noncumulation of Normal Social Science," *Sociological Forum,* December 1992, Vol. 7, No. 4, pp. 701—710.

2. Adrienne Rich, "Resisting Amnesia: History and Personal Life,"*Blood, Bread, and Poetry* (New York: Norton, 1986), p. 145.

3. Thomas Kuhn, *The Structure of Scientific Revolutions*. (Chicago, IL: University of Chicago Press, 1970).

4. See Robert Staples, this volume, p. 162.

5. Ralph Ellison, this volume, p. 84.

6. Gerrit Huizer and Bruce Mannheim, eds., *The Politics of*

Anthropology: From Colonialism and Sexism Toward a View From Below (Paris, France: Mouton Publishers, 1979); Gloria Hull, Patricia Bell Scott, and Barbara Smith, eds., *All the Women Are White, All the Men Are Black, But Some of Us Are Brave* (Old Westbury, NY: The Feminist Press, 1982).

7. Mary Beth Norton, David Katzman, Paul Escott, Howard Chudacoff, Thomas Patterson, and William Tuttle, *A People and a Nation: A History of the United States,* third edition (New York: Houghton Mifflin, 1990), p. 936.

8. These murders were committed on September 15, 1963. See Angela Davis, "Remembering Carole, Cynthia, Addie Mae and Denise," *Essence,* Volume 24, September, 1993, No. 5, p. 92, 122, 123, & 126.

9. Leonard Peltier was first jailed in 1972 after being attacked by two off-duty policemen, beaten severely, and then charged with the attempted murder of one of the police. The confrontation at Pine Ridge occurred in 1975, during which time an FBI agent was killed. Peltier's trial for his alleged involvement was in 1976–1977. See Jim Vander Wall, "A Warrior Caged: The Continuing Struggle of Leonard Peltier," in Annette Jaimes, ed., *The State of Native America* (Boston: South End Press), p. 298.

10. Within the discipline of theology, normative ethics offers moral evaluations of actions and institutions and their effects on humanity. Liberation ethics is considered a subfield that has historical relation to theology in many ways similar to Black sociology's connection to mainstream sociology.

11. Katie G. Cannon's definition is from a course entitled "Resources for a Constructive Ethic: The Black Woman's Literary Tradition," which she taught at Episcopal Divinity School in Cambridge, Mass., Fall 1987.

12. Katie G. Cannon, *Black Womanist Ethics* (Atlanta, GA: Scholars Press, 1988), p. 2.

13. Ibid.

14. Patricia Hill Collins, *Black Feminist Thought: Knowledge, Consciousness and the Politics of Empowerment* (New York: Routeledge, Chapman and Hall, 1990).

15. This document is published by the American Sociological Association (1722 N St. NW, Washington, D.C. 20036. See also the association's web page at www. asa.net.org).

16. Kenneth Clark, this volume, p. 409.

17. Katie G. Cannon, *Black Womanist Ethics,* p. 105.

18. Ronald G. Walters, this volume, p. 198.

19. Janet Koenig, "Commemorative Stamp Series," *Heresies: A Feminist Publication on Art and Politics,* 4, no. 3 (1982), p. 8 cited in Adrienne Rich "Resisting Amnesia: History and Personal Life," in *Blood, Bread, and Poetry* (New York: Norton, 1986), p. 141.

20. Joyce Ladner, this volume, p. 415.

21. Clark, this volume, p. 409.

22. Robert Blauner and David Wellman, this volume.

23. Richard Hernnstein and Charles Murray, *The Bell Curve: Intelligence and Class Structure in American Life* (New York: Free Press, 1994); Daniel Patrick Moynihan, "The Negro Family: A Plan for National Action" (United States Department of Labor Office of Policy, Planning, & Research: Washington, DC 1965).

24. Patricia Hill Collins, *Black Feminist Thought: Knowledge, Consciousness and the Politics of Empowerment,* p. 209.

25. See Toni Morrison, ed., *Racing Justice, Engendering Power:*

Essays on Anita Hill, Clarence Thomas, and the Construction of Social Reality (New York: Pantheon, 1992); Evelyn Hammonds, "Clarence Thomas, Affirmative Action and the Academy," in *Beyond A Dream Deferred: Multicultural Education and the Politics of Excellence*, edited by Becky Thompson and Sangeeta Tyagi (Minneapolis, MN: University of Minnesota Press, 1993), pp. 66–82.

26. Lynn Wilson, "Epistemology and Power: Rethinking Ethnography at Greenham," in *Anthropology for the Nineties,* ed. Johnetta B. Cole (New York: The Free Press, 1988), p. 47.

27. I would like to thank Elizabeth Higginbotham for her insightful discussion on this point.

28. The reason I clarify "partly" is that much of the impetus for revisioning ethical codes in the 1960s and early 1970s, both in the sciences and social sciences, can be traced to the growing influence of the law and institutional attempts to protect against lawsuits. See Tom Beauchamp, Ruth R. Faden, R. Jay Wallace, and Leroy Walters, eds., *Ethical Issues in Social Science Research* (Baltimore: Johns Hopkins, 1982), pp. 5 and 7.